PRAISE FOR *ZEITGEIST 2025*

"Tom Horn's writing always sizzles...but *Zeitgeist 2025* absolutely blazes! Hang on for the ride of your life as Dr. Horn catalogs how the New World Order is already embracing...and preparing for the second coming of...its cherished new gods!"

　　—Pastor Carl Gallups, bestselling author of *Masquerade* and
　　The Summoning

★★★★★

"Tom Horn's writing always sizzles...but *Zeitgeist 2025* absolutely blazes!
Hang on for the ride of your life as Dr. Horn catalogues how the New World Order is
already embracing... and preparing for the second coming of... its cherished new gods!"

– Pastor Carl Gallups, bestselling author of *Masquerade* and *The Summoning*

THOMAS R. HORN

With Contributors Bob Maginnis, Allie Henson, Josh Peck, Donna Howell, Derek Gilbert, Sharon Gilbert

ZEITGEIST
2025

Countdown to the Secret Destiny of America,
the Lost Prophecies of Qumran, and the Return of Old Saturn's Reign

DEFENDER

CRANE, MO

ZEITGEIST 2025: COUNTDOWN TO THE SECRET DESTINY OF
AMERICA… THE LOST PROPHECIES OF QUMRAN, AND THE
RETURN OF OLD SATURN'S REIGN
by Thomas Horn

Defender Publishing
Crane, MO 65633
© 2021 Thomas Horn

A CIP catalog record of this book is available from the Library of Congress.

Cover design by Jeffrey Mardis.
All Scripture quoted is from the King James Version unless otherwise noted.

CONTENTS

CONTENTS

ZEITGEIST
2025

SWAMP CREATURES, BRAHMA, AND THE SECOND COMING OF OLD SATURN'S REIGN

I f you read my last book, *The Messenger*, you may immediately have a hint as to what is behind the unusual title of this work, *Zeitgeist 2025*. If you do not understand the connection, I highly recommend you read *Messenger*, as it is filled with the most incredible discoveries involving how, exactly three and a half years before the original date set by NASA for the asteroid Apophis (which I argue is biblical Wormwood at the middle of what most evangelicals and some Catholics call the seven-year Great Tribulation period) to come crashing down on this planet (April 13, 2029), the high holy days of the Feast of Tabernacles will be unfolding on earth. Just a few days before that will be the Feast of Trumpets, and 120 days (biblical numerology for the end of mankind) earlier is Pentecost. All three of these festivals are strongly tied by eschatologists to the Second Coming of Jesus Christ.

Now, you may have seen recently where NASA is repeating their position that Apophis will likely not impact earth in 2029, but will instead barely skim safely past the world while knocking out some of the satellites in orbit around our planet. But just one of many scientists is warning that NASA's trajectory calculation of Apophis is off by as much as six hundred thousand miles,[1] which Harry Lear implies could very well send Apophis crashing into earth just eight years from now. Lear sent an open letter to the president and US government scientists begging them to cross check these calculations immediately, even though he ends his dispatch with an ominous admonition that we may already be out of time.

Besides Lear, top-one hundred scientist Nathan Myhrvold, in a recent peer-reviewed paper, "An Empirical Examination of WISE/NEOWISE Asteroid Analysis and Results," refutes much of the data from NASA and in fact charges them with deliberately misreporting threats by near-earth objects and of behaving "extremely deceptively" with deliberate "scientific misconduct" in a cover-up of very real and potentially imminent space threats.[2]

Even famous planetary scientist and astrophysicist Neil deGrasse Tyson admits that, on April 13, 2029:

> Apophis will come so close to Earth that it will dip below our orbiting communication satellites. It will be the largest closest thing we have ever observed to come by earth…the orbit we now have for it is UNCERTAIN…because these things are hard to measure and hard to get an exact distance for—WE CANNOT TELL YOU EXACTLY WHERE THAT TRAJECTORY WILL BE."[3] (Emphasis added)

That said, in *Zeitgeist*, I argue that mankind has indeed likely entered the last decade of history as it has been known—what prophecy teachers call the Church Age—and how the several unusual things you will read herein set this work apart from all other books on prophecy.

Among the amazing things you will discover within these pages is how the Essenes of Dead Sea Scrolls fame were only one of the ancient prophecy communities to predict more than two thousand years ago that mankind would indeed enter its final age (Jubilee cycle) four years from now, in 2025—three and one-half years before Apophis smashes into our world.

Assuming for the moment that I am right, and that the asteroid Apophis is biblical Wormwood and therefore 2029 represents a time around the middle of the Great Tribulation period when the trumpet judgments begin, Monday, October 13, 2025 (April 13, 2029, minus three and a half years), would be the approximate start date of the seven years of Tribulation foreseen in Scripture (see Matthew 24:21; Revelation 7:14; and Daniel 12:1).

The year 2025 is also the one envisioned ten years ago in a series of studies co-organized by the Atlantic Council and government organizations from Europe, the US, Beijing, Tokyo, Dubai, and other partnering nations that led the US National Intelligence Council and the EU Institute of Security Studies to produce a report titled *Global Governance 2025: At a Critical Juncture.*[4] In this document, the highest-level intelligence agencies in the world determined that a global government could emerge around 2025 from "an unprecedented threat" that would materialize requiring all nations to lay down their differences and come together in mutual defense of one another against an unprecedented "menace." In particular, they foresaw an incoming asteroid, a new pandemic (which I believe Apophis is bringing with it via an extremophile microorganism with a virus), as well as a biotech-created "new form of human" representing existential threats.

Having said that, and realizing what must happen for the world stage to align in preparation of Antichrist's seven-year reign and world government, I am sitting here in my home office today contemplating how to start chapter 1 of this most important treatise in light of recent geopolitical events.

It's a chilly Missouri afternoon outside; it isn't supposed to be warmer than thirty-eight degrees all day, just a bit better than Washington, DC, at forty-five degrees, where Nancy Pelosi and company are working hard to refill the swamp and initiate this end-times alignment while also making

Donald Trump feel it's even colder than the thermometers say—at least in the air around their shoulders.

I'm sure they think of what they're busy doing as payback, as it was only four years earlier when, on January 20, 2017, with former presidents George H. W. Bush, Bill Clinton, George W. Bush, and Barack Obama sitting behind him, the highly unexpected, newly elected Donald J. Trump addressed America and the world by criticizing the former presidents and their establishment buddies in a way nobody had seen or heard before. He made it clear that his agenda for the people had not ended on the campaign trail, and that he had gathered on the west front of the Capitol to announce more than the orderly and peaceful transition of power from the Obama administration to his. I wrote about that amazing day at the time, noting how he began:

> Today's ceremony has very special meaning. Because today we are not merely transferring power from one administration to another, or from one party to another—but we are transferring power from Washington, D.C., and giving it back to you, the American people.

Then, with former presidents squirming in their seats, wishing they could be somewhere else, he offered no quarter, adding:

> For too long, a small group in our nation's Capital has reaped the rewards of government while the people have borne the cost.
>
> Washington flourished—but the people did not share in its wealth.
>
> Politicians prospered—but the jobs left, and the factories closed.
>
> The establishment protected itself, but not the citizens of our country.
>
> Their victories have not been your victories; their triumphs have not been your triumphs; and while they celebrated in our

nation's Capital, there was little to celebrate for struggling families all across our land.

That all changes—starting right here, and right now, because this moment is your moment: it belongs to you.

It belongs to everyone gathered here today and everyone watching all across America.

This is your day. This is your celebration.

And this, the United States of America, is your country.[5]

Whether he knew it or not, with that declaration of war, Mr. Trump had set himself against very powerful enemies—visible and invisible, ancient and contemporary.

To the illumined elite, the inaugural address was a clear salvo that promptly drew a line in the sand from which was made an unholy covenant: "The Donald" would have to learn a lesson about "pulling the drain plug from the swamp" in Washington, DC. The entities entrenched there are ancient, powerful, and far harder to expel than mere political diatribe would muster. What has transpired since reflected this response and was even predictable, though I and half the nation had hoped for more time.

What do I mean?

Secular and biblical scholars, historians, prophets, and even occultists have understood for thousands of years that a very dark time has long been forecast for the nation's immediate future, and that this destiny would not be delayed forever.

FORESEEN BY HISTORIANS AS THE LEAD-UP TO ZEITGEIST 2025

In 1997, in a work describing itself as a thesis "that turns history into prophecy," professors William Strauss and Neil Howe released their groundbreaking book, *The Fourth Turning*, which examined Western historical paradigms over the past five centuries and discovered cycles of life and generational archetypes that reveal an astoundingly prescient pattern of incidents that ultimately lead to chaos and a so-called Fourth Turning.

The authors describe a "Turning" as "an era with a characteristic social mood (a zeitgeist), a new twist on how people feel about themselves and their nation. It results from the aging of the generation [before it]."[6] A society enters a Turning once every twenty years or so, when all living generations begin to penetrate their next phases of life. The living generations, or *saeculae*, comprise four cyclical Turnings, characterized as:

- **The First Turning (THE HIGH):** An era of enthusiastic collective strengthening and civic development, having burned the brush and swept the ashes of preceding structure.
- **The Second Turning (THE AWAKENING):** Built on the energies and accomplishments of the High, but finds increasing yearning for introspection with a high tolerance for spiritual expression outside the parameters of predetermined standards.
- **The Third Turning (THE UNRAVELING):** Begins as the "society-wide embrace of the liberating cultural forces" loosed by the Awakening shows signs of civic disorder and decay, a heightened sense of self-reliance, and an increasing withdrawal of public trust. This builds to a near crisis of downcast pessimism and a palpable pall that can only be remedied by yielding to the next.
- **The Fourth Turning (THE CRISES and the era we have now entered):** By far, the most perilous, as societies pass through the greatest and most dangerous gates of history. As desperate solutions are sought for "sudden threats" on multiple cultural fronts, confrontation is passionate and decisions are often reactive, aggressive. "Government governs, community obstacles are removed, and laws and customs that resisted change for decades are swiftly shunted aside. A grim preoccupation with civic peril causes spiritual curiosity to decline…. Public order tightens, private risk-taking abates, and…child-rearing reaches a smothering degree of protection and structure. The young focus their energy on worldly achievements, leaving values in the hands of the old. Wars are fought with fury and for maximum result."[7]

Through the examination of an enormous amount of political and cultural history, Strauss and Howe processed more than five hundred years of such Anglo-American cultural Turnings into remarkable, well-organized, and predictable cycles, and it is from this reservoir that they finally staked an uncanny claim about America (keep in mind they made these predictions twenty-five years ago, long before the September 11, 2001, attacks on America, the pandemic of today, and the January 6, 2021, riots at the US Capitol and subsequent prosecution of Donald Trump). Among the scenarios they foresaw were:

- A terrorist attack involving an airliner, a military response, authorization for house-to-house searches, and false-flag accusations against the administration.
- An eco-environmental malaise with the Centers for Disease Control announcing the spread of a new communicable virus (like COVID-19) with quarantines and relocations.
- Growing anarchy throughout the world largely generated along racial divisions leading to unprecedented government suppression of personal freedoms.

In describing these insightful scenarios, Strauss and Howe felt a catalyst would unfold as a result of a specific dynamic, and "an initial spark will trigger a chain reaction of unyielding responses and further emergencies."[8]

They further warned:

Just after the millennium, America will enter a new era that will culminate with a crisis comparable to the American Revolution, the Civil War, the Great Depression, and World War II. The very survival of the nation will almost certainly be at stake.[9]

Strauss and Howe saw the United States of that time (1997) in the Third Turning, "midway through an Unraveling":

America feels like it's unraveling. Although we live in an era of relative peace and comfort, we have settled into a mood of pessimism about the long-term future, fearful that our superpower nation is somehow rotting from within.

The next Fourth Turning is due to begin shortly after the new millennium.... Real hardship will beset the land, with severe distress that could involve questions of class, race, nation, and empire....

The very survival of the nation will feel at stake.

Sometime before the [zeitgeist] year 2025, America will pass through a great gate in history, commensurate with the American Revolution, Civil War, and twin emergencies of the Great Depression and World War II.

The risk of catastrophe will be very high. The nation could erupt into insurrection or civil violence, crack up geographically, or succumb to authoritarian rule.[10]

The risk of such sacrificed civil liberties under government authoritarianism was also foreseen by the brilliant English novelist George Orwell, who had endured the heartache, delusion, fears, and cultural shocks of the pre- and post-World War II Britain and portrayed the ultimate goals of such totalitarianism and total government surveillance through his novels *1984* and *Animal Farm*.

Orwell died in January of 1950, long before the actual emergence of the very society he so feared: a world of mechanized eyes and software slogans; a realm of memespeak, thought police, and the false perception of universal exceptionalism (which by its very nature makes everyone the same—except for "protected classes"). However, this oppressive and fear-based environment predicted by Strauss, Howe, and Orwell is but the harbinger of darker worlds still to come.

Ordo ab chao. Order out of chaos. Apophis. Set. The return of old Saturn's reign.

If this phrase is new to some of you, you're not alone, but it has percolated through elitist brains for centuries in one form or another. In 2010, Richard Florida, a sociologist who studies economic cycles in city systems, authored a seminal book called *The Great Reset*. The primary thesis of this sleeper seed-book is that major paradigm and organizational shifts occur in economic systems when cities lose sight of diversity and creativity. For Florida, it's the creative classes of individuals who stoke the engine of innovation and hence drive invention and industry. Without such big thinkers, Florida would assert, mankind's forward momentum grinds to a halt.

Of course, critics of Florida's metropolitan model disagree on the grounds that he insists this so-called creative class must be composed of a high percentage of gender-fluid individuals. Yes, you read that correctly. To achieve the "great reset" of mankind, cities must be restructured with a new elitist class whose ideologies skew heavily to socialism. Florida's logical end, therefore, is socialist Darwinism. Such a philosophy paints mankind as ever striving towards greater levels of achievement and centralized organization. First, he moves from living alone in caves to hunter-gatherer tribes, followed by agrarian communities, then to industrialized cities where farming is no longer required, to today's information-addicted, hashtag-loving big thinkers who can't fix their own flat tires, much less grow a tomato—and finally, the cities die and the community disbands. The only way to fix this, Florida asserts, is to inject cities with socialists, who will kick us into a new age of innovation.

We are being forced into this very shift right now. Don't believe it? Just recall the social-media-driven hashtag revolution that is currently overwhelming cities and law-enforcement agencies across the globe. At present, thousands of protesters bearing slogans and signs, neatly printed with the most fashionable hashtags (#fillintheblank), have taken to the streets—with Molotov cocktails in hand—ready to defend their right to desecrate our homes and sow destruction in our towns. They seek to erase more than history, more than statues—the current age itself. And in an era in which nearly all learning is digital, it's easy to imagine how history might be changed to suit a rising dictator. Like the Nazis, book-burning removes old ideas and brands them heretical or damaging, but if a child's only source of information is the Internet, then all knowledge is subject to editorial alteration and erasure.

With the loss of printed history and commemorative structures and statues—without a hard copy of humanity's flawed past—future generations will have to rely upon the plays, poetry, and propaganda written by government-approved authors via online sources and the approved tech oligarchs that can instantly be updated to reflect the ideology of the moment. With a single keystroke, what has been will cease to be.

In Orwell's dystopian *1984*, the fictional setting of Oceania depicted the era we've now entered and the four "Ministries" he envisioned under the figurehead of Big Brother: Love, Peace, Plenty, and Truth.

The Ministry of Peace actually perpetuated unending wars; the Ministry of Love oversaw suffering and torture against those who would not adhere to the Party line; and the Ministry of Plenty weaponized starvation through socialism. Then there was the Ministry of Truth—the propaganda arm of the government media that employed fake-news "Doublethink" and "Newspeak" as the official dialectic of the state.

> "Newspeak" is the term Orwell invented for controlled language: restricted grammar and limited vocabulary as "a linguistic design meant to limit the freedom of thought—personal identity, self-expression, free will—that ideologically threatens the régime of Big Brother and the Party, who thus criminalized such concepts as 'thoughtcrime' contradictions of the English Socialist Party orthodoxy" (INGSOC).[11]

Today, in America, the nonfiction version of the Ministry of Truth has materialized and is fully operational through the Orwellian tools of modern Marxists and social media manipulators including Twitter, Google, Facebook, and "news" organizations that blacklist Christian and conservative commentary by burying search results and exhibiting bias in their artificial-intelligence, shadow-banning algorithms and reporting.

Like Representative Alexandria Ocasio-Cortez (NY) and other Democrats are now openly pushing even against conservative Democrats,[12] INGSOC controlled her citizens' thoughts and activities by requiring each to communicate using only Newspeak. The concept of free speech had vanished in Oceania in favor of ironically positive and often self-contradictory words and phrases.

Joycamps replaced labor camps, presumably making them "fun" (not).

Goodthink was any thought that supported the ruling political Party.

Oldspeak was the former English language (one can see our current trends towards shorthand communication—i.e., emoji—replacing actual, cogent expression through entire sentences).

Oldthink was outdated ideas held by individuals before the rise of the current regime.

Thinkpol was the thought police, who used false-flag operations to lure unsuspecting renegades into "outing" themselves.

Teledep, was the Ministry of Truth's telecommunications department of the regime, which broadcast Big Brother's daily briefings and propaganda.

Telescreens provided two-way communication between government entities and citizens.

Thus Orwell foresaw our current society, where social media and twenty-four-hour news cycles invigorate the cancel mob into tyrannizing anyone who holds what they consider to be the wrong opinions, says the wrong words, or points out the dangers of progressive (regressive) ideology's new "truths." Think of how the hashtag generation is using peer pressure to force netizens to rethink their positions and beliefs. We are being changed, dear friends, and we will dive deeper into that investigation in the next chapter. But for now, recognize that we're slowly being moved toward a new paradigm by a maniacal minority of keyboard, "cancel culture" warriors who have metastasized in the American sociopolitical environment via Stalin-like efforts to purge anyone they consider a threat to their position. If your dialogue doesn't bend to their will, you will be removed. Depending on how large your audience is, you may even just disappear or conveniently commit "suicide." Power is being concentrated into the hands of fewer and fewer individuals, and soon it will reside in only *one*.

J. R. R. Tolkien would call it the "One Ring to rule them all." Today's community organizers might paraphrase it as "One Meme to rule them all."

But before you can restructure society—before you can design a new Tower of Babel, raise Sauron's Dark Tower, or lay the foundations for Orwell's Oceania—all the old foundations must be destroyed and forever removed from memory. That is what's happening right now, the most vivid recent example being the burning down of all things Donald Trump, his brand, and anything or anybody that appeared to support him.

As Bob Weir for *American Thinker* said when reminiscing about racketeers who will do anything to keep from being exposed:

> From the moment [President Trump] declared war on the corruption in D.C., he became a target of all those entrenched power brokers who have been able to hide their venal activities from an unsuspecting public. Trump became the loudest whistleblower in history when he talked about draining the swamp that had been operating like an organized crime family for generations. In order for a Mafia-like mob to operate effectively, it must keep its nefarious pursuits from public exposure. Hence, President Trump had to be destroyed![13]

This is reflected by Florida's "Great Reset" and today's hashtag movement, which is intent on destroying all of humanity's past, leaving behind a void that requires filling. Think of this as societal brainwashing that leaves the formerly filled and "prejudicial" brain empty and ready for Orwell's Newspeak to take hold.

This is why, although the authors of *The Fourth Turning* note that the events described in their thesis are not absolute, they also insist that the cycles, these Turnings, cannot be interrupted. As summer follows spring, an Unraveling precedes a crisis of Faustian proportions:

> It will require us to lend a new seasonal interpretation to our revered American Dream. And it will require us to admit that our faith in linear progress has often amounted to a Faustian bargain with our children.
>
> Faust always ups the ante, and every bet is double-or-nothing. Through much of the Third Turning, we have managed to postpone the reckoning. But history warns that we can't defer it beyond the next bend in time.[14]

In Strauss and Howe's vision, Faust's "deal with the devil" ultimately includes the arrival of an unexpected national leader who will emerge during this current Fourth Turning from an older generation and lead the globe into a New World Order, which they envisioned developing by 2025. This commander—whom they call the "Grey Champion" (and who some of us might worry could be—or could pave the way for—Antichrist)—would come to power as a result of the nation losing faith in existing government and desperate for a political savior to arrive and "calm" nerves by offering to "Build Back Better" a socialist governance with welfare for the masses. This leadership would seize what can only be described as a cancel-culture crusade warm to promulgating Oceania-like suppression of unapproved dialogue in order to rein in any and all challenges to the new social construct.

Is this starting to sound familiar?

On November 3, 2020, after most had gone to bed with incumbent US President Donald J. Trump on track to handily win reelection including in so-called swing states, around two o'clock in the morning, a phenomenon unfolded, and votes seemed to magically appear from out of nowhere in astonishing numbers favoring Joe Biden.

Within forty-eight hours, claims of voter fraud erupted across the nation, including in Georgia, where, after observers were told to go home, video cameras mounted in the building recorded suitcases of votes being pulled from under tables by three Democratic operatives who were filmed running the ballots through counting machines over and over. This was followed in the days ahead by allegations of hundreds of thousands of late-night votes arriving for Joe Biden in states like Pennsylvania, where GOP poll Watchers had been blocked from observing tallies.

Other anomalies quickly emerged. Forensic examination of Dominion vote-counting machines determined the devices may have been used to flip votes from one party to another, and more than two thousand eyewitnesses lined up to testify in sworn affidavits of various irregularities they saw, which appeared to them to be obvious acts of fraud on Election Night and the day after.

That list goes on, but it doesn't matter. Even though Senator Rand Paul (R-KY) says you are a fool if you doubt there was a "great deal of evidence of fraud"[15] and illegal election law changes, it's now forbidden for you to question anything regarding the veracity of the above claims, even if at one time this was a nation known as "the land of the free" that cherished the First Amendment ("Congress shall make no law...abridging the freedom of speech, or of the press; or the right of the people peaceably to assemble, and to petition the Government for a redress of grievances"). Just ask *Mandalorian* star Gina Carano,[16] conservative actor, and pro-life advocate Kevin Sorbo,[17] or the alt-tech microblogging and social networking service Parler. It's a very good way to get de-platformed, shadow banned, publicly scorned, or worse under the new Oceania rules. At SkyWatch TV, we are all too familiar with such shadow-banning of our reports, getting kicked off our newsletter email service for conservative Christian commentary, and I myself once more being mislabeled by Professor S. Jonathon O'Donnell[18] (a Fellow in the Clinton Institute for American Studies) in the peer-reviewed journal *Religion* as a "Christian nationalist," which *USA Today* calls "a threat...embedded throughout our governing institutions—courts, military, legislatures, agencies, police,"[19] which I certainly am not. As anybody who has read my warnings against Dominionism could attest, I am a patriotic American and I vote. But first and foremost, I am a born-again believer committed to advancing the Gospel of the Kingdom of God.

It would be so nice if people would just read the Federalist Papers, including the tenth one, in which James Madison argues that "faction" is what motivates Americans. Our strength lies in passions and opinions on different things, and it is (or should be) our ability to learn from one another and compromise or peacefully disagree that lies at the foundation of greater resolution and civility. But alas, it seems political commentator Dennis Prager may have been correct when, at the time he was watching unfolding events at the close of 2020, including the subsequent actions by Big Tech to censor commentary from the sitting president, he said: "This is the Reichstag fire relived. We're living in a gigantic lie that is reminiscent of the Reichstag fire!"[20]

If you don't know what Prager was talking about, the Reichstag fire was an arson attack on the Reichstag building, "home of the German parliament in Berlin, on Monday 27 February 1933, precisely four weeks after Adolf Hitler was sworn in as Chancellor of Germany. Hitler's government stated that Marinus van der Lubbe, a Dutch council communist, was the culprit, and it attributed the fire to communist agitators. A German court decided later that year that Van der Lubbe had acted alone, as he had claimed. The day after the fire, the Reichstag Fire Decree was passed. The Nazi Party used the fire as a pretext to claim that communists were plotting against the German government, which made the fire pivotal in the establishment of Nazi Germany."[21]

The Nazis capitalized on the fire and quickly moved with a vengeance to cement their authority and grant the state unprecedented power (in the name of "public safety"), which resulted in suspending "most civil liberties in Germany, including habeas corpus, freedom of expression, freedom of the press, the right of free association and public assembly, and the secrecy of the post and telephone. These rights were not reinstated during Nazi reign. The decree was used by the Nazis to ban publications not considered "friendly" to the Nazi cause.

With Communist electoral participation also suppressed (the Communists previously polled 17% of the vote), the Nazis were able to increase their share of the vote in the 5 March 1933 Reichstag elections from 33% to 44%. This gave the Nazis and their allies, the German National People's Party (who won 8% of the vote), a majority of 52% in the Reichstag.[22]

Strauss and Howe, when they wrote their thesis over twenty-five years ago, were convinced something very similar would unfold in the years immediately before Zeitgeist 2025. They saw the United States in the Third Turning then, and that the next crisis period or Fourth Turning would erupt around 2025, which I contend is more likely than not to represent the start of what dispensationalist Christians call the "Great Tribulation" period (more on that later).

Will the suppression of free speech under the new administration's tech oligarchy and the George Soros and Barack Obama-backed agitators who continue to threaten havoc across America ignite the circumstances that lead to the Grey Champion's authoritarian rule? America has experienced three such major crises before—the Revolutionary War, the Civil War, and the Great Depression and World War II, each followed by their respective periods of reconstruction. These times were marked by social decay and civil dread that required Americans to carry a tremendous burden after massive conflict and substantial loss in order to try and rebuild a better future.

And don't forget, it was Barack Obama who, after designating America as "no longer a Christian nation," declared just days before his election in 2008: "We are five days away from fundamentally transforming the United States of America."[23] His wife, Michelle Obama, echoed these sentiments earlier, saying, "We're going to have to change our traditions, our history; we're going to have to move into a different place as a nation."[24]

This intentional redefining of the nation and attempt at changing the course of the United States was partly what Donald Trump was determined to stop and why, in his State of the Union address (February 2019), he declared that, so long as he was president, "America will never be a socialist country."

Did all that change January 20, 2021, with the inauguration of Joe Biden? As the oldest American president ever, is he Strauss and Howe's Grey Champion? According to the Christian end-times blog, *Signposts of the Times*:

> We as Christians, and in particular, those that understand and follow Bible prophecy will be watching with much interest over the next days, weeks and months ahead to see how God will use President Joe Biden to put in place the final pieces of the Last Days puzzle that will usher in the Tribulation period and the system of Antichrist.[25]

Are they right? Are we nearing the trigger event(s) or chaos stage of a final Fourth Turning?

Besides professors of history like those above who foresaw what the actions and reactions of policy makers and social engineers would generate, behind such political players and master manipulators at cultural helms, an invisible order—vividly described in Scripture—holds deeper insight into where we are today and the influences guiding us to where we wind up next.

INVOKING THAT DARK DESTINY

Before and after the presidency of Donald Trump, the United States was—and now is again—on an intentional trajectory to fulfill what famous Freemason Manly P. Hall described as *The Secret Destiny of America*, which includes future national and global subservience to the god of Freemasonry, a deity most Americans would not imagine when reciting the Pledge of Allegiance to "one nation under *God*." In fact, the idea by some that the United States was established as a monotheistic "Christian" nation by those who designed Washington, DC, and that the "God" referred to on American currency is a Judeo-Christian one, is a puzzling conclusion when reflected against the deistic beliefs of so many of the Founding Fathers (as perpetually viewed in the "Supreme Architect" deism of Freemasons and in the "Supreme Judge of the World" and "Divine Providence" notations in the Declaration of Independence) and the countless pagan icons that dominate the symbols, statues, buildings, and seals carefully drafted under official government auspices. The Great Seal of the United States, which Hall rightly called "the signature" of that exalted body of Masons who designed America for a "peculiar and particular purpose," bears rich symbolism forecasting anything but Christianity. In fact, when Christians in the 1800s argued that a hypothetical annihilation of the US would lead to "antiquaries of succeeding centuries" concluding that America had been a heathen nation based on symbolism of the Great Seal, Congress was pushed to create something reflecting the Christian faith of so many of its citizens. US President and Freemason Theodore Roosevelt strongly opposed this idea, while other Masons weren't as frustrated with the plan because, given the ambivalence of the term "God" and the axiom that, interpreted within the context of the Great Seal symbolism, this certainly would not infer the biblical Christian God, the slogan, "In God We Trust," (whomever you believe "God" is) was accommodated by Masons and other illuminatus and so was approved as the official US motto.

In my book *Zenith 2016* (which, among other things, noted that the year of Trump's presidential election had been foreseen by prophets and sages for thousands of years as the apex date when governments would begin shifting toward the spirit predicted on the Great Seal [Antichrist], followed by the Man of Sin's actual arrival and acceptance on the global stage [in 2025?]), to illustrate the point that one definitely would not determine the "God" in America's official motto refers to the Father of Jesus Christ or a biblical Trinity, I wrote:

Imagine yourself as a space traveler who visits earth in a fictional, post-apocalyptic world. Digging through the rubble of the once-thriving planet, you come across a copy of a U.S. one-dollar bill with the two-sided Great Seal of the United States joined in the middle by the phrase, "IN GOD WE TRUST."

Upon consideration, you ask yourself, "What *god* did this refer to?" With no preconceptions, you allow the symbolism on the seal to speak for itself, from which you quickly determine that this had been a great culture who worshipped Egyptian and Greek deities, especially a particular solar one whose all-seeing eye glared from atop an unfinished Egyptian pyramid. Upon further investigation into the specific beliefs of the strange group whose members had influenced the Great Seal, you discover from their highest masters, including one "illustrious" Albert Pike, that the sun god they venerated so highly had been known to them at various times in history by the names *Apollo, Osiris*, and *Nimrod*.[26]

I made this argument in *Zenith 2016* because, unknown to most Americans and certainly to average Christians, the Great Seal's mottoes and symbolism relate to both Osiris and Apollo specifically, yet as one. Osiris is the dominant theme of the Egyptian symbols, his resurrection and return, while the *mottoes* of the seal point directly to Apollo, and the eagle, a pagan emblem of Jupiter, to Apollo's father. For instance, the motto *Annuit Coeptis* is from Virgil's *Aeneid*, in which Ascanius, the son of Aeneas from conquered Troy, prays to Apollo's father, Jupiter (Zeus). Charles Thompson, designer of the Great Seal's final version, condensed line 625 of book IX of Virgil's *Aeneid*, which reads, *Juppiter omnipotes, audacibus annue coeptis* ("All-powerful Jupiter favors [the] daring under-takings"), to *Annuit Coeptis* ("He approves [our] undertakings"), while the phrase *Novus Ordo Seclorum* ("a new order of the ages") was adapted in 1782 from inspiration Thompson found in a prophetic line in Virgil's *Eclogue IV*: *Magnus ab integro seclorum nascitur ordo* (Virgil's *Eclogue IV*, line 5), the interpretation of the original Latin being, "And the majestic roll of circling centuries begins anew." This phrase is from the Cumaean Sibyl (a pagan prophetess of Apollo, identified in the Bible as a demonic deceiver) and involves the future birth of a divine son, spawned of "a new breed of men sent down from heaven" when he receives "the life of gods, and sees Heroes with gods commingling." According to the prophecy, this is Apollo, son of Jupiter (Zeus), who returns to earth through mystical "life" given to him from the gods when the deity Saturn-Jupiter returns to reign over the earth in a new pagan Golden Age—what the alignment of Jupiter and Saturn on December 21, 2020, forecast, which many (including pastors) erroneously referred to as the "Christmas Star"[27] (according to the Greek text, the magi followed an asteroid, not a stationary star alignment, whose trajectory led them to Bethlehem). It was the closest the two planets have appeared together in approximately eight hundred years, and did indeed forecast the arrival of a "messianic son"—the false one, whose spirit will reside in the Beast of Revelation 17:8.

From the beginning of the prophecy referenced on the Great Seal of the United States we read:

> Now the last age by Cumae's Sibyl sung Has come and gone, and the majestic roll Of circling centuries begins anew: Justice returns, returns old Saturn's reign, With a new breed of men sent down from heaven. Only do thou, at the boy's birth in whom The iron shall cease, the golden race arise, Befriend him, chaste Lucina; 'tis thine own Apollo reigns.
>
> He shall receive the life of gods, and see Heroes with gods commingling, and himself Be seen of them, and with his father's worth Reign o'er a world....
>
> Assume thy greatness, for the time draws nigh, Dear child of gods, great progeny of Jove [Jupiter/Zeus]! See how it totters—the world's orbed might, Earth, and wide ocean, and the vault profound, All, see, enraptured of the coming time![28]

According to Virgil and the Cumaean Sibyl, whose prophecy formed the *Novus Ordo Seclorum* of the Great Seal of the United States, the New World Order begins during a time of chaos when the earth and oceans are tottering—a time like today. This is when the "son" of promise arrives on earth—Apollo incarnate—a pagan savior born of "a new breed of men sent down from heaven" when "heroes" and "gods" are blended together. This sounds eerily similar to what the Watchers did during the creation of Genesis 6 giants, and why many believe Antichrist also represents the return of the Nephilim. But to understand why such a fanciful prophecy about Apollo, son of Jupiter, returning to earth should be important to you: In ancient literature, Jupiter was the Roman replacement of Yahweh as the greatest of the gods—a "counter-Yahweh." His son Apollo is a replacement of Jesus, a "counter-Jesus." This Apollo comes to rule the final New World Order, when "Justice returns, returns old Saturn's [Satan/Lucifer as the god of the air] reign." The ancient goddess Justice, who returns Satan's reign (*Saturnia regna*, the pagan Golden Age), was known to the Egyptians as Ma'at and to the Greeks as Themis, while to the Romans she was Lustitia. Statues and reliefs of her adorn thousands of government buildings and courts around the world, especially in Washington, DC, as familiar Lady Justice, blindfolded and holding scales and a sword. She represents the enforcement of secular law and is, according to the Sibyl's conjure, the authority that is going to require global compliance to the zenith of Satan's dominion concurrent with the coming of Apollo. What's more, the Bible's accuracy concerning this subject is alarming, including the idea that "pagan justice" will require surrender to a satanic system in a final world order under the rule of Jupiter's son.

In the New Testament, the identity of the god Apollo, repeat-coded in the Great Seal of the United States as the Masonic "messiah" who returns to rule the earth, is the same spirit—verified by the *same name*—that will inhabit the political leader of the end-times New World Order. According to key Bible prophecies, the Antichrist will be the progeny or incarnation of the ancient spirit, *Apollo*. Second Thessalonians 2:3 warns:

> Let no man deceive you by any means: for that day shall not come, except there come a falling away first, and that man of sin be revealed, the son of *perdition* [*Apoleia*; Apollo]. (Emphasis added)

Revelation 17:8 likewise ties the coming of Antichrist with Apollo, revealing that the Beast shall ascend from the bottomless pit and enter him:

> The Beast that thou sawest was, and is not; and shall ascend out of the Bottomless Pit, and go into *perdition* [*Apolia*, Apollo]: and they that dwell on the Earth shall wonder, whose names were not written in the Book of Life from the foundation of the world, when they behold the Beast that was, and is not, and yet is. (Emphasis added)

Among other things, this means the Great Seal of the United States is a prophecy, hidden in plain sight by the Founding Fathers for more than two hundred years, foretelling the return of a terrifying demonic god who seizes control of earth in the new order of the ages. This supernatural entity was known and feared in ancient times by different names: Apollo, Osiris, and even farther back as Nimrod, whom Masons consider to be the father of their institution.

In the last chapter of this book, we will circle back to this prophecy to expose the most insidious aspects of the scheme counting down to the year 2025.

INVITING THOSE PAGAN ENTITIES TO RULE OVER AMERICA
AND GUIDE US INTO THE NOVUS ORDO SECLORUM

When US Representative Nancy Pelosi, on January 4, 2007, assumed her role as Speaker of the House at the opening of the 110th Congress, she followed the pattern set by George W. Bush and his old man, infusing a loaded statement concerning the Founding Fathers, saying they were so confident in "the America they were advancing, they put on the seal, the great seal of the United States, '*Novus Ordo Seclorum*'—a new order for the centuries." Pelosi did not go into detail as to why she considered the phrase *Novus Ordo Seclorum* important dialectic during the momentous changeover of the control of Congress, nor did she add why this expression exists beneath the unfinished pyramid and the all-seeing eye (eye of Horus/Osiris/Apollo) in the Great Seal of the United States in the first place. But her allusion to it was not coincidental. I believe it was framed against January 20, 2001, when her dynastic establishment pal President George W. Bush, during his first inaugural address, faced the obelisk known as the Washington Monument and twice referred to an angel that "rides in the whirlwind and directs this storm." His reference was credited to Virginia statesman John Page, who wrote to Thomas Jefferson after the Declaration of Independence was signed, "We know the race is not to the swift nor the battle to the strong. Do you not think an angel rides in the whirlwind and directs this storm?"

Five weeks after Bush's inaugural, on Wednesday, February 28, 2001, Congressman Major R. Owens of New York stood before the House of Representatives and prayed to this "angel in the whirlwind." He asked the spiritual force to guide the *future* and *fate* of the United States.[29] Twenty-eight weeks later (for a total of thirty-three weeks from the day of the inaugural—a number invaluable to mysticism and occult fraternities), nineteen Islamic terrorists attacked the United States (according to the official story), hijacking four commercial airliners and crashing two of them into the Twin Towers of the World Trade Center in New York City. They slammed a third into the Pentagon, and a fourth, which had been directed toward Washington, DC, crashed near Shanksville, Pennsylvania. What happened that day resulted in nearly three thousand immediate deaths, at least two dozen missing persons, and the stage being set for changes to the existing world order.

When Bush was giving his second inaugural speech four years later, he again offered cryptic commentary, saying:

> For a half century, America defended our own freedom by standing watch on distant borders. After the shipwreck of communism came years of relative quiet, years of repose, years of sabbatical— and then there came a day of fire.

A few paragraphs following, Bush added:

> By our efforts, we have lit a fire as well—*a fire in the minds of men*. It warms those who feel its power, it burns those who fight its progress, and one day this untamed fire of freedom will reach the darkest corners of our world. (Emphasis added)

The phrase, "a fire in the minds of men," is from Fyodor Dostoyevsky's nineteenth-century book, *The Possessed* ("The Devils"), a novel set in pre-revolutionary Russia, where civil resistance is seen championed by nihilist Sergei Nechaev, who tries to ignite a revolution of such destructive power that society will be completely destroyed. The fact that a United States president would quote this phrase in an official speech of record was astonishing to many analysts, given that *The Possessed* is about violent government crackdown on dissent that sparks civil unrest and revolution marked by public violence, something eerily reminiscent of today.[30] *Fire in the Minds of Men* is also the title historian James H. Billington chose for his famous book on the history of revolutions, including the origin of occult Freemasonry and its influence in the American Revolution. In his closing comments, Bush himself tied the inaugural crypticisms to the Masonic involvement in the American Revolution, saying, "When our

Founders declared a new order of the ages, they were acting on an ancient hope that is meant to be fulfilled." The phrase, "a new order of the ages," is taken from the Masonically designed Great Seal (*Novus Ordo Seclorum*), and Bush further acknowledged that the secret society members were acting on an "ancient" hope that is "meant to be fulfilled."

Fast forward to the election of Joe Biden and Kamala Harris, and the surreal, illicit invocation to dark supernaturalism tied to those governing entities intent on fulfilling—as Bush prophesied—that ancient conspiracy from the Great Seal of the United States has been immediately revived. Right on cue, we find Democrat representative Emanuel Cleaver offering the congressional prayer opening up the 117th Congress "in the name of the monotheistic god, Brahma, and god known by many names by many different faiths."

Setting aside the numerous incorrect assumptions by Cleaver involving Brahma, the entreaty to such a Hindu god was highly appropriate, given that Vice President Kamala Devi Harris' name also invokes deities from Hindu mythology—illusionary and destructive ones.

From "The Surprising Meaning of Kamala Harris' Name" at thelist. com, we discover:

> Kamala is another name of a well-known Hindu goddess, who is probably better known as Lakshmi....
>
> Devi is a Hindu goddess as well. It is a Sanskrit word that means "goddess," but it is also the name of the Hindu mother goddess. Devi is considered to encompass womanhood completely...[but] does have a fierce side, and is involved in not only creating worlds, but destroying them as well.
>
> Her sister's middle name matches Kamala"s—Maya's middle name is Lakshmi. Maya is also a Sanskrit name meaning "illusion," and is another name of Durga, a Hindu goddess.

Thelist.com goes on to explain that Kamala's mother, Shyamala, chose these names specifically because, "A culture that worships goddesses produces strong women," she told the *Los Angeles Times*.[31]

Perhaps this explains why those "strong" women and men have taken to the streets of Portland, Oregon, over the last two years to feed the spirit of chaos beneath the shadow of Portlandia, the second-largest copper statue (after the Statue of Liberty) of a goddess in the United States, at thirty feet, ten inches tall and weighing six and a half tons. If standing, she would tower at approximately fifty feet.

The Portlandia repoussé is located above the entrance of the City of Portland Office Buildings downtown and is implicative of the goddess of witchcraft, Hecate.

Supposedly designed after "Lady Commerce" on the Portland City Seal, she holds a trident—considered of the utmost importance for sorcery and indispensable to the efficacy of infernal rites—under a six-pointed star, also an important instrument of dark arts and Hecatian witchcraft.

As occultists know, the metal (copper) that Portlandia is crafted from was sacred to ancient goddess worshipers. In early Rome copper was called cyprium, due to being primarily mined from Cyprus, the birthplace of the goddess Aphrodite. It was also sacred to the Sun God of Babylon and similar deities, some of whom required human sacrifice.

A plaque beneath Portlandia offers disquieting connections between her influence over that city and the souls of those citizens she reigns over, saying:

> She kneels down, and from the quietness of copper reaches out. We take that stillness into ourselves, and somewhere deep in the earth our breath [souls] becomes her city. If she could speak this is what she would say: Follow that breath. Home is the journey we make. This is how the world knows where we are.

Thus, the pattern continues between some of America's recent national leaders whose invitations (unlike Donald Trump's habitual recognition of the Judeo-Christian God of the Bible) have been to dark supernaturalism for ruling over and guiding the souls and destiny of this nation into an occult World Order. This now includes the new vice president (who could certainly become the actual president if aging Joe Biden—whom former White House stenographer Mike McCormick, who worked for Biden for six years, says "has lost 50 percent of his cognitive abilities"[32]—becomes incapacitated or otherwise incapable of fulfilling his four-year term), who bears the name of Hindu entities connected with "illusion" and the "destruction of worlds." (By the way, Robert Oppenheimer, the "father of the atomic bomb," upon witnessing the first detonation of a nuclear weapon on July 16, 1945, actually quoted the related Bhagavad-Gita, a Hindu text, declaring, "Now I am become Death, the destroyer of worlds.")

Joe Biden's name is likewise intriguing. A Jewish scholar points out that the Hebraic name for Joe Biden translates "Alas! Judgment!"[33] while other experts note that it beckons the arrival of a promised son, a "messiah," according to prominent Rabbi Aryeh Weingarten, who says Biden's name (בידן) contains the letters *yud daled* (יד), which spell out the word *yad* ("hand").

An article at Israel365.com explains:

Rabbi Weingarten [states] the first and last letters of "Biden" spell out the word "ben" (בֶּן), meaning son, which hints at the process of Moshiach (messiah) which will come through Moshiach ben David (the anointed son of David) and the Moshiach ben Yosef (the anointed son of Joseph). Rabbi Weingarten added that the gematria (Hebrew numerology) of "ben" is 52, equaling the name of Eliyahu (Elijah the prophet) who is the harbinger of the Messiah.

"This is not to say that Biden is the Messiah or will announce the Messiah," Rabbi Weingarten said. "This is simply a reminder that even a path that we would rather not choose can be God's method to bring about the redemption."

Rabbi Weingarten then noted the inner letters of the name Biden, yud and dalet (יד). The gematria of those letters equals 24.

"Many times in the Bible, David's name is written with a yud (דויד instead of the more common דוד) bringing the numerical total of his name to 24," Rabbi Weingarten explained. "Biden's last name is coming to remind us that we are on the verge of Elijah's arrival to re-establish the Davidic dynasty."[34]

The problem is, for Christians and Messianic Jews, the Messiah already arrived in the New Testament. His name is Jesus. Thus, the prophetic suggestion involving Biden's name more likely indicates a role he may play with the coming of the false messiah, the Antichrist.

Even some orthodox rabbis seem to agree, connecting the election of Biden and Kamala with the return of the days of Noah.

Rabbi Yoel Schwartz, the head of the Sanhedrin's Noahide Court and a highly respected Halachic (Torah law) authority, produced a video in which he commented on the divergent possibilities of the US presidential election.

"The elections were held on the 17th of Cheshvan," Rabbi Schwartz said. He noted that according to Jewish tradition, rains that caused the flood in the time of Noah began falling on the 17th of Cheshvan. "It was also on that day that here in Israel, the first rains of the season fell in earnest. They should have been rains of blessing but since Biden was elected, these rains became, like the rain on the same day in the time of Noah, a harbinger of the coming flood."[35]

Rabbi Schwartz adds: "The Democrats are spreading the very same sins that forced Noah into the ark," while another rabbi similarly notes that in Hebrew, "Harris" (הריס) means "destruction."

So, with Trump out of the way (at least for the time being), the dark side of the Deep State is quickly reviving efforts to get America back on track to its Secret Destiny, summoning those agents of chaos whose ancient scheme will culminate in arrival of the dreaded Man of Sin.

Joe Biden himself pledged allegiance to this New World Order in the *Wall Street Journal* op-ed, "How I Learned to Love the New World Order," in which he detailed his vision of surrendering American sovereignty to a new global government via the United Nations.

"Most Americans, myself included, reject 1930s-style isolationism. They expect to see the strong hand of American leadership in world affairs, and they know that...many security threats...require global solutions," he extolled.[36]

Will Biden's vision quickly unfold in the countdown to Zeitgeist 2025? "People who are not governed by God will be ruled by tyrants," said William Penn, founder of the English North American colony, the Province of Pennsylvania.

And for all those now bidding the return of "Old Saturn/Jupiter's" reign, we would also remind them of the ancient Greek tragedian Sophocles' warning: "Those whom Jupiter wishes to destroy, he first deprives of reason [drives mad]."

That said, it appears that left-leaning Americans are nevertheless rushing to embrace the newly appointed Zeitgeist gods, as vividly illustrated on the Spring 2021 cover of *Jacobin* (a leading voice of the American left, offering socialist perspectives on politics, economics, and culture), where the apotheosis of Joe Biden, Barack Obama, and Bill Clinton with the Hilarion are accompanied by lessor *elohim,* Nancy Pelosi and Chuck Schumer, as angels.

Biden's larger-than-life, bare-chested figure is shown surrounded by "holy spirits" of Twitter and "saints." The latter include kneeling Democrat leaders in the US Congress, Dr. Anthony Fauci, fawning journalists and manager-class devotees eagerly consuming the "holy scripture" from what is probably the latest Barack Obama memoir. The former president himself is shown as a six-winged seraphim bracketed by the likewise angelic [Obama], Hillary and Bill Clinton, with the trio gazing benignly from the heavens. A crowd of mask-wearing suburban laymen on Earth celebrate Biden's ascension.[37]

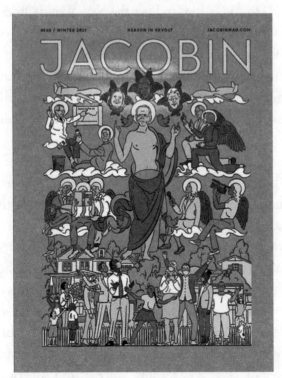

Spring 2021 cover of Jacobin conveying Joe Biden as an ascending Christ-like figure with Barack Obama, Bill and Hillary Clinton, accompanied by lesser elohim, Nancy Pelosi and Chuck Schumer, as angels.

BIG OLIGARCHY'S
COUNTDOWN TO 2025

2

[This is written] to the future or to the past, to a time when thought is free…to a time when truth exists and what is done cannot be undone: From the age of uniformity, from the age of solitude, from the age of Big Brother…greetings![38]

The above segment, from George Orwell's *1984*, was a diary entry written by main character Winston, who sought to connect with people who had previously or would one day exist in a time different than his own: an era when people did not live under constant control via programming that not only inserted governmental agenda into the psyches of the general public incrementally and at will, but where, also, members of society were not surveilled 100 percent of the time by the same powers. The book outlines a man's inner struggle between rebellion and compliance in the face of extreme population scrutiny and control by governmental powers. Such forces, in *1984*, regulate and enforce every aspect of a man's life, down to his very thoughts. By even writing a journal at all—an endeavor the man kept hidden—Winston violated laws stating that both independent speech and expressions of free thought were equal to insurrection, their very existence a usurpation of the authorities that ruled.

In this novel, the earlier-mentioned branch of the government known as the Ministry of Truth oversees all "news, entertainment, education, and fine arts."[39] This force utilizes its powerful and influential outlets to continually program the audiences, glorifying certain leaders as nearly god-like, while others are propagated as hated figures. Such personalities are often even the focus of a routine called a "Two Minutes Hate," an aptly-named period of time wherein a face of an individual who is pinpointed for revulsion appears on all surrounding screens, sending the crowd into a frenzy of screaming, throwing items, and even violence at the sight of the character. Such power-orchestrated periods provide the dystopian society's tired and weary populace an outlet for mounting frustration as they go about their micro-controlled lives.

In our modern world, some have made comparisons between Orwellian assertions and the real world, while others have maintained that Orwell was a genius of fiction and nothing more. After all, our modern population would *never* stand for the blatant conditioning that occurred in *1984*'s Two Minutes Hate. Such an obvious tactic would be recognized and dispelled immediately. Furthermore, many who state that modern media is used to target and coerce the animosity of specific political figures and movements come from a conservative crowd, meaning that those who would defend the media are often of the liberal slant. Since most of the left-leaning populace is made up of educated, degree-holding citizens,[40] the accusation that they would be the first to succumb to such primordial manipulation tactics would seem to insult our most matriculated consensus. Thus, if any comparison to Orwell's Oceania can hold water, we must observe a subtler tactic than the brutish ones controlling Winston's world. It would have to be more covert, incremental, persistent, and even civilized-looking. Perhaps it would be in the form of a continual inundation of headlines that villainize a targeted political figure, movement, or demographic, while, on the other hand, the elevating of a glorious counter-hero or movement is contrasted. Such an approach would coerce a culture into embracing one style of thinking and voting, and would impress them upon their daily philosophies, while those positioned as a public enemy are embraced as such. And, in response to the nonstop flood of messages that specifically work to shape the public's position on everything from politics to which shoes to purchase, a tired community begins to passively intake what they are spoon-fed, because many of them, like Winston, fight the mental onslaught until they can no longer will themselves to perceive reality. Sadly, many end up like Winston, who, at the end of *1984*, can—spoiler alert—no longer wage war with his own instincts and shuts down:

He had won the victory over himself. He loved Big Brother.[41]

Now, *that* is a strategy for controlling the mindset of the masses that just might catch on, were the media to think of it.

Wait a minute. Perhaps that is precisely what we've been seeing. If this is the case, those figures unfortunate enough to be positioned as deserving of public disdain would, perhaps, be relieved to *only* be the focus of a Two Minutes Hate, as opposed to the all-day, every-day animosity that's aimed in their direction.

Are you willing to challenge your thinking? With knowledge comes power; do you dare to continue reading, knowing that what is unraveled here may cause you to see the world around you differently?

In truth, we are surrounded by cultural associations that tell us what to purchase, like, wear, eat, drink, drive, and even how to vote. In fact, a societal agenda is being played out via our media each day that—albeit more tactful than Orwellian literature—programs our public mindset in nearly the same way. Better yet, the subtlety employed nearly guarantees that, as we embrace the narrative being carved, we additionally perceive accrued thought patterns to be our own.

Just as Winston's inner conflict was derived in his own instinctive resistance to the Big Brother forces, it is understandable if the current inundation of media into the common mindset causes us to feel wariness and distrust toward an unseen power that drives an agenda and utilizes multiple angles to continually program the minds of the masses.

Many people have heard the line "Big Brother is watching" and likened it to the surveillance that occurs in our modern setting.[42] But more covert in our condition is the fact that not only are we increasingly watched, we are being programmed. When there are central, controlling entities that feed the narrative of thought throughout a nation, they tell us how to think, what is appropriate to say, how to feel, what to believe, and what to be passionate about, let alone how we are to spend our money. But, the modern-day equivalent to the Orwellian Thought Police maintains control with a softer finesse than those in *1984*.

At least, that's the case so far.

Consider the revolution of occurrences over the past few years. Does it seem as though political alliances in the public sphere have become more aggressively polarized than in recent decades? Perhaps you've noticed that phrases such as "hate speech" have become more common—perpetually causing people of traditional or religious values to grow silent about their beliefs? Or, maybe you or someone you know has been banned from social media for statements that—while legal under the First Amendment of the US Constitution—were deemed "too offensive" to be posted publicly. Maybe you've noticed specific individuals who have been victims of continual headline-bashing, while others are repeatedly glorified by the same news outlets.

If you've observed these things occurring simultaneous to the gratuitous oversaturation of media-related themes in increasing areas of our daily lives (memes, advertisements, news updates continually buzzing on our smartphones, and more), you may be wondering if there is a more powerful force attempting to empty the public's minds of certain thoughts, while overwhelming them with other content. Or, perhaps the proximity of distraction itself is becoming a weapon of choice by powers that be. It would seem that the same icons of media that once pervaded our television screens now follow us everywhere we go. Via smartphones, tablets, computer laptops, and other devices, we are never alone anymore. In the digital age, we have a universe of information at our fingertips. Conversely, the very same universe intrudes upon us every other minute. We're rarely afforded an undistracted moment wherein we can have a conversation with a friend or loved one that isn't interrupted by a series of beeps, dings, and other distracting tones, each announcing political upheaval somewhere in the world, proclaiming the divorce of a celebrity couple, or promising to divulge the weight-loss secrets of the rich and famous.

At the price of connectivity, we lose our privacy, our autonomy, even our individuality. We are witnessing a revolution of Orwellian proportions. Next, those who employ such tactics will come after *your* right to free speech—and soon, that of independent thought. The continual "paid programming" that flows through our countless devices and keeps us at the beck and call of every ringtone doesn't come without cost. Our minds are, at cue, being trained to respond to a corporate chronicle that the public is slowly forgetting how to live without. There is an agenda behind the script, a conditioning that occurs with every new "ding" that commands our attention. Most people will dismiss this important detail, but it is vital—forming the crux around which this chapter is shaped:

Big Brother is not merely *watching*.

Big Brother is *speaking*.

IT'S EVERYWHERE

In order to fully expose the level of control media has over our thinking, it's important to illustrate its vast reach. When one says the word "media," people usually visualize a television news channel or perhaps a single social-media platform. Unfortunately, those images are remnants of yesteryear, when a type of simplicity attached itself to broadcasting, when the power knob of a television could cut off the intrusion it placed on our lives, and when ownership of outlets was limited so that each had a restricted realm of influence. Later we'll delve into how much of this has changed, but a small exposé of reach-potential will help us understand the sheer force behind the element we sum up with the single word "media."

An easy way to begin to grasp this factor can be found by playing a little game. Next time you visit a local, big-box brand department store (such as Walmart, Target, or Kmart), imagine that you have the power to remove anything from the store's inventory that you see fit. Let's pretend that your criteria for removal is any reference—however big or small—to any type of content related to television, movies, modern music, magazines, *and* news stories including reporting on the realms of politics, sports, natural disasters, etc.

As you tour the store, mentally remove anything with branding or advertisement that falls within this category. This will be easiest if you start in an area such as the cereal or cookie aisle, since examples here will be the most obvious. If packaging features a cartoon character, remove it from your visual. If a product is branded with a superhero, take it out. Apply this principle to everything as you walk through the grocery section of this building. If such a maneuver of inventory were in your power and you carried out this directive, what would be left on the shelves? Taking this activity a step farther, wander away from the food section of the building and roam through the other departments: clothing, shoes, toys, and electronics. If you followed the initial instructions for this exercise—removing all references to anything existing in modern media—what would remain? It's likely the store would be nearly empty, with the leftover stock strangely mirroring the inventory lining the shelves of a general store of yesteryear.

This simple exercise helps us begin to get an idea of how far into every aspect of our culture this inundation extends. We're surrounded at every turn by items branded by associations—not because they're related, but because the one will help generate sales for the other.

For example, a few years back, many kids were captivated by the cartoon *SpongeBob SquarePants*. This goofy-faced, yellow dude was everywhere: bubble bath, shampoo, shoes, t-shirts, pajamas, bedding, cookies, cereal, crackers, fruit snacks, coffee mugs, school supplies, backpacks, myriad toys, and even appliances such as waffle makers and toasters—the list goes on and on. All the revenue from sales of these products represents millions of dollars annually, *completely aside* from the money made by the actual cartoons and movies starring the animated character. For several years, SpongeBob's face was everywhere as part of a vast franchise of money-making endeavors, via which Nickelodeon saw proceeds soaring to $8 billion annually, which involved "more than 700 license partners worldwide…[and became] the most widely distributed franchise in MTV Networks history."[43]

Consider another example: In 2013, Disney released its $1.28 billion box-office hit *Frozen*, which became so popular that merchandise sales soared to more than $100 billion in retail gains, flooding the markets with so much *Frozen* inventory that even other Disney franchises were off-put by the overwhelming saturation, which they called "brand fatigue."[44] As for me, I'll never forget the day I saw Disney's *Frozen* characters branded across the labels of three-pound bags of apples sold at our local grocery store. This is an example of the previously mentioned strategy of sales by association—what that cartoon's princesses had to do with these orchard-produced fruits, other than to entice parents of young children to purchase them, I could never begin to comprehend (that is, other than to say that the fruit's appeal is bolstered by the pictures of the Disney princesses on the labels). My point in discussing both *SpongeBob SquarePants* and *Frozen* is to illustrate the depth of the media's saturation into our society. One simple animated character created for entertainment purposes is backed with enough resources to launch its image on everything—related or not!—from apples to toothpaste. Imagine then, the kind of power that these forces have at their avail, should they decide to use the same resources to push an agenda.

Oh, wait—they already are.

If you were to extend the grocery store activity to the outside world, you would quickly visualize a place where little remained. Imagine visiting a city where no signs or billboards, advertisements, product displays, restaurants, etc., referenced any type of media. Like the store whose inventory was reduced to a small, general-store assortment of necessities, metropolises would quickly seem quiet, desolate, and barren after all such links were removed. (We would feel as though we had gone back in time!) The truth is, we're besieged with media 24/7. When we really study our surroundings and analyze the impact it has on our lives, it's a bit overwhelming. Yet, there is more to this revelation. In tandem with all that's been said, consider that 90 percent of all the media we see—which so vastly impacts the spaces where we spend our lives—originates from only six sources.[45]

Let's put this together: Only six companies control 90 percent of *all* the media hiding in plain sight each day, appearing—through branding or otherwise—on our clothing, groceries, and other merchandise. It is in the scenery (via billboards and advertisements) we see while driving to work, and it permeates social media and online connections. The incoming messages often influence our decisions, shape the way we spend our time and money, and even sway our philosophy about moral and religious aspects of life (if you doubt this, notice the increasingly immoral correlation between the media and the current public worldview). If the notion that our psyches are progressively flooded still leaves you unconvinced, consider that the average consumer now sees five thousand ads each day. That's a tenfold increase since the 1970s, when that number was only five hundred.[46] And, as if it isn't alarming enough to realize that only six sources launch this barrage, we may find it even more distressing to learn that many of these corporations are held jointly via shared stocks, which often have interlocked interests.

Were you beginning to see how a few key voices narrate the story of society?

The Hand That Rocks the Boat

> Infancy's the tender fountain,
> Power may with beauty flow,
> Mothers first to guide the streamlets,
> From them souls unresting grow—

Grow on for the good or evil,
Sunshine streamed or evil hurled,
For the hand that rocks the cradle
Is the hand that rules the world.[47]

When this poem was written in the nineteenth century, it glorified mothers (and others involved in child-rearing) whose influence was so profound that it carved the condition of the upcoming generation. Back then, the caregivers' philosophies and principles were woven into the fabric of emerging leaders and citizens. The concept of the entire world being ruled by the cradle-rocking hand acknowledged that children are impressionable, capable of being sculpted in every way throughout their formative years until they grow up to apply the principles of their upbringing to their own role in society. Thus, seeds sown into the youngest generations sprout the worldview of the next.

However, in subsequent centuries—especially in recent decades— caregivers no longer have sole responsibility for shaping the paradigm and attitudes of children. Intrusive forces such as television series, movies, propaganda asserted in educational settings, social media, and even commercials inserted concepts—good and bad—into children's outlooks as they grow. And, since more parents now work outside the home than ever before, daycares, public schools, and media of all types seem to claim more of our children's time than do guardians. In fact, statistics show that "as few as 14 percent [of Millennials] were cared for at home by a relative"; thus, we can see that more than 85 percent of our youngest generations are influenced by sources outside the home and/or immediate family.[48] As the world changes, the digital availability of communication and information fosters an era in which upcoming generations' views are increasingly sculpted not by parents or caregivers, but by those on social media, news outlets, and even TV shows and movies that foist any—and all—agendas into the minds of our most impressionable. The notion that technology has usurped the parental role in modern society has credibility: Most children ages two to five watch more than thirty hours of television each week, and six- to eleven-year olds average twenty-eight hours of TV watching weekly. Additionally, 71 percent of those ages eight to eighteen have a television in their bedroom, meaning they have no parental supervision while taking in such content.[49] Worse, all too often, these avenues of information don't seek to better our world or promote peace, but instead influence the masses to embrace a dark agenda. In this way, the powers that be often exploit the resources of our modern digital age to manipulate the public and sow discord.

But what, you may ask, does this have to do with modern media outlets? How are these issues related?

Few would argue that powerful figures, agencies, and political movements often use such resources to their advantage when pushing their own agenda. Crowds are, unfortunately, relatively easy to manipulate with access to the right avenues of influence. And, when it becomes observable that the public is not embracing a notion, movement, or legislation that leading powers desire to promote, often the solution can be as easy as tweaking the headlines or television programming to incite public response. When degenerate sources wish to create a certain large-scale reaction, all they must do is rock the proverbial boat. And, unfortunately, since the guidance of family or caregivers has waned across the years and digital preoccupation has taken its place, many people don't have a philosophical or religious platform from which to pull and respond. Instead, modern generations have been conditioned to seek guidance from Internet memes, television programming, social media, and other sources of electronic information—or *mis*information. And, since there are devious powers that would use these outlets to promote their own agenda rather than serve the public via earnest journalism, we risk falling prey to sensationalistic stories rather than insisting on obtaining truth. The result is zealous droves of impressionable young adults who embrace headlines enthusiastically—even when they lack the whole truth. On a large scale, this means that a few in power have the means to steer society with craftily spun stories.

Thus, the hand that previously rocked the cradle is replaced by a new hand—one that, instead, rocks the boat.

The Internet

The news industry has changed vastly over the past century. There are several reasons for this, one of the primary being the emergence of the Internet. In fact, this single entity has revolutionized how nearly the entire world operates. Of course, its benefits have been obvious, from facilitating information-gathering and instant communication to enhancing corporate and industrial practices and simply making our personal lives run a little more smoothly. For example, the Internet has given us the ability to find just the right product, company, or service without limiting our options to what's in our local phone book or nearby retail shops. And, during recent COVID-19 shutdowns, the World Wide Web seemed at times to be a lifeline for households in need of supplies amid pandemic-prompted shortages and brick-and-mortar store closures.

But, as with so many good things, there's a dark side of the Web as well, one that, for example, fosters malevolent trade practices and adversely affects the reporting and circulation of news. With more and more people obtaining their news digitally, distribution costs have plummeted. The trend toward paperless distribution of news hasn't only increased profit margins, but has also opened up opportunities for real-time reporting. In previous decades, newspaper reporters covered breaking stories by traveling to the location, researching events, conducting interviews, writing the articles, and seeing them published no sooner than the next morning's paper. In contrast, today's journalists can cover and write entire stories remotely from their desks in the newsroom or from their homes, often simply by gathering the facts from Internet sources.

Director of the Tow Centre for Digital Journalism at Columbia University, Emily Bell, commented on the way a new form of journalism emerged around the time of the September 11, 2001, World Trade Centers attack, stating:

> Linear TV just could not deliver. People used the web to connect…in real time…then [posted] on [online] message boards

and forums…[with] bits of information they knew themselves and aggregated it with links from elsewhere.[50]

With the speed at which technology can now provide updates, few people now have the patience to wait for a print article (where they're even still available, as many newspapers have gone to online-only formats) in the next morning's newspaper when they're wanting more information on a hatching story. The Internet has afforded immediate connection to worldwide events as they happen.

Unfortunately, the down side of this instant news production is that it has become a breeding ground for misinformation, with little accountability for incorrect or false reporting. Blogs, vlogs (video blogs), user-edited sites (such as Wikipedia), social media, personally/privately contracted Internet domains (such as www.<anynamehere>.com), memes, and so many other currently available ways of moving information across the globe have given all individuals platforms by which they can present any information they want as news—with nearly no accountability.

During the days when all news was in print format, most information was vetted through editors and others who fact-checked and proofread stories. Granted, there was still the opportunity for agenda-influenced information (or downright lies) to be released, but those stories had to survive a selection and approval process before going to press. For example, if two newspapers in the same town told different versions of a story, readers could be aware that one of the journalists wasn't telling the truth or that the whole story wasn't being fully disclosed. Any corrections or updates could be printed in a subsequent edition (albeit, sometimes in an inconspicuous area where readers would likely overlook it; these corrections often seemed to be more of a token effort than a real one to publicly set the facts straight). However, all this aside, what the public had access to was multiple news sources printing stories as they saw them to be true, researched by reporters who often traveled to the source of the event or had trusted sources of information, and that were fact-checked and edited by news companies that hung their credibility on the notion that the public could *and would* expect trustworthy reporting. The Internet's impact on the press today, however, has made it so that consumers often see reports with different or conflicting facts. For the average reader, true accounts become more difficult to discern with each passing day.

The vehicle by which the public obtains its news has changed vastly across the decades as well. What began a century ago as a daily printed form of the news slowly evolved to include news broadcasts from radio stations, television networks, and finally to Internet sources, which are available through a variety of devices, including personal computers, tablets, and smart phones.[51]

> Each shift [of public news intake] rendered the prior form of media slightly more obsolete and identified a universal theme:… people…will embrace any technology that permits them to… [obtain news at greater speed and incrementalism].[52]

Because the Internet is a resource that gives a platform to anyone who creates a social-media profile, composes emails, contracts a "www.<anynamehere>.com" website, has enough graphic arts skill to create the most rudimentary of memes, or generally knows how to type an opinion, it is daily flooded with stories that don't benefit from the scrutiny print news underwent in eras gone by. Millions of opinions taint articles that *appear* to present credible investigations. Sources of "facts" are dubious and sometimes unverifiable.

Not only does the Internet itself create a forum wherein any users can post their version of news, but technology has also brought us to a place where nearly any story can be contrived by folks at home on a simple computer. Deepfake, Photoshop, graphic design, film editing, artificial intelligence, and other technology provide limitless possibilities for presenting any information, whether valid or not, as "real." As stated before, truth has become a "buyer beware" market.

One meme floating around the Internet says, "'Don't believe everything you read on the internet.'—Abraham Lincoln."[53] This very image makes the point: It only takes a moment for most viewers to recognize that Lincoln *never* could have said this, since the Internet didn't come on the scene until more than a century *after* his death. However, youngsters who are unaware of this chronological gap may accept the words as fact. (And, as we'll discuss later, then they'll repeat them to comrades as truth.) Herein lies yet another way the Internet has contributed to the public's inability to trust the news. This newer vehicle for circulating news greatly complicates matters for readers looking for truth, because instead of having access to only a couple of news sources with an established journalistic process of ensuring reliability and scrutiny, we have at our fingertips thousands of versions of the same story—many of which are based on unprofessional journalistic practices, personal opinions and biases, secondhand information, rumors, and—at times—even outright lies.

With such a playground of false information available to anyone who chooses to report a story, and with no accountability for falsehoods or errors, a new problem emerges for professional news reporters. These, who once had daily deadlines for stories to be included in the following morning's print newspapers, now find that the immediacy of the Internet, combined with its availability for any to report on, fosters a setting wherein they must work 24/7 to stay ahead of the continual feed of unreliable information posted. Reporting now happens around the clock, and the true professional must work tirelessly to stay ahead of the game, and they do so for reasons ranging from duty to true journalistic ideals in order to prevent public panic in response to published untruths. The flipside of this issue is that, while journalists now have access to much more information by which to feed their own stories via the Internet, they must scrutinize the information's credibility before using it. And, the corporation that loses too much time to such analysis risks breaking stories "days after they've appeared on Twitter" as tweets from eyewitnesses who may not have full details of the event.[54] The resulting conundrum for the journalist becomes whether to publish a story before all details are verified or to run the article so late that the world has moved on and the content is no longer relevant. As a result of this dilemma, the quality of the news often suffers.[55]

Remember the Abraham Lincoln meme mentioned earlier? It likely originated as a joke. This brings up another valid point regarding misinformation on the Net. Nearly any story, hoax, meme, or social media rant, removed from its context, can be (and often is) circulated and perceived by some as fact. In this way, reporters seeking to share true information are, again, vastly outnumbered by news that derives from false origins—whether intentionally or not.

From Journalism to Media Consolidation

> We know that no one ever seizes power with the intention of relinquishing it.[56]

Those who have attempted over the past centuries to share true and credible news with the public follow five core elements of good journalism. These should be followed by anyone presenting themselves as members of an honest press.

1. **Truth and reliability.** Just as the oath one must take before giving a sworn testimony in a court of law, reporters should give the truth, the whole truth, and nothing but the truth. When they can't verify information that seems relevant, its unconfirmed status should be relayed to the reader/viewer.
2. **Independence of agents**. Those call themselves reliable sources shouldn't operate on behalf of anyone who might gain financially or otherwise from the information being disseminated. Facts should be presented without sway by any "political, corporate, or cultural" conflict of interest.[57] Affiliations with those who may profit should be made public.
3. **Lack of bias.** When stories are relayed as factual, they should include all details and events, not only those that skew the article to sway readers' opinions in one direction or another. Opinion pieces should be disclosed as such.

4. **Objectivity.** False reporting can lead (as we've often seen) to impassioned responses from the public that can escalate into all types of problematic behavior. If journalists seek to carry out a public service, then it's necessary to present fact-based, objective reporting that doesn't manipulate the public's emotions.

5. **Accountability.** This is to be done with professionalism, the willingness to correct any errors, and the motivation of building—and keeping—the public's trust.[58]

Some of the obstacles standing in the way of honest journalism have been outlined. It has been asserted that there is a powerful hand that rocks the boat society rides in. But, if this is the case, then precisely *whose* hand is it that reaches out to shake up the public's mindset? A couple of decades back, we began to see a shift in the answer to this question.

In returning to our earlier example of two newspapers in the same town, there was a time several decades ago when it would have been legally mandated for the two entities to be separately owned. In fact, several laws were in place that regulated and limited ownership of television stations, news outlets, and radio stations. As a general rule, in most markets, only one could be owned at a time per region. Cross-ownership, meaning proprietorship of multiple types of companies, was also usually prohibited. Such laws were set into place by the FCC (Federal Communications Commission) to avoid biased reporting and over-conglomeration of news. In the late 1990s, however, some within the industry began to fight these rules (more on this in a bit). In June of 2003, the FCC updated its rules to allow television broadcasters to expand ownership to reach "a combined 45 percent of the national audience," allowing news sources to extend their reach beyond the previously held 35 percent cap.[59] Simultaneously, guidelines were updated to allow cross-ownership of multiple forms of media outlets—television, radio, newspaper, etc. Additionally, companies whose reach was previously limited to only one station were now permitted to own multiple, depending on the size and spread of their market and the ratings of each outlet under same proprietorship.[60] In simpler terms, this extended reach from *one* outlet, capped at 35 percent of national audience, to multiple *and* various means of broadcasters, who were then *each* allowed to obtain 45 percent of the national audience. The overlap potential within same-possession allowed conglomerates nearly unlimited scope.

Some among the FCC expressed concern over this legislative overhaul, worried that "the changes would concentrate ownership in the hands of a few, reduce the diversity of viewpoints and stifle reporting of local news."[61] ("Local news" includes much more than reporting stories that occur in one's hometown; it also refers to the representation of small group points of view, localized political or economic issues, lesser-known political candidates, and even the assurance that special-interest concerns—such as "consumer advocates, civil rights and religious groups, small broadcasters, writers, musicians, academicians and the National Rifle Association"[62] just to name a few—are not replaced with generic, nationalized rhetoric.)

The heart of the issue was this: The previously held policies existed to keep news diversified, independent, and competitive. With these qualities in mind, each station would be held accountable—by both its consumers *and* opponents—to provide true, vetted, and well-researched news. By limiting cross-ownership (the holding of television, radio, and newspaper outlets simultaneously) sources were, again, forced to do diligent reporting or be eliminated by more responsible contenders. Those who challenged these rules did so on the grounds that many of the laws were several decades old—seemingly archaic in light of such new innovations as cable TV, satellite, and even a newly budding World Wide Web.[63] Existing laws, instated between 1941 and 1975, were set in place specifically to "encourage competition and prevent monopoly control of the media;"[64] but were declared by many to be outdated in light of these newer information vehicles. Essentially, networks retaining only the remaining audiences of analog television claimed that the era of a few major networks, paired with small, localized channels, was in the past, rapidly being outpaced by newer ways of consumers selectively acquiring programming in the home (such as those just mentioned). As a result, companies that had been disallowed to pursue expansion of their audience beyond the 35 percent cap—and who likewise claimed that they barely turned profits as is—claimed they were being pigeonholed into continual financial struggles.[65]

For this reason, in 1996, a law was instated that forced the FCC to revise and restructure older legislation that was no longer deemed to be in the public's best interest every two years.[66] While larger networks sought to remove the 35 percent audience cap completely, smaller stations prophetically claimed that this would "allow the networks to gobble up [smaller] stations and take away control of programming."[67]

In fact, Commissioner Michael Copps' apprehension of the changes was so severe that he stated that, under the new laws, "America's new media elite [has been given] unacceptable levels of influence over the ideas and information upon which our society and democracy depend."[68]

Ironically, many of the outlets that made a case for necessary expansion are still the largest media outlets controlling the market today: ViacomCBS, Newscorp, Fox, Disney, ABC, General Electric, NBC, AOL, Time Warner, CNN/Money, and Warner Bros.[69] (More on specific media companies in the upcoming pages.) Suffice it to say, despite whatever economic "threat" these felt that they were facing prior to 2003, they actually weathered the storm quite well.

In June, 2003, CNN Money reported:

The…[FDC] approved new media ownership rules…allowing television broadcasters to expand their reach, despite fears the move may reduce the variety of viewpoints available to consumers.[70]

Since these changes began, perpetual consolidation of media ownership has become more of an issue. Before this occurred, higher numbers of media outlets were locally owned or owned by a greater number of sources, meaning that viewpoints represented had influence from a more level "playing field," and that news was better primed for its own viewer locale and was better customized to its location/demographic.

Many experts who weighed in on the changes in June of 2003 voiced forewarning fears in response to the changes. Those who saw the imminence of bias in reporting, diminishment of small-group viewpoints, and over-conglomeration of coverage—particularly as it pertains to political commentary—have been proven right nearly two decades later. Perhaps one of the most alarming remarks given was by executive director for the Center for Public Integrity, Charles Lewis, who immediately expressed concern regarding how the mainstreaming of media would be abused politically:

> The most powerful special interest in America is the media…if you're a politician, they control whether your face and your voice is on the airwaves. That's power. If you're not on the airwaves, backed with constituencies, you're going to lose.[71]

Critics of media consolidation express several concerns. One is that when competition is consolidated, the lack of rivalry erodes the drive to remain truthful in reporting, to offer edgy information represented in full factual objectivity, and the diversity of small-groups' voices becomes lost amongst a larger rhetoric. Additionally, when news outlets focus solely on reporting, those who seek coverage do so intentionally. When stories are presented between modes of entertainment, viewers perceive themselves to be informed, but their intake has been passive—randomly interspersed amid what they are otherwise doing. Since they don't go looking for updates, they aren't in an active mindset to objectively take in the information that may be lined with bias, *and* they're only presented with the stance that merely floats across the screen. Naturally then, they haven't heard both sides of a story. But, because they aren't seeking out news coverage in the first place, it's unlikely they will research to find the truth.

Another element of conglomeration is that media is often represented with one homogenized voice. This misrepresents the spoken opinions of controlling entities as a collective public consensus, which isn't always accurate. Complicating this matter is the fact that consolidation only represents national and global information. The lack of local news is more than the loss of reporting regarding geographically close events. This means that if a portrayed position doesn't align with nationally asserted rhetoric (as has been mentioned regarding civil-rights groups, special-interest groups, lesser-known candidates, etc.), it runs the risk of being diminished. When considering the passivity with which people will receive news, the national/global filter stories will be put through, and the potential for representing opinion or bias as factual or public consensus, we can see how these elements can be combined with the sheer saturation available to our modern press to create a setting wherein a single event, movement, or voice could sway political momentum, possibly even worldwide. Since sensationalism drives sales, there is always a risk that mere "drama" will equate itself with credible news in the public eye, while investigative, fact-driven stories garner less attention.

All of this is *before* we consider how much money networks make running paid advertisements for political groups or campaigners, which undoubtedly skews objectivity between such political agents and their cooperative advertising networks. Putting all this together, it becomes obvious that we have evolved from a place where the press exists to inform the population to it being abused to *manipulate* and *steer* it.

This transition represents a crucial (and devastating) rotation in the history of media influence. The cross-ownership of television and radio stations, along with newspaper outlets, has deeper implications than just dual proprietorship. Sources that previously focused on news for the purposes of reporting events were now in a position to see increased profits for cinematic and merchandising endeavors. If political reporting caused adverse responses from viewers, there was the additional threat that their purchase or entertainment decisions would see an impact as well. Additionally, the power of media quickly became a vehicle for furthering political undertakings. The lines between reporting and media for entertainment blurred, and financial potential quickly marred lines between the varying realms, causing cross-ownership to become a form of cross-contamination between conflicting interests.

On one hand, television and movies still existed as entertainment.

After the appearance of a television in every home in the mid 1940s to the mid 1950s, advertisers soon figured out that they were sitting on a gold mine if this new innovation was used properly. Previously limited to print media, they found that television allowed their advertising to enter each home. Early on, their target audience was mostly women, since they were most likely to be at home during the daytime. Soon, marketing to kids was added to TV commercials that aired during cartoon productions. Nowadays, nobody is safe from the barrage of commercial advertising.

On the other hand, TV also quickly became an outlet for news reporting. Ideally, the public enjoyed truth in reporting—so long as it was kept separate from the sales side of media. This was largely accomplished via the rules that regulated/limited ownership of varying outlets. As time progressed, television and radio became increasingly popular sources of news, but it was still understood that entertainment and reporting occurred in separate arenas. However, on another plain, the government, like advertisers, quickly realized that TV was a great tool for mainstreaming campaigns and for other political announcements. It was easy to integrate, since so much of the news overflowed into political realms and vice versa. Furthermore, TV served to "[bring] the candidate and the voter into more intimate contact than was formerly possible," and "no candidate for high national or state office can afford to ignore a medium that reaches at least 98 percent of all American households."[72] Mainstreaming of issues, debates, interviews with candidates, and virtually all other aspects of political interaction became information that television quickly carried into each voter's living room. We don't need to spend much time imagining all the ways that the introduction of TV entirely changed the scope of political campaigning. Yet, for a time, they were still held as separate spheres from commercial media.

Through cross-ownership, and later, conglomerate consolidation, these various media realms (entertainment, advertisement, and politics) have collided. Much of the corporate ownership of these entities has intertwined, and the resulting cross-*contamination* tends to allow each agenda to inundate the others. Over time, political agendas, marketing ads, and entertainment have come to be delivered in the same field, with the messages easily confused. This makes it harder for people to know what is real, what is procured from political agendas to drive votes in a certain direction, what is merely for entertainment purposes, what is orchestrated to generate commercial sales, and what theatrics are contrived to rouse passions in viewers for deviant, ulterior motivations.

After all, when news outlets are owned by entertainment companies, can we ever be certain that reporting is credible, untainted by sensationalism for entertainment purposes? But then again, when entertainment is owned by news outlets, can we be certain that products made for our amusement are merely that? Or could it be that they are created and used to condition the population to accept what's being asserted within political spheres? It's no coincidence that a currently trending movement will at some point become the topic of television shows and movies. Many times, the companies pushing such issues are owned by the same parent corporation.

BIG MEDIA

It has been stated that 90 percent of all media we see daily derives from six controlling corporations that have become known as "Big Media." Though they appear to be separate entities, we find, upon digging, many mergers and bidding wars to acquire and innovate new assets and means of profit. As such, many networks or companies are owned by more than one company on this list at a specified percentage of shareholdership. This is worth noting, since many are perceived as competitors by the outside world, yet their interests—and investments—are intertwined. Further complicating ownership is the fact that, as negotiations are in the works, many place chronological stipulations on the conversions, making their ownership transferable at a *future* date, convoluting present possession of assets. With all of this said, here is a current overview of the conglomerates that influence nearly every moment of our lives.

AT&T

Each of the following is directly owned or is a subsidiary of AT&T: Warner Media LLC, Warner Brothers, DC Entertainment (DC Comics and DC Films), New Line Cinema (made famous recently by *The Lord of the Rings* film franchise), HBO, Otter Media, DirecTV, Cricket Wireless, and Turner Broadcasting System, which comes loaded with its own list of subsidiaries. These include CNN, Boomerang, Cartoon Network, Turner Classic Movies, TNT, TBS, and Turner Sports (which includes several sports website outlets such as NBA.com and the Bleacher Report). Because AT&T has evolved from the earliest of telephone companies—originally called American Telephone and Telegraph Company—it likewise still owns some of the more archaic relics of the telephone industry, such as the Yellow Pages, and "almost anything with the name 'Bell' in it."[73, 74, 75]

Walt Disney Company

The following are either directly owned or are subsidiaries of Disney: ABC News, Disney Media Networks, ESPN (80 percent), Touchstone Pictures, Marvel, Lucasfilm, A&E (50 percent), Pixar, Hollywood Records, Vice Media (10 percent), Core Publishing, The History Channel (50 percent), Lifetime (50 percent), and many others too numerous to list. Then, countless movie franchises are owned by Disney, such as *Indiana Jones*, *Star Wars*, *The Muppets*, and *Marvel*. On top of all this is the obvious ownership of Walt Disney theme parks and Disney television channels worldwide. In addition, Disney recently completed a $71 billion merger with Fox, obtaining assets such as Fox's television and movie studios, FX, National Geographic, and stakes in some assets in London and India. Disney obtained Fox's 30 percent stake in Hulu, which, added to Disney's previously held 30 percent, gives it a controlling stake at 60 percent. Also acquired were such film franchises as *Avatar*, *X-men*, *The Simpsons*, and *Deadpool*. An interesting exchange took place during the proposal of this merger, however. Originally, the offer for

the acquisition was $52 billion, which had been discussed and even casu-
ally accepted between Disney executive Bob Iger and Fox executive Rupert
Murdoch in 2017. However, several months later, Comcast attempted to
outbid Iger for the assets, offering Murdoch $65 billion. Iger's response was
to counteroffer, outbidding Comcast at $71 billion. Here's the twist: The
structure of the sale contract gave Murdoch the option of taking his payment in cash or in shares of Disney stock, which the Murdoch foundation
opted to do. Thus, the transaction is really more a merger than a sale, ensuring a type of cross-collateralization of interests between previously competing entities. Murdoch is now a powerful shareholder in Disney, in addition
to retaining his hold of certain Fox assets such as Fox Business Network,
Fox News Network, Fox Broadcast Network, Fox Sports, and Fox television
stations.[76, 77, 78, 79, 80]

Comcast

Comcast has been named the biggest broadband provider in the US,
"with over 22 million internet customers" reported in 2017.[81] It also has
assets in the filming and television industries, including the movie-making
giant Universal Studios, which in turn operates Universal Pictures International, Universal Studios Home Entertainment, Universal Animation
Studios, Universal Interactive, and other smaller filmmakers such as Illu-
mination Entertainment, Focus Features, and Working Title Films. The
following are all directly owned by or are subsidiaries: MSNCB; NBCU-
niversal, which also operates NBC, NBC News, NBC Studios, and NBC
Sports (along with several other lesser-known sports outlets), along with
NCBUniversal cable (which operates a chain of cable channels such as
Bravo, USA Network, CNBC, MSNBC, E!, SyFy, Sleuth, and many others) and DreamWorks Animation Studio; Universal Studios; Fandango;
New Era Tickets; the Platform; StreamSage; Universal Pictures; and Hulu
(which Disney is currently negotiating with to purchase and obtain full
control). Comcast also owns the Weather Channel and Internet accom-
paniments such as theweatherchannel.com and related apps and Xfinity

branding (which includes Xfinity TV, Xfinity Voice, and Xfinity Internet). Among its assets is also XUMO, an online streaming video service offering nearly two hundred channels. Also included in its subsidiaries are several extra-American ventures such as Telemundo, Latin America Pay Television Service (LAPTV), and many other Hispanic television channels.[82, 83, 84]

National Amusements

The following are either directly owned or are subsidiaries of National Amusements: CBS (80 percent) Viacom, Paramount Pictures, Paramount Communications, Blockbuster, Comedy Central, MTV, VH1, Nickelodeon, BET, CMT, Showtime Networks, and Simon & Schuster, and cinema companies such as IMAX (in several US states), Cinema de Lux, Showcase Cinemas, and Multiplex Cinemas; it also holds part stock in Fandango.[85, 86, 87]

News Corp/FOX Corp

News Corp owns the *New York Post*, HarperCollins, the *Sun* newspaper (UK), the *Sunday Times* (UK), and Dow Jones & Co., which operates the *Wall Street Journal*. It also owns 20th Century Fox Film Corp., Fox Television, Fox Broadcasting, Fox News, and Fox Sports (As stated previously, these assets were retained by Murdoch during the merger with Disney). The Murdoch Family owns 39 percent shares in both News Corp *and* the Fox Corp.[88, 89, 90] Rupert Murdoch, the former CEO of 21st Century Fox, chairman of News Corp, "controls 120 newspapers across five countries."[91] Because of the merger between Fox and Disney, he now owns huge stock that Big Media contender as well.

Hearst Communications

Hearst Communications' worldwide spread is nearly incalculable, with hundreds of businesses that range from magazines, newspapers, and radio stations to television stations, cable networks, and even software providers across the globe. Only some of these are the History Channel (50 percent), A&E (50 percent), Lifetime & Lifetime Movie Network (50 percent), ESPN (20 percent), NorthSouth Productions (50 percent), Complex Networks (50 percent), and Intermedia Group (50 percent). Only a few newspapers owned are *Houston Chronicle*, *Times Union* (NY), *San Francisco Chronicle*, *Advertiser*, *Canyon News*, *Foothills Trader*, and Seattlepi.com. Magazines include, to name only a few, *Esquire*, *HGTV Magazine*, *Popular Mechanics*, *Seventeen*, *Woman's Day*, *Town & Country*, *Food Network Magazine*, *Good Housekeeping*, *Country Living*, *Men's Health*, *Car and Driver*, *Cosmopolitan*, *ELLE*, and many more. The company also owns partial shares in VICE Media and VICELAND, Iflix, Kobalt Music, and BAMTech. Also included in assets are several syndicates and media affiliates, including Cowles Syndicate, King Features Licensing & Syndicate, Reed Brennan Media Associates, North America Syndicate, and Litton Entertainment. Likewise operated by the Hearst conglomerate are Hearst Health, The Fitch Group, and CAMP Systems. Even with such an extensive list, we've barely scratched the surface of the inventory of Hearst assets.[92, 93, 94]

AND NOW, IT'S CONSTANT

These are the corporations that determine most of the media that impacts *our* worldview. However, they don't act alone. They gain power daily, which is delivered via their new, silent partners in the emergent, modern-day "Big Brother." These are the corporations that propel the saturation of media *content* even farther into our lives by devising ways of pumping it into our psyches 24/7. If life were as simple as it was a few decades back, we would simply have the option of switching off the radio and television or stepping away from media. But the modern world isn't so cooperative with our need for silence. We may try to get a break from the barrage, but then the smartphone goes off. The tablet dings with a social media notification.

A hollow "konk" sound announces the arrival of a priority email. Another ringtone alerts our attention to breaking events that refuse to wait.

And that's when it happens. Those of us who thought we could easily free ourselves from the presence of Big Media find that the silent partner—broadcasting's shiny new vehicle—has crept in to our quiet domiciles, setting off a series of dings, tweets, and beeps. Truly, thanks to this more intrusive agent, no one is ever alone anymore.

Big Tech

As stated, Big Tech is the mode by which the agenda of the select few is driven into our homes, brought to our dinner tables, or left at our bedside to greet us in the morning (or awaken us in the night). It is a bold, brazen personality, which will unapologetically interrupt the deepest of conversations with a spouse or child, intrude upon final moments with a loved one, or even embarrassingly announce the most trivial of events in a silent moment during church services or a wedding ceremony. Thanks to digital devices, we never experience true solitude anymore. The continual presence of our technologies keeps us from allowing our thoughts to wander far from whatever is currently being put forward as the necessary thing to think about. Headlines are carefully chosen, memes are constructed, and via this means, a disturbing number of us are programmed how to think. Even though we perceive ourselves to be discerning these matters independently, many of us don't realize we're being constantly, albeit subtly, influenced. (Recall that 90 percent of what is being delivered via media comes from six corporate-origin voices.[95]) In addition, Big Tech assures that the way people are coerced to think is equally narrow in origin, yet its broad reach gives this agenda the appearance of being inescapable and of reflecting the majority mindset. This is done to shape and homogenize the masses to embrace whatever narrative is being sent down the pike, and to create a generation whose philosophies, thoughts, and actions are reliably similar across the populace. It's *1984*-ishly familiar:

The ideal set up by the Party was something huge, terrible, and glittering…a nation of warriors and fanatics, marching forward in perfect unity, all thinking the same thoughts and shouting the same slogans, perpetually working, fighting, triumphing, persecuting—three hundred million people all with the same face.[96]

With an understanding of who Big Tech is and what its objectives are, the following is a recap of the companies that currently monopolize the digital world—and thus determine how and when *our* thinking is dictated.

Facebook

In 2004, Mark Zuckerberg and a few acquaintances launched Facebook "as a school-based social network at Harvard University."[97] In 2006, the site became a public platform, and it has since grown to be a point of connection for friends, a photo and video exchange, and a source of entertainment, news, advertising and business promotion, networking, sales, and much more. It currently boasts two billion monthly subscribers, and, as has been stated, has rapidly become one of the first places people turn for news and information. While Facebook is singled out as one of the leading social-media platforms, many others serve the same general purposes, such as Facebook's Messenger, WhatsApp, Twitter, YouTube, Instagram, Tumblr, TikTok, and many others. Most of these sites are free and rake in their extravagant revenues through advertising. On that note, 98 percent of Facebook's monies are brought in courtesy of ads (comparably, Twitter's is 85 percent).[98]

Amazon

Founded in 1994 by Jeff Bezos, Amazon began as an online warehouse for media such as books and compact discs, then broadened its market to include online sales of nearly anything that can be purchased, from

clothing, housewares, and furniture to jewelry, electronics, and even groceries. Further, the company has expanded into video streaming, online
music memberships, Cloud-based accessory software, Kindle books, and
electronic publishing/reading accessories. Via Prime and its acquisition
of Whole Foods Market, it has become a monster in its own category,
employing 180,000, "building a retail powerhouse with a market capitalization of $250 billion,"[99] and has now built its direct access into many
homes with its Alexa and Echo virtual assistant artificial intelligence. In
2013, Bezos purchased the *Washington Post* newspaper.[100]

Apple

Apple Inc. was founded in by Steve Jobs in 1976, and was originally
formed as a personal computer manufacturer. Starting out with such
innovative technologies as the Macintosh computer, available for retail in
the mid 1980s, the corporation soon added software, graphic interfaces,
information technology helps, and myriad consumer electronics to it rep-
ertoire. Among these are the iPhone, iPod, HomePod, the Apple (smart)
watch, AirPods earbuds and AirPods Max headphones, and the iPad tablet to name a few. Software products include Final Cut Pro X, Xcode,
Logic Pro, iPadOS, iOS, tvOS, and more. Other ventures initiated by
Apple are Apple TV+, iTunes, Mac Apps, iOS Apps, Apple Music, Apple
Arcade, iCloud, AppleCare, Apple Pay, Apple Card, the Apple Store, and
the Genius Bar.

Google

Google, launched in 1998 by Larry Page and Sergey Brin, began as an
online search engine with an interface for advertising. Since then, the
company's reach has extended to include a variety of online interfaces such
as Google Chrome browser, Gmail, Google Maps, Google News, Google
Earth, Google Podcast, YouTube (formerly Google Video), Google Photos, Google Keep, Google Play Apps, and many classroom helps such

as Google Docs, Google Slides, Google Calendar, Google Workspace, Google Classroom, and many more.

Microsoft

In 1975, Bill Gates and Paul Allen founded Microsoft Corp., which was originally a computer software company. Seeing vast success in the mid 1980s thanks to its MS-DOS programming, the company maintained a competitive edge through the emergence of the personal computer by introducing (and incrementally *re*introducing) such innovations as Microsoft Windows, Microsoft Office Suite, and the Internet Explorer browser. Other ventures include Skype, LinkedIn, Microsoft Surface, Xbox video game products, and consumer products such as personal computers, laptops, MSN digital products, tablet computers, HoloLens, Visual Studio, and Azure.

CAN'T LIVE WITHOUT THEM

Each company named as one of the five Big Tech companies has both innovated and dominated its market. Each seems to specialize in something different, and each far surpasses its competition. In its own way, each provides a unique vehicle for furthering the saturation of Big Media into our daily lives, and we've become perpetually more dependent on the services that they offer. For example, since its emergence as an online search engine that quickly became a valuable tool in both homes and businesses, Google has additionally cornered the market in the education system, delivering software, apps, and even hardware to public education as it is quickly moving towards more and more technology-based instruction. During the lockdowns of 2020, any lingering doubt regarding whether Google had taken over mainstream education with its tools and apps quickly vanished when school closures demanded that nearly all schooling be moved to the online realm Google had so "graciously" set into place. Yet, despite its many successes, Google makes most of its money from collecting data on people, which it then uses to direct appropriate advertising to potential consumers.[101] With this in mind, some are concerned about the potential child profiling that *could* be occurring via these school-directed resources.

Amazon has taken over a vast majority of e-commerce since its origination, but perpetually so since the COVID-19 crisis ensued. With people locked at home and unable to go out for supplies, this market-cornering gargantuan now enjoys revenues brought by people worldwide who have acclimated to getting everything—even groceries—from an online source. However, this giant corporation and others like it have not elevated without a secondary consequence to the convenience they offer: brick-and-mortar stores everywhere have taken a large hit economically, and many have even closed, unable to compete. This is troublesome for our local economies, but could pose a worse threat in the long run. If, for whatever reason, this service was to be interrupted, it could mean worldwide shortages.

Facebook is the world's leading forum for social media, connecting as many as "2.3 billion monthly active users, as of December 2018."[102] While it may seem like an innocent place for people to chat with friends, it also provides a "news feed" that continually inundates the user with preselected headlines, misleadingly portrays memes and headlines as fact, and often removes stories that are "politically incorrect" under the heading of being empirically false (these are two different issues that will be addressed in just a bit). Confusing about Facebook is that its claims of "fact-checking" causes it to appear credible as a news outlet, while in fact it is a social outlet. After all, a user-edited website can *never* claim that all its content has been vetted. (Note that while Facebook is the largest of social media platforms, the problems discussed are not unique to it, but apply to nearly all other social media forums as well.)

When we study Big Tech and how its innovations fuel our daily lives, new revelations of our dependence on these corporations reveal themselves into perpetuity. We can also see how the need for these resources has increased drastically over the past several years. We must worry when our society's *entire* infrastructure and lifestyle are supported by such a short list of corporations.

If the grid upon which Big Tech is built were ever to falter, disastrous effects could be felt worldwide. Should a few malicious or control-hungry individuals decide to use it (or cut it off) as a tool to manipulate the entire population, it *could* be the most powerful weapon the world has ever known.

THE THOUGHT POLICE

"Hate speech" has become the phrase by which modern-day censorship has driven some to privatization—silencing or withholding their own views because they are perceived as unpopular or unacceptable. Sites that claim to be user-friendly, user-led, or even visitor-edited offer the notion that they are free-speech platforms, but often this is not the case. Even in regions such as the United States, where the First Amendment offers us the privilege of free speech—at least for *now*—these forums reserve the right to enforce their own codes of conduct. This censorship gives the public the illusion that content seen is a representation of the general consensus, and thus quietly influences some users to perceive their own beliefs as unfounded, untrue, or held by the minority. By seeming to be a "public" forum, it appears that the platform welcomes all positions, but by "fact-checking" or otherwise eliminating select perspectives from user posts, the content is indeed filtered, which alters the understanding of the majority opinion or mindset. This deceptive tactic makes users feel that *they* are wrong when their opinions don't align with "popular" belief.

In this way, the public is tricked into embracing the "updated" consensus—one that doesn't offend social media friends. Those who perceive themselves to be in the minority thinking subscribe to the notion that their ideas must be outdated or archaic, and that they should be more open-minded about accepting the expressions that *are* allowed to remain on social media—since those are acceptable/approved. This is how selective propaganda is refined and fed to the public by means of Big Tech. The desire to be mainstream, up to date, and even progressive becomes the filter by which an independent mindset and traditional ideas are strained from common thought: It's a regulatory purging of any ideals deemed "politically incorrect."

In part, this is the consequence of a world that has accepted postmodernism as its standard. On one hand, absolute truth has become a casualty of everyone's prerogative to interpret everything according to his or her own convictions rather than accepting truth for what it is. To compound the issue, when a worldview lacks biblical foundation, it is usually filled by the media and surrounding worldly influences that serve as the criteria by which individual perceptions are built. On the other hand, because secular standards are the basis for the predetermined narrative asserted to the public by Big Media, the crowd will embrace and defend it, calling those who take all other stances an enemy.

Then, when those who believe in a cause or have an agenda have resources of mass propaganda through which to report events, the job of programming people into homogenized thinking takes precedence over reporting events or relaying the truth, especially when such resources earn their vast revenues commercially and not by being outlets of credible journalism. As a result, events are truncated or elaborated upon, facts are skewed or selectively reported, and even entire stories are misrepresented, taken out of context, or downplayed—depending on how their telling may impact the psychology of readers/viewers or call them to public response.

BIG BROTHER AT THE DINNER TABLE

In the fall of 2020, regions of the UK began to discuss enforcement of laws that prohibit "threatening, abusive, or insulting words," in defense of "people with protected characteristics, including disability, sexual orientation and age."[103] Particularly, in Scotland, the Hate Crime and Public Order Bill seeks to inflict criminal penalty—potentially even prosecution—on those who make statements that violate such criteria. This includes journalism and theatrical settings, and could even extend to homes: "Conversations over the dinner table that incite hatred must be prosecuted under Scotland's hate crime law, the justice secretary has said."[104]

This situation has incited passionate responses on both sides of the issue. As a Bible-believing Christian, I hold that God loves *all* equally, that we are *all* made in His image, and that none of us should speak ill of or demean others—regardless of their lifestyle, ethnicity, or any other reason. The matter of speaking kindly of others is not where my concern falls. What I find alarming is the eerie comparison to the Orwellian Oceania's poor Mrs. Parsons, whose playfully bloodthirsty children were so enamored with the Thought Police that they emulated these authorities in their childhood games. Mrs. Parsons' skittish demeanor is perpetually agitated by their continual running around with toy guns and shouting at passersby, accusing them of being "traitors," "spies," or "Thought-criminals," and even begging their mother to take them to see public executions by hanging.[105] These children are, as the book insinuates, a product of societal conditioning that occurs around them during their formative years.

But, here is another disturbing thought. Perhaps you're unaware that, in January of 2021, new US House rules moved to prohibit such gender-oriented terms as "father, mother, son, [and] daughter" from the federal code. Such regulations will update language to include only gender-inclusive terminology, omitting what is offensive to some. In fact, "the rules include 'sweeping ethics reforms, increases accountability for the American people, and makes this House of Representatives the most inclusive in history.'"[106] For some who wish to cite a gender that isn't covered by masculine or feminine pronouns, it's becoming increasingly popular for additional language to be added. For example, some embrace the newly utilized, gender-neutral pronoun "ze" rather than "he" or "she." Setting aside my own convictions regarding the matter of gender and viewing it from a strictly legal standpoint, the *inclusion* of this term is different from the *banning* of older language that specifies male or female. It's one thing to say that there are some who wish to be called "ze"—and entirely another to say that "he" and "she" are now outlawed words. If this is increasingly enforced, by disallowing traditional references, everyone could find themselves a "ze." In attempting not to offend some, the gender identification of others could be forcibly reclassified.

In considering the mandates in Scotland and the revolution of verbiage in the House, the broad potential impact of such updates is something I find disturbing. What happens when we are required, even in our homes, to make sure that our very language complies with conformities not only chosen by other people for their *own* lifestyles, but that are imposed on us—regardless of whether we agree with the philosophy or morality surrounding them? For example, removing the words "mother" and "father" from the federal code is only a start. Where does it go from there? Do these words become prohibited on the street? Current legislation in the UK could be the beginning of a new trend. What about people who still believe in and wish to use gender identity that involves words such as "mother," "father," "aunt," and "uncle"? Do we risk these terms being prohibited on the streets, in public places, or even our homes? What will happen to those who choose to use such language, only to have an offended guest—or worse, their *own child!*—report them to the authorities? Is there a day in our future when our own conditioned children will run around our homes accusing us of being criminals if, before dinner, we pray to our Heavenly *Father*?! This is only one of the many ways that censorship could lead to a breakdown of fundamental civil rights—and even the freedom—of citizens around the world. The potential is both baffling and formidable.

SOCIAL MEDIA'S IMPACT ON REPORTING

These days, much of the public is tired of feeling as though they've been manipulated by the press, never knowing whom to believe, what is true, and whose agenda is fueling the narrative reported to society. In fact, recent years have shown a decline in confidence in the press' investigative reporting, which fell gradually from 72 percent in 1972 to 18 percent in 2016.[107] Why did this deterioration of trust in our media occur? According to an article in *The Guardian*, it is because news outlets are now "focused on maximizing profits, catering to what is popular or sensational rather than what citizens need to know…[transforming] journalists from investigators and analysts offering serious news to 'content providers' competing for attention."[108] If this is the case, then the press has evolved to become a disservice to society, and acceptance of reporting has, again, become a "buyer beware" market.

However, it would be wrong to state that the world is now completely devoid of journalists who strive to provide honest and factual assessments of events occurring around the world. There are still individuals who perceive this as their life's mission, but they work in the minority, against the elements outlined thus far in this chapter. And, their contenders are large corporations that have seemingly limitless resources in comparison to them. *And,* there is a self-defeating element to be found in a public that turns to unreliable sources like memes and social media for their news. After all, it is a bit oxy-moronic to state that the public's confidence in reporter accuracy has declined when the same folks have practiced diminished diligence in sourcing the information they trust in the first place. For example, recent studies have shown that memes have played a large (and ever-increasing!) role in presidential elections. Yet, they're not a credible source of news. The meme mentality of our culture can be seen as reflecting our most important decisions. Take, for example, the fact that, in campaigning for the 2008 presidential election, the major television news outlets averaged 220 minutes covering candidates' stances on issues pertinent to the election, which declined to 114 by 2012 and plummeted to 32 in 2016.[109] The fact that these were able to get by with such increasingly minimal coverage speaks to the fact that our society has become a "quick-snap-decision," meme-fueled mindset. In fact, nearly 70 percent of the US population now reportedly keeps up with headlines via social media outlets,[110] which we've already stated can never claim their content is thoroughly vetted. There's simply no way around the fact that these outlets are a faulty place to perceive news. Anyone can create and post memes, which are often later recalled as though they were actual headlines. Memes, however, can be hoaxes, jokes, lies, or even created for comedy, but once viral, they're often perceived as truth.

As has been mentioned, another issue with such platforms being considered news sources is that they have no obligation to truth in reporting or removing bias. About their "fact-checking" claims, we must wonder *who* these "fact-checkers" are and what their criteria is. When information deleted from public forums is removed because the information is deemed *offensive*, but is subsequently reported as *untrue*, the platform has misused its power. Also, when "politically correct" data *appears* to render an honest representation of the common consensus, but does not, it ostracizes those whose political, philosophical, or personal views don't align with the "whitewashed" version of political correctness displayed by those who are allowed to remain. But worse, the censorship imposed on users is done so under language that attaches hostility or violence to the material removed, as though an unappealing opinion equates to public threat. *And*, it's often that enforcement of varying policies is disproportionate.

For example, one public forum's guidelines state a prohibition against nudity, sexually explicit content, hate speech, threats, or attacks on a particular group of people (which can be connected via race or ethnicity, religion, sexual orientation, gender or gender identification, disease or disability, to name just a few). So, if someone holds a value that contradicts those of another group, the mere fact that he or she disagrees means that counterparts can report the verbiage as hate speech, which then flags a user as having made "violent or dehumanizing speech, harmful stereotypes, statements of inferiority, or calls for exclusion or segregation."[111] The problem is that ambiguity surrounds such terminology. A statement that one doesn't agree with another's lifestyle can be made constructively and isn't equivalent to hostility or a desire for violence. (This is aside from the fact that, despite rules barring anti-nudity/sexually explicit content, it is often allowed to remain on such sites, revealing a lopsided enforcement/censorship).

As stated before, once a message has been removed from its original context and goes viral, it can be hard to pinpoint the intent of that first post. This is a problem for those whose "hate speech" statements are isolated, changing the point it relays. Similar to the aforementioned Abe Lincoln meme, it is also a problem when independent users post their opinions about news events. Unlike reading publications produced by trusted sources that strive for journalistic integrity, a public forum claims to "fact check" its content while being a setting wherein contributors could be your local pastor, a businessman looking to promote his commerce, your aunt, the twelve-year-old who lives down the street, or the neighborhood criminal. Thus, the irony of public mistrust in "news" is partly found in the shift in sources the same public follows. It isn't possible for a forum to keep tight reins on all content, and making such claims only further discredits society's view of broadcasting outlets as a whole.

As such, social media serves a unique purpose. On one hand, it becomes the quick, meme-driven way to introduce ideas to the public (more on this in a bit), while asserting a false sense of security that such sites have the infrastructure to maintain *any* control over what is posted, which portrays the appearance of truth in reporting when in reality it isn't possible to ensure with such a platform. The result is a breeding ground for false information disguised as truth, one in which nearly 70 percent of the American populace, as stated earlier, claims as its newly established source for headlines. This creates disastrous scenarios, such as one that was blocked in the nick of time during the already-tumultuous summer of 2020, when a meme nearly went viral indicating that—due to COVID-19—there would be no 2020 election. While the site was able to remove the meme (suspending many accounts in the process) a rumor like this *could* have sent a tense and already-rioting public out of control. Yet, the only reason the meme was pulled down was the disastrous potential it held. Others that—for whatever reason—might be allowed to remain can cause vast damage. Yet, the rules of these forums admittedly allow some posts to remain despite their false status, when they are deemed to be made of non-serious intention. This is a subjective call, often made by digital algorithms, with the capability of over- or under-censoring with unlimited possible consequences.

To further illustrate, recall that Facebook does not claim to be a news outlet, yet it's one of the leading sources users are turning to for coverage of events. Facebook states only that it is a community goal to "[reduce] the spread of false news...[not always by removing it completely, but reducing] its distribution by showing it lower in the news feed."[112] Since Facebook itself holds no liability for user posts, the entity admits that sometimes the removal is based on feedback from third-party fact-checkers who report to Facebook that the news is false. In turn, Facebook doesn't conduct its own investigation. This means that, even if news posted *is* true, anyone claiming that it's false could be named as a fact-checker, report the message as false, then possibly even launch a counter report debunking the initial (possibly true) story.

What a mess.

(This is what results from making all interpretation of truth subjective to individual scope and launching public-media platforms wherein everyone—vetted or not—has a voice.)

In this way, social media serves well any sources wishing to sow misinformation in the public arena. Those who want to see the public confused, disempowered, or accepting political candidates or policy that isn't in society's best interest can sway the public's view by adding myriad memes, or by sending out memes with the plan of taking them down as "untrue." What a tool. And when followers of social media already have the notion that real news is a fading concept—that the story is always changing and that, in general, news outlets can't be trusted—a "why try?" idea is fostered, and the public grows weary of seeking anything real. So, they slowly surrender, unable to distinguish the voice of certainty from the millions of others, and relinquish control to a Big Brother who will filter out what they need to know and feed it to them in a quick, ready-to-eat meme (which, consequently, contributes to society's newfound inclination to accept news at a quick glance).

After all, if people aren't sure it's credible information to begin with, they certainly don't want to invest much of their valuable time in reading any fine print on the matter.

Headlining "Facts"

"Clickbait" is content written and posted by advertisers that has as its number-one purpose attracting Internet users to "click" on a link to the advertiser's website. One of the pithiest and most effective tools used online today is the clickbait headline. Often, those who want to cast doubt on a person or event or shape the public's response about nearly anything presented in the news can do so by using one of the oldest tools in social manipulation tactics: the rumor. Unfortunately, society is full of folks who often see a headline and investigate the matter no further. So, by posting captions that have false tales in them, an individual or news outlet has the power to circulate a fabricated version of the story—without being guilty of telling an outright lie. After all, often captions state the most sensational line in a story, then the article itself clears up the gossip. But how many people take the time to read the whole thing? It turns out that "most readers spend most of their reading time scanning headlines rather than reading the story," since we're so busy these days that we find it hard to dedicate the time to taking in the entire article.[113] Thus, the headline has the power to tell its own, separate saga.

As such, sensationalistic captions—credible or not—are posted in visible areas in hopes of accruing traffic from the curious who will click on a story to learn more. Once the digital traffic has moved to a site, ad revenues are paid to the host site, and few care whether the story is tabloid-worthy or authentic. And, since (as has been stated) most people don't keep reading past the headlines, clickbait banners are *particularly* alluring in their sensationalism, since the goal is to incite enough curiosity to prompt the reader to make the "click." Additionally, by design, headlines aren't intended to summarize an article's content. They highlight a shocking or attention-capturing element of the story, bringing it front and center in the hopes that while the busy reader skims past other stories, *this* one will command attention.[114]

Pairing the sensationalistic nature of headlines with the busy-ness (and short attention spans) of most adults, we have a breeding ground of misinformation. As Professor Patrick Egan, associate professor of politics and public policy at New York University, put it, "We're in this kind of Wild West world in social media where it's very difficult to attribute where sources of ads and other political messages come from."[115] Consider the many celebrities' lives that are on display for the public eye, and how often rumors of pregnancies, divorces, affairs, and other drama make headlines, but are later refuted. Such initial misinformation can be as simple as a title that suggests a compromising photo was taken or a "baby bump" was spotted, and the gossip is launched. Even if the ensuing story puts the proper perspective on the situation and reinstates a truer picture of the situation, readers will probably never get that far. In this way, sensational headlines are allowed with a free hand, with no accountability, as long as the story suggests circumstances rather than facts. Since readers see captions and interpret them as accurate, there is likewise no accountability; it's simply written off as human error.

Such situations are bad enough when they're accidental, or when they're a misinterpretation the subsequent story clears up, but often, they are strategically placed so that the repetition of the message will cause the misinformation to be accepted as documented in the public eye. Fake headlines designed specifically for spreading misinformation is a tactic "as old as time" because it settles into our social and community spheres and permeates the places where we obtain and discuss updates on stories and events.[116] In other words, these one-liners pop up in our daily lives: "Did you see that so-and-so is pregnant?" "I couldn't believe [enter celebrity couple's names here] are getting divorced!" When broadcast on public forums or even news outlets, and it is rarely called out for what it is, it's simply corrected in the fine print or written off as human error.

When the spread of misinformation occurs as a result of *true* error or misunderstanding, it can be damaging enough. But there is another angle to consider. The ambiguity in tracing false reporting back to the source fosters a setting wherein a small group of headline-controlling individuals holds great power in spinning the publicly accepted narrative in one direction or the other.

For those looking to control the population's emotions, purchases, or even votes, all they need to do is send out accounts that make the desired statement and see that they're never traced back to their source and corrected. (Or, if such wrongs *are* righted, it only needs to be a quiet fix, one the public doesn't need to be made aware of, despite that victims' lives may never be the same.) Once launched, readers will see the headline and later remember it—and declare it to their peers—as fact. Because origins can remain elusive, reporting entities can escape accountability, and the public's belief on an issue is forever swayed. This tactic is one Joe Biden himself discussed in January of 2021, stating that, to coerce the public to embrace falsehood, "You keep repeating the lie; [and] repeating the lie."[117] (Of course, in this context, Biden was accusing Donald Trump of using this tactic.)

Context

Part of the headline's power is wielded by its use of context. For example, before the January 6, 2021, run on the Capitol building in Washington, DC, Trump had said the following before an assembly of his followers regarding his stance on the outcome of the 2020 election, which he contended had been pilfered:

> All of us here today do not want to see our election victory stolen by emboldened radical left democrats…[and] the fake news media…we will never give up. We will never concede. …we will stop the steal![118]

He then discussed how Republicans needed to remain stronger than ever, and said that they would have to "fight like hell"[119] to maintain electoral honesty in the face of what he perceived to be a bogus election outcome in favor of Democratic Joe Biden and Kamala Harris. In context, many might say that the words sound patriotic and defensive of the American electoral process. However, later the same day when the Capitol was stormed, resulting in five deaths and up to one hundred fifty injuries, headlines popped up all over the world accusing Trump of "inciting violence" against the American governmental building. Naming Trump nearly a traitor to our country, hatred for the man—who was already staunchly disliked by some—spread like wildfire, while others sprang to his defense. (Many conspiracy theorists blamed other sources for the storming of the building, stating that the damage was done by groups other than Trump followers to solidify disdain for him. These, some of whom deserve reflection, are outside the scope of this work.)

Worth noting is that Trump's words, in context, could have easily seen the word "fight" traded for the term "advocate," which never would have been construed as inciting violence. The word was used metaphorically, *and* in conjunction with the words "peacefully and patriotically."[120] If the public can no longer take phraseology in the context of their figurative meaning, then we have troublesome waters ahead, since nearly every political campaigner in the history of our country has used such terminology at some point, with no intention of seeing its literal meaning played out. (Beyond this, the inability to keep the word "fight" in context means that many football games I've attended would have been bloodier battles than indeed they were, and that cheerleading is a *very gory* sport.) In fact, if the public were to consistently hold this standard to each candidate serving now, it may be very alarming that Joe Biden, on January 8, 2021, stood in a public forum and stated of Republicans, "We need a Republican party. We need an opposition that is principled and strong."[121] However, later in the same speech, he was asked if he thought some leading Republicans ought to resign as a result of the post-January 6, 2021, friction. His answer was: "I think they should just be flat beaten the next time they run."[122] If our public has lost the ability to place metaphorical context around statements made, and thus presume *literal* intentions by the speaker, then we are reduced to conditions where a quickly chopped sentence fragment can be used to transform figurative dialogue into literal intentions and threats. If this is the case, then many may as well have *also* posted headlines stating that Biden had threatened to "flat beat Republicans." Perhaps we could even raise the stakes by tweaking the language to say, "Biden wants to beat Republicans until they can't [physically] run," or, "Republicans should only ever walk, or the Democrats will wallop them." See how fast this game gets out of control? Of course, all it would take is to view the full context of Biden's speech to acknowledge that such a statement is a ridiculous reach. That wasn't the context of his message, which referred to political campaigning and victory and loss. Yet, it would seem that nearly every statement that came out of Donald Trump's mouth made contemptuous press for the duration of his presidency *and* during both the 2016 and 2020 campaigns. So, how does it come to be that certain candidates are targeted for press exploitation and others are not?

Therein lies the crux of how headlines are selectively used to prop up one candidate while villainizing another. Regardless of whether you are a Trump supporter—even aside from whether you believe that he incited the violence at the Capitol—there can be no denying that captions have sensationalized everything dislikeable about him. In all fairness, his abrasive manner, unpolished demeanor, and (at times) rough speaking style hasn't helped matters in his defense. But is there more to it? Perhaps his conservative stances, his assertion of family values, the stand he took for the unborn, and his decisive foreign policies had something to do with it. If a politician can't be controlled—as many knew that Trump could not—then perhaps key voices in powerful places opted to disparage him for easy removal.

Under the consolidation of the media, it becomes apparent that manipulation using headlines is more easily achieved now than ever before. And, considering the speed with which our thinking can be shaped via strategically worded headings, advertisements, or memes, an entire narrative can be crafted by careful selection of words or emphasized facts.

What Do You Meme?

If using headlines as a rumor mill isn't alarming enough, it's worth repeating here that memes are often mistaken for headlines by people who then perpetrate misinformation. Memes are a digital spin-off of what originated in newspapers as comic strips. They can be humorous, political, or commercial in nature. The previously referenced meme mentioning Abe Lincoln is a perfect example of one that originated as a joke but that could be misconstrued.

Memes have become powerful marketing tools in the advertising world, which illustrates precisely how powerful their pithy nature is. We can read them at a glance and take in the point with no time investment. In addition, their humorous, tongue-in-cheek nature allows them to remain on our phones, tablets, and computer screens (who hasn't turned a screenshot of a favorite meme into their wallpaper at one time or another?) whereas a headline may be quickly passed by. In this way, memes are covert ways of relaying one-liners for those with an agenda. For example, consider the thousands of memes featuring phrases such as "You can't fix STUPID," "Please go home!" and "Over my dead body!" along with a picture of a political candidate or a still frame that encapsulates a political movement. These quickly circulate to bolster opinionated public response, particularly during elections. Memes are such powerful tools, in fact, that marketing agencies are still attempting to quantify their full impact.

MEDIA AFFECTS POLITICS

Even before the 2020 election, sources predicted that social media- and other Internet-based platforms would greatly influence the election's outcome, especially amongst Millennials. This dynamic impacts the types of candidate coverage that is then taken on by different news outlets and their dedication toward unbiased coverage. This is vital, because the amount of coverage allotted to a particular hopeful has a large impact on voter decisions, *especially* since votes rely so strongly on name recognition.[123] In this way, candidates who emerge with unpopular or "politically incorrect" views could lack the coverage to even get their campaign launched in the first place.[124] Thus, they receive few votes.

News outlets have become so wired for instant gratification (recall that news reporting is 24/7 now) that news released in the morning can change the trajectory of the day's remaining narrative.[125] This provides a new tactic for candidates aggressive enough to pursue it: Politicians tweeting or posting early can command the direction of news throughout the rest of the day by inciting response from counterparts.[126] In this way, individuals in high places who have headline-swaying power can hijack the captions in the morning and force their agenda into a particular day's news. (This makes for handy campaigning and pushes name recognition.) In conjunction with this, independent social media profiles made by powerful individuals amplify "America's already polarized bubbles."[127] Thus, just by making drama, candidates raise hype, which keeps their names popping up all over regular and social media, *and* diverts headline action toward being all about themselves for the rest of the day—and sometimes longer. This is problematic, because there is—as has been stated repeatedly—no accountability on matters of memes or false headlines. One can raise Cain, then later simply claim to have been joking, mistaken, or quoted out of context. This sabotages opportunities for credible journalism (and honest campaigning) and sends authentic news outlets into damage-control mode, while public emotions run high and votes are decided based on passion rather than fact.

We've discussed how headlines are used as tools regardless of whether they are accurate and how receptive the public is to them—even in meme form—on social media platforms. Additionally, the influence of "fact-checking" on social media platforms has the power to skew public perspective. Likewise, through micro-targeting (using data about consumers obtained by tracking their online purchases, app preferences, demographics, "likes" on social media, and other factors), campaign ads are directed at specific citizens to recruit their votes.[128] This is very effective, because studies in social science have shown that those who have strong opinions on certain issues, when facts reveal an economic or political condition that contradicts their belief, are likely to cling to their older misconceptions. On this matter, Professor Patrick Egan states, "There is political science research that indicates…[people] reject facts…at odds with their [own] beliefs [or stance]…and they readily accept…[statements] that comport with their beliefs."[129] Also, media outlets that assert a certain political stance (conservative, liberal, etc.) attract consumers of similar positions, and often report by selective exposure—only seeking information that fits the anticipated outcome of the consumer's desires—truth regarding candidates is muddled because the full story isn't told. Or, if it is, the individual merely tunes it out, because it is an undesirable truth.[130] In simpler words, people often hear what they want to hear.

But there's a more underhanded turn to all of this, and that's found in controlling entities' capacity for choosing who *they wish to see win* an election, and then spam the candidate's name relentlessly during the months beforehand. The opponent of the pre-chosen one receives no press—thus, no name recognition. If the less desirable candidate proves difficult to diminish in the public's view, he or she is increasingly villainized—true or not—until the public has a distaste for the candidate. This is often done by "character-based scripts" written by media: "Al Gore was a pompous bore," "George W. Bush…wasn't very smart," and "Trump is a racist."[131] Strategic headlines, filtered social media posts, and witty memes drive the agenda that decides the public's ballot decisions along with nearly everything else media can reach with its broad limbs. It may all *appear* to be random, generalized public consensus, but a darker script is being written, and the authors are surprisingly few.

OLIGARCHY

When the word "oligarchy" is mentioned, many are disinclined to believe that things have really progressed to such a point. After all, the very term brings to mind leaders of war who, after violently conquering a territory, hold it in a tight grip while ruling with a totalitarian thrust. However, there are several types of oligarchy, some of which require warfare and others that operate with more subtlety. Recall that the powers that be are aware that their audience is highly educated and intellectual. Thus, a more delicate approach is required to maintain power. What we see today is, as author Jeffrey A. Winters calls it, a *civil* oligarchy, wherein the ruling individuals "are fully disarmed, do not rule, and submit to the property-defending laws of highly bureaucratic institutional states."[132] Additionally, civil oligarchy is characteristically marked not by one leader, but by an entrenched collective who often operates cooperatively but separately in pursuit of the same interests.[133]

Sound familiar?

These conditions occur when gratuitous quantities of wealth and its accompanying influential power are accumulated by the disproportionate few.[134] This power is often the type that has become so innate that it is impossible to remove from the setting because it cannot be fully filtered out.[135] Considering the multifaceted attributes of our modern tech/media collective, this would seem to be the perfect instrument.

Civil oligarchs manage to obtain and keep great wealth and power while maintaining a somewhat low profile politically. That's not to say they're not famous, but they are much more powerful than they appear to be to the public. This is an intentional strategy: Protecting wealth requires either a firm hand in retaining it (strong, governmental rule) or a compliant, "you scratch my back, I'll scratch yours" interaction with higher powers. Those with great wealth often find that the right contributions, favors, or purchases in high places afford them powerful friendships and wealth shelter. The governmentally powerful and the extremely affluent often become an intertwined class of characters who can't easily be separated.[136] Similarly, those who obtain great prosperity also acquire great political power, despite their apparent uninvolvement in government. Their authority is derived via their commerce. These are often people who pursue their agendas behind the mask of large enterprises, contracting masses of "worker bees" who, possibly unknowingly, labor for a deviant schema and a much larger machine than they realize, fervently working "year-round as salaried, full-time advocates and defenders of core oligarchic interests."[137] In such conditions, the most powerful people in the world are able to blend into the background, fueling the cycle but keeping a low profile.

As stated, oligarchs usually aren't political leaders. They're those who own or command such great resources that they can hold sway over their regions with great influence. Consider what author Jeffrey Winters states regarding the concept:

> Oligarchs can be sole or controlling owners of corporations and can use them as personal instruments of power...corporations serve as vehicles to amplify the interests of the oligarchs who command them...[and can] be owned in ways that are highly diffuse and impersonal...run by managerial strata that sometimes include workers or the state.[138]

The idea of people who hold great power but aren't political rulers goes way back. Winters states that the concept of oligarchy is far predated by corporations, and that they are merely newer tools to implement a much older strategy of influence. Thus, corporations are not oligarchies within themselves, but are "instruments" used by them.[139] However, oligarchs have a great need to defend their accumulated wealth, so they often establish and rely on a multifaceted "power substratum" that may involve a political presence or involvement via influence, but often doesn't include direct governmental involvement. "Instead, the political involvement of oligarchs becomes more indirect as it becomes less focused on property defense—this burden having been shifted to an impersonal bureaucratic state."[140]

The current uprising civil oligarchy generated through Big Media and Big Tech presents a setting wherein a select few voices are now positioned to influence media, which inundates the population continuously and demands compliance—or it will silence them. This oligarchy steers the plot by which people will choose, buy, vote, live, perceive truth, and so much more. And multitudes of tools and resources are available to these powers. Politicians are stationed strategically; media then reinforces ideas asserted in politics via TV shows, movies, and music. Don't think it's an accident that the emergence of nearly every political hot topic is quickly followed by the broadcast of a movie or television series that romanticizes the issue. It's an attack from all sides. Society is conditioned by headlines, which are reinforced by entertainment, then followed up politically or philosophically by the introduction of new, more "evolved" ways of thinking. The masses are persuaded that the assertion is the answer to their problems, and they take that brainwashing to the voting booth, to retail lines, and into every other aspect of their decision-making. Some may think this doesn't sound controlling until they realize that, in this sequence, the oligarchy has utilized one of its most compelling and subtle, dual-level resources: *mobilizational power.*[141] This cunning tactic operates by stirring and manipulating the masses so they will rally to support an oligarch's cause *for* them:

> It refers to the individual capacity to move or sway others—the ability to lead people, persuade followers, create networks, invigorate movements, provoke responses, and inspire people to action (including getting them to take risks and make great sacrifices).[142]

This is the weaponry of the new oligarchy.

AN ORWELLIAN TRINITY?

It would appear that a third player is emerging in the scheme of controlling partners of world dominance. "Fintech" (financial technology) is the new word referring to organizations that conduct banking and many other transactions through digital means. It represents "an industry encompassing any kind of technology in financial services—from businesses to consumers…through software or other…[digital means] and includes anything from mobile payment apps to cryptocurrency [bitcoin and litecoin, for example]…[and includes transactions made via] the internet, mobile devices, software technology, or cloud services…[and later] funds, trade stocks, pay for food or manage insurance…(and often on your smartphone)."[143] This includes crowdfunding websites such as

GoFundMe and Kickstarter, any and all consumer- and business-oriented online banking, purchasing, and selling.

At the hub of the Fintech movement stands what is known to some as the Big Three: Vanguard, State Street, and BlackRock. These are the monster corporations that facilitate resource management and financial technology for the largest conglomerates in the world. The most prevalent is the nearly $9 trillion corporation BlackRock,[144] which started as an asset-managing company in 1988. Growing over the next three decades to be a super-player in its field, it has even developed a huge impact in Washington, DC, and is now "the largest money manager in the world,"[145] operating seventy offices in thirty countries and servicing clients in more than one hundred countries, extending its global reach throughout "North and South America, Europe, Asia, Australia, the Middle East and Africa."[146] This firm runs a gargantuan technology operation that manages nearly $22 trillion in assets, and it has influential shares with Alphabet Inc. (Google's parent company)[147] and "a stake of 5 percent or more in nearly 98 percent of firms in the S&P 500 index including Apple, Microsoft, J. P. Morgan Chase, [and] Wells Fargo...[and is the] world's largest shareholder in fossil fuels."[148] (Do you see how all the superpowers seem to be sitting at the same table?) Its assets and managed assets include nearly everything covered in the earlier explanation of Fintech, but this anomalous company also owns such curious resources as "stakes in Mexican toll roads, hospitals, gas pipelines, prisons, oil exploration businesses, and a coal-fired power plant," along with interests in some of Canada's road and bridge projects and other surprising holdings.[149] The corporation's executive staff has been made up of many who have worked in prominent political positions, such as Barack Obama's national security advisor Thomas Donilon and Coryann Stefansson, who served in the New York Federal Reserve Bank.[150]

Particularly interesting about BlackRock is that it is slated to play a key role in Biden's administration; in fact, the recently inaugurated has seated several BlackRock figures in Washington. For example, Biden named former BlackRock global head and Obama administration economic advisor

Brian Deese as director of the National Economic Council.[151] BlackRock global chief investment strategist, Mike Pyle, holds experience in Washington, DC, via his position serving the Obama administration, and was named to serve the Biden administration in the capacity of chief economic advisor for Vice President Kamala Harris.[152] It is also noted that the Biden administration set its sights on BlackRock former chief of staff Adewale Adeyemo, and it was rumored that Chief Executive Larry Fink "will serve as a top official at Treasury," although, as of now, Fink asserts he plans to stay at BlackRock.[153]

Fintech is the means by which the entire world's money will soon be moving. It will be controlled by oligarchs who use big corporations to control the cultural and political narrative, the constant digital delivery of propaganda, and…the *supply of nearly all material necessities around the globe*. The way our needs are met is rapidly becoming all-digital, all-controllable, all-*obstructable*. Access can be cut off immediately, and in a cashless society, what are we to do but comply with powers that be in order to keep access to our livelihood? If you don't think this is already on the horizon, ask yourself this question: How many cash or check transactions have you conducted in the past few years—*especially* after the onset of the COVID-19 crisis? How much did you begin to purchase online rather than from a physical store? How many times—even at a restaurant or grocery store—have you conducted the entire selection and payment transaction from your smartphone or home computer before merely driving up and receiving your purchases? Even more, despite the hit that the economy took as a byproduct of the COVID-19 crisis, do you find it surprising that BlackRock's assets rose 19 percent between December of 2019 and January of 2021?[154] While our local economies struggled, Fintech made a killing. On the matter of transitioning toward a world more reliant on Fintech during the pandemic, Larry Fink stated, "It has led to a profound shift in economies and how societies even operate, creating opportunities to redesign our society."[155]

So what type of "redesign" could we be looking at? It would certainly appear that the system is coming into place, with key corporations, people, and powers waiting at the ready for their final quest. Recall that this one firm (BlackRock) has a global reach, agents in the White House, and a stronghold on digital banking, which impacts nearly everyone on the planet.

Putting this all together, we begin to see the pieces form an unholy trinity, of sorts. Big Media asserts the agenda and propaganda, but cannot carry out its directive without its vehicle, Big Tech. This powerful partner drives the message into the homes, schools, workplaces, scenery, and even the pockets and purses of the entire population until the saturation seems inescapable. The third partner in this, Fintech, works to pull all financial transactions and banking into digital format, which will keep the population obediently connected, for fear of losing access to their monies.

WE TEN KINGS...

There is an interesting and potentially prophetic element where this Orwellian trinity is concerned. In Revelation 17, we see a series of events unfolding that lead to the rise of the harlot of Babylon, the ascent of the Beast's power, and eventually the devouring of the harlot and Babylon's fall. Without delving into a huge study of Revelation here, I will summarize a potential interpretation of some key passages in light of all we've discussed in this chapter.

First, notice that Revelation 17:12–13 states:

And the ten horns which thou sawest are ten kings, which have received no kingdom as yet; but receive power as kings one hour with the beast. These have one mind, and shall give their power and strength unto the beast.

Next, let's take a moment to investigate the picture Revelation chapter 17 is revealing: In verse 7, we see the Beast carrying the woman, whom many believe represents the apostate church.[156] The oft-debated seven mountains mentioned in verse 10 symbolize a seat of power in prophetic language.[157] (This could mean seven prominent dominions from the time of Rome moving forward, *or* it could mean, as some believe, that "the reference to the seven mountains identifies the city as Rome, the place from which the false religious system of the last days will be directed.")[158]

Moving forward, let's connect the shocking dots between verses 12 and 13, and the subsequent events:

> And the ten horns which thou sawest upon the beast, these shall hate the whore, and shall make her desolate and naked, and shall eat her flesh, and burn her with fire. (Revelation 17:16)

Next, in Revelation 18, we see Babylon fall, ending an era wherein the kings of the earth have enjoyed time of drunkenness and fornication with her—a time when "the merchants of the earth…[were] waxed rich through the abundance of her delicacies" (verse 3). When Babylon falls, observe the type of devastation that is foretold. Particularly, notice the vast list of industries affected by this catastrophic event:

> And the kings of the earth, who have committed fornication and lived deliciously with her, shall bewail her, and lament for her, when they shall see the smoke of her burning…. And the merchants of the earth shall weep and mourn over her; for no man buyeth their merchandise any more: The merchandise of gold, and silver, and precious stones, and of pearls, and fine linen, and purple, and silk, and scarlet, and all thyine wood, and all manner vessels of ivory, and all manner vessels of most precious wood, and of brass, and iron, and marble, And cinnamon, and odours, and ointments, and frankincense, and wine, and oil, and fine flour, and wheat, and beasts, and sheep, and horses, and chariots, and slaves, and souls of men. And the fruits that thy soul lusted after are departed from thee, and all things which were dainty and goodly are departed from thee, and thou shalt find them no more

at all. The merchants of these things, which were made rich by her, shall stand afar off for the fear of her torment, weeping and wailing…And they cast dust on their heads, and cried, weeping and wailing, saying, Alas, alas that great city, wherein were made rich all that had ships in the sea by reason of her costliness! for in one hour is she made desolate. (Revelation 18:9, 11–15, 19)

We see that ten mysterious, kingdom-less kings stand with the harlot for one hour (not a literal sixty-minute period, but a measured era of time). When judgment falls, it appears that a cataclysmic, *worldwide economic shutdown* occurs. This is an event so devastating that merchants are stunned, commerce is halted, and there is no apparent strategy for recovery. Everyone simply stands paralyzed, in a state of mourning.

As the harlot facilitates the Beast's rise to power, the ten rulers of intangible dominions are key players, operating "with one mind…[giving] their power and strength unto the beast" (Revelation 17:13). In a possible interpretation, these rulers of immaterial provinces use their resources—which seem to operate with a strange type of "sameness"—to prop up the Beast's system, by which "no man might buy or sell, save he that had the mark, or the name of the beast, or the number of his name" (Revelation 13:17). However, when Babylon and the Beast fall, the ten kings are defeated as well. Notice also that the ten kings loathe the harlot and make war with her (Revelation 17:16).

So, what do these prophetic elements represent?

If the harlot is the apostate church, then it appears that powerful people make nice with her, exploiting her naiveté while she endorses the Beast, until the first opportunity surfaces for her to be taken out of the picture. This is happening now. As high-end religious leaders call for a one-world religion that increasingly sells out for a syncretistic, new, "politically correct" assembly, the Beast-facilitating, apostate following is already rising to power while the harlot's counterpart—the true and faithful Body of Christ—is being driven toward privatization via such elements as "hate speech." The Church is heading for a split, one that drives the *true* Body of Christ underground while the "Hooray for Everything"[159] bunch plays in high places with no idea it's soon to fall prey to the big dogs.

But, consider the ten anomalous rulers who facilitate the Antichrist's economic system—one that will prohibit any kind of buying or selling without proper access (mark). The kings who operate with an enigmatic "sameness" have "no kingdoms."

Their dominion is intangible. Perhaps it is digital…

And when they fall, so does the world's economy.

As has been stated, Big Media is currently dominated by six corporations. Big Tech holds five. Somewhere in the middle of all this, Fintech is made up of three, but is rapidly falling under the domain of one, which is asserting its dominance worldwide, and in high places. As of today, this totals fourteen entities if we count the entire Orwellian trinity. We could likely be only a few corporate buyouts away from seeing ten world-ruling powers who have no palpable kingdoms.

Just a few more conglomerate mergers, and the ten could ascend to claim their thrones.

In fact, looking back on chapter 1 of this book, the importance of the names of Joe Biden and Kamala Harris, and the biblical argument that providence often connects the meaning of national leaders' names to the destiny of nations will help us dive deeply into revelations about America's Orwellian future that few have ever contemplated.

NAMES OF NATIONAL FIGURES AND DESTINIES OF NATIONS

3

Readers may have wondered why I took time to point out the meaning of the names of Vice President Kamala Devi Harris and President Joe Biden. Spiritually and biblically speaking, names are especially important when connected to national leaders at pivotal points in history. They may even be the result of providence. Because the typical individual is unaware of how profoundly significant this is in the prophetic scheme of things, I asked theology and history major Donna Howell to contribute to the following information, so that all may perceive how truly important names are at this time in history and what this has to do with *you* if you are a member of the Body of Christ.

But first things first.

Our culture in the modern West is, shall we say, more than just a trifle different than those of the Bible when it comes to naming our children. Actually, that's true regarding some distant societies thriving in the world today as well. Here, it's not unusual that we discover a pregnancy, pick up a book of baby names, and make a list of ones we simply like the sound of—all well before the child is born and regardless of the name's meaning. We may not consult the Lord in prayer, fast, or have any kind of naming ritual for our offspring. And, for the most part, we largely don't believe a person's name means anything other than the noise we make with our mouths when we want to make sure our little one doesn't stick his or her finger in an electric outlet.

But this definitely was *not* the case for the ancients. As for the Bible's "main characters"—that is, the Jews—they lived by their wisdom writings and traditions, most of which are heavily linked to an interpretation of Scripture.

CHOOSING A NAME: THE APPROACH OF THE ANCIENTS

Let me explain briefly how this manifested into the importance of naming rituals. As one example, Deuteronomy 32:46–47 states:

> And [Moses] said unto them, "Set your hearts unto all the words which I testify among you this day, which ye shall command your children to observe to do, all the words of this law. For it is not a vain thing for you; because it is your life: and through this thing ye shall prolong your days in the land, whither ye go over Jordan to possess it."

The overarching theme of these verses, though they don't directly address naming a child, ensures that younger generations are brought up to understand, appreciate, cherish, and respect the Law of God given through Moses. This, these verses clearly recognize, will lead to a long life of spiritual prosperity in the Promised Land.

The Jews committed themselves to a communal reading of the Torah. The verses we just reflected on are from Haazinu, the fifty-third weekly Torah reading in the Jewish cycle. With this established, it would not be easy for God's people to forget the emphasis that He (again, through Moses) placed on the importance of raising up children in the community of Yahweh. For a deeper understanding and reflection, the Jews also committed these traditional, "community" values to writing, many works of which are reflected in the ancient commentaries. Scriptures read from the Haazinu are covered in the Midrash Tanhuma 1 commentary (also known as "Tanhuma A" or "Tanchuma Buber"). One of the first things that it relates to the Jewish community about a fresh young life entering the nation of God is what a child should be named: "One should ever examine names, to give his son a name worthy for him to become a righteous man, for sometimes the name is a contributory factor for good as for evil."[160]

Jewish-tradition expert Dr. Ronald L. Eisenberg discusses this concept further in his book, *The JPS* [Jewish Publication Society of America] *Guide to Jewish Traditions*: "A person's name is thought to define and control his or her soul and destiny (Ber[achot] 7b). Therefore, the selection of an appropriate name is a critical decision."[161] And, in sharp contrast to practices today, there was no hiding whom one was related to, since names stemmed from the family line…which also meant that any shame a person accrued by committing a sinful act would be undivorceable from his or her relatives as well.

See, in the beginning, "family names" (surnames) were nonexistent for the Jews. One merely went by a first name, then the Hebrew *ben* ("son of") or *bat* ("daughter of"), and finally the father's first name. Using my own name as an example, I would be known only as "Thomas ben Clarence." If the father's name was very common, then other information was needed, such as what city one was from (or known in). At times, for clear identification *and* for distinction, the tribal lineage was mentioned (especially in the cases of men from the Kohen or Levite tribes after the Babylonian division). For instance, at the town market trading grain for a sheep, I might be called "Thomas ben Clarence ha-Kohen." But, if I was caught at the town market *stealing* a sheep, aside from my own personal punishment, there would be a grandiose and long-lasting layer of dishonor and shame placed upon Thomas, Clarence, and the entire Kohen tribe as far back as my ancestors could be traced. It was anything but a casual affair. This is why we don't read any verses in the Bible stating that a parent cradled a newborn and said, "I think I'll call him Seth; it has a clever ring to it," or, "Didn't you have an uncle with a nose shaped like that? What was his name again? Yeah, Joseph. That'll do, since I can't think of anything else." A name was almost always assigned to a new life as a way of ritualistically dedicating the baby to the Lord and to his or her "Yahweh community" for life. If a baby was named after a relative, it was for that namesake's *legacy* and the new parents' hope that the youth would walk in the same or similar footsteps as another who had already demonstrably lived for God.

Of course, the subject extended beyond merely naming newborns. So important was the marriage between a person and his or her name that some Jewish communities resorted to a name-change for a loved one on his or her death bed. As an example: All signs point to the notion that cousin Joseph is not going to recover, because God has ordained that he will die soon. A copy of the Scriptures is brought in and opened to the first random page (or paragraph of a scroll), and a learned member of the family begins to read. The first Jewish man of merit, long life, and generally good works who happens to appear in the Word is David. So, a renaming ritual involving close family members occurs right there at the bedside of Joseph. If Joseph—now called David—does rise again and recover, he will keep his new name for the rest of his life (assuming he is not renamed a second time). This is done as a sort of "covenant name" (my words, to avoid a lengthier and more complicated explanation).

Dr. Eisenberg's *Guide to Jewish Traditions* acknowledges that this would look like odd superstition to an outsider, but to a Jew, if nothing else, it shows the enormity of the power, authority, and influence assigned to a name in relation to the mystical and unseen operations of God.[162]

Regardless of ancient traditions, communities, and cultural norms, however, can an argument actually be made that points to the spiritual/mystical significance of a person's name? Or is it all mere superstitious nonsense and folk beliefs? Is there possibly anything to "the ancient notion that names give power over [people's] souls and fates"?[163]

THE FALLACY OF JULIET LOGIC

What's in a name? I mean, *really*. A rose, by any other name, *would* smell as sweet, would it not? Let's be mature about this. Spoken names are just a sound in the air. It doesn't have to be mystical. We don't choose our names, anyway, so there are no spiritual or numinous implications behind names, right? It's not like it's a destiny…

Not exactly. It's more complicated than that, as folks familiar with their Bibles will know. The Shakespearean argument put forth so influentially by Juliet on the balcony of our most iconic stage romance seems sound enough initially…but it has a giant hole in the center where logic goes to die.

Well, technically, you might be thinking, a rose really would smell the same regardless of what we call it…

True. Scientists in the field of horticulture will say that, regardless of the name, the "complex mixture of low molecular weight compounds emitted by flowers into the atmosphere and its structure"[164] is a factor regardless. Our olfactory systems will take in the same sensation and report that incoming information to the human brain in the same way, no matter what name tag we want to slap on a plant from the Rosaceae family. This is because the purpose of the flowers' scent isn't about you or me; God designed the mechanism to attract pollinators who contribute to the continuing ecological function of the planet.

But there's an obvious error in this romanticized Juliet-ism: A flower doesn't have a soul *or* a destiny—Romeo does. Beautiful poetry aside, it's a silly thing to present the idea that a flower's name, and a human's name, would have an equivalent link to the universe, the unseen realm, God, destiny, etc. Yet, there is a "mini-Juliet" alive in most of us. We may not hang our arguments on a rose like Juliet did, but we commit a similar grievance when we assume that names have no meaning but "a sound in the air." Or that, just because a baby doesn't choose his or her own name, there's nothing to the idea that a name might be supernaturally or prophetically linked to a person's role in the universe.

Some may remember, when President Donald Trump was first announcing his intention to run for president prior to the 2016 campaigns, the spike in online discussion regarding the meaning of his name. "Donald" is derived from the Gaelic *Domhnall*, meaning "world leader." "John" is Hebrew, and it means "God is gracious." The surname "Trump" is "trumpet" or "drum" in German; in modern English, it's "to excel, surpass, outdo"; or, in earlier English, it is "triumph." Not surprisingly, the collective name—which could be read, "a world leader who will triumph under the grace of God"—wasn't lost on those whose ears were piqued to the prophetic when 2016's election suddenly flipped in Trump's favor— and remember, Donald Trump didn't choose *his* name, either.

So, our "it doesn't matter" Juliet-isms would only be fair if considered within the framework of what the Bible (and human history) says about the mysterious link between *people* and the title that represents them… not roses. With that in mind, reconsider Juliet's reasoning: Calling a rose "skunk cabbage" (a wetlands plant here in the States that smells horrid, especially after a fresh rain) or perhaps "corpse flower" (a real flower from the rainforests of Indonesia with vampiric fangs in the center that smell like a rotting dead body) would, in human equivalent terms, be an injustice to "the calling placed upon this flower's life." It would be "an insult to its destiny." Maybe, after God had used this flower to accomplish great things, He would have changed its name to "Rose."

But one thing Shakespeare and his lovely heroine did get correct was the desperation that drives the dialogue. Just to get in the right headspace, let's take a peek back at the lady standing at the edge of that infamous balcony, using brackets to indicate clarification:

JULIET: O Romeo, Romeo! wherefore art thou Romeo? [Literally, "Why are you Romeo?"; the word "wherefore" is commonly understood to mean "where," though the true meaning is "why." She is asking why he has to have this name.]
Deny thy father and refuse thy name;

Or, if thou wilt not, be but sworn my love,
And I'll no longer be a Capulet [i.e., "If you can't refuse *your* name, then I will refuse mine, if you swear to love me"]....
'Tis but thy name that is my enemy;
Thou art thyself, though not a Montague ["You are simply *you*; your surname doesn't define you"]....
What's in a name? that which we call a rose
By any other name would smell as sweet;...
Romeo, doff thy name,
And for that name which is no part of thee
Take all myself.
ROMEO: I take thee at thy word:
Call me but love, and I'll be new baptized;
Henceforth I never will be Romeo.

And where did they end, these young lovebirds? It's Shakespearean Tragedies 101: They did *not* get married, have children, and attend potlucks at a local church where Romeo was baptized anew and freed from the binds that held him to the House of Montague. In the end, their *names* had more power to speak of their destiny than *they* ever had. And whereas I understand perfectly well that the play *Romeo and Juliet* is a fictional as well as an exceptional situation, the error of Juliet logic (that moment when the meaning of names is considered a flippant nonissue) is alive and well for many folks.

So, grab your Bible. Let's see what the Good Book actually says on the matter.

BIBLICALLY SPEAKING, IT'S MORE THAN A "SOUND IN THE AIR"

Bible characters and locations throughout the Word undergoing name changes during times of historical and spiritual significance; the Lamb's Book of Life being checked for the saints' entry through the pearly gates of heaven; the dominion of Adam over the animal kingdom through the ceremonial naming of each beast; saints receiving instruction to ask of things "in the name" of the Lord…

What do all these factors, and so many others, have in common?

AS IT PERTAINS TO PEOPLE

Collectively, they illustrate, even to the newest of Bible students, that the Word takes names very seriously. *Baker Encyclopedia of the Bible* states:

> In the Hebrew language, the term for "name" most probably meant "sign" or "distinctive mark." In the Greek language, "name" (*onoma*) is derived from a verb which means "to know"; a name then indicates that by which a person or object is to be known.[165]

And the *Evangelical Commentary on the Bible* acknowledges that "a new name indicates a new destiny."[166] Often, this is shown quite transparently. For example, consider Genesis 17:5:

> Neither shall thy name any more be called Abram, but thy name shall be Abraham; for a father of many nations have I made thee.

In this case, we needn't look any further than the immediate context to see the purpose behind God's decision to rebrand Abram. It's right there in plain sight that He planned to multiply Abram's seed tremendously. The promissory note upon this covenantal act is manifest in the changing of what every person from that day forward would call Abram; every time his name was uttered, the promise of God would ring in the ears of those present, reminding him and his people that God would do what He said He would. In Hebrew, "Abram" is made up of *'ab*, which means "father," and *rām*, "high" or "exalted." God, by tweaking "Abram" to "Abraham," fused in the Hebrew *hămôn*, or "multitude," ultimately rendering the name to mean "high father over a multitude."

Does the rose smell as sweet by just any ol' name in this case? Sorry to disappoint you, Juliet, but the answer is no. The rose is much, *much* sweeter as the sun sets for the first time over Abra-*ham*, the father of many nations, than it would have been over the "high father," generically. And his wife, Sarai-turned-Sarah (Genesis 17:15), wasn't left outside of the promise, though the etymology behind that switch is much harder to nail down. Most commentaries and discussions on this moment in Scripture acknowledge that the Hebrew roots of both "Sarai" and "Sarah" mean "princess." Naturally, to go from "princess" to "princess" doesn't make sense, so much earlier scholarly discussion posed the interpretation that "Sarai" was a title chosen by man over a certain earthly tribe, whereas "Sarah" was a God-given designation stipulating that she would be the princess "of all mankind." This theory, though beautiful, was hard to prove, and for some time, the full explanation was unattainable. However, in the nineteenth century, brilliant German theologian and biblical exegete, Heinrich Ewald, pointed out something that should have been glaringly obvious. Of the possible meanings of the Hebrew *sarai*, one was a verb meaning "to contend, to strive...contentious, violent, which suggested unpleasant ideas of temper." The change from this pejorative moniker to the feminine derivative of "prince," *sarah*, "was an honourable distinction conferred on the wife of Abraham."[167] In other words, Abraham's wife's name changed from meaning something like "to fight and struggle" to "princess."

In a similar vein, establishing what a location would be called based on an important event was also commonplace. In one story, both a person *and* a place were reborn into a new identity. The night Jacob wrestled with God, we happen upon this exchange:

And he said unto him, "What is thy name?"
    And he said, "Jacob."
    And he said, "Thy name shall be called no more Jacob, but Israel: for as a prince hast thou power with God and with men, and hast prevailed."

And Jacob asked him, and said, "Tell me, I pray thee, thy name."

And he said, "Wherefore [again, it's actually "why"] is it that thou dost ask after my name?" And he blessed him there.

And Jacob called the name of the place Peniel [literally, "face of God"]: "for I have seen God face to face, and my life is preserved." (Genesis 32:27–30)

Though Abram was rebranded "Abraham" for the purpose of a future promise through his offspring, Jacob's new identity, "Israel," represented his current relationship with God and the relationship the twelve tribes would have with God, as well as a release for him from his former life and reputation. "Jacob" meant "holder of the heel" or "one who supplants," and though our culture today celebrates the name as a reference to the man who would father the twelve tribes of the covenant nation, the origins of "Jacob" are a bit unscrupulous. As his brother, Esau, is lamenting to their then-blind father, Isaac, about the blessings that Jacob deceitfully stole by impersonating him, he angrily asserts his cynicism: "Is not he rightly named Jacob? for he hath supplanted me these two times" (Genesis 27:36). Translate that to modern terms, and it's as if Esau shouted, "This brother of mine keeps stealing from me! How appropriate that his name would be *Jacob*! That swindler!"—the implication being that "Jacob" was synonymous to "trickster" or "manipulator."

The new name that Jacob was assigned after his "face to face" with God at Peniel was "Israel." As Logos Bible Software's prized *Faithlife Study Bible* commentary acknowledges: "Here, the reasoning for the name Israel (*yisra'el*, in Hebrew) is the verbal phrase 'you have striven with (or struggled with) God.'" Again, *yisra'el* is partially derived from the *sarai/sarah* roots, which, as stated a page or two back, relates to the meaning "'to struggle,' 'to strive,' or 'to fight.' The name *yisra'el* itself could mean 'God will struggle,' 'May God struggle' or 'God fights.'"[168]

So, considering that this conversation between God and Jacob occurred just after Jacob wrestled and struggled with God (in a theophany; appearing as "a man," Genesis 32:24) all night until the break of dawn, the Julietism here would be: "Jacob wrestled/struggled/fought with God at Peniel. Obviously he was given the name that means 'wrestled/struggled/fought' for that event, alone. It doesn't have to be a prophecy." But then we are given the *rest* of the Old Testament. It's a little more than coincidence or irony that *the nation* called "Israel" (not the man, Jacob) would go through such *intense* times of struggle with Yahweh in the generations to follow this astounding moment in Scripture. "Israel" ended up being the very description and definition of the nation long after Jacob was gone.

This could be why the ancients believed in the more mystical connections between that seemingly meaningless "sound in the air" and destiny. Biblically speaking, names are more than just a moniker or a sticker the Israelites put on their T-shirts at social mingles and tea parties. To the people of God, the *Holman Illustrated Bible Dictionary* states, "a name expressed essence." This source immediately goes on to say:

> To know the name of a person was to know that person's total character and nature....
>
> The knowing of a name implied a relationship between parties in which power to do harm or good was in force. That God knew Moses by name occasioned the granting of Moses' request for divine presence (Exod. 33:12, 17). The act of naming implied the power of the namer over the named, evidenced in the naming of the animals in Gen. 2:19–20 or Pharaoh's renaming Joseph (Gen. 41:45; cp. Dan. 1:6–7; 2 Kings 24:17).[169]

Both men and women were allowed to name their children (somewhat surprising considering how infrequently women were given authority over the household or its dealings in nearly every other way). Choosing a name for one's offspring could be related to how a mother or father felt about the birth, or just after it; to commemorate a special event; to mark them for a high purpose or destiny; to dedicate them to God and His will; to keep strong familial bonds or alliances; or to carry a message from God, such as some of Jesus' names would do for His people (for instance, "Immanuel," meaning "God is with us" [Matthew 1:23]).

So, do children grow up acting in a way that suits their name because this is what is expected of them, and this title is all they believe themselves capable of? Or do they grow up fulfilling their name as a destiny because there was a mystical, prophetic connection between their soul and name at birth, and they never truly had a choice concerning what they would become? It's easy to assume the former: Toddler Jacob feels rebellious during time-out one day and says, "Mom and Dad wanna name me 'trickster'? Fine! I'll show them 'trickster'!" Then he spends the rest of the afternoon devising plans to take all he can from Esau...I mean, why not? It's a decent theory.

On the very heavy other hand, there are occasions in history when people have accomplished something astounding that their names prophetically pointed toward, and there is *no explanation* for how they could have known to arrange that—even if they had wanted to.

As only one example, consider Daniel. The name is derived from the Hebrew *din*, "judge" and *el*, "God," which translates, "God is my Judge." The meaning here is that there is no other—no human nor little-*g* god— that would suffice as the guiding judge over this man's life from birth. The biblical account of Daniel shows that, through the Babylonian captivity and within circumstances outside of his own control, Daniel was repeatedly placed before *human* judges and subjected to laws that were not of Yahweh. It was as if sinister forces were alive in the universe at that time that wanted him to be stripped of his name and any association that he may have had to it. In fact, when Daniel was first brought to Babylon, the chief official declared that his new name would be Belteshazzar ("Bel protects his life," an appeal to the Babylonian god Bel for provision) as a way of divorcing Daniel from any connection to the God of his people. (This was done to Daniel's friends, also [Daniel 1:7]; Hananiah ["Yahweh is gracious"], Mishael ["who is what God is"; "high place"], and Azariah ["one whom Jehovah aids"] all had their names changed to references of Babylonian deities. Hananiah became Shadrach ["command of Aku"]; Mishael became Meshach ["who is what Aku is"]; and Azariah became Abednego ["servant of Nebo"].) One important thing to note about this particular renaming, however: Unlike the other accounts mentioned wherein *God* changes what someone will be called for a divine purpose, in the case of Daniel, pagan captors made the decision. Daniel's destiny would therefore remain tied to the "God is my Judge" moniker that he was given prior.

The attack on Hebrew names was only the first act the Babylonians carried out in an attempt to place distance between the Jews and their God. From the moment they were brought into the new, dark land, Daniel and his friends were expected to eat and drink the king's food and wine, which were spiritually unclean as per Israel's laws (cf. Daniel 1:8–16). When Daniel requested to eat only vegetables and drink only water, the chief servant of the king—the earthly judge over Daniel's spiritual matters in that moment—stiffened, afraid that Daniel and his friends would not work as hard, and the chief would be held accountable to *his* earthly judge (the king). But Daniel's True Judge had given Daniel "favor and compassion" in the eyes of the chief (1:9). He suggested a ten-day trial wherein the Hebrew servants would eat only vegetables and drink only water, and the chief could observe for himself whether their work achieved, or lacked, the necessary ethic. Amazingly, the chief agreed to the trial—submitting himself, as well as Daniel and his friends, to the Judge who was by his very name the One presiding over Daniel in the spiritual realm—and the results were surprising. Not only did Daniel's Judge come through to sustain him to accomplish all the work on his docket for that ten days, the Hebrew servants actually looked healthier—"fatter in flesh"—than the non-Hebrew servants (1:15).

This chief would *not* be Daniel's judge. Nor would this Babylonian king. Daniel was "marked," or "destiny-ed" if you will. (Yes, I'm aware that "destiny-ed" is not a word. But it fits here; it should be read differently than "destined," which our culture has made synonymous with "determined." Besides, it's fun to say…) Daniel would have his actions ultimately judged by Yahweh and no other.

Really, Tom? A guy hatches a plan to eat garden salad, and you see a connection between names and destinies?

Not by any means would it stop there. Many who are familiar with the book of Daniel know where this is going, and how it climaxes in the supreme judge/Judge showdown. As often happens in the Word, when dealing with real men and women and their finite strength, one test leads to another, each becoming grander than the last. Small victories beget greater tests, which beget more astounding victories, and so on. We should never despise small beginnings (Zechariah 4:10), because, when we are faithful with little, we will be trusted with much (Luke 16:10).

So, fast-forward a short time, and King Nebuchadnezzar was experiencing disturbing dreams and night visions that would not let him rest. He called for the "magicians, the enchanters, the sorcerers, and the Chaldeans" (2:2) to come and interpret his dreams. When they failed, Nebuchadnezzar ordered that *all* wise men of Babylon be killed (2:12), including Daniel and his friends. Without panicking, crying, or stopping to write a last will and testament, Daniel calmly, "with prudence and discretion" (2:14), asked for the cause of the death sentence.

Why did he react this way? Because he was fearless? Because he loved the Babylonians he worked for and was willing to march into the execution room to prove a point for his king? Because the other Hebrews looked up to him and he didn't want to cause a panic amidst his people? I suppose some of those reasons could have been a factor, also. But in my personal opinion, Daniel remained calm because *he already knew who his Judge was.* He was aware of what he had been "destiny-ed" to be through the calling of his name.

Nevertheless, there stood Daniel cooperating with his own death warrant as the king's men came to collect him for execution. When he discovered that it was a matter of dream interpretation, he requested an appointment with the king, went home, and asked his three best friends—now known by their Babylonian names Shadrach, Meshach, and Abednego—to pray for guidance from the Judge he already knew would have the last word over his own destiny. Then, believe it or not, he went to bed and slept on it. (Who else, besides a *very* confident man, would be able to sleep at a time like that?) In the night, the same Judge who was knitted into the fabric of Daniel's very name revealed all of what the king's dreams meant, and Daniel awoke with praises on his lips.

The next morning, he was brought to Nebuchadnezzar. Unlike the others before him, Daniel had not been told the dream before the interpretation was expected. On the contrary, as soon as Daniel entered the room, the king asked if he knew *both* the dream *and* its interpretation (2:24–26). Daniel explained that no wise men, magicians, enchanters, or any other mystics of that sort would be able to help Nebuchadnezzar, because the king's dreams were actually from the God of the Hebrews!

I imagine in this moment Daniel standing there observing the king's reaction carefully yet confidently as he proceeded to tell Nebuchadnezzar the secret thoughts of his slumbering mind that nobody could possibly know, *followed by the interpretation* of these thoughts nobody could know. I can almost see Daniel watching the countenance of his earthly judge—the man who only the day before had decreed his death—alter from pompous disbelief to skepticism to surprise and then to worshipful gratitude for Daniel's God. When Daniel finished speaking, Nebuchadnezzar fell on his face, declared that the Hebrew God was greater than all others ("God of gods") and the Leader of every high seat upon the earth ("Lord of kings"), and then promoted Daniel to rule over all of Babylon (2:47–48). Daniel was immediately granted his only request: that Shadrach, Meshach, and Abednego be assigned to rule alongside him.

That's right, I like to imagine Daniel thinking at that moment, *I was never destiny-ed to die today. God, alone, is my Judge.*

Poetic, isn't it? It's almost as if no other baby name Daniel's parents could have chosen would have more integrally related to God's plan. But, we are far from finished.

Unbelievably, though Nebuchadnezzar had *just* acknowledged that Yahweh was the "God of [all] gods" and "Lord of all kings," he quickly went on to build an idol of gold, demanding that everyone was to stop what they were doing and worship the idol anytime they "hear the sound of the horn, pipe, lyre, trigon, harp, bagpipe, and every kind of music" (3:5). If they refused, they would be thrown into a fiery furnace and burned alive. At this proclamation, some Chaldean opportunists who weren't fond of their Hebrew supervisors stood and officially accused Shadrach, Meshach, and Abednego of disobeying the idol-worship law. The king was naturally enraged, so he sent for the Hebrew administrators and made sure they heard, and understood, his expectations. After repeating the law they were to obey and the death verdict that would be carried out if they didn't, Nebuchadnezzar essentially asked, "What god is gonna save you *then*?" (3:15). Obviously, the king didn't know the destinies these Hebrew men *also* had embedded into their original names (again: Hananiah ["Yahweh is gracious"], Mishael ["who is what God is"], and Azariah ["one whom Jehovah aids"]) before the Babylonian officials rebranded them. (Had he known, his experience with the other Hebrew lad, whose name was "God is my Judge," may have given him a heads up regarding what was to happen next. But since this reflection is more about Daniel than the story of the furnace, I will be brief.) In an answer to the king's taunt, the three Jews explained that they would be delivered from the furnace, but that, even if they were *not*, they would give up their lives before they worshiped any idol or any god other than Yahweh Jehovah.

Nebuchadnezzar, more livid than before, had the furnace heated to seven times its usual temperature and ordered his men to throw Shadrach, Meshach, and Abednego into the flames. The furnace blazed so hot that it killed Nebuchadnezzar's men who drew near. The three Jews, however, walked amidst the flames unharmed, and the king was shocked when he saw that they were joined by a fourth man (at least an angel, though most theologians agree this is a theophany [appearance of God as a man], and many believe it was a Christophany [appearance of Christ as a man]). Nebuchadnezzar then called to Daniel's friends, and as they emerged from the fire without so much as a singed hair on their heads, the king once again acknowledged and magnified the glory of Yahweh throughout the kingdom, declaring that death would befall any person found slandering the Hebrew God. The three victorious men were, once again, promoted.

Later in Daniel's story—after he had interpreted the second dream of Nebuchadnezzar that announced his downfall…and the subsequent handwriting on the wall that announced his son Belshazzar's downfall— King Darius the Mede, who had taken the kingdom from Belshazzar, appointed Daniel as a high official over all other officials and satraps (viceroys, of sorts, to the king, with a high level of authority and autonomy). The satraps were (not surprisingly) jealous of Daniel's position and, just like their conniving predecessors, set out to sabotage his relationship with the king. After joining in number, they went to the king and convinced him to make a new law stating that, for thirty days, nobody in the kingdom would be allowed to worship or pray to anyone except the king. Those found in defiance of this law would be thrown into a den of hungry lions and devoured alive. Darius, probably without giving the matter much thought, signed the injunction. Daniel, as faithful to Yahweh as ever, made no changes to his daily routine of prayer and supplication to the God of the Hebrews, and he was spotted by the con artists who had set him up praying in his usual place by the window. They fled to the king to report him, and Darius, who cared about Daniel, fretted until sundown trying to think of a way to intervene on Daniel's behalf. Sadly, however, it was a law of the Persians and Medes that once a king set forth an injunction, it couldn't be revoked.

When Daniel was, in fact, cast into the den of lions, the king shouted after Daniel that his God might deliver him, and then the opening to the den was sealed with the king's signet. From there, King Darius spent a sleepless night without food or entertainment, fearing what he would find when the den was opened the following day.

But Daniel knew something Darius probably didn't know…Daniel had been "marked" for such a time as this. He had been "destiny-ed" to escape the judgment of an earthly, human king with his vain and finite decrees. "God is my Judge" was written upon Daniel's spiritual nametag, and it would be this very night that his name fulfilled the pinnacle test of providence and calling.

In the morning, the distressed King Darius ran to the den, calling out to see if the innocent, condemned Daniel might offer an answer from the darkness below. Considering that this would be a literal impossibility on so many counts, the king must have looked irrational and overcome by lunacy to his men as he sought a response from someone whose alternate name may as well have been "the lions' most recent meal." After all, those lions had been starved to the point that a human surviving in their midst was inconceivable, and the kingdom officials knew it. Immediately after the whole ordeal, when Daniel's several conspirators and their families were thrown into the den all at once (the condemnation of the wives and children being sanctioned by Persian law, *not* by the God of the Bible as a revenge endorsement, by the way), their bones were broken in midair by the jaws of the leaping, starving predators[170] before their bodies ever hit the floor (6:24). *That's* how hungry those massive felines were intentionally kept. So Daniel's deliverance was far more than merely doubtful.

It simply wasn't to be. Daniel was a goner. His life was over. Ended. Finished. Terminated. Devoured.

…Except that it wasn't.

Why? Because, as Daniel's birth name now declared with more miraculous authority from the Almighty and all the powers of heaven than ever before in his life, *God* was Daniel's Judge. Not Nebuchadnezzar, not chief servants of the king, not Darius or his foolish advisors, not any little-*g* god or statue…just El, and El alone.

As the anxious king leaned over the sadistic feeding hole listening, the Hebrew promise upon the head of *din el* reverberated from that gnarly pit like a shout of rebuke to any person or pagan god that would oppose Yahweh in that moment: "O king, live forever!" Daniel's voice rang out:

> My God sent his angel and shut the lions' mouths, and they have not harmed me, because I was found blameless before him; and also before you, O king, I have done no harm. (6:21–22)

Following this, King Darius wrote a doxology and spread it throughout the land, a word of widespread praise for the God who had saved Daniel from the mouths of lions.

Juliet, sweet Juliet…a rose doesn't *always* smell as sweet by another name. Even a group of hungry, mangy lions from a sixth-century BC feeding hole could have told you that—that is, if they could have figured out how to unclench their jaws to do so.

And before it's assumed that every account was as inspiring, there were a few "skunk cabbages" and "corpse flowers" in the Word, too. For instance, Baasha, meaning "wicked," "offensive," or "he who lays waste" was the name of the king of Northern Israel who gained his throne through offensive military maneuvers. Later he was told by the prophet Jehu that his rule would be like the house of Jeroboam as a result of his wicked leadership (1 Kings 15–16). Another is Bera, meaning "son of evil" or "to be wicked"; this was the name of the king of the morally dead city of Sodom (Genesis 14:2), which God destroyed. And these are only a couple of examples that could be grabbed from the beginning of the "B" section of *The Exhaustive Dictionary of Bible Names.*[171] I could go on for a while longer, but you get the idea.

I think that, by now, the point has been made that, even if our *modern* world approaches choosing names with the same gravity as they do when choosing between Taco Bell, Burger King, or whatever sounds good today, that's not the casual treatment that the Bible assigns to the subject.

There is no better proof for that fact than in the way the Word treats the names of *God.*

AS IT PERTAINS TO GOD

Dishonoring a person's name is an insult. But, did you know that dishonoring the Name of God can be a serious—and possibly fatal—offense (Exodus 20:7; Leviticus 19:12; 22:2, 32; Psalms 74:10, 18; 139:20; Ezekiel 43:7–8; Malachi 1:6)? Are you aware that sometimes the Name of God was encapsulated in how He identified His people (Deuteronomy 28:10; 2 Chronicles 7:14; Isaiah 43:6–7; Micah 4:5; 5:4)? Did you know that He is revealed to us via His Name (Exodus 3:13–15; 33:19; 34:5–7; 6:3; Genesis 14:18–20; 17:1; 21:33; 32:29–30; Judges

13:17–18; Jeremiah 16:21), and that His Name declares His presence in our lives (Numbers 6:22–27; Deuteronomy 12:5–7; 1 Kings 8:15–21; 2 Chronicles 6:4–11; Nehemiah 1:9; Psalm 20:1; 54:1; 74:7; 75:1; Isaiah 30:27; John 17:11–12)?

Readers of the Word will recognize early on that the Bible lists many names for God. Unlike us, God is infinite, and therefore, a single title representing one aspect of His being is insufficient. He doesn't have a destiny in the way that we do. Instead, humanity and the world are destined to dip and climax in whatever waves of history come into conformity with His fixed, inflexible will. Unlike us, He is stable and immutable, so His Name will never "change" from one to another like "Abram" to "Abraham." Rather, He has *numerous names that always simultaneously apply* as each identifies and describes merely one facet of His whole being.

Even then, with what some scholars identify as the existence of more than a thousand names of God—as enormous a number as that is for us to wrap our heads around—the unfathomably complex and infinite Person of God could not be efficiently summarized in any human language…not even if we pooled every word from every culture of the world. This is because the God of the Bible, though *revealed* in the Bible, is not limited to what we make of His self-revelation. The conclusions mankind comes to while studying the Word and the character of God are, even by the brightest and sincerest theologians, still *interpretations* of God's self-revelation, conducted by men and women who are affected by the Fall. Therefore, we can't count on any list of His names to be all-comprehensive, forever-conclusive, and complete.

That said, it continues to be important for believers to have at least the most basic, healthy understanding of the varying titles of God and what they describe, simply because, while He owes us nothing and we are forever indebted to Him, He still provided a way for us to comprehend His nature and His ways as much as we can. That was His gesture, His own "reaching out to us" that He gifted us with in the interest of drawing us into an increasingly intimate relationship with Him. *Holman* weighs in:

The name of God holds an important key to understanding the doctrine of God and the doctrine of revelation. The name of God is a personal disclosure and reveals His relationship with His people. His name is known only because He chooses to make it known. To the Hebrew mind, God was both hidden and revealed, transcendent and immanent. Even though He was mysterious, lofty, and unapproachable, He bridged the gap with mankind by revealing His name.[172]

The sharing of the Lord's Name with us is no small matter, as shown in the fact that even one of the Ten Commandments addresses the correct respect for and use of it. It's therefore asking very little for us to take the hand He offered and draw nearer to Him in understanding who He is through what He is called, and then to honor that, and keep it holy (Exodus 20:7; Deuteronomy 5:11).

In that interest, we'll touch on just a few of what I believe are the most fundamental and doctrine-central names of God. (Keep in mind that, although some might speak to us more powerfully or personally than others, the lens we should view these through requires us to understand that *every Name of God is* "synonymous with his person, his presence and his power, and is therefore held in the highest honour."[173] We can't accept the titles/layers of God that we like, but reject those that we don't find as appealing.)

El

The Hebrew *el* or *El* is most simply translated as "god" or "God," though that interpretation alone is a bit ambiguous and attempts to weave a massive, ancient concept into the fabric of our contemporary culture. It is true that the word *was* used in various little-*g* god references outside of Yahwism (and, in those cases, was uttered far more casually), but, when in reference to the Hebrew God, it held an air of warning. Simply saying "El means God" depletes the fullness of what that primitive Semitic root—that first uttered sound by the Jews—would have implied to the Yahweh-fearing listener in the beginning.

Today, we say "God" as if it's just another vocabulary word. We get a break in traffic and say, "Thank God." We see cousin Sally's preposterous new haircut and say, "Oh my God…" We stub our toe on the counter and say, "God, that hurt!" In church, the pastor makes jokes, "My wife told me not to have a doughnut today, but I asked God and He said it was alright." Whether any of these uses is disrespectful or sinful is between the reader and, well, God. The point here is not to expose bad habits, but to express how desensitized we are (culturally if not individually) to the most common references to "God." The original treatment of that word in Hebrew would have been sacred, and its impact on its listeners would have been dramatic. The sound "El" instilled "a mysterious dread or reverence" to the earliest Jews.[174] In one syllable, it announced an invisible accountability, a pair of watchful eyes from an entity you couldn't escape and could never possibly dare to challenge.

Not surprisingly then, "El" became the ultimate prefix for more specific, descriptive references to God, such as:

El Shaddai, "God Almighty": This was used when God forged the covenant with Abraham (Genesis 17:1–2) and when He provided a name to the patriarchs Abraham, Isaac, and Jacob (Exodus 6:3). Though the original meaning and etymology of *shaddai* is technically unknown, the most popular two theories are that it derives from: 1) *sha* ("the one who") and *dai* ("is sufficient"), or 2) *shadad* ("to overpower, to deal violently, or to devastate").

Despite potential ambiguity of the original meaning, however, the translators behind the LXX (Septuagint)—men who were far less removed from Semitic lingual roots than we are today—translated *shaddai* to the Greek *Pantokrator* ("All Ruler" or "Sovereign One"). Additionally, scholars have studied its appearance throughout the Word and noted that the context is always associated with Someone all-powerful, omnipresent, omniscient, and far above mere humanity in His power and supervision of the universe.[175] In that regard, "God Almighty" seems as appropriate a transition into English as anything else in our secondary language, though again, the depreciation of respect for that title in our culture is a tragedy.

El Elyon, "Most High God" (or "God Most High"): By itself, the Hebrew *elyon* is an adjective meaning "highest." When joined to "El," it clearly designates a God who is exalted far above any other god or being anywhere in the cosmos or beyond. In many scholarly reference materials, the title *El Elyon* is first and foremost mentioned for its appearance in Genesis 14:18–22, the string of verses that most profoundly assigns Melchizedek as the "priest of the most high God."

El Olam, "Everlasting God" (or "Eternal God"): Not only was *olam* a term used to imply the never-ending "beyond" of the afterlife in a literal sense, but it could also be used figuratively as an homage to royalty, as we see in 1 Kings 1:31:

> Then Bathsheba bowed with her face to the earth, and did reverence to the king, and said, "Let my lord king David live for ever [*olam*]."

As a suffix to "El" and a name for Yahweh, *Olam* "designates the 'fullness' (totality) of the experience of time and space."[176] In other words, He is the only Being who can claim that He has experienced this extreme extent of eternality. Unlike us, El has had no beginning, and He will have no end. He is the "fullness" of the eternal God: "from everlasting [*olam*] to everlasting [*olam*], thou art God" (Psalm 90:2).

Many other examples could be given of the Lord's titles as they describe His unspeakable enormity and magnitude over and above anything the wildest of human imaginations could conceive. Three other well-known references among these are *Adonai* ("Lord"; more specific to biblical contexts would be "Lord with Complete and Total Authority"), *El Roi* ("God Who Sees Me"; the tone is that He sees *everything*), and *El-Berith* ("God of the Covenant").

Jehovah/Yahweh (YHWH)

The Tetragrammaton (four-lettered name), appearing in our alphabet as YHWH, is made up of the Hebrew consonants *yod*, *he*, and *waw*, followed by another *he*. It's widely known that the pronunciation of this name is merely the best guess of even the most brilliant, scholarly minds. The short explanation for this is that ancient Hebrew manuscripts were written consonantally—that is, without vowels. The reason we came to eventually know what vowels would/should be inserted into all the other Hebrew words is because the Scriptures were read aloud and the pronunciations were passed down throughout generations of oral tradition. Then, the Masoretes transcribed all the holy texts sometime before AD 900, inserting vowels as the Hebrews would have pronounced them. This translation became the Masoretic Text so heavily prized in the academic world today.

However, because YHWH—the most direct and personal Name of God in all of Scripture—was so sacred, there *was* no oral tradition or pronunciation history that carried on into the Masoretic generations. Historically, when a rabbi arrived at this word when reading Scripture, he would verbally adjust the text on the spot (called *qere perpetuum* reading), saying instead *Adonai* or an equivalent instead of the consecrated Name that was written. It has therefore remained a mystery what the first vowels (and vowel sounds) would have been (or sounded like) in YHWH, and therefore how to pronounce it.

According to some scholars, the decided "Yahweh" configuration we're familiar with today draws its roots all the way back to the time of the Amorites, when historical evidence shows similar derivatives of divine titles, such as *yah*, *yahu*, and *yahwi*. Others claim it connects to Aramaic in ancient Egypt, when the divine name appears as *yhw*, which would have been pronounced "yahu." The four letters, when transliterated to Latin equivalents (likely in AD 1518 by Petrus Galatinus—confessor to Pope Leo X), became JHVH; then, adding the transliterated vowel sounds of the stand-in *Adonai*, we arrived at "Jehovah."

But apart from letters and sounds, the word's *meaning* is, quite unbelievably, unknown…at least on a purely technical level. Sure, a multitude of lay sources claim to know the secret, and most agree with the most widely accepted theories. But for each of those sources, another—such as *The Anchor Yale Bible Dictionary*—brings the overly ambitious world of academia back to reality, reminding us that "the meaning of the name is unknown."[177] One would think that something as important as at least one solid record of the very personal Name of God would be kicking around somewhere throughout the globe's ancient biblical and historical documents. Many guesses have been put forth, such as one that connects to *haway*, an earlier form of the Hebrew verb *hayah* ("to be"). This, among several other similar ideas, points to a serious and reasonable possibility that Yahweh/Jehovah was originally an ontological term: simply the state of being, one who *is*, one who exists. This aligns with the Lord's vital self-revelation in Exodus 3:14, when that exact name appears in Hebrew: "And God said unto Moses, I Am [YHWH] That I Am [YHWH]: and he said, Thus shalt thou say unto the children of Israel, I Am hath sent me unto you." Collectively, it expresses that God simply *is*, He didn't rely on anyone to create Him or place Him in a position of authority, and He doesn't owe anybody an explanation for why He wants things the way He does.

If this is, in fact, what the name YHWH intends to communicate, then it makes a lot of sense what that would have meant to earlier generations of humanity. To use Moses as an example: Strutting in and demanding that an old-world leader as powerful as Pharaoh to simply let his slaves go free is the purest definition of insanity to anyone alive in that day. That messenger would have to have been sent by a ruler far more powerful than Pharaoh—one with soldiers in much grander numbers and more cutting-edge military equipment than the Egyptian king at his most threatening hour—for it to even be considered worthy of an audience with the throne. This other ruler who sent Moses would have to be of the most impressive and royal earthly bloodline, with riches that bore witness to his successful leadership and allies in all surrounding territories who would jump at the chance to back him in any crusade he saw fit to launch. Anything less would be laughable.

Suddenly, the name YHWH makes the rest of that list seem tiny.

For Moses and Aaron, the Ruler who sent them was the great "I Am": The One whose Name is by its very nature ontological; the One who "simply is" and owes no explanation, existing in and of His own power, who was there before the beginning and who will remain for all eternity… and whose army is therefore all of creation, manifesting in whatever series of devastating plagues He sends with a mere nod in Pharaoh's direction.

Boom.

That is what YHWH most likely meant. It's far more than just saying "He is what He is," as if God is capricious and refuses to self-reveal. The entire Bible is an account of God's self-revelation—one that He doesn't owe us, but provides to us anyway, that communicates an extension of His willingness to reach to earth and develop a true relationship with His creation.

The very fact that the sound of the word was too sacred to repeat aloud—for so many generations that the pronunciation, spelling, and root meaning were eventually lost—speaks volumes for what the ancients believed about the power *behind* it. They held that:

> The name held magical power. One who knew the name [Yahweh] could wield power over [God] and summon him to his/her aid, e.g., against one's enemies. The importance of the name is underscored by the story of Jacob wrestling with a divine being who was reticent to reveal his name to Jacob (Gen 32:24–30; cf. Judg 14:17–20).[178]

And certainly, the ancient belief that one could wield power over God by saying the "magic" word is preposterous, *but* the authority held by the Name Yahweh/Jehovah is demonstrably certain. Scripture recognizes YHWH specifically as the:

- Thrower of lightning and the voice of thunder (Exodus 19:16–19; 20:18; Psalms 18:14; Job 37:5; Amos 1:2; Habakkuk 3:11);
- Regulator of the rain (Genesis 2:5; 1 Kings 17);
- Governor over all lakes, rivers, and the sea (Exodus 14:21; Jonah; Josh 3:16–17);
- God over all the mountains (Exodus 19; 1 Kings 20:3);
- God over all the deserts (Judges 5:4);
- One who appears as fire, and who commands fire like a weapon (Exodus 13:21; 1 Kings 18:38);
- …and many more demonstrations of supremacy.[179]

And, similar to El, YHWH eventually became the first half of some very powerful compounds, such as:

- *Jehovah Jireh*, "The Lord Will Provide"
- *Jehovah Nissi*, "The Lord Is My Banner"
- *Jehovah Mekaddesh*, "The Lord Sanctifies"
- *Jehovah Shalom*, "The Lord Is Peace"
- *Jehovah Sabaoth*, "The Lord of Hosts"
- *Jehovah Rohi*, "The Lord Is My Shepherd"
- *Jehovah Shammah*, "The Lord Is There"
- *Jehovah Tsidkenu*, "The Lord Is Our Righteousness" (remember this one for later, in our discussion of Melchizedek)

NAMES FROM HUMAN TERMS

Another entire subsection could be placed here discussing at length where so many other names of God appear in Scripture, what they mean, their context, and how these names and the details around them can breathe life into our relationship with God in the same way that studying El or Yahweh/Jehovah can/has. For space reasons, however, here's the most basic list. I strongly encourage you to do some digging on your own. For each of these titles (and *so* many others not on this list!), God is taking on a description that is closer to our human experience than El or YHWH. He is allowing Himself to be imagined in human word-picture terms so that we can connect with who He is and what He does in our own limited understanding.

"Rock" (Deuteronomy 32:18; Psalm 19:14; Isaiah 26:4): The idea of God as a "rock" is not to be taken lightly or misunderstood. It's not the same as calling God a thing we would pick up and throw, like a pebble, or as saying that He's anything like a heavy, motionless being apparently serving no purpose but to be opulent and commanding. (The latter of these two images does sound a little like the "absent landlord" god of the deists, however.)

The symbolism here is of a mighty, giant stone that no mere human could move, one not washed away in the tide or given over to mood swings, but strong, immutable, and impenetrable. God was the Rock of Israel, and He is the Rock of our salvation. He can be counted on to never move or change concerning His promises to us. If we build our relationship with God on sand, just like a house, it will fall away. A relationship with God built upon rock, however, will last forever (Matthew 7:24–27). Thankfully for us, He is the kind of Rock that can be counted on when we build such a thing.

"Refuge," (Psalm 9:9; Jeremiah 17:17) "Fortress" (Psalm 18:2; Nahum 1:7), and "Shield" (Genesis 15:1; Psalm 84:11): A fortress or refuge of strength for us, or the shield in our arms over our hearts, behind which we can seek safety from our enemies. God *is* stronghold and He *is* protection, as these names reveal.

"Sun" (Psalm 84:11): God is, Himself, the source of all light. As Creator, He is the source of life, also. As far back as the time of the earliest humans (and in every culture from Adam down, as anthropology studies indicate), the sun has been seen as the most powerful force in existence from our earthly perspective. The oldest anthropological data we have shows that the earliest, non-Hebrew cultures believed the sun to be a god itself, rising and setting regularly only if the people down below pay the right kind of spiritual homage (which obviously differed from culture to culture).

In an extreme, yet beautiful contrast to the beliefs of those primitive peoples, the psalmist here calls the Hebrew God "a sun" that will not withhold any good thing "from them that walk uprightly."

"Refiner" (Malachi 3:2–3): Like the finest metals in the ancient times that had to be plucked from the ore veins and put through a purification system to rid it of debris and dross, God is our purifier. He is the Refiner who helps us in the process of sanctification and holiness. Without the God of perfect goodness, there would be no refinement for the fallen world.

SPECIFIC TO THE HOLY SPIRIT

Whereas many of the names shared so far could effectively apply to all Persons of the Trinity equally (though the historical context of the El and YHWH references were often allusions to Father God's relationship with Israel), there is a short, fascinating list of names that are specific to the Holy Spirit. At times, these names are even acknowledged in the Old Testament, showing quite beautifully that the Spirit, though written about more in the New Testament than in the Old, has been active from the beginning (as the Word says in Genesis 1:1–2).

It's likely that anyone reading this book has some familiarity with the New Testament, at least to the point that he or she has heard all about the astounding intervention of the Spirit on the Day of Pentecost and the mighty wonders He enacted through the disciples. If so, you would also know that the Spirit's miraculous intervention carries on through the end of the Book and into our daily lives today. You would also be familiar with the fact that the Spirit is called "Comforter" and "Counselor" (John 14:16, 26; 15:26; Romans 8:26; and others). You may also know that when He appeared to Mary, He was called the "Power of the Highest" (Luke 1:35). But being reminded of a few of these other titles can be helpful in getting us thinking outside "the box" regarding the Holy Spirit. Let the following sink in:

"Breath of the Almighty" (Job 33:4): The context of this verse in Job leads scholars to believe credit is being given to the Holy Spirit, directly, for the act of breathing life into creation (a role typically reserved for God the Father in most casual sermons today). The takeaway can easily be that the Holy Spirit's role is more active than we sometimes think in our relationship with God.

"Good Spirit" (Nehemiah 9:20; Psalm 143:10): Even as far back as the time when the books of Nehemiah and the Psalms were written, the writers of the Word leaned on the help and guidance from the Spirit of God.

"The Spirit of Might" (Isaiah 11:2): This Old Testament verse refers to the helps that the Holy Spirit will minister unto the coming Messiah. It lists six others—rest, wisdom, understanding, counsel, the spirit of knowledge, and of the fear of the Lord—rounding out to *seven*, the Lord's number.

However, thanks to much modern teaching on the Person of the Spirit, we tend to be familiar with His associations with rest, wisdom, understanding, knowledge, etc., but we forget sometimes that He is the Spirit of *Might!* The word alone inspires imagery of a soldier outfitted in the armor of God, setting His brow against the enemy who knows in advance he will be trampled under the weight of God's limitless power.

I might offer another, human-coined title in light of that reflection: He is the "Spirit I Want On My Side"!

"The Spirit of Adoption" (Romans 8:15): This reference is more than just precious. It speaks to an internal longing many young people have today to know that "healthy father figure" that we have addressed so many times in our culture in the last couple of decades. But also, if certain scholars and linguist experts are correct, the *Abba* at the end of this verse referring to the Holy Spirit as the Adopter actually means "Papa" or "Daddy."[180] (Advocates of this view acknowledge that theirs is not the "only" explanation for the ancient use of the Aramaic/Hebrew *abba* in this instance, and that the usage here might be more formal ["Father"], but that the term was certainly used in common language between sons and fathers at the time, so it's unlikely to be dismissed or unproven as well.)

If this is true, we not only have a great Father in God and the Person of the Spirit, we have a great "Papa," too, which adds a whole other layer of treasurable intimacy our Lord freely gives to His children—the *adoptees*.

"The Spirit of Judgment" and "The Spirit of Burning" (Isaiah 4:4; 28:6): Even Jesus acknowledged that the Spirit would convict and judge the entire world (John 16:8). Here in Isaiah, we get a glimpse of the Holy Spirit in His position of Judge by fire, a purification or cleansing of sorts. Yet a deeper analysis of this messianic, prophetic verse doesn't just identify the Holy Spirit as an angered, righteous arbiter doling out what evil people deserve on the Day of Christ, but instead as One with the intent to preserve the people of God—the Remnant who were for God and with God from the beginning.

SPECIFIC TO THE SON

Much like the Spirit, God the Son appears in our corporate thoughts in a way that only partially recognizes who He is. Typically, we know that He is the Resurrection and the Life (John 11:25); the Almighty (Revelation 1:8); the Author and Finisher of our faith (Hebrews 12:2); the Bread of Life (John 6:32–35); the Bridegroom (Matthew 9:15; John 3:29; Revelation 21:9); the Chosen of God (Luke 23:35); the Cornerstone (Isaiah 28:16; Psalm 118:22; Ephesians 2:20; 1 Peter 2:6); the Door (John 10:9); the Head of the Church (Ephesians 5:23); the High Priest/Apostle (Hebrews 3:1, 2); the Image of the Invisible God (2 Corinthians 4:4; Colossians 1:15); the Light of the World (John 8:12); the Lion of the Tribe of Judah (Genesis 49:9, 10; Revelation 5:5); and many others.

These glorious names are only magnified when we're reminded that He is humbly called "the carpenter" (Mark 6:3).

But, like with the Spirit, let's not assume we know enough about Him that it isn't worthy of our taking time to check back in on what else He might be known for. Consider these other names by which He is called:

"Bright Morning Star" (Revelation 22:16): I personally love this one. Scholars often make the connection, but not everyone in the Church sees the obvious juxtaposition between this title for Jesus and the enemy, who is called "morning star" and "son of the dawn" (Isaiah 14:12).

The context of the reference in Isaiah is of a *fallen* star; the context in the messianic verse is of our beautiful Messiah, the "offspring of David," correcting the Church in the last days. One (the enemy) is always trying to "look like" the other (Jesus), and he continues to fall short of fooling true followers of the real One (Christ).

"Emmanuel"/"Immanuel" (Isaiah 7:14–8:8; Matthew 1:23): This term means "God [is] with Us." The first time a young believer hears that Jesus is "Immanuel, God with us," it might sound complicated and raise questions about how God can any more be "with us" now that Jesus is ascended back to the Father (and therefore whether the label is now moot), *or* it can sound too simple, as if it only refers to the event of the Incarnation. Actually, it's both, and more.

Jesus condescended Himself to become a human (much like a human might become an ant in order to save an anthill, as many preachers and teachers relate), and this act alone is one of the most complicated theological concepts within Christianity. When He was here, physically, He was literally "God with [i.e., amidst] us" at the time. But His work on the cross united us with His Father, whose standards of holiness could not previously allow for the perfect relationship because of our sin. In that regard, Jesus' sacrifice literally joined us, even in our fallen state, to God, and He is now "with us" as a result of the Messiah.

"The Father" (Isaiah 9:6; 1 John 1:1–3): This is not a reference to Jesus being just "one *with*" the Father, as He is in the High Priestly Prayer of John 17 (also John 10:30; 14:9). These verses refer to Jesus, the Son, as "the Father." Yet, as mind-blowing as this concept is—and as much as it appears to be confusing one of Jesus' definitive titles with the Father Person of the Trinity (which is not the case)—what *is* being communicated here is fundamentally awe-inspiring.

"Father," when in reference to the Son, "speaks of his concern (Psalm 65:5), care and discipline (Psalm 103:13; Proverbs 3:12; Isaiah 63:16; 64:8); cf. Psalm 72:4, 12–14; Isa. 11:4."[181] In other words, though the Son is not the Father in respect to His role in the Trinity, Jesus' perfect behavior on earth set a "fatherly" example for the rest of us regarding how we should live and love the way He did, showing (inasmuch as we humans can) that level of "concern, care, and discipline" in our lives and when interacting with others around us.

"Firstborn" (Hebrews 12:23; Revelation 1:5): Similar to the "Father" references, Jesus is here depicted as our oldest brother (also see Hebrews 2:11; this context makes it more clear that He is the Firstborn of Christianity as the original member of the brethren). Biblically speaking, being the oldest brother makes Him the heir of the Father's blessings, as well. (Unlike in the Jacob and Esau story, however, no one can trick the Father into accidentally giving His blessings to another!)

Interestingly, the firstborn son of every Hebrew family was saved by the first Passover during the Exodus by the blood of a lamb. Jesus, Himself, *was* the Lamb whose blood was shed once and for all (John 1:29, 36; 1 Peter 1:19; Revelation 5:6–12; 7:17), thereby becoming the Passover sacrifice who died so we all might live. But our oldest brother was raised after three days, and, like the eldest of a Hebrew family that night in Egypt, would not be owned by the grave!

What a cool thought—Jesus, our "older brother." It's endearing and sweet to think of Him in that way! (See how studying the names of God can revolutionize our Christian concepts? His character has so many layers! It's important that we don't get stuck in a rut with our pet theologies and forget that He's bigger than our grandest perceptions.)

"Word" (John 1:1, 14): Jesus is literally the Word. This means that He is the walking, talking, example-setting speech of the Father, and of all standards of holiness.

"Son of Man" (throughout the New Testament): Have you ever wondered why Jesus called Himself the "Son of Man"? Why "man"? Why not always "Son of God"?

One popular explanation is that "the Son of Man" identifies the *human* aspect of His mission. According to this view, He set aside His divinity in the sense that He came to be an unfallen man (as opposed to men in general) who would lay down His life for humanity as a sacrifice, thereby connecting Him to His prophetically human-messianic role. For example, the book of Revelation refers to "one like a son of man" that also reflects the dual role of Son of God and Son of Man. In Daniel 7:13, the prophet also foresaw "one like the son of man" in a more ethereal light as He received all glory and power from the Ancient of Days (the Father). So this title was protoevangium (*protos*, "first," and *evangelion*, "good news" or "Gospel"; a term therefore meaning a prophetic, pre-Gospel message or signal [such as the crushing of the serpent's head in Genesis 3:15]). "Son of Man" foresaw that the Messiah would become a man, born of a woman for First Advent purposes, but that He would also be "the second [or last] Adam" (1 Corinthians 15:45) in that He was unfallen and the offspring of God—a part of the Trinity, etc. (More on the "Last Adam" title in a moment; it's my favorite!)

However, next to this truly respectable and theological rationalization of "Son of Man" is a surprising turn of events since 1947, when the Dead Sea Scrolls provided "the other side of the story." Christian apologist Dr. William Menzies (no relation to the earlier film producer by the same name who died in the 1950s) explains:

> Even the term *Son of Man*…has been better understood in more recent times with the finding of ancient manuscripts such as the Dead Sea Scrolls. This term was *not at all a reference to the humanity of Jesus*, as many scholars previously understood. Instead, it is a powerful assertion of His deity and messiah-ship. The term *Son of Man* was [historically, for Israel] another way of referring to the triumph of the Messiah! Jesus not only claimed to forgive sins, but by describing himself as the *Son of Man* He also claimed to be the fulfillment of biblical prophecy. He claimed to be the Anointed of God for whom Israel had longed and yearned. Is it not striking that almost without exception this is the designation He used of himself?
>
> It is also important to note that Jesus received worship. When the Magi saw Him, "they bowed down and worshiped him" (Mat-

thew 2:11). When the blind man whom Jesus had healed expressed his belief in the Son of Man, he worshiped Jesus (John 9:38).[182]

If Dr. Menzies (and other scholars who have taken this position since the discovery of the Dead Sea Scrolls) is correct, then Jesus wasn't nearly as quiet about His messianic mission as we previously thought. In the past, reading so many times that He called Himself merely "Son of Man" gave the impression that He was keeping His true identity as the Son of God on the down low so as not to arouse suspicion and more opposition than necessary before due time. But if the Jews had long believed that the "Son of Man" was going to be the promised Messiah, then Jesus was quite open about who He was—at least as that applied to His people. (The Jews would have understood it far more than, say, the Romans.) Another useful purpose of the term was that it had *not*—as had many other messianic names—been dragged through the muck of misinterpretation by religious authorities and married to the "soldier messiah who would take down Rome" idea that the oral traditions had started to solidify in the minds of the Jews. "The Son of Man" was *clean*, exempt from miscalculation, and therefore perfect for Christ to claim while also openly asserting who He truly was. *Baker Encyclopedia of the Bible* explains:

["Son of Man" was not about] his human nature or humanity, as some church fathers or contemporary scholars believe. Rather, it reflects on the heavenly origin and divine dignity of Jesus.... Jesus used the term as a messianic title for himself…with considerable originality because the term was not fraught with popular misconceptions concerning messiahship.[183]

With those "misconceptions" in mind, understand that almost every other word, phrase, or name that could have been chosen to describe the Messiah while He lived would have conveyed something that was no longer accurate to His being or mission, at least regarding how those alternative choices would have landed on a Jewish audience's ears. So convinced were the Jews that Jesus was going to be a different kind of Savior than He was, He chose to stick with a "clean" term, one that had a reference to humanity in the title. That is *not* to say, however, that the use of "Man" was in any way linked to humanity historically.

We too often look at just what the Bible says, divorcing its texts from their historical context. For instance, Ezekiel preferred the phrase "Son of Man" ninety-three times in reference to humanity in the Jews' earlier history (e.g., Ezekiel 2:1; 3:1; 4:1; 5:1; 6:2; 7:2; and so on). Old Testament poetic parallelism did the same (Numbers 23:19; Job 16:21; 25:6; 35:8; Psalms 8:4; 80:17; 146:3; Isaiah 51:12; 56:2; Jeremiah 49:18, 33; 50:40; 51:43; and on it goes). Alone, these references could make "Man" in the phrase "Son of Man" more emphatic and central to pop culture's definition or interpretation of the term than it should be. But outside of what *we today* consider to be Scripture, the apocryphal books the Hebrews also studied mentioned this "Son of Man" figure as a consistently mighty, "authoritative heavenly figure [who] appears at God's side to judge the world and bring salvation."[184] Concepts like these are from texts such as 1 Enoch 46–71 (which contains the Jewish culture's most crucial "Son of Man" sayings) and 4 Ezra 13, neither of which is included in today's canon and therefore is given much less attention by biblical interpreters as time goes on. However, these ancient apocryphal texts played "a major role in the Jewish concept of the Messiah."[185]

Perhaps most easily put: "Son of *Man*," without glancing backward to history, sounds like a simple reference to something human while in contrast to the deity that Jesus was (and *is*, obviously). And this is why we have modern scholars stating that this Name of Jesus identifies the human aspect of His mission when it doesn't. To the original audience, God's covenant people, the Hebrews, the term "Son of Man" was intrinsically and unbreakably woven to mean "Son of God"—the concept of a coming Messiah Savior. It therefore pointed to the *opposite* of a human mission.

Yeah, but all the scholars are basically saying the same thing, aren't they? I mean, isn't this kind of a silly semantics game?

Not really, *especially* not to any new believers who might be reading this book. The Jews, as Dr. Menzies stated, *always* understood "Son of Man" to be a direct reference to the triumphs of the Messiah because of how the Messiah figure was described in Daniel, Ezekiel, and other apocryphal works important to their culture and cultural identity. Those precious people who may be a little newer to the faith than others might be earnestly trying to seek Jesus through the Gospels and finding themselves tripping on why, more than any other Name, Jesus calls Himself "Man." They may be wondering why, if Jesus knew who He was and truly believed it, He would keep choosing to reveal Himself as a being no more powerful than another Adam. For any such readers, once the history is explained more deeply than many contemporary sources do, then Jesus suddenly comes to life off the pages of the Gospels like one who boldly *owns* His purpose amidst the Jews instead of trying to hide it in ambiguous terms.

As to whether Jesus and Adam had anything in common, however, that much is clear upon studying the next name on our list.

"Last Adam" (1 Corinthians 15:45): I will conclude our list with this one, because it is, quite frankly, a staggering fact that will make you rethink everything you *thought* you knew about humanity. Donna Howell, an author who works with Defender Publishing, recently shared something with me from one of her Bible and theology classes that floored me. When we think of Jesus as the Last Adam, we commonly understand that Adam brought sin and death, and Jesus, also wholly human, brought forgiveness and life, and the contrast of these two characters makes one the first, and the other the last. (That is an oversimplification, I know; I just want to draw attention to this powerful concept.) However, when we think like scholars do, we realize this verse might just as well be referring to the idea that Adam and Jesus shared another trait: They were the *only two humans who ever existed on earth*...at least as far as that aligns with what God the Father originally created. Adam was perfect before the Fall, and nobody after him was perfect until Jesus; Jesus was perfect always, and since then, none of us have been. In their perfection—and in the form that God first intended—they were what humans were *supposed to be* in the beginning. Consider this quote by Dr. Millard J. Erickson, author of almost thirty books in systematic theology, including the revolutionary 1985 work, *Christian Theology*:

> In thinking about the incarnation, we must begin not with the traditional conceptions of humanity and deity, but with the recognition that the two are most fully known in Jesus Christ.... For the humanity of Jesus was not the humanity of sinful human beings, but the humanity possessed by Adam and Eve from their creation and before their fall. There is no doubt, then, as to Jesus' humanity. *The question is not whether Jesus was fully human, but whether we are.* He was not merely as human as we are; he was *more* human than we are.[186]

Imagine that: Adam and Jesus were the only people in history who were "fully" human. Adam ended his life "not fully human," based on the forbidden fruit sin stain that contorted his otherwise perfect design. That means Jesus was the only human who began, lived, and completed His life as the kind of human God originally made. The rest of us... The only way I can put it is that we have a sort of *spiritual* genetic mutation that makes us "less than human" on this side of eternity.

THE MYSTERY OF MELCHIZEDEK

On the coattails of the discussion of Jesus' names comes a very bizarre, almost alarming question of one aspect of His deity. The Word says that Christ was/is/always will be our High Priest (Hebrews 4:14–16). But the Word *also* says that one has to be a descendant of Aaron in order to be a priest (Exodus 28:1). (Or, one has to at least be a Levite through direct patrilineal descendants of the original Levi, if not a direct Aaronic descendant through the fathers' sides alone. For the record, this is what separates today's first two of three post-exilic Jewish tribes. The three altogether are the Kohen tribe, the tribe of Levi, and Yisrael. Yisrael is anyone who is not of the priestly bloodline, while Levites are *all* of the priestly bloodline, "set apart" for their refusal to worship the golden calf [Exodus 32: 26–29]. Within the parent tribe of Levi is the bloodline of Aaron. From Aaron forward, and only through those who descend directly from Aaron through their *fathers*, is a smaller Aaronic tribe, the Kohenim. For the purposes of this study, and because interpretations of the matter differ from scholar to scholar, we will assume that the treatment is the same: *One had to be a Levite/descendant of Aaron to have a place in the priesthood.*)

That said, it was prophesied as far back as Micah (5:2) that the Messiah would not be from the Levite bloodline, but from the tribe of *Judah*!

What do we make of this apparent contradiction?

This is the mystery of Melchizedek.

(Special thanks to my brother in the Lord, Dr. Michael Heiser, a scholar behind the development of many Logos Bible Software resources, for his assistance and direction throughout this section of this study on biblical names.)

Who Really Is Melchizedek, Anyway?

What a complicated question this turned out to be when I recently asked it, myself. Genesis 14:18–20 states:

> And Melchizedek king of Salem brought forth bread and wine: and he was the priest of the Most High God. And he [Melchizedek] blessed him [Abram], and said, "Blessed be Abram of the Most High God, possessor of heaven and earth: And blessed be the Most High God, which hath delivered thine enemies into thy hand." And he [Abram] gave him [Melchizedek] tithes of all [or a tenth of everything].[187]

Did you happen to note that these two men—a non-Israelite and an Israelite (or *pre*-Israelite, that is, since Abram was a father of Israel but Israel was a couple of generations later)—were both respectfully and worshipfully acknowledging the same God?

In trying to better understand this somewhat obscure character, we must first look at his name. Melchizedek is the Hebrew *Malki-Tsedeq*, and it's not pronounced mel-chiz-eh-dek like in most Christian circles today, but mal-kee-tseh'-dek. For good reason, many scholars interpret the meaning of this name to be "king of righteousness," from what is stated in Hebrews 7:2: "To whom also Abraham gave a tenth part of all; first being by interpretation King of righteousness." The ESV renders this verse in a way that reads more closely to the way we speak today: "And to him Abraham apportioned a tenth part of everything. He is first, by translation of his name, king of righteousness." However, though this is the *translation* of his name, there are also good reasons—namely potential pagan origins—some scholars say "not so fast" on the seemingly too-easy conclusion. Nobody is suggesting that the book of Hebrews is wrong, as any true, believing scholar of the Word knows that its contents are inerrant and infallible. But many scholars acknowledge that the Hebrews passage doesn't go into the background detail necessary to explain how a name could translate to one thing, but have roots in another explanation.

The etymology of "Melchizedek" is technically impossible to know, though we can formulate some educated theories. Keep in mind as you read the following that Melchizedek was *not* an Israelite (and he certainly wasn't a descendant of Aaron, Levi, or even one of the patriarchs—Abraham, Isaac, or Jacob—for that matter), so he would not have come by his priesthood of the "Most High God" Yahweh through that means. Also, since he wasn't born and raised in the nation of God's people as an Israelite, it shouldn't be alarming if some of his roots are buried in the Canaanite system.

First, *tsedeq* in Hebrew means "righteous," while *malk* is "king." However, quite confusingly, Tsedeq is also the proper name of a Canaanite god. This means that "Melchizedek" could be "King of Righteousness," like the title of the righteous king of Salem (as he was); or, it could be "My King Is

Tsedeq." Some scholars, like Dr. Michael Heiser in his *Naked Bible Podcast*, note that the typical rules of Hebrew grammar disallow for the *i* at the end of *malki* without switching from "king of [something]" to "my king is [something]." In this case, the name must become "My King is Righteous" or "My King is Tsedeq [the deity]."[188] There are exceptions to this that suggest the *i* in the name *Malki-Tsedeq* might be a "vestige of the case system" (meaning a more ancient form of writing Hebrew letters),[189] but it isn't the likeliest possibility. It was at this point that Dr. Heiser saw my knitted eyebrows and raised me a double-take. The "wild card," as he puts it, is that the Hebrew *malk* for "king" could *also* be the Canaanite god *Malk* (or *Melek*), giving a third possibility here that Melchizedek was actually named "Malk [the deity] is Righteous." Elsewhere in the Old Testament (Haggai 1:1; Ezra 3:2), Heiser points out, we also run across the terms *yotsedeq* and *yehotsedeq*, both of which (for reasons complicated enough that I'll refrain from elaboration) mean "Yahweh is righteous," which means that *Malki-Tsedeq* could additionally be translated "Yahweh is Tsedeq."

Clear as mud?

I know…*pant, pant.* Me too…

But even theologians like Heiser—who spend their very lives attempting to make it simpler for readers to understand the Bible—acknowledge that this one is a toughie. He concedes:

> Again, all these things are possible with Melchizedek. It could be "my king is righteous," "my king is Tsedeq," "king of righteousness," "Malk is righteous," or "Malk is Tsedeq." It could be any of those five things just in this one little name.[190]

Still later in the discussion, the possibility is introduced that it could also mean "My King is Just."

And even if the exact name were to be decided, there's a whole second line of questioning in relation to the source of the name: Was Melchizedek's name assigned at birth, like something we would expect to see on an ancient certificate? Did he take it upon himself in some act of devotion?

Did he carry out some feat or participate in an event that attached him to it or earned it for him? Or was it just an adjectival epithet—would it appear as a mere epitaph on his grave, "Here lies that king who was righteous"?

Perhaps the *most important question* we could be asking, however, is this: If the *i* in *malki* is a factor that forces the "my king is" translation, as just explained, then Melchizedek's name would have nothing to do with himself as king; his name would be an honorific name of some *other* king who was "Melchizedek's king" in some way—and who would that be, if not Tsedeq? Doesn't it seem a little desperate to say that we would assume this to be some other distant ruler when Melchizedek lived right there in Canaanite territory with a deity named Tsedeq?

If we're being as honest as the best scholars out there, we simply don't know. That's why the research has to visit other connections to arrive at any possible conclusions.

Now, the territory that Melchizedek presided over was Salem. The Sumerian word for "city" was *uru*. So scholars believe one major possibility is that *uru* and *Shalem* together would have been the root derivatives of *urusalim*, which is one variation of how "Jerusalem" was spelled in some existent tablets, manuscripts, and early diplomatic correspondence among leaders of that day. Though there are other possibilities (and traditions, like those from our Latin Vulgate translator, Jerome), once one is equipped with all the information available (a luxury not afforded to scholars in the past prior to the discovery of the Dead Sea Scrolls or the invention of tools like Logos Bible Software), the signs most heavily point to the idea that Melchizedek was the king of Jerusalem. Given, that's *early* Jerusalem, during the days of the Jebusites and before the city would have been associated with Jehovah at all...but still Jerusalem. It's important to acknowledge and remember that *names* at this primitive point in history and in this area of the globe would have been principally Canaanite/pagan still, until Israel's Davidic rule later on (2 Samuel 5:6–7). With this detail in the back of our thinking cap, we hit our first reliable consistency within this etymological soup.

After *Malki-Tsedeq*, there was another ruler of the city by the name of *Adoni-Tsedek*, mentioned in Joshua 10:1–3 (with the alternate "zedek" transliteration spelling often given to Melchizedek; i.e., Adonizedek). What does *his* name mean? Remember our reflection on Adonai? Without doubt, *Adoni-Tsedek* means "my lord is Tsedeq." This is glaring evidence that Melchizedek's name would be tied to the same Canaanite deity, thus translated as "my king is Tsedeq."

Some get to this point in the reflection—just as I originally did and as Heiser predicts his listeners will—and wonder why a priest of the Most High God, Yahweh, would be named "My King Is Tsedeq." Who in the otherworld is Tsedeq, anyway, and why would a servant of Yahweh have anything to do with "another god"?

And here's a telling question: Why does *tsedek* mean "righteousness" in Hebrew, anyway? If you're familiar with how etymology works, you will know where this is going already. If the Israelites said it first, then there's a possibility that a god by the same name in a pagan culture is coincidence (though, an unlikely one, considering how condensed the world population was at the time, and how neighbors' language influenced surrounding people groups). If the pagans said it first and the word was adopted into the Hebrews' daily language, the implications go berserk in another, more exciting direction.

Don't worry. More answers are coming quickly, and they will fall like a sedative to your frazzled nerves and splintered thoughts. Getting to the *end* of this trail will be worth it, I promise.

In getting to the bottom of who Tsedeq is, we see that he can be traced as far back as the Babylonian pantheon and the Amorite pantheon. That links this deity to a vast number of ancient people groups and their languages, pulling in all sorts of names of this same god that don't sound anything like Tsedeq (such as Kittu, Isar, and others). But in some of the personal, theophoric names (or names including deities) recorded in Ugaritic texts, we find *Sdqslm*, or, literally, "Tsedeq is Salem."[191] The latter half of Jerusalem's name, in context of this etymological journey, would have also pointed to the Canaanite deity, Shalem, who was also—*wait for it*—

the god of justice (*misor*) and righteousness (*tsedeq*)! So, if Tsedeq *is* Salem, as the texts illustrate, then the ruling deity of "Jeru-salem" (literally "city of Shalem"), for time immemorial before Abraham and his family would have been greeted by Melchizedek, would have been Tsedek, the deity of righteousness, justice, and probably peace, if the scholarly links between the deity Shalem and the Hebrew word for peace (*shalom*) are as reliable as they appear to be. This also explains why, later on when Jerusalem has become the capital of Yahweh's people, it is still referred to as "the city of righteousness" (Isaiah 1:21, 26).

Throughout the links, we see that Tsedeq is repeatedly connected to the sky, and more specifically, to the sun. At times, this is vaguer, whereas for other peoples, the worship of Tsedeq involved full-fledged worship of the sky's celestial objects, which we all know Yahweh wouldn't have anything to do with.

Nevertheless, putting aside all other cultures for the moment, consider Melchizedek in light of all we've covered:

- He is a priest of the Most High God (*El Elyon*)—i.e., Yahweh, Himself, as acknowledged in both Genesis 14 and Hebrews 7.
- He and Abraham (a clear follower of Yahweh) worship the same deity.
- He is named after a "deity king," Tsedeq, who is now shown to be the god of peace, justice, and righteousness.
- He is ruler over a city dedicated to and named after traits that are *central and essential* to our very own Jehovah God, especially as He interacted with His people in the Old Testament.

If you haven't yet spotted the pattern, I'll let Heiser point it out, as he does so in the best way:

Let's just go all the way back. Abraham worships Yahweh. It's just Abraham! He has some kids, he's got some servants. Those are the Yahweh worshipers around. They're living in Canaan because

God told them to go there. Everybody else is a Canaanite. So of course, you're going to run into people who are Canaanites, and they're going to be people like this Melchizedek guy who is a priest of the Most High God.... If you walked up to Melchizedek and said, "Hey, who's the Most High God?" he would say "Tsedeq!" All right?...

It means that we have a different name for the same deity....

It's difficult for us, looking at this, to think how this system worked. Maybe this is a poor analogy, but think about the way we refer to God. We refer to him as God, Yahweh, El, El Shaddai, Father. If we really sat down and thought about it, we've probably got ten or fifteen ways that we refer to God. We don't theologically have any other deity above Him, yet we use all these different names. What if we were doing that in a historical context where some of the people who heard us use these names thought we were referring to other deities? That's the kind of thing you have going on in biblical times....

His covenantal name is Yahweh. He could go by these other names—and did. We have biblical evidence for that....

Consequently, Melchizedek could bear the name of Yahweh or Tsedeq and not violate the theological proposition that Yahweh or Tsedeq.... In the final form of the biblical text, they're one and the same. He could bear the name Tsedeq and refer to him as Most High because Tsedeq was Yahweh.[192]

Heiser does go on to acknowledge that not every scholar comes to this conclusion. However, I want to leave Heiser's podcast for a moment and go on my own scholarly trail of thought: Back to the "who said it first?" question... Why does *tsedeq* mean "righteousness" in Hebrew if that was the preexistent name of a pagan god unrelated to Yahweh? And on whose human authority would it *ever* be a good idea to retain that title as one for Yahweh, as we know already that they did (*Jehovah Tsidkenu*, "The Lord Is Our Righteousness")? Why would the biblical writers make

Yahweh's very Name "Righteousness" in so many verses within the Old
Testament using variations of the age-old "Tsedeq-deity" spelling, as we
know they did (Isaiah 41:10; 45:19; 51:1, 5; 61:3; Psalm 4:6; 9:9; 17:1;
48:11; 58:2; 94:15; 98:9; 118:15–20; Jeremiah 33:16)? The very association to "a pagan deity" would force a more creative work-around than for
the Israelites to retain that term for their *true* Most High God. To keep a
pagan name for Him would be ludicrous and unfaithful, a total "Jezebel"
move on the proverbial chessboard with God that has no other result but
a smack-down checkmate from an angry God.

Not convinced? Think of it this way: In today's Western, English-
speaking culture, that would be like deciding that, because the deity
name "Lucifer" means something as beautiful as "morning star" or "light-
bearer," we could make "Lucifer" at least a part of one of our names for
Jesus, since Jesus *also* brought light into the world. Heaven forbid that
our logic would ever allow for us to associate Christ's powerful name with
Lucifer just because they had a common trait or characteristic. It's absurd
that we would do that, and it's equally absurd that the Israelites would
commit that grievance…*unless* Tsedeq and Yahweh were actually the same
deity. Then it all clicks into place.

We might get to this point and wonder why, if Jerusalem was already
known as a territory dedicated to and even named after this same Yahweh
under the Canaanite pronunciation "Tsedeq," the Israelites would have
been sent to conquer that area. If it was already territory that, etymology
aside, belonged to the God of the Bible, then, regardless of how one pro-
nounces a name, it seems odd that the Israelites were sent to take it over
during the Davidic rule. Right?

Sure it does. But remember, there were hundreds of years between the
Most-High-God-worshiping Melchizedek and the Adonizedek of Joshua
10, and there are many links between Tsedeq and sun worship in some of
the neighboring cultures. Heiser explains:

> What we know for sure is that by the time you get David coming
> in there and taking control of the city, there's no ambiguity as to

who David is worshiping. When the historical books get written, they're going to reflect a theological revolution that, "No, we're not going to come into this place called Jerusalem as Yahweh worshipers and you guys are doing your Tsedeq thing over here…." David goes in there and says, "We are claiming this turf because this was given to our ancestors by Yahweh, the Most High God. We're claiming this turf—this city. This is going to be my capital. I am the one chosen by God to be king. This is going to be his place, and we're not messing around with all these other deity names. If there's talk of the Most High going on here, we're not going to use the term Tsedeq, we're going to use the term Yahweh."[193]

I think we've proven to this point that it's not an impulsive or reckless conclusion to assume that Melchizedek was the king-priest of Tsedeq-Yahweh. Over in Psalm 110, verse 4, we catch another glimpse of this historical character, in a verse describing the Messiah: "The Lord hath sworn, and will not repent, 'Thou [Jesus] *art* a priest for ever after the order of Melchizedek.'"

Christ Never Had to Be "Of" the Aaronic Bloodline!

First, let's understand that we shouldn't take this too far. There's no evidence within the Word indicating that we should assume that Melchizedek's appearance to Abraham was a Christophany, or that he was any kind of a divine being. He is identified in these verses as the king of Salem, and painting him in light of a Christophany, theophany, or angelic being would create more questions than answers about his being known as the current ruler over pre-Israeli Jerusalem on the day he met Abram and that entire conversation occurred in Genesis 14. However, it's a responsible, logical conclusion to suggest that Melchizedek was a "type" or "picture" of Christ.

We looked at a list a couple of pages earlier that showcased the extraordinary familiarity between this character and the Word of God.

With his name having now gone from "My King Is Tsedeq" to effectively "My King Is Yahweh," we can proceed to reflect on the other elements: He's associated with the Father, kingship, Jerusalem, righteousness, justice, peace, and the priesthood. Folks during the Second Temple Period are going to start building a profile of what they believe the coming Messiah will look like, and by Psalm 110, the biblical writers directly state that the Messiah will be a priest "after the order of Melchizedek," or a priest whose order can be traced to something older and higher than a Levitical ancestry rule from the Mosaic Law. How much more astounding, then, that Christ fulfilled these expectations, even though His coming and His work would not look anything like what the Jews of His time thought they would. The connection is even more unbelievable when we calculate the odds of Christ fulfilling this one parallel, never mind the countless prophecies!

It's not a coincidence that Abraham ("Abram" at the time) came into contact with this king by the name of "My King Is Yahweh"—and it's likewise no coincidence that Israel's conquests led God's people to claim this as their Promised Land—officially linking the first king under Yahweh to David, whose bloodline would produce the Messiah, Christ. The original king of Jerusalem, under our very precious Lord Jehovah, wasn't David, but Melchizedek! And Melchizedek was not merely a king, but a king-priest! His order or priesthood was the first, the oldest, and the highest, and therefore took precedence over the later Aaronic order of priesthood that was born from what many scholars (not just Heiser) would consider to be God's "secondary plan" when Moses' lack of faith angered the Lord.

Consider this: Throughout Exodus 3 and 4, there is a repetitiously argumentative nature in the communication between God and Moses: God tells Moses to do something, and Moses gives reasons God's plan will never work. This happens over and over, until it climaxes in Moses' outright plea that God just "send someone else" to fill Moses' shoes (Exodus 4:13). In the next verse, we read that God's anger is "kindled" against Moses, and He announces that Moses' brother, Aaron the Levite, will now be the speaker for God since Moses' faith is a growing issue. Aaron is now a sort of equal leader with Moses over the people of God, which leads to his fulfilling the role of High Priest.

> This would mean that the Aaron[ic] priesthood is, at best, a concession or an accommodation to Moses. At worst, it's a punishment. In other words, Moses is not allowed to approach the Most Holy place later on, but Aaron is.... Aaron's priesthood is a result of Moses' unbelief from the very beginning.[194]

If Moses hadn't goobered too many times in his faith, our God likely never would have set his brother as the official bloodline in the first place, and it likely wouldn't have had anything to do with who someone in Israel was related to. The order of the priesthood under Melchizedek, then, is the Higher Order that the Messiah would inherit.

You know, though, after all this reflection, Jesus' *true* paternal bloodline on His Father's side (Father God) was of a Higher Order anyway, so, spiritually speaking, the *Son of God* should not be limited to the tribe of Levi...but if He *is* going to be accountable to some "priesthood order," it stands to reason that it would be established under the very first king of Jerusalem in the Word who is irrefutably coupled with the Father God's original covenant man, Abraham.

Now, fast forward to the messianic references in Psalm 110 again, specifically verses 1–4, and note that "Zion" is *Shalom*—in other words, Jerusalem (!!!):

> The Lord [Father] said unto my Lord [Son], "Sit thou at my right hand, until I make thine enemies thy footstool." The Lord shall send the rod of thy strength out of Zion [Jerusalem; ruling place of the ancient Melchizedek]: rule thou in the midst of thine enemies. Thy people shall be willing in the day of thy power, in the beauties of holiness from the womb of the morning: thou hast the dew of thy youth. The Lord hath sworn, and will not repent, "Thou art a priest for ever after the order of Melchizedek."

With that in mind, let's return to what the book of Hebrews says of our great Messiah, who has inherited His priestly status from this higher order, and let's reflect what we now know (with my brackets added) of this relationship in light of these new insights.

Jesus, made an high priest for ever after the order of Melchizedek.

For this Melchizedek, king of Salem, priest of the Most High God, who met Abraham returning from the slaughter of the kings, and blessed him; To whom also Abraham gave a tenth part of all; first being by interpretation King of righteousness [we're getting to this...], and after that also King of Salem, which is, King of peace....

Now consider how great this man [Melchizedek] was, unto whom even the patriarch Abraham gave the tenth of the spoils [why would Abraham pay tithes—money that has historically been given to the Hebrew/Christian God—to the king of Salem if he was a corrupt, pagan king?]. And verily they that are of the sons of Levi, who receive the office of the priesthood, have a commandment to take tithes of the people according to the law, that is, of their brethren, though they come out of the loins of Abraham: But he whose descent is not counted from them received tithes of Abraham, and blessed him that had the promises. And without all contradiction the less is blessed of the better. And here men that die receive tithes; but there he receiveth them, of whom it is witnessed that he liveth. And as I may so say, Levi also, who receiveth tithes, payed tithes in Abraham. For he was yet in the loins of his father, when Melchizedek met him [meaning Levi wasn't born yet, but as Levi was at this moment still "in the loins" of the patriarch, Levi, *himself*—the very father of the priestly bloodline—is subject to this payment of tithes to Melchizedek, the higher priestly order].

If therefore perfection were by the Levitical priesthood, (for under it the people received the law,) what further need was there that another priest should rise after the order of Melchizedek, and not be called after the order of Aaron? For the priesthood being changed [note that the priesthood is "being changed" here, from Levi to the higher Melchizedek], there is made of necessity a change also of the law [and therefore, even the *Law* must be changed to reflect this higher order!]. For he of whom these things are spoken pertaineth to another tribe, of which no man gave attendance at the altar [Jesus is from "another tribe" altogether, of which no man of Israel ever had anything to do with during His priestly rituals around the altar]. For it is evident that our Lord sprang out of Juda; of which tribe Moses spake nothing concerning priesthood [this tribe was even above the knowledge and authority of *the* one and only Moses, who "spoke nothing concerning" it!].

And it is yet far more evident [the writer of Hebrews essentially just said, "Guys, this is *obvious*, now," so we shouldn't try to make it more complicated than what follows next in the text]: for that after the similitude of Melchizedek there ariseth another priest [or, "there arose another priest who is a 'type' of Melchizedek"], Who is made, not after the law of a carnal commandment [the ESV says, "not on the basis of a legal requirement concerning bodily descent"; i.e., it's not a matter of who He's related to], but after the power of an endless life. For he testifieth, "Thou art a priest for ever after the order of Melchizedek." For there is verily a disannulling of the commandment going before for the weakness and unprofitableness thereof. [This verse from the KJV is very wordy... A modern rewording (mine) would say: "The prior commandment is weak and useless, so verily, right now, we are observing an exchange of the old priesthood commandment/ Law for something newer, stronger, better, and more profitable for all."] For the law made nothing perfect, but the bringing in of a better hope did; by the which we draw nigh unto God.

And inasmuch as not without an oath [i.e., don't assume this new order was established without an oath or covenant] he was made priest: (For those priests were made without an oath [the priests of the bloodline of Levi/Aaron became such by birth, not by oath]; but this [Jesus as High Priest] with an oath by him that said unto him, "The Lord sware and will not repent [He will never change His mind], Thou art a priest for ever after the order of Melchizedek:)

By so much was Jesus made a surety of a better testament [that is, a newer, better covenant than the old]. And they [priests of Levi] truly were many priests, because they were not suffered to continue by reason of death [their natural, human death excused them (obviously) from being a priest and carrying those responsibilities]: But this man [Jesus], because he continueth ever, hath an unchangeable priesthood [He will *always*, unchangeably, be our High Priest!]. Wherefore he is able also to save them to the uttermost that come unto God by him [meaning He can save them completely and radically], seeing he ever liveth to make intercession for them.

For such an high priest became us, who is holy, harmless, undefiled, separate from sinners, and made higher than the heavens; Who needeth not daily, as those high priests, to offer up sacrifice, first for his own sins [Jesus clearly never did, and never will, offer a sacrifice for His "sins," as He is sinless], and then for the people's [and He needn't offer up a sacrifice for *our* sin]: for this he did once, when he offered up himself [because He already accomplished this!]. For the law [the *old* way] maketh men high priests which have infirmity [men who are imperfect]; but the word of the oath, which was since the law, maketh the Son, who is consecrated for evermore [our High Priest is forever perfect]. (Hebrews 6:20, 7:1–28)

Okay, okay, Tom. But you can't just say that the book of Hebrews is "wrong" when it says that Melchizedek's name means "King of Righteousness," right?

You're correct. But, the answer to that conundrum is a) more in front of you than you might have seen, and b) buried in a lengthy explanation regarding how the Jews of the Second Temple era wrote and spoke about the then-coming Messiah.

As a reminder, the book of Hebrews was written to the Jews, not to modern Christians. The Jews already had a Second Temple-era concept of who the Messiah (the ultimate King of Righteousness) would be, as He was described throughout the Old Testament—as well as how those Old Testament Scriptures would have been interpreted by a Jewish audience at the time. The writer of Hebrews wasn't trying to convince *Christians* that Jesus was of the line of a higher order of priestly lineage (though we benefit infinitely that this material was written). He (or she, if some scholars are correct when they link the writer of Hebrews to Priscilla of Pauline association) was intending to inform a *Jewish* audience that Christ was a valid High Priest, as under an order of ancient origin that even the psalmist understood. The point was to show that Melchizedek, a king named "My King Is Yahweh," was a clear "type" of Christ. When viewed from the etymological roots of the name that was over and over and over again dropped in oral tradition throughout that era, what *else* could this Melchizedek/Christ-type's name possibly mean, prophetically, other than the very fulfillment of the supreme King of Righteousness?

In the interest of not steering this study too far down a theological rabbit hole that has already consumed the entire life's work of countless scholars, I will leave the etymology of "Melchizedek" here and move on. (However, I'm sure inquiring minds out there simply *must* have the "full explanation" of how scholars arrive at harmony between "King of Righteousness" and "My King Is Tsedeq/Yahweh." If that is the case for you, a good place to start would be Dr. Michael Heiser's "Naked Bible Podcast," episodes 166, 167, 168, 170, and 172. Further information regarding these shows and their transcripts is at this endnote.[195])

This is all fascinating, isn't it? I only wish I had another five hundred pages to keep reflecting on the importance of names as they pertain to God. Hopefully by now, the point has been made: Names are *much more* than a "sound in the air" or any other errant Juliet-ism. Names represent a destiny and a promise.

But they also represent a *covenant*.

PEOPLE "OF" THE NAME

So far, we've looked at how the Word of God treats the issue of names and naming, and we've taken time to consider examples as it pertains to people, and then to God. Second, we established what importance the name "Melchizedek" holds in establishing Jesus as our High Priest. Now, let's put these three in a blender and see what delicious, soul-feeding substance comes from it.

"The Name" As Term of Personhood

Even the term "the Name" (Hebrew *ha-shem*), in and of itself as it appears throughout the Word of God, is a reference to personhood. It is, in a way, anthropomorphic all on its own, taking on a level of interventional activity on the behalf of humanity. Consider Isaiah 30:27–28:

> Behold, the name of the Lord cometh from far, burning with his anger, and the burden thereof is heavy: his lips are full of indignation, and his tongue as a devouring fire: And his breath, as an overflowing stream, shall reach to the midst of the neck, to sift the nations with the sieve of vanity: and there shall be a bridle in the jaws of the people, causing them to err.

In such usage (and others; see Psalm 20 and Isaiah 60:9 for a couple of examples), "the Name" *is* God, and God *is* His Name. The authority of one is inseparably conjoined to the power of the other and vice versa, forever, throughout the universe and into perpetuity.

Deuteronomy 12:11 covers a telling moment in early Scripture:

Then there shall be a place which the Lord your God shall choose to cause his name to dwell there; thither shall ye bring all that I command you; your burnt offerings, and your sacrifices, your tithes, and the heave offering of your hand, and all your choice vows which ye vow unto the Lord.

From this, we see that part of the purpose of having a *physical* location of worship for Israel was so that God's Name could "dwell" therein. Later in Scripture, when this place was, in fact, established, the presence of Yahweh, as it dwelt above the Mercy Seat, was identified as "the Name" (Chronicles 22:19).

Having said this, let's fast forward to the New Testament. Jesus, in His High Priestly Prayer of John 17 (which should mean more to us all now that we've reflected on His following the Higher Order of Melchizedek), acknowledges this Name as His own, as one with the Father's (the central theme of this prayer is oneness with the Father), and therefore as unto His own charge:

And I am no longer in the world, but they are in the world, and I am coming to you. Holy Father, keep them in your name, which you have given me, that they may be one, even as we are one. While I was with them, I kept them in your name, which you have given me. I have guarded them, and not one of them has been lost except the son of destruction, that the Scripture might be fulfilled....

...that they may all be one, just as you, Father, are in me, and I in you, that they also may be in us, so that the world may believe that you have sent me. (John 17:11–12, 21, ESV)

At this moment in the life of Christ, Jesus boldly and directly acknowledges that the Name of God was that which was "given [Him]." There is no basis to refute the idea that the personification of "the Name" is thus transferred onto the Man behind our sin atonement. (For more examples of how Jesus *is* the same Name as the Father, see Acts 5:40–42 and Romans 10:9–13, which partially quotes Joel 2:32.)

The fact that Jesus prayed to the Father that we—*we!!!*—would be kept "in [the/His] Name" (v. 11) means that we have inherited something very important. It's crucial that we don't miss it.

We are now people "of" the Name. How? Because we are people "of" the covenant—first the old, as Israel, and then the new, under Christ. Watch this...

First, the people of God from the beginning were essentially told that "the Name" was too grand a power for humans to know, and when asked, God essentially let us know that it doesn't concern us (Genesis 32:29; Exodus 3:14). As has been made generally clear up to this point, to the ancients, knowing the name of a powerful entity meant that the authority would be shared with the one who knew:

> To the ancient, the name was an element of personality and of power. It might be so charged with divine potency that it could not be pronounced [like YHWH]. Or the god might retain a name hidden for himself alone, maintaining this element of power over all gods and men.[196]

This could potentially throw off the balance of the deity's power and present harm to humanity. Yet, something quite bizarre and unprecedented occurs *after* God has deemed Moses worthy of the knowledge of His Name:

> And he (God) said, I will make all my goodness pass before thee [Moses], and I will proclaim the name of the Lord before thee. (Exodus 33:19a)

Whoa—oh goodness! That's a game changer. You caught that, right? Yahweh just proclaimed His Name to Moses on Israelites at Mt. Sinai! Note:

Giving the name entails a certain kind of relationship; it opens up the possibility of, indeed admits a desire for, a certain intimacy in relationship. A relationship without a name inevitably means some distance; naming the name is necessary for closeness. Naming makes true encounter and communication possible. Naming entails availability. By giving the name, God becomes accessible to people. God and people can now meet one another and there can be address on the part of both parties.... Naming also entails vulnerability. In becoming so available to the world, God is to some degree at the disposal of those who can name the name. God's name may be misused and abused as well as honored. For God to give the name is to open himself up to hurt. Naming entails the likelihood of divine suffering, and so this act of name-giving is decisively continuous with 3:7: "I know their suffering." This shows why there is a commandment regarding the name of God.[197]

In this act of sharing the otherwise unspeakable and unknowable title of God with His people, God has chosen to solidify His covenant and deepen His relationship with them...even to His own vulnerability. No other nation or people of the old world would know this secret. The Israelites now had a tool they didn't have before; this made them "people of the Name." If the countless scholars weighing in on this moment are correct, this gave the Jews the authority to call upon the Name when they needed God's assistance and favor. This kind of intense power *could* be abused! Over time, in the sincere interest of keeping what God dared share with His people holy and sacred, Jews gradually embraced the practice of not uttering God's Name at all, which is where we stumble upon things like "G-d" in modern Judaism. (Hopefully by now, most readers have picked up on why the crasser equivalent of "Gosh, darn it" at a toe-stubbing is *not* what the Third Commandment is all about. Using the Name in vain meant to drop the authority of God on some matter of one's personal gain or vainglory. That said, the "Gosh, darn it" equivalent would still be using one of the titles of God uselessly and without intention other than to let out some pessimistic steam, so it's obvious we shouldn't be using it that way, either.)

Then, as we saw earlier, Jesus also *was* "the Name," as it *was* Him also, because Jesus was "one with" Yahweh, and Yahweh had "given" Jesus His Name. The Old Covenant was sealed by the sharing of Yahweh's secret Name, which was a mystery until that point (and because of its sacred treatment from the Jews after that, it largely remains a secret to scholars who, today, argue all over the place what it should be and what it means). We know Jesus, and therefore, we know the Name—literally and spiritually—of the New Covenant. This is why we have such verses that make names synonymous with personhood. For example, Acts 1:15:

> And in those days Peter stood up in the midst of the disciples, and said, (the number of names together were about an hundred and twenty).

Take that same application over to Acts 15:14:

> Simeon hath declared how God at the first did visit the Gentiles, to take out of them a people for his name.

This is a clear reference to the concept that God wants, if I might speak in an adoptive terminology, "a people that belong to Him."

We are that people!

Though we speak Jesus' Name with boldness now, as opposed to trying to keep it secret, we do so with intention and purpose. We are no less the people *of* the New Covenant because we utter His many precious titles aloud and in text (such as this book), which now extends to any Jew or Gentile to claim for his or her own, if he or she can cast off the shackles of doubt and accept the free gift that was the sacrifice of the Son.

And if we are people *of* the New Covenant, then we are people *of* the Name.

If you have already accepted Christ as your personal Lord and Savior, welcome to the family, to the fellowship of the Name!

Have you been baptized yet? Whether you have or haven't, there is something about that sacrament you should know about.

Baptism "in" the Name of? Not Exactly...

To begin, there's an odd (but rewarding!) bit of linguistic intel I would like to share. Just as a reminder, the symbolism of baptism is that a person is brought to the water in his or her sinful state, *publicly* (in front of witnesses) submitting himself or herself to be submerged into the water, representing a spiritual cleansing by the blood/living water of the Lamb, and then that person is brought back up anew. It is the enactment of the outward sacrament that shows a man's internal invitation to Christ—and therefore the spiritual transformation into a new creation in Christ (2 Corinthians 5:17)—is serious and complete. (The act of sanctification has also begun.) The water, itself, has no power. But the *words*...that's a different matter.

Do you remember the words spoken at your baptism, or have you been to another's lately and heard what was said just before the dunk? More than likely, it was, "I baptize you *in* the Name of the Father, the Son, and the Holy Spirit." Right?

Actually, though this is beautiful, this is not what the Word tells us to say during the official sacrament of baptism. Not exactly, anyway...and the early Church Fathers, Church historians, and biblical commentators almost all attest to this. (Donna Howell has also written about this a time or two in previous works.)

The Greek preposition translated as "in" here in the baptism sacrament verse (Matthew 28:19) is more accurately translated as "into." You are not just being baptized "in" the name of the Father, Son, and Holy Ghost, as if this is a stamp of God's acknowledgment and approval of a symbolic act. Something done "in the name of" someone else means you have their permission and authority to do something. But when "in" becomes "into," the phrase is no longer about *consent*…it becomes *familial!* Being baptized "into the name" means you "take on that name" like a child does today when he or she is adopted into a new family. He or she "becomes" a Smith or a Johnson. In equivalent terms: Adopted children don't just dip in water because their new parents give their permission, authority, or consent to join the family. We, in joining the family of God as His children, are being placed "into the name."

I was astounded when I had first heard this theology, simply because it was never even questioned around me, but it's legitimate. Stuart Weber, in the *Holman New Testament Commentary*, the *Matthew* volume, states:

> The believer who chooses to submit to baptism into this name identifies with God's name as well as the spiritual family of all others who are identified with this same name.[198]

We take on the family title, as well as the family *charge* and *mission!* It means "no less than entering into covenant with a person, as God; professing faith in Him as such; enlisting one's self into His service; and vowing all obedience and submission to Him."[199] As R. T. France's commentary on the book of Matthew attests:

> But while John's baptism was only a preparatory one (3:11), Jesus now institutes one with a fuller meaning. It is a commitment to (*in the name* is literally "*into* the name," implying entrance into an allegiance) *the Father, the Son and the Holy Spirit* (all three of whom, interestingly, were involved in the event of Jesus' own baptism, 3:16–17). Jesus thus takes his place along with his Father and the Spirit as the object of worship and of the disciple's commitment. The experience of God in these three Persons is the essential basis of discipleship. At the same time the singular noun *name* (not "names") underlines the unity of the three Persons [i.e., "the Father, the Son, and the Holy Spirit" as the Trinity, all three involved in the "entrance into an allegiance"].[200]

The *Didache* (one of the earliest didactic works compiled by the Christian Church)—also known as *The Teaching of the Lord through the Twelve Apostles to the Nations*—was compiled circa AD 100–150. In its "CHAP. VII.—CONCERNING BAPTISM," we read:

> And concerning baptism, thus baptize ye: Having first said all these things, baptize *into* the name of the Father, and of the Son, and of the Holy Spirit.[201]

This work was written so near the time of Christ that it's logical to assume its authors knew better what our Lord ordered for His own sacrament than the writers of our English translations do. Many of our modern translations have been heavily associated with, or influenced by, the Latin Vulgate. This creates some confusion, as the *Pulpit Commentary* shares:

> In (**into**) **the Name of the Father, and of the Son, and of the Holy Ghost.** Our version follows the Vulgate, **in nomine,** which does not give the right force to the expression. The phrase does not mean merely invoking the Name, under the sanction of the great Name, but something more than this. It signifies into the power and influence of the Holy Trinity, into faith in the three Persons of God, and the duties and privileges consequent on that faith, *into the family of God* and obedience unto its Head. The "into" shows the end and aim of the consecration of baptism.[202]

But, in case that's not enough to convince some skeptics, here are a few more sources to reflect on:

- "baptizing them in the name of the Father, and of the Son, and of the Holy Ghost—It should be, 'into the name'; as in 1 Co 10:2, 'And were all baptized unto (or rather "*into*") Moses'; and Ga 3:27, 'For as many of you as have been baptized *into* Christ.'"[203] — *Commentary Critical and Explanatory on the Whole Bible, Volume 2*

- "in = into. Ap[pendix] 104"[204]; and from the noted Appendix 104: "[The Greek word] *eis*…denotes motion *to* or *unto* an object, with the purpose of reaching or touching it";[205] in other words, merging or interacting with a thing ("into") as opposed to observing or allowing something—*The Companion Bible: Being the Authorized Version of 1611 with the Structures and Notes, Critical, Explanatory and Suggestive and with 198 Appendixes*

- "in (or rather, *into*)… What is meant by being baptised 'into a name'? The answer is to be found in the fact so prominent in the Old Testament (*e.g.* Exodus 3:14–15), that the Name of God is a revelation of what He is. Baptism was to be no longer, as it had been in the hands of John as the forerunner, merely a symbol of repentance, but was the token that those who received it were brought *into* an altogether new relation to Him who was thus revealed to them."[206]—*Ellicott's Commentary for English Readers*

- "But we are here instructed respecting the appropriation of this institution to the Christian dispensation, in its most complete form. The apostles, and their successors in the ministry of the word, are ordered to baptize those whom they made Christ's disciples, *into the name*."[207]—*Benson Commentary*

- "*in the name*" Rather, **into** the name. Jewish proselytes were baptized **into** the name of the Father; Jesus adds the names of the Son and of the Holy Ghost."[208]—*Cambridge Bible for Schools and Colleges*

- "Rev[ised], correctly, 'into the name.'… Baptizing *into* the name of the Holy Trinity implies a spiritual and mystical union with him….[and] 'into' is the preposition commonly used with 'baptize.'"[209]—*Vincent's Word Studies*

Our choosing to become a "new creature" in Christ—and the corresponding outward sacrament that accompanies that decision—was always going to be "with the authority of God's name" anyway. If you'll remember, it was through the mouth of Jesus, Himself, that the sacrament was established in the first place (Matthew 28:19). So although it's conceivable to think that Jesus would have said, "Go ye into the world and baptize people in the authority of my Name," there's the natural question of why that would need to be stipulated. The authority of Jesus' aname was implied when *He, Himself* charged the apostles with this responsibility. Everything—*everything*—changes when we realize He really meant (in modern words), "Go ye into the world and baptize people into my family, so that they might join me in my mission to save"!

Adoption Adaption

Now, with our being placed "into" the family and mission of God—which requires a full surrender of self and cause for the rest of our existence to the three Persons of the Trinity and all they require—we, the "people *of* the Name," have a duty to uphold. As adoptees, it is our responsibility to grow in the Lord personally and to contribute to the increase of our fellowship.

An adoption is a change into a new family. It's covenantal. Those who are adopted take on a new life from many angles, from a name change to new dinner-table traditions. The ways of the old family, the old life, are no more. The memory of that life may always remain, but the former is shed and replaced by the new that we step into. We are now owned and loved by someone who will care for us in a way we haven't been cared for before, and the greatest void of our lives is filled.

Unfortunately, many folks with selfish intentions have manipulated the foster-care system to collect a paycheck (or worse), and there have been many tragic tales of adoptions that ended only in neglect or relinquishment of the child the second the "honeymoon phase" is over and the responsibility of parenthood kicks in. Because of this, it's hard for some to fully grasp the beauty of these care concepts apart from the stories of those who have exploited them. Nevertheless, for the following comparison, we will proceed, assuming a best-case scenario with an adoption the way God would wish it.

Follow this trail of thought for a moment: Robert Jones (a fictional name I just grabbed out of thin air) is a man of the greatest integrity. He's an amazing guy with a large home and an enormous heart for children in need. He chooses to adopt a troubled child named Billy into his family, and Billy takes on his new name. This boy "becomes" Billy Jones. He is now Billy *of the name* Jones. There is a covenantal covering over Billy that is solidified the day the adoption papers go through and the name "Jones" is now legally bound to the boy. The sacred agreement Robert makes with Billy in this legal transaction of adoption is a promise, a *vow* that he gifts to this boy to care for him, bring him under the covering of Robert's roof and protection, let him occupy Robert's space, be a part of all Robert's family fireworks barbeques, come to Robert with questions and needs, etc.

Many things about Billy will always be the same: He will always love the soothing sounds of classical symphonies, his hair will continue to grow in blond, he will prefer to wear red when he practices on his skateboard in the neighborhood park, he'll keep enjoying slapstick comedy, and so on. But there will be many changes as well. As Billy gets used to his new home and learns to put more and more faith and trust in the relationship Robert is forming with him, his decisions and habits will shift into a new place. The goals he had in his previous, tormented life—such as running away from home and finding some way to be rich and self-reliant so he never has to depend on anyone—start to seem less appealing. As Robert sets the example of perfect love and care, slowly but surely, Billy begins to adapt into newer, healthier thought patterns. Though it takes a while, Billy eventually comes to trust that Robert isn't going to leave him like his first family did, and he starts to wonder how he ever could have lived without a father like Robert. Day by day, he releases the internal baggage that plagued him in his former life, replacing that pain with hope for brighter tomorrows and a genuine kindness for other hurting kids he meets.

He soon finds that his habits are changing as well. Whereas Billy used to pull the blankets over his head in the morning and refuse to get up because he didn't want to face another round of his parents fighting, now he can't wait to get to the kitchen first thing every day to share breakfast with his new daddy. In the past, he lived with earbuds in his ears even when music wasn't playing so he could remain socially aloof and disconnected, but now he can't wait to visit with his friends! Before, when another kid at school picked a fight with him, he saw only a punk who deserved to be punched…but now when that happens, he recognizes the internal hurt and rage that drives another child to act out, so he finds a way of steering the negative energy in a more neutral or positive direction. He finds himself making decisions for the good, the pure, and the virtuous things each day now, and for the first time ever, he's beginning to taste what it's like to *thrive* in this life instead of just fighting to *survive*.

In addition to the internal transformations is an environmental conversion. At his old place, Billy would have been allowed to sit in the basement in front of a computer, looking at any poisonous imagery he wanted to put into his mind while his parents were upstairs getting high. But in this new home with a loving father, Billy is expected to clean up after himself and help with the household chores, and all extracurricular activities he participates in have to pass a moral standards check. There are certainly moments when Billy is tempted to smart off, sneak to the computer at night and look at things he shouldn't, or pull the blanket back over his head when he hears his dad announce first thing in the morning that the lawn needs mowing. And because Billy is human, he absolutely does give in to temptations and fails sometimes, doing things like shouting a curse word on the basketball court, slamming the door when Robert tells him to get off the phone, or mocking his Sunday school teacher at church. But Robert continues to lift Billy up, love him, and believe in his ability to do better while consistently presenting him with a firm, unchanging list of rules and expectations that, Robert says, will lead to the happiest possible life for Billy down the road.

As time goes on, the bond is strengthened between Robert and Billy to the point that Billy can't stand idly by when he sees another young person hurting the way he used to, like Ted, a foster kid down the road with "skateboarding bruises" where skateboarding bruises wouldn't naturally be. Ted's situation looks so much like Billy's old life of sadness and despair that Billy is eaten alive with the desire to help his friend. One day, out of desperation, he approaches Robert with what he feels is a preposterous request: Would Robert adopt Ted, too?

Imagine the surprise a character like young Billy would experience if Robert says yes, then finds a way to make the adoption process both immediate and pain-free. Now consider how exciting the scenario would be if Robert tells Billy, "Go, you, to the ends of the neighborhood and tell the good news to every living creature that my house will never be too full to welcome in new children or teens, no past baggage will ever be too much, and I will always be personally available for everyone who comes into my presence, forever." Wouldn't *that* be a cool addition to the story of Billy and Robert?

But, you see, that's the miracle of what God has *already* done.

When we, the adopted, come into the Family, the Body of Christ, we experience something very close to what Billy experiences with Robert, except *our* encounter is with a perfect, infinite Being whose house truly will never become too crowded with family and whose omnipresence really does allow for personal availability for all. God really and truly *is* standing there with open arms, ready and willing to accept *any and all* into His Family and His presence. His invitation is eternal, and there is never an admission fee. No false advertising draws in a weary soul with promises that can't be kept, for He is immutable, unchanging and steady. Because He is omniscient, He is Lord over every force of the universe, and because He is omnipotent, He has the power necessary to execute the vows written in His Word; no child of God's will lack for anything on His watch. Oh, what a mighty God we serve!

Hang on a second, though. That's not all there is to this picture. There's only one problem, and it's doesn't have to do with God, but with where *we* choose to place the period.

Like Billy, we, too, are required to shake off the old, former life and take on the new one that comes with stepping into our new family. We can't enjoy the benefits of God's free gift of salvation without understanding that such an adoption is a legal transaction in the spiritual realm, requiring changes on our end, too. When we give our hearts to the Lord and make the eternally rewarding decision to become a part of the Body of Christ, we become a new creature entirely:

> Therefore if anyone is in Christ, he is a new creation; the old things have passed away; behold, new things have come. (2 Corinthians 5:17; LEB)

Being spiritually adopted by God places us in the army of the "people *of* the Name of Christ."

Our very names are recorded in heaven (Luke 10:20), written in the Lamb's Book of Life (Revelation 3:5)! We're "destiny-ed" to a calling so much higher than our wildest imaginations from the very *second* we sincerely accept salvation. Whatever our spiritual nametags said before, it's all "skunk cabbage" and "corpse flower" compared to the identity He brings us into. Through Him we can overcome the temptation of our sin, as well as the damage to our hearts that the sin has caused, and in fact, we are given a brand new name (Revelation 2:17)! Top scholars even acknowledge that this is "to receive Jesus' victorious, kingly name… [B]elievers' reception of this name represents their final reward of consummate identification and unity with the intimate, end-time presence and power of Christ in his kingdom and under his sovereign authority… [T]he 'new name' is a mark of genuine membership in the community of the redeemed" who will go on to enter the blessed City of God![210]

And whereas that status means *everything* for you and me in the light of the world and all eternity, it also means we must release the past person and take on the attributes of the Father. We're charged to be better people and examples with our behaviors, because Jesus' final words before His ascension was that we really *are* to go to the ends of the earth and tell every creature the Good News that Christ has a family and a Name for them, too.

Recall the heroes of the faith. Take a minute to think about those men and women who radically revolutionized the way the secular world viewed

Christianity or Jesus. In fact, let's narrow the list down to just a few stars from the "Preachers of the Great Awakening" list: John Wycliffe, Jan Hus, Martin Luther, Jonathan Edwards, George Whitefield, Dwight Moody, John and Charles Wesley, Charles Finney, and James McGready—or more recent names, like Billy Graham, Kathryn Kuhlman, Carmen, or Keith Green. As vastly different as any one of these ministers is from the others, they all hold one thing in common: Their names will never be forgotten, not because they had a nice ring to them, but because they took their spiritual adoption papers seriously; the assumed the character attributes of the Father after the grace of the Son and through the power of the Spirit, giving their whole lives as innovators of the Gospel message. We are called toward increase! We're not only *allowed* to share our family with others, but we're *commanded* to do so. We've taken on *ha-shem*—the Name.

The "sound in the air" Juliet-ism suddenly seems absurdly superficial. What's on *your* name tag?

A LONG RITUAL,
A DARK WINTER, AND
THE AGE OF AQUARIUS

by Sharon K. Gilbert

4

The really dangerous people believe they are doing whatever they are doing, solely and only, because it is without question the right thing to do. And that is what makes them dangerous.
—Neil Gaiman, *American Gods*

You know how to interpret the appearance of the sky, but you cannot interpret the signs of the times.
—Matthew 16:3b

And we know that all things work together for good to them that love God, to them who are the called according to his purpose. What shall we then say to these things? If God be for us, who can be against us?
—Romans 8:28; 8:31

began working on this contribution for Dr. Horn's *Zeitgeist 2025* before Christmas 2020, but a pulled muscle in my back forced me to abandon typing for those intervening weeks to let the muscle and inflamed tendons heal. During that time, I continued to research, keep up with the latest news, and occasionally post to social media from my phone while resting on a heating pad. But God is good and works all things together, according to His plans; thus, that "down" time allowed me to observe the machinations of the spirit realm within our nation's capital and the hidden hand behind their recent speeches and actions.

Needless to say, these events have been eye-opening.

I got saved at a very young age, not much more than four or so. My parents didn't allow me to announce it publicly for many years, fearing I didn't understand the implications or the reasons for it, but I did. I'd been conversing with the Lord since my earliest moments, talking to Him out loud and in my head as though He were right there beside me.

Which He was, and is, and always will be.

Almost from the beginning, I asked Jesus to grant me the ability to see the world as He saw it, to understand people and events as He does. Of course, no human can ever truly comprehend the intricacies and infinite wonders of the universe, but there are times when God has graciously allowed me to see into that darkling glass that Paul describes in 1 Corinthians 13:12. Because of our frailties and human limitations, we cannot see with clarity, but we are sometimes able to perceive shadows and movement, signs of things that are or will soon be. What I've "seen" happening over the past few weeks is warfare, not just between the Deep State and Donald Trump, but between ancient spirits warring with God and even with one another. The big clue came on January 6, 2021, when a ragtag bunch of hooligans apparently broke into the Capitol building and ran amok.

Some on the radical left even claim they attempted a *coup d'état*.

If you're my age, then you remember the John Frankenheimer's 1964 film, *Seven Days in May*, starring Kirk Douglas, Eva Gardner, and Burt Lancaster. The movie was based on a best-selling, 1962 political thriller of the same title by Charles W. Bailey II and Fletcher Knebel. The screenplay was written by the brilliant storyteller Rod Serling of *Twilight Zone* fame.

The action is set in 1970 and involves an attempted *coup d'état* by the Joints Chief of Staff, led by Air Force General James Mattoon Scott, played by Lancaster. General Scott commands a super-secret unit called

ECOMCON, which trains at a covert base in Texas and has the ability to commandeer all the nation's communications systems under states of emergency. General Scott is presented as highly conservative and an over-the-top patriot who's convinced a planned nuclear disarmament treaty with the Soviets will weaken the United States and lead to our annihilation. Scott decides to use his secret unit to seize control from President Lyman (played by Frederic March) and prevent Congress from ratifying the dangerous treaty.

The film depicts President Lyman as kindly and humanitarian (liberal) and General Scott as wild-eyed, willful, and war-mongering. In a very real way, this 1964 film is a strange prophecy about Donald Trump, but instead of a wild-eyed Air Force general, we have a wild-card outsider whose policies seek to leave the New World Order (NWO) and return America to nationalistic values. It's Trump versus the entrenched Deep State of Washington, who prefer to remain in the NWO.

And what super-secret unit of hardened soldiers would the so-called sore loser, wild-card President Trump, use to overthrow American "democracy" and the "rule of law"? Not a highly trained team of warriors and mercenaries. Not a super-secret cabal of military experts.

No, Trump uses a cosplay version of the Village People.

Really?

The response? Mainstream media pundits fan the flames of leftist indignation and fears by inciting virtual riots and populating the Internet with a constant stream of photos of "Q-Anon Shaman" in his crazy buffalo hat along with his selfie-taking hooligan buddies. This event did nothing to alter government, but it succeeded in further dividing America straight down the middle, with both sides shouting out hateful memes and demeaning posts on social media and some even calling for the heads of those on the other side.

While such behavior provides a cathartic release of pent-up anger and grief, it does nothing but stokes the fires of this spiritual war and incite the spirits to riot. It provides them with energy and purpose.

Meanwhile, we're missing what's really going on here. It is not a *coup d'état.* This strange bit of theater in Washington is actually part of a long *ritual* intended to allow the fallen realm to complete their plans to found the new Golden Age as described in Virgil's *Eclogue IV*:

> Now the last age by Cumae's Sibyl sung
> Has come and gone, and the majestic roll
> Of circling centuries begins anew:
> **Justice returns, returns old Saturn's reign,**
> With a **new breed of men sent down from heaven.**
> Only do thou, at the boy's birth in whom
> The iron shall cease, the golden race arise,
> Befriend him, chaste Lucina; 'tis thine own
> Apollo reigns.[211] (Emphasis added)

Many who quote the above lines choose to emphasize the return of Saturn or the reign of Apollo, but notice that *before* mentioning Saturn, Virgil tells us that "Justice returns." What might that mean? Hint: It's much deeper and far more sinister than you might imagine.

We of the twenty-first century think of "justice" as a concept, a representation of fairness or of our legal system, and to a certain extent, that's true. But to Virgil, it refers to a *goddess* called *Themis* in Greek, but the Latin is *Justitia*.

Justitia (or Themis) was a Titaness placed in charge of overseeing the divine order. You've seen many statues and paintings of the goddess. Usually, she wears a great crown with long rays, as though representing the sun. In many ancient Near East cultures, the sun (Utu or Shamash) was the lawgiver. Therefore, seeing Justitia crowned with the solar rays of this lawgiver shouldn't surprise us, because this Titaness taught mankind the idea of laws and of justice. Indeed, this casts Justitia in a role, similar to Inanna (sister of Utu/Shamash), who gave mankind the *mehs*, a collection of rules and skills that provide civilization with rules and order.

In addition to her crown, Justitia holds a sword and a balance—just like all our statues of Lady Justice that stand before our courts. The scales depict her position as our judge. Interestingly, the Olympian Zeus is also given a set of scales in Homer's *Iliad*, and he uses it to decide who will win in the winner-takes-all fight between Hector and Achilles at the Battle of Troy. Zeus decided who would live and who would die.

You might even say that the scales can weigh souls.

Earlier, I stated that the cosplay show in Washington on January 6 was part of a long ritual. Here's what I mean by that. First of all, understand that the spiritual war in which you and I are engaged (and all of humanity participates, either as a Christian, clad in Christ's armor, or as an unwitting pawn of the enemy) began long ago, probably before Adam was created. If you want a full "unpacking" of this concept, I refer you to the book Derek and I released in 2020, *Giants, Gods, and Dragons.*[212]

The basic idea is that Genesis 1:2 implies the existence of a universe that is no longer perfect, according to God's original design and vision. Something has happened to unsettle it, to corrupt and mar it, to render it empty and chaotic. In fact, the prime suspect behind this corruption is very likely called Chaos, an ancient dragon sometimes called Tiamat, Yamm (represented by the sea), Leviathan, and Judge Nahar (representing the rivers). We even see Chaos depicted by the Ouroboros, a twisting serpent or dragon.

In Genesis 1:2, we read:

And the earth was without form, and void; and darkness was upon the face of the deep. And the Spirit of God moved upon the face of the waters.

The actual Hebrew in this verse is *'erets hayah tohuw bohuw.* Literally, one might render this as "earth became Tiamat." *Tohuw* is a cognate (same word, different language) for the name of the ancient dragon, Tiamat.

Derek and I believe this verse reveals the indescribable aftermath of a war so violent and long that it corrupted the entire face of God's creation. Chaos's attempted coup failed, and God reset the world and created the very first prison with Chaos as its first prisoner—and the Spirit of God hovers over the deep as warden. This Chaos dragon was the first rebel and the first inmate, Prisoner Zero of the long spiritual war, and he/she/it still resides beneath the waters.

It may even be that the seven-headed dragon of Revelation depicts this very entity. Think about that for a moment.

But to return to our idea of a pre-Adamic world, at some point in the distant past of earth's existence, a long war began between God Almighty and some of the brethren within the first family of created beings. Sometime after the imprisonment of Chaos/Leviathan, God decided to create Adam, whose existence served as a lightning rod that further divided the heavenly realm. Some truly hated these humans, perhaps even envied Adam and Eve, for these weakling entities, created a "little less than the angels," were to become part of the Divine Council! But worse, humans were given *dominion of the earth* and even the ability to procreate! How dare God do such a thing?

What did this mean? It meant that human numbers could multiply into many generations, but rebel angels could NOT. The bottom line: The fallen realm's army needed numbers if they wanted to topple God from His throne.

So they decided to co-opt mankind. First of all, an entity called a Nachash (a type of dragon) would tempt Eve, causing her and Adam to sin by eating the fruit of a forbidden tree. Then, when these two were cast out of the Garden of Eden, more of the rebels would descend to Mt. Hermon and begin to build a fallen, hybrid army. This led to a universal "reset," which we call the Flood of Noah. After Noah and his sons rebuilt the world of men, a fallen spirit or demonic coalition would convince a human generally named as Nimrod to build a great portal, called the Tower of Babel, to return "Old Saturn's Reign," but God stopped it by dividing the nations into tribes with different languages. This led to a third reset.

God then sent seventy of his "loyal" angels to govern these tribes, but these failed the test and allowed men to worship them as gods. The LORD then commenced a new plan by calling Abraham to leave the pagan world and found a new and unique people, who would call upon the Name of Jehovah. During all of this, the fallen realm, possibly influenced and even supernaturally directed by Chaos, continued their plans and plots to unseat YHWH from His throne.

Remember, pagan rites and rituals—whether hidden or overt—provide the energy and legal permission to these fallen warriors to rise and overcome the earth. Now, let's examine how recent political events reveal aspects of this long, spiritual war.

A TEMPLE FOR THE END

During his inaugural address on January 20, 2021, incoming President Joseph Biden quoted a particular Bible verse:

> I promise you this: as the Bible says *weeping may endure for a night, but joy cometh in the morning.* We will get through this, together.
> The world is watching today. (Emphasis added)

This quote comes from Psalm 30:5, but the president's writers left out the beginning of that verse, which states: "His anger is but for a moment, His favor is for life." Does this administration prefer to avoid any mention of God's anger? Probably. But this psalm is far more than just a pleasing promise for joy in the morning.

Here is Psalm 30:1 in the ESV:

> A Psalm of David. **A song at the dedication of the temple.** I will extol you, O LORD, for you have drawn me up and have not let my foes rejoice over me. (Emphasis added)

Two things stand out regarding the speechwriter's decision to use this particular psalm. First of all, note the phrase "dedication of the temple." You may be wondering what temple the psalm means. After all, it was Solomon, not David, who constructed and dedicated the Temple. However, the line doesn't actually say the Temple of YHVH. The original Hebrew is *chanukkah bayith David*, meaning the "dedication of the house of David." We could translate this as the dedication of a temple, because—as king— David represented the House of Israel, which served as the embodiment of YHWH's presence.

Returning to our theme of the goddess Justitia returning and a long pagan ritual, very shortly after the so-called coup failed, Senator Chuck Schumer described the January 6, 2021, incursion into the House of Representatives this way:

> It is very, very difficult to put into words what has transpired today. I have never lived through or even imagined an experience like the one we have just witnessed in this Capitol. President Franklin Roosevelt set aside Dec. 7, 1941, as a day that will live in infamy. Unfortunately, we can now add Jan. 6, 2021, to that very short list of dates in American history that will live forever in infamy.
>
> This **temple to democracy was desecrated**, its windows smashed, our offices vandalized.[213] (Emphasis added)

Senator Schumer's speech is certainly laced with the hyperbolic, but two things emerge.

One: The senator invokes the ghost of the late Franklin D. Roosevelt, which is rather ironic, because FDR said this to the Federal Council of Churches in 1933:

> Early Christians challenged the pagan ethics of Greece and of Rome; We are wholly ready to challenge the pagan ethics...of our boasted modern civilization.[214]

Two: Schumer actually calls the House of Representatives a temple of democracy! AND, he says that temple *was desecrated!* My friends, understand this. As newly elected leader of the Senate, Chuck Schumer is now the highest-ranking Jewish politician in American history. Why would he make the claim that a comic-book crew of bison men somehow per-formed a desecration of a holy temple? By doing so, he is deliberately par-alleling the "abomination of desecration" spoken of in the book of Daniel!

And Senator Schumer's alarmist battle cry was taken up two weeks later at the inauguration by Senator Amy Klobuchar:

> Two weeks ago, when an angry, violent mob staged an insurrec-tion and **desecrated this temple of our democracy**, it awakened us to our responsibilities as Americans. This is the day when our democracy picks itself up, brushes off the dust, and does what America always does. Goes forward as a nation under God, indi-visible, with liberty and justice for all.[215] (Emphasis added)

In other words, the CAPITOL BUILDING, and in particular the HOUSE OF REPRESENTATIVES, is A TEMPLE TO DEMOC-RACY. Are these politicians imaginative, or is there a darker purpose at work here?

Dr. Thomas R. Horn explored the idea of Greco/Roman temple refer-ences within the design of Washington, DC, in his seminal book *Zenith 2016*:

> Thomas Jefferson, who shepherded the antichristian "Roman Pantheon" design, wrote to the Capitol's architect, Benjamin LaTrobe, defining it as "the first temple dedicated to…embellish-ing with Athenian taste the course of a nation looking far beyond the range of Athenian destinies" (the "Athenian" empire was first known as "Osiria," the kingdom of Osiris). In 1833, Massachu-setts Representative Rufus Choate agreed, writing, "We have built no national temples but the Capitol." William Henry and Mark Gray in their book, *Freedom's Gate: Lost Symbols in the U.S. Capi-tol*, add that, "The U.S. Capitol has numerous architectural and other features that unquestionably identify it with ancient tem-ples." After listing various features to make their case that the US

Capitol building is a "religious temple"—including housing the image of a deified being, heavenly beings, gods, symbols, inscriptions, sacred geometry, columns, prayers, and orientation to the sun—they conclude:

The designers of the city of Washington DC oriented it to the Sun—especially the rising Sun on June 21 and December 21 [the same day and month as the end of the Mayan calendar in 2012]. The measurements for this orientation were made from the location of the center of the Dome of the U.S. Capitol, rendering it a "solar temple." Its alignment and encoded numerology point to the Sun as well as the stars. A golden circle on the Rotunda story and a white star in the Crypt marks this spot.... **It is clear that the builders viewed the Capitol as America's** sole temple: a **solemn...Solar Temple** to be exact." (Emphasis added)

So, the Capitol building was intentionally constructed to serve as a temple, and President Biden quotes a psalm which was written for "'the dedication of the temple." Oh, but there's more to those post-coup speeches. Let's take another look at that Bible verse quoted by incoming President Biden. The Septuagint translation (Brenton English version), tell us the timing of Psalm 30—for the first three words in verse one read: "For the end."

Huh? Wait! WHAT END?

Is there something prophetic about Psalm 30 that's escaped our notice? Yes, I think so.

David tells us this in verse 3:

O LORD, you have **brought up my soul from Sheol**; you **restored me to life** from among those who go down to the pit. (ESV, emphasis added)

This is a psalm of resurrection, which does indeed make it a psalm of praise 'for the end'! In verse 2, David thanks the Lord for healing, but in the context of "end times," the king is most likely referring to *eternal* healing, not temporal healing from some virus like COVID-19.

Now, let's assemble these two clues.

One: Senator Schumer and his fellow senator, Amy Klobuchar, both used the singular idea of a *desecration of the temple of democracy.*

Two: The psalm in President Biden's speech refers to resurrection from Sheol, healing, and a time of "THE END."

Gentle reader, is the fallen realm signaling something?

The end? Resurrection? A false abomination of desolation? If the Capitol is a temple, then it must house a "god," right? I would argue that this god—or rather goddess—is Justitia or Justice, who heralds the return of "Old Saturn's reign." Our country is about to become part of a New World Order that commences with the Great Reset. I explored the chaotic shift required to achieve the Great Reset at length in my chapter for the 2020 book, *The Messenger.*

> Recall the social-media-driven, hashtag revolution that is currently overwhelming cities and law enforcement agencies across the globe. At present, thousands of protesters, bearing slogans and signs, neatly printed with the most fashionable hashtags (#fillintheblank) have taken to the streets—with Molotov cocktail in hand—ready to defend his or her or their right [pronouns are now tricky and change daily] to desecrate our homes and sow destruction in our towns. They seek to erase more than history, more than statues, but the current age itself. And in an era where nearly all learning is digital, it's easy to imagine how history might be changed to suit a rising dictator.

Now, if pronouns and gender identity politics aren't enough to enlist a generation into the armies of the fallen realm (who masquerade as "social JUSTICE," by the way), then what other hashtag-branded crisis might lead us into Virgil's Golden New Age?

Two words: dark winter.

DARK WINTER IS COMING

To begin this section, let's take another look at President Biden's inaugural speech. This paragraph precedes his reference to Psalm 30:

> My fellow Americans, in the work ahead of us, we will need each other. We will need all our strength to persevere through **this dark winter**. We are entering what may well be the toughest and deadliest period of the virus. We must set aside the politics and finally face **this pandemic** as one nation. (Emphasis added)

In recent months, this same phrase, "dark winter," coupled with the idea of a pandemic, has slowly propagated throughout numerous speeches from the Democratic camp, almost always referring to our present COVID-19 challenge, both as a country and as part of the new global village.

Here are a few examples:

- The Dark Winter of COVID-19 Overshadows the Debate (*The Nation*)[216]
- Dark Winter Coming (*Minot Daily News*)[217]
- Plunged into Virus "Dark Winter," Biden Must Lead Us Out (ABC News)[218]
- US Plunges into Coronavirus "Dark Winter" (*Chattanooga Times Free Press*)[219]
- Sending Vaccine to Cities One Way Out of "Dark Winter" (*Express News*)[220]
- Governments Need to Keep Providing Support through "Dark Winter": IMF Economist (Yahoo Finance)[221]

This is just a tiny sampling of headlines of news articles, editorials, and social media posts regarding "dark winter," beginning in the final weeks of the presidential debate season. It's unlikely that multiple sources suddenly decided *en masse* that the phrase "dark winter" would resonate with voters.

For those who've lived through decades of Oval Office changes, the idea of "talking points" is familiar. Consider the infamous "talking points" memo that Monica Lewinsky gave to Linda Tripp regarding President Bill Clinton's sexual conduct. We all know about it, because this same memo was presented as evidence in his impeachment trial. Some of you might hear "dark winter" and think of the tagline HBO chose to use to promote its drama series *Game of Thrones*, but the very moment I discovered the media repeating the phrase "dark winter"—each one echoing Joe Biden's use of it—I connected the phrase with something else, and it's very much virus-related.

On June 22 of 2001, one day after the summer solstice (a high pagan holy day), the following political power brokers assembled to consider a tabletop exercise dubbed by the Johns Hopkins Center for Health Security as "Dark Winter."

Each of these well-known individuals played a role in a mock government response to the theoretical crisis:

- US President: The Honorable Sam Nunn
- National Security Advisor: The Honorable David Gergen
- Director of Central Intelligence: The Honorable R. James Woolsey
- Secretary of Defense: The Honorable John White
- Chairman, Joint Chiefs of Staff: General John Tilelli (USA, Ret.)
- Secretary of Health & Human Services: The Honorable Margaret Hamburg
- Secretary of State: The Honorable Frank Wisner
- Attorney General: The Honorable George Terwilliger
- Director, Federal Emergency Management Agency: Mr. Jerome Hauer
- Director, Federal Bureau of Investigation: The Honorable William Sessions
- Governor of Oklahoma: The Honorable Frank Keating

- Press Secretary of Governor Frank Keating (OK): Mr. Dan Mahoney
- Correspondent, NBC News: Mr. Jim Miklaszewski
- Pentagon Producer, CBS News: Ms. Mary Walsh
- Reporter, British Broadcasting Corporation: Ms. Sian Edwards
- Reporter, *The New York Times*: Ms. Judith Miller
- Reporter, Freelance: Mr. Lester Reingold

The scenario for the Dark Winter exercise is described thusly at the Johns Hopkins website:

> With **tensions rising in the Taiwan Straits**, and a major crisis developing in Southwest Asia, a **smallpox outbreak** was confirmed by the CDC in Oklahoma City. During the thirteen days of the game, the disease spread to 25 states and 15 other countries. **Four-teen participants and 60 observers witnessed terrorism/warfare in slow motion.** Discussions, debates (some rather heated), and decisions **focused on the public health response, lack of an adequate supply of smallpox vaccine,** roles and missions of federal and state governments, **civil liberties associated with quarantine and isolation,** the role of DoD, and **potential military responses to the anonymous attack.** Additionally, a predictable 24/7 news cycle quickly developed that focused the nation and the world on the attack and response. Five representatives from the national press corps (including print and broadcast) participated in the game and conducted a lengthy press conference with the President.[222] (Emphasis added)

It sounds eerily similar to our current pandemic crisis, doesn't it? Quarantine, isolation, possible bioterrorism (we still don't know the true origin of the initial outbreak, though the World Health Organization insists that China engaged in no subterfuge—*really?*). But we also get a hint in the phrase "tension rising in the Taiwan Straits."

Only a couple of weeks ago, CNN gave us this headline: "China Flies Warplane Close to Taiwan in Test of Biden."[223]

A very long enmity exists between mainland China (the People's Republic of China [PRC]) and Taiwan (called the Republic of China [ROC] since 1949). The PRC lays claim to the island, using the phrase "one-China policy" to preclude any notion of a separate and non-Communist Republic of China. President Jimmy Carter initiated the one-China policy in 1979 by refusing to recognize the ROC. This lack of action affirmed our support of China's hegemony over Taiwan. This remained our official US position until President Trump, whose political views on China varied. The Associated Press reported this in February of 2017:

> President Donald Trump sharply reversed himself Thursday after months of suggesting he wouldn't hold himself to the long-standing "one China" policy, under which the United States only maintains unofficial ties with Taiwan.[224]

President Trump's views of the one-China policy may never have been codified into law, but it's well known that President Joe Biden is a friend to China, and may very soon have to decide HIS policy on Taiwan.

China has recently tested the new president by flying sorties over the Taiwan Strait. Taiwan responded by deploying missiles. The island nation of Taiwan is just one hundred miles from the mainland of China, but it's also a strategic military and shipping lane, leading into the South China Sea. China sees any US resistance to their dominance of this shipping lane as contrary to their military options, for the strait is a choke point, which leads to access of islands of the central Pacific such as Guam and the Marianas. Japan claims governorship rights to parts of the South China Sea, and Japan is our ally. Therefore, any mounting military tension in the region could lead to another Pacific War.

It's possible that we are headed into the same geopolitical conditions as those of the June 2001 smallpox scenario, Dark Winter.

Remember, my friends, that an attack of a different sort came to our country just a few months following the Dark Winter exercise: September 11, 2001. There was no release of smallpox, but in the wake of the World Trade Center Towers attacks, we saw many releases of anthrax, which caused everyone to look carefully at incoming mail for signs of tampering. Even a misaligned stamp or unknown sender caused hundreds to return the envelopes unopened to the post office for investigation. Most of America was terrified—which, of course, was the point.

The limitations of a single chapter preclude a recitation of the many domestic incidents of "intentional release" of biological agents—not by a foreign entity, but by our own government—so I recommend the book *Clouds of Secrecy: The Army's Germ Warfare Tests Over Populated Areas* by Leonard A. Cole[225] to learn more about a very dark history that's escaped the notice of most.

Returning to our earlier question, one has to wonder why the Biden team chose to use "dark winter" as a key talking point for debate and media articles. Yes, it evokes the popular phrase "winter is coming," used repeatedly in the HBO series *Game of Thrones,* but as the expression is linked to our current pandemic, it's far more likely that "dark winter" is a troubling hint at what may soon be coming to the real world: a severe and sudden biological attack of biblical proportions. After all, the Democrats claim the so-called coup on January 6 was a desecration of their temple (one that worships the goddess Justitia, presumably—but also deifies George Washington in its rotunda), and their language evokes the last days.

> When he opened the fourth seal, I heard the voice of the fourth living creature say, "Come!" And I looked, and behold, a pale horse! And its rider's name was Death, and Hades followed him. And they were given authority over a fourth of the earth, to kill with sword and with famine and **with pestilence and by wild beasts of the earth.** (Revelation 6:7–9, emphasis added)

The Greek word translated as "pestilence" in the English Standard Version is actually *thanatos,* which means "death." But since death is implied already, there must be an alternative meaning to the word. The Septuagint authors, who translated the Hebrew Old Testament into Greek, translated the Hebrew *deber* into Greek as *thanatos*.[226] According to *The Dictionary of Deities and Demons, deber* ("pestilence" or "plague") was actually the name of an entity. For more on this idea, see our books *Veneration* and *Giants, Gods, and Dragons*.

Now, as terrible as SARS-Cov2 has sometimes seemed, there are other *deber* weapons that are far more destructive. Smallpox is a particularly nasty kind of pestilence. In the twentieth century alone, it killed at least three hundred million people worldwide. Presumably eradicated in 1980, this DNA virus has slept and given mankind decades of relief from its ravages. Yet, frozen reserves of smallpox virus are maintained by the United States and Russia. Presumably, these are secured in armed freezers and are tightly inventoried and controlled, right?

Not necessarily. Rumors abound of thefts in Russia during the confusing and chaotic (there's Chaos again) transition period from the Cold War days of the USSR to today's bold, new Russian Federation (cue President Vladimir Putin astride a massive brown bear). Defectors like Dr. Ken Alibek,[227] formerly of the Russian biological weapons program *Biopreparat*, insist that thefts and inventory "mistakes" have occurred, which could have placed smallpox samples into the hands of other countries, known as "state actors," but also into the hands of terrorist organizations, either state-sponsored or independent. It is, therefore, plausible to assume that a sudden terrorist event could occur involving the intentional release of smallpox virus or of some other deadly biological agents here in the United States.

One way would be to infect a person with the disease and then send him or her to one of our largest cities. Or a pathogen might be released into our water systems. Cholera and typhoid fever proliferate in water and spread rapidly, as do dysentery and Hepatitis A. Smallpox, anthrax, and even Ebola could be released in aerosolized form.

By the way, in case you've missed it, Ebola has reared its ugly *deber* head in Africa once more. As of this writing, there are ten cases with five deaths in the West African country of Guinea, with another 125 individuals being monitored for symptoms. Simultaneously, in Congo, eight people have been diagnosed with Ebola, and three have died. It's believed that patient zero in Congo was infected through sexual contact with her husband, an Ebola survivor. If this mode of transmission is new to you, understand this: The virus has been found in breast milk and semen as long as *two years* following recovery.

Meanwhile, in Guinea, the index case was an infected nurse, whose funeral provided the context for the subsequent infections. One of these managed to enter Liberia before that country closed its borders, and she is being monitored for signs of Ebola. Liberia is right to be cautious. During the West African outbreak of 2014–2016, more than 11,300 people died of Ebola virus disease (EVD).

COVID-19 has provided the impetus for worldwide change and a prelude to the Great Reset, but imagine something as deadly as Ebola running through the densely packed high rises and slums of our first-world megalopolises. Indeed, the 2014–2016 outbreak caused panic here in the US—all because one man decided to fly to Texas.

Now, let me add one other, little known, exercise to this possible future scenario. It's quite likely that you've read or heard about the October 2019 Johns Hopkins exercise called Event 201, which explored the possible consequences of the intentional release by a terrorist group of a novel coronavirus in multiple locations. But there's another coronavirus scenario that may have escaped your notice.

In 2017, the team from the Johns Hopkins Center for Health Security prepared an exercise booklet called the *SPARS Pandemic Scenario,* described as a:

> [The] self-guided exercise scenario for public health communicators and risk communication researchers covers a raft of themes and associated dilemmas in risk communications, **rumor control**, interagency message coordination and consistency, issue management, **proactive and reactive media relations**, cultural competency, and ethical concerns....

Its purpose is to prompt users, both individually and in discussion with others, to imagine the dynamic and oftentimes conflicted circumstances in which communication around emergency MCM development, distribution, and uptake takes place. While engaged with a rigorous simulated health emergency, scenario readers have the opportunity to mentally "rehearse" responses while also weighing the implications of their actions. (Emphasis added)

Feel like your head just exploded? Well, you're not alone. Mine certainly did when I found this booklet. The big takeaway from this exercise is that it's training regional and local authorities to govern response to an outbreak by using media propaganda and rumor control. This is precisely what we've seen during the COVID-19 outbreak! Interestingly, the pathogen imagined in this fictional scenario that commenced in in Minnesota was dubbed SPARS.

Here is the scenario as described on page 4 of the booklet:[228]

In mid-October 2025, three deaths were reported among members of the First Baptist Church of St. Paul, Minnesota. Two of the church members had recently returned from a missionary trip to the Philippines, where they provided relief to victims of regional floods. The third was the mother of a church member who had also traveled to the Philippines with the church group but who had been only mildly sick himself. Based on the patients' reported symptoms, healthcare providers initially guessed that they had died from seasonal influenza, which health officials predicted would be particularly virulent and widespread that fall. However, laboratory tests were negative for influenza.... A week later, the CDC team confirmed that the three patients were, in fact, infected with a novel coronavirus, which was dubbed the St. Paul Acute Respiratory Syndrome Coronavirus (SPARS-CoV, or SPARS), after the city where the first cluster of cases had been identified.

You'll notice that the disease is named for the area where it first occurred, which is normal for such events. Why COVID-19 doesn't include a reference to Wuhan, China, is an indication of how much clout China really has in our world. One of these days, Derek and I will have to research the ancient spirit rulers of China, but for now, realize that most of this booklet is about media and social media actions to control the narrative—not as an exercise to help local and regional authorities control the disease.

It's all about using a crisis to force the Great Reset.

THE DAWNING OF THE AGE OF AQUARIUS

God ended Noah's world with the Flood, and by doing so, He reset Noah's world and destroyed the bodies of the Nephilim. Over the course of my life, I've had half a dozen or so dreams that felt "important." Two of these are Rapture dreams, but I won't get into them here. A few are dreams of a prophetic nature. One has to do with our nation.

On January 9, 2009, I can still remember the details and the general feeling of doom as I awoke. The content of my dream so shook me that I immediately wrote it all down and emailed a description of it to two friends. I also wrote an entry about it on my personal website. The idea of water and geopolitical/spiritual bankruptcy were connected in the dream, and the two seem even more connected now. Why? Because, Chaos is still controlling the world, even though he/she/it has been imprisoned since before Adam walked with God in the Garden of Eden. Remember, Chaos is also known as Yamm, often translated as "the sea," but also as Leviathan, that twisting serpent (dragon).

Here's the dream, as I recorded it in 2009:

Last night, I dreamt that I was visiting Washington DC—perhaps I lived close to it. I remember seeing large books in a major, domed building that looked like a mausoleum—in fact, a cemetery was also housed inside and out. Honored dead.

Great books by Hamilton and Jefferson and Franklin, original documents, collections in bound volumes stood on shelves like end caps in a grocery store. I remember thinking that these should be protected. No one seemed to care.

Later in the dream, I was close by, visiting a friend, when a great storm blew in—I could see the domed building from our window—the winds and rains blew with hurricane force, and literally knocked the domed building off its foundations. We screamed—but we were protected—the winds didn't seem to hurt us—however, the building with all the books and the dead was being pushed back into the graveyard—it even spun around and tilted!

The next morning, we rushed to the building—it was in ruins—the books, however, were still there, but they needed to get out of the rain. Several of us decided to move them into our cars, other rooms, anywhere to protect them from further harm. Employees and other visitors to the building didn't seem to care— they didn't even notice the storm.

I left to find help while the others moved the books. Oddly enough, I came to a room filled with George Washington impersonators. They were busy putting on makeup and practicing lines. They didn't know what I was talking about, when I told them about the storm. Stranger still, I also found Liz Taylor there! She said she would help, but she seemed to be doing it to get attention. I left with Taylor, and we returned to the domed building.

Most of the books were rescued by then, but some of the major collections had been badly damaged—Hamilton's original letters and documents were falling apart. Bodies from the honored dead burial crypts had been unearthed, and it was impossible to tell who they were.

I cried and cried. I remember someone trying to rebury these dead heroes, but it was so hard.

Outside, I could see that the building had moved because

it had come "unhitched" from its foundation. My friends and I managed (amazingly) to pull the entire building out of the water and mud and align it with the "hitch" once again, but the **linchpin** was missing, so it couldn't be secured.

As I woke up, these words spoke clearly in my mind, spoken by a male voice in my right ear—"fayit, fayit, fayit."

I quickly dressed and opened my computer to look up the word "fayit." It is Indonesian for "bankrupt."

I can still hear those words, as if that strong male voice still whispers into my right ear. By the way, whenever I hear audible whispers (rarely, but when they do happen, it's startling), they always come from the right side of my head.

As I write this chapter, I once again used the Internet to find the word "fayit." This time, instead of translating it as an Indonesian word, the algorithm called it Haitian-Creole meaning "bankrupt" or "failure." It's possible, I suppose, that translation algorithms have improved since 2009, but it's odd that the software's erased all possibility of its being Indonesian. Now, why does that matter? In 2009, President Obama was about to be inaugurated, and he spent some of his youth in and even went to school in Indonesia.

But here is why I relate this "flood" dream.

On the twenty-first of December, 2020, an alignment occurred in the heavens that the mainstream media hailed as the new "Christmas Star." This conjunction of Jupiter and Saturn had nothing to do with the star that heralded the birth of Christ but everything to do with heralding a new "Savior," anointed by the fallen realm. It is Virgil's return of Saturn/Kronos, a Titan who is presently residing in Tartarus.

President Joe Biden is calling for unity and a world of fellowship and love, and some commentators are claiming we've entered a New Age governed by the sign of Aquarius. In case you don't know, Aquarius is a "water bearer," which might relate back to my dream, for in many ways, this Biden administration is actually the third Obama administration.

Aquarius is also called "the cup-bearer," which takes us back to the research conducted by Derek and myself for our book, *Veneration*. You see, in antiquity, the position of "cup-bearer" referred to the eldest son or other male relative who would provide the drink offering during something called the "kispum" ritual. The Aquarius constellation itself dates back to antiquity and was called "GU.LA" or "the Great One" in Babylonian catalogues and may have represented the god Ea, patron god of the city of Eridu.

Greeks associated the constellation with Deucalion, son of Prometheus, who built a ship to survive a coming flood (rather like Noah). Chinese astronomers envisioned these stars as Yu-Lin-Kium, or "Army of Yu Lin," considered a great army of mounted soldiers far to the north. The Chinese pagans believed this army would one day invade the earth—in the end of days.

Interestingly, the Saturn Nebula lies within this constellation. The nebula bears a vague resemblance to the planet Saturn, but looks a bit like a great eye to me. Recall that Virgil's Eclogue IV refers to the return of "old Saturn's reign" as the beginning of a New Age of Men, comingled with gods.

The idea of a new age of peace and love harkens me back to my teenage years (yep, I'm that old), when this song was popular:

When the moon is in the Seventh House
And Jupiter aligns with Mars
Then peace will guide the planets
And love will steer the stars
This is the dawning of the Age of Aquarius
Age of Aquarius (Aquarius, Aquarius)
Harmony and understanding
Sympathy and trust abounding
No more falsehoods or derisions
Golden living dreams of visions
(Mystic crystal revelation)

And the mind's true liberation, Aquarius
Aquarius[229]

Note that Jupiter is mentioned as aligning with Mars, not Saturn, but the conjunction in December of last year was hailed as the arrival of Aquarius. One highly respected astrologer put it this way:

The great Saturn-Jupiter conjunction which happened on 21st December 2020 has a biggest role to play in this present decade 2020 to 2030 and the outcome of this decade **will create a new order** which will be applied for the next 70 years from 2030 to end of this century.[230] (Emphasis added)

You might not expect me to leap from tales from astrologers to meetings of the world's most powerful men and women, but there is a very strong thread that does so. It's known as the World Economic Forum.

Dr. Klaus Schwab, the forum's founder, believes that our world is about to enter a New Age; a great New World Order, that precipitates from something he calls the Great Reset. As I wrote in Tom Horn's 2020 book, *The Messenger*, this is sometimes styled as the "RE:SET," implying something else coded within the single word.

Indeed, we can see the names of two gods here, Re and Set. In a very real way, these two combine to indicate destruction and rebuilding—or "Build Back Better," which is another favorite phrase used by President Biden and many other world leaders today. In fact, in a virtual meeting of the global leaders known as the G7, Prime Minister Boris Johnson teased Biden for stealing his catch phrase![231] Apparently, Johnson claims he invented "Build Back Better," but it is actually part and parcel of Schwab's Reset plans. Another way of looking at this idea of RE:SET is *order ab chao*, or "order out of chaos."

Let's put all these clues together.

Jupiter's conjunction with Saturn on December 21, 2020—the winter solstice—somehow announced the arrival of a NEW AGE, overseen by a "water bearer," who will pour out his love and hopey-changey pixie dust on all the world. The governments will look to an overarching body like the World Economic Forum to lead them into this new order, right? We're to believe that "order out of chaos" is a good thing, and we'll all love our new masters, and the Earth Mother and her children will rule over all humans benevolently.

Yeah, right.

TEACHING THE WORLD TO PRAISE THE OLD GODS

Ever since the Age of Reason divorced us from the God of the Bible and substituted our former religious allegiance to obeisance at the altar of science, Mankind has stood upon the precipice of a very slippery slope. Darwinian evolution has led to social Darwinism, which in turn led us to eugenics, and thence to transhumanism. We're now told that humanity should not only upgrade to a new form, but we should *worship old gods*.

Pope Francis, a leading cheerleader for the World Economic Forum, is also the first Jesuit pope, so in essence sits upon dual thrones: that of the "Black Pope" (historically, the general of the Jesuit Order) and the "White" or official papal throne. Strangely enough, we have two white popes as well, in that Benedict resigned to allow a Jesuit to assume command.

Pope Francis has been a great supporter of universalism and open borders, where property is no longer private, but shared with the worldwide community, an idea given the trendy new name of "shareholder capitalism" by Dr. Klaus Schwab, the founder of the World Economic Forum. However, despite his public claims of mutual ownership, it's doubtful that either Pope Francis or Schwab would approve, if we tried to remove anything from *their* homes or from the Vatican.

But returning to the idea of paganism and our mandate to worship at a new altar, Francis's 2015 encyclical quotes his namesake, St. Francis of Assisi, and strikes this paganism drumbeat:

"LAUDATO SI', mi' Signore"—"Praise be to you, my Lord." In the words of this beautiful canticle, Saint Francis of Assisi reminds us that **our common home is like a sister** with whom we share our life and **a beautiful mother** who opens her arms to embrace us. "Praise be to you, my Lord, through our Sister, **Mother Earth**, who sustains and governs us, and who produces various fruit with coloured flowers and herbs."[232] (Emphasis added)

Later, in 2020, the pope returned to St. Francis for inspiration and dedicated that year's encyclical to fraternity and social friendship:

This saint of fraternal love, simplicity and joy, who inspired me to write the Encyclical *Laudato Si'*, prompts me once more to devote this new Encyclical to fraternity and social friendship. **Francis felt himself a brother to the sun, the sea and the wind**, yet he knew that he was even closer to those of his own flesh. Wherever he went, he sowed seeds of peace and walked alongside the poor, the abandoned, the infirm and the outcast, the least of his brothers and sisters.[233] (Emphasis added)

It's strange that a man who serves as the public face of the Jesuit Order, a socialist and science-based fraternity of belief, would spread the false gospel of Mother Earth, Sister Earth, and a being called a brother to the sun, sea, and wind. These are inherently pagan ideas, and they seek to divorce mankind from science and return us to ancient beliefs and worship.

Lest you doubt the idea of "brother sun," here is another excerpt from the pope's 2015 encyclical:

87. When we can see God reflected in all that exists, our hearts are moved to praise the Lord for all his creatures and to worship him in union with them. This sentiment finds magnificent expression in the hymn of Saint Francis of Assisi:

Praised be you, my Lord, with all your creatures, especially **Sir**

Brother Sun, who is the day and through whom you give us light. And he is beautiful and radiant with great splendour; and bears a likeness of you, Most High. Praised be you, my Lord, through **Sister Moon and the stars**, in heaven you formed them clear and precious and beautiful. Praised be you, my Lord, through **Brother Wind**, and through the air, cloudy and serene, and every kind of weather through whom you give sustenance to your creatures. Praised be you, my Lord, through **Sister Water**, who is very useful and humble and precious and chaste. Praised be you, my Lord, through **Brother Fire**, through whom you light the night, and he is beautiful and playful and robust and strong.[234] (Emphasis added)

Why am I quoting Pope Francis? Because of two things:

1. Francis wholeheartedly supports the RE:SET agenda of the World Economic Forum.
2. Joseph Biden will be the second Catholic president. In fact, he has boasted on television that Francis has been very supportive of him.

This quote is from a November 12, 2020 article in *America: The Jesuit Review*:[235]

According to a statement from Mr. Biden's transition team, the former vice president thanked the pope for his "leadership in promoting peace, reconciliation, and the **common bonds of humanity around the world**." Mr. Biden also said he hopes to work with the Vatican "on issues such as **caring for the marginalized and the poor**, addressing **the crisis of climate change**, and welcoming and **integrating immigrants** and refugees into our communities."

Welcome to the Age of Aquarius, my friends, when the gods of harmony and understanding define us all as bigots and haters. Social justice is being poured out like water from the NEW GODS of Capitol Hill, Saturn, and Justitia, and we're expected to enjoy owning nothing. By the way, if you want something that's really going to make your head explode, know this: Capitol Hill is modeled after Capitoline Hill in Rome, one of that city's seven hills. It was once known as the site of Jupiter's Temple, but then later, it added a temple to—you guessed it—Saturn. One might say, our Capitol is based on the conjunction of Jupiter and Saturn.

But here's the good news, my friends. Jesus Christ is still on the throne, and He foresaw all of this. Not one headline, not one tweet, not one election has surprised Him. He is head of a vast army, and we're not talking about the Chinese army of soldiers hiding within the constellation of Aquarius. No, these are fierce angelic warriors, who fight alongside each of us on this field of spiritual warfare.

I'll end with this encouraging passage from Psalm 23, verses 4–6 (ESV):

> Even though I walk through the valley of the shadow of death,
> I will fear no evil,
> for you are with me;
> your rod and your staff,
> they comfort me.
> You prepare a table before me
> in the presence of my enemies;
> you anoint my head with oil;
> my cup overflows.
> Surely goodness and mercy shall follow me
> all the days of my life,
> and I shall dwell in the house of the LORD forever.

Christ, our Shepherd, leads us into the very heart of the fallen realm, the valley of the shadow of death, and He prepares a table for us and pours us a cup that overflows. He is the True Cupbearer, the True Source of life-giving water.

It is HIS BLOOD that protects us. Christ is king—not Saturn or Jupiter, and HE is the arbiter of true justice.

All those who want to RE:SET this world and set themselves upon thrones should take warning from this passage. For Christ is your king, too. He rules over all worlds and thrones and dominions—even Chaos.

And He is coming back. *Soon*

Hallelujah! Even so, come, Lord Jesus!

But, before His arrival, another is coming…and bringing hell with him.

BIDEN MAKES WAY FOR
THE KINGS OF THE EAST

5

This chapter has been scrapped and restarted several times. As this is being written in December 2020, events keep overtaking it. Revelations about China's relationship with the Biden family and with America as a whole have been more substantial than could be captured with a few quick edits.

The mainstream media has finally acknowledged the existence of an official investigation into financial dealings between Joe Biden's son, Hunter, and business partners in China who may be connected to the Chinese Communist Party. The rollout of the story by the media has been almost comical; one is reminded of Claude Rains as Captain Renault in *Casablanca*, shutting down Rick's Cafe Americain and declaring that he's "shocked, shocked to find that gambling is going on in here!" If you've seen the film, you know that Captain Renault barely finishes his line when a croupier appears with a wad of cash in hand: "Your winnings, sir." Obviously, Renault was not only aware of the gambling; he facilitated it by turning a blind eye until it was no longer expedient.

Likewise, the media was aware of the story nearly two months before the wall of silence around it began to crumble:

In October, left-wing sites such as the *Daily Beast* were featuring headlines that read, "Russian State Media Is Desperately Trying to Keep the Hunter Biden Story Alive" and "FBI Examining Hunter's Laptop As Foreign Op, Contradicting Trump's Intel Czar." Today we learn from the same outlet that "evidence of [a money laundering] probe [into Hunter Biden] was apparent in the markings on a series of documents that were made public—but went largely unnoticed—in the days leading up to the November election."[236]

Those key details weren't "largely unnoticed," they were largely ignored. And now that the election is safely past, they are shocked, shocked to find a federal investigation going on in here.

The mainstream media's "breaking news" on December 9, 2020, of a probe by the US attorney for Delaware into Hunter Biden's tax affairs surprised only those who depend on the mainstream media for information. As noted elsewhere in this book, several weeks before the 2020 US election, the *New York Post* disclosed the existence of a laptop, evidently abandoned by Hunter Biden in April of 2019 at a computer repair shop in Wilmington, Delaware. The hard drive of the laptop contained, among a large number of disturbing digital photos, evidence of substantial business dealings between Chinese companies and Biden. But, as detailed in another chapter, any mention of the laptop or its contents was considered bad form by the mainstream press, and social media sites Twitter and Facebook openly admitted their efforts to suppress the story.

However, by the second week of December 2020, media gatekeepers have decided that it's safe to allow at least some of the Biden-China story to see the light of day. Why? Why now? Wasn't this a story eight weeks earlier? Certainly, the voters thought so; as we note in another chapter, some 17 percent of Biden voters in seven key swing states, six of which were awarded to the former vice president, would not have voted for him had they been aware of the story. That would have been enough to swing those six states to President Trump, giving him 311 electoral votes and sparing the country weeks of legal challenges.

Even with the many credible accounts of voting irregularities across the country, without an assist from the media, Joe Biden wouldn't have come close to victory.

The question now is where this leads. If we step back and look at the big picture, a disturbing pattern emerges. The geopolitical pieces are being arranged in a manner that would probably shock Joe Biden, his son, and their associates both here and on the other side of the Pacific. What's emerging is the fulfillment of prophecy, a New World Order that results in humanity—what's left of it—subservient to the charismatic leader of a global government. In short, a coalition is forming with the goal of creating the one-world kingdom envisioned by Nimrod more than five thousand years ago.

This coalition includes globalists in the United States, including leading members of both major political parties; Western elites, represented by those who are regularly invited to exclusive gatherings like the annual meetings of the Bilderberg Group and the World Economic Forum; and China, whose technocratic leadership has emerged as an unlikely but willing partner, at least for now, of the globalists of the West.

Not surprisingly, the media paid little attention to the source of Joe Biden's alliterative but uninspiring campaign slogan, "Build Back Better," possibly the worst presidential campaign slogan since Democrats declared 170 years ago, "We Polked You in '44, We Shall Pierce You in '52."[237]

Those of us who pointed out that "Build Back Better" was lifted directly from the United Nations and the World Economic Forum were labeled conspiracy theorists who were needlessly worrying over an imaginary threat to our national sovereignty.

Except the conspiracy isn't a theory. COVID-19 brought it out into the open as WEF founder and CEO Klaus Schwab enlisted the crowd that flocks to his annual, exclusive event at Davos, Switzerland, in a grand plan to fundamentally reshape human civilization—a plan he's dubbed the Great Reset.

The title is lifted from a 2010 book by Richard Florida, who argued that the economic crisis of 2007–08 was a golden opportunity for a "great reset" of civilization that would put humanity on the path to sustainable prosperity. Florida's thesis was that the rise of a "creative class" living in growing urban areas would drive the recovery from the economic downturn, and that cities with high exposure to the so-called "creative economy"[238] would be best positioned to lead this economic reset.

Florida's book hasn't aged well. Just ten years after its publication, some of the urban centers named by Florida as examples of the creative economy, especially New York City and San Francisco, are hemorrhaging population at a startling rate as residents flee taxes and crime that's risen to unbearable levels.

Still, the term "Great Reset" has found a new champion in Klaus Schwab and the World Economic Forum. Schwab describes the Great Reset as "a rare but narrow window of opportunity to reflect, reimagine and reset our world."[239] That sounds fine, even visionary, but what does he actually *mean* by that? To Schwab and his colleagues, it's a technocratic utopia where engineers and bureaucrats monitor, measure, and mete out the essentials of life based on their expert assessments of who needs what, where, and when.

"What gets measured gets managed," according to the World Economic Forum's website,[240] and they mean everything: Wealth and energy consumption must be redistributed, businesses must make protecting the global climate a core principle, and outmoded notions of private property must be abolished. This, by the way, is the driving force behind the Internet of Things, an initiative to connect everything through the web, and 5G cellular service, to serve up the bandwidth needed to track things like telephones, TVs, electric "smart meters," and the movement of ships, planes, trains, and automobiles.

The main obstacles standing in the way of the Great Reset is the persistent habit of humans to live near and associate with others who are similar to them, desires for privacy and liberty, and private ownership of property.

In mid-November of 2020, the World Economic Forum released a video to social media titled "8 Predictions for the World in 2030."[241] Those predictions are enlightening:

1. You'll own nothing. And you'll be happy. Whatever you want you'll rent and it will be delivered by drone.
2. The US won't be the world's leading superpower. A handful of countries will dominate. (*Note: The Chinese flag is featured prominently in the shot.*)
3. You won't die waiting for an organ donor. We won't transplant organs; we'll print new ones instead.
4. You'll eat much less meat. An occasional treat, not a staple—for the good of the environment and our health.
5. A billion people will be displaced by climate change. We'll have to do a better job at welcoming and integrating refugees.
6. Polluters will have to pay to emit carbon dioxide. There will be a global price on carbon. This will help make fossil fuels history.
7. You could be preparing to go to Mars. Scientists will have worked out how to keep you healthy in space. The start of a journey to find alien life?
8. Western values will have been tested to the breaking point. Checks and balances that underpin our democracies must not be forgotten.

It comes across as the type of future depicted in the *Star Trek* franchise—a world free from want, where food and organ replacements are available at the nearest replicator, and scientific enlightenment has lifted humanity out of the superstition of religion.

From a prophetic perspective, it's the Tower of Babel writ large. You can see how the bold predictions of the WEF conflict with the American ideals of life, liberty, and the pursuit of happiness. While the world after the Great Reset is described as a high-tech utopia, one doesn't need to read many of the glowing articles and white papers at the World Economic Forum's website to realize that one very important aspect of this New World Order is not mentioned at all: Who's in charge?

Those drone-delivered goods we'll be happily renting will be owned by *somebody*. Who? Somebody will decide where those billion refugees will be resettled, how much meat we're allowed to eat, who gets first dibs on printed replacement organs, and where you can set your thermostat. *Who?* Schwab never says, but it's a safe bet that it won't be you or me.

Six thousand years of recorded history offers some insight into human nature. The Golden Rule is generally twisted to mean that those with the gold make the rules. There's no reason to suppose that the technocratic panopticon envisioned by Schwab and his allies would be any different. They believe they're uniquely qualified to tell us how to live (for our own good, of course), and the Great Reset is their move to grab this power.

A quick word of explanation: The "panopticon" was a new type of prison designed by philosopher Jeremy Bentham in the late eighteenth century. Bentham's design placed the cells in a circle around a central observation tower from which guards could observe any prisoner at any time without the inmates being able to tell whether they were being watched. The concept, Bentham thought, was that the uncertainty of knowing when they were under observation meant that prisoners would effectively guard themselves by following the rules. Bentham believed this concept could be applied to factories, hospitals, asylums, and schools.[242]

Schwab proposes to go Bentham one better and turn the entire planet into a panopticon. This goal is within reach, thanks to 5G cellular broadband technology, which offers download speeds up to one hundred times faster than 4G cellular service. This new, higher data rate facilitates the Internet of Things, so that every aspect of our lives can be monitored, measured, and managed. You don't need to believe in end-times Bible prophecy to see how useful that will be to a future global government.

By this point in the chapter, you may be wondering about the connection between Joe Biden's alleged links to China and the Great Reset. Here it is: China has been building closer relationships with Western leaders in banking and business through the World Economic Forum for the last forty years, a period that corresponds with China's emergence as an economic powerhouse. It's our view that while Klaus Schwab and his cabal of Western globalists see China as a partner in a new technocratic world order, China is playing the WEF to get what it wants, which is unrivaled status as the world's only superpower. China's ruling elites may also be looking to get some payback for the "Century of Humiliation," the period from 1839 to 1949 that includes the Opium Wars, the Sino-French War, the Sino-Japanese Wars, the Boxer Rebellion, the Invasion of Manchuria, and World War II.[243] In other words, China intends to make this the Chinese century, just as the twentieth was the American.

Obviously, China's nationalistic drive is at odds with the globalist goal of a group of nations sharing power in harmony, but there is another, more powerful force behind the scenes of this drama, one that isn't mentioned by any geopolitical analyst working in major media today. That force resides, of course, in the spirit realm—the principalities and powers that Paul wrote about in his letter to the church of Ephesus about two thousand years ago. Chinese nationalists and Western globalists will undoubtedly be shocked to discover, as they eventually will, that they've build the infrastructure for a kingdom ruled by an entity which most of them don't believe is real. We mean, of course, the Antichrist.

How would this work? To build this global kingdom, the middle class in the West, particularly in the United States, must be destroyed. A people that can support itself without the government is liable, even likely, to resist. Even though this independent spirit has weakened in the US, it's still strong enough to present a challenge for an outside power—especially since Americans, despite representing just 4 percent of the global population, own about 40 percent of the world's civilian-owned firearms. That's 393 million weapons, or about 120 guns for every one hundred Americans.[244]

Now, please understand that we're not calling for an armed insurrection, just noting a fact—one suggesting that surrender of our national sovereignty, when it comes, is most likely to happen during a global crisis similar to the COVID-19 pandemic. It will be a conquest without a shot fired as people willingly trade liberty for "salvation." Sadly, the savior they'll get will be the one they deserve and not the One who takes the field at the Battle of Armageddon.

As new disclosures about the investigation into Hunter Biden's taxes have found their way into the mainstream press, we've learned that the relationship between the elder Biden and one of Hunter's Chinese business partners was much closer than the former vice president admitted.

Hunter Biden called his father, Joe Biden, and his Chinese business partner "office mates" in a September 21, 2017, email to the general manager of his former Washington, DC, office building.

"Please have keys made available for new office mates," Hunter Biden wrote in the email before listing Joe Biden, his stepmother Jill Biden, his uncle Jim Biden and Gongwen Dong, who he identified as the "emissary" for the chairman of the now-bankrupt Chinese energy conglomerate CEFC.

Hunter Biden also requested that a sign be made for his office stating "The Biden Foundation" and "Hudson West (CEFC US)."

Hunter Biden's dealings with CEFC in 2017 were at the center of allegations from his ex-business partner, Tony Bobulinksi, who said in October that Joe Biden was "plainly familiar" with his family's business dealings in China. Bobulinski was one of the recipients of the much-publicized May 2017 email purportedly referencing Joe Biden as the "big guy" who would hold 10% in a joint-venture deal with Hunter Biden and CEFC.[245]

Hunter Biden's contacts with CEFC included Patrick Ho, who was sentenced to thirty months in prison on charges of bribing officials in Chad and Uganda to secure oil drilling rights, and Ye Jianming, who served from 2003 to 2005 as deputy secretary general of the China Association for International Friendly Contacts (CAIFC).[246] A 2018 report by the US-China Economic and Security Review Commission identified the CAIFC as a front for China's People's Liberation Army, performing "dual roles of intelligence collection and conducting propaganda and perception management campaigns."[247]

This potential breach of national security is not limited to the Biden family, or to the US, for that matter. Over the weekend of December 12–13, 2020, Sky News Australia and the UK's *Daily Mail* disclosed the leak of a database containing the names of nearly two million members of the Chinese Communist Party (CCP). Many of these CCP members worked in the West, in sensitive areas such as defense, banking, and pharmaceuticals. The *Daily Mail* noted that Pfizer and AstraZeneca, both involved in the development of COVID-19 vaccines, employed 123 CCP members who'd sworn an oath to "guard Party secrets, be loyal to the Party, work hard, fight for communism throughout my life…and never betray the Party."[248]

Of concern to the British government was the revelation that defense contractors Rolls-Royce, Boeing, and Airbus each had "dozens" of party members on their payrolls. Major British banks HSBC and Standard Chartered employed "hundreds." None of those companies reportedly have policies against hiring members of the CCP.[249]

The relationship between China and the West began to thaw half a century ago, during the Nixon administration. In February of 1972, President Richard Nixon visited the People's Republic of China for a week, allowing Americans to see images from inside China for the first time since the Korean War, twenty years earlier. And things took another turn in 1979, when the Chinese sent a delegation to Davos.

When Deng Xiaoping started China's "reform and opening up" policy in 1978, Mr. Schwab showed up in Beijing to ask Mr. Deng to come speak at what was then called the European Management Forum. Mr. Deng declined. But he sent a small team of free-market economists led by Mr. Qian in 1979, a month after the Chinese Communist Party Central Committee approved the new policy.

After his visit to Davos, Mr. Qian quickly arranged for the Chinese Academy to establish a partnership with Mr. Schwab and the forum. The forum had the benefit of Switzerland's reputation for political neutrality. Beijing and Washington had backed opposite sides in the Vietnam War, which had ended only four years earlier, so business and economic contacts with the United States were mostly politically off limits in China.

The forum quickly began playing a key role in bringing European investment and business ideas to China. Concepts like joint stock ownership of businesses, instead of cooperative or communal ownership, were developed in China in the early 1980s partly through contacts and discussions at the forum.

Today, the leaders of China's state-owned enterprises use their attendance at the forum to allay any overseas concerns about their expansion into international markets, said Justin Lin, the director of the Center for New Structural Economics at Peking University.[250]

China's engagement with the US and the world grew exponentially in 2001 when it joined the World Trade Organization. America's trade balance with China shifted from nearly even in 1985 to a $419 billion deficit by 2017. It accelerated after 2001, and has cost the US an estimated 3.7 million manufacturing jobs.[251] President Trump's emphasis on redefining America's relationship with China has reduced the annual trade deficit to $345 billion in 2019, and it appears that it will be smaller yet in 2020.[252]

President Trump's "trade war" with China has generally been criticized in the press. Proponents of free trade tout its advantages, mainly the alleged availability of cheaper goods as items are produced where they can be made least expensively. In the real world, however, that only works when nations play on a level field. If one side subsidizes its manufacturing, artificially lowers costs by easing regulations or manipulating its currency, or places tariffs on import goods, then that nation gives its economy an unfair advantage.

A growing issue in recent years between the US and China is the theft of intellectual property. By some estimates, IP theft by the Chinese costs the United States between $225 billion and $600 billion a year.[253] China's Thousand Talents Plan has recruited thousands of scientists and engineers at Western universities, both Chinese expats and foreign nationals, by making lucrative deals with academics to send their research back to Beijing.[254] The program was declared a threat to American interests by a Senate subcommittee in 2019,[255] and in early 2020, the chair of Harvard's chemistry and chemical biology department, nanotechnology expert Charles Lieber, was indicted for lying about his financial ties to China.[256] The National Association of Scholars identified thirty-nine cases of American professors, administrators, students, and government researchers charged for crimes stemming from illegal ties to China in 2020. Compromised institutions included UCLA, Texas A & M, West Virginia University, Indiana University, UC-Davis, Stanford, Ohio State, UC-San Francisco, Case Western, Emory University, University of Tennessee, Boston University, University of Florida, University of South Florida, University of Kansas, UC-San Diego, University of Texas, Virginia Tech, Duke University, Los Alamos National Laboratory, NOAA, and NASA.[257]

We understand that nations spy on one another. That's part of the geopolitical game. Moses and the Israelites sent a covert team into Canaan to spy out the land more than thirty-four hundred years ago, and it's a safe bet that espionage wasn't a new concept then. But the Chinese government has used scholarly collaboration as cover to place "dozens, or even hundreds" of agents inside American institutions to funnel research and technology to Beijing.[258]

And this isn't news in Washington, DC. As Lieutenant Colonel Robert Maginnis (US Army, Ret.) noted in his 2018 book *Alliance of Evil*:

> FBI Director Christopher Wray testified before the Senate Intelligence Committee in February 2018 that the Bureau is investigating many Confucius Institutes, the Chinese-funded language and cultural centers located on more than one hundred American universities. The US intelligence community warns that these institutes are potential spy tools and thirteen of them are located on universities that host top-secret Pentagon research, such as Arizona State, Auburn, and Stanford. Wray warned that "naiveté" in the academy aggravates the risks, and he asserts that the Chinese exploit "the very open research and development environment that we have" on college campuses.[259]

Interestingly, the Democrat-led House of Representatives appears reluctant to annoy the Chinese by targeting the Confucius Institute branches active on sixty-five American college and university campuses.[260] Despite passing the Senate unanimously in July 2020, House Democrats voted against bringing the CONFUCIUS Act to the floor for a vote.[261] The bill would strip government funding from universities without direct control over Confucius Institutes on their campuses to limit the ability of the Chinese government to spread propaganda and, presumably, use those facilities for intelligence gathering. As of this writing, five months later, House Speaker Nancy Pelosi still hasn't allowed the bill out of committee.[262]

In response, the Senate added the provisions of the bill to the 2021 National Defense Authorization Act, which passed the Senate by a vote of 86-14.[263] House Democrats amended the NDAA to authorize the Defense Department, rather than the Department of Education, to withhold funding from universities that do not comply. That narrowed the focus of the bill to protecting Defense-funded research, rather than the broad range of protections envisioned in the original CONFUCIUS Act.[264]

This is an odd political move for Speaker Nancy Pelosi, who's apparently gambling that the American public doesn't know or care about the security threat posed by China, even as a member of her caucus, Rep. Eric Swalwell (D-CA), has come under fire for a two-year relationship with an attractive young Chinese woman named Fang Fang (or Christine Fang, as she was known). Fang met Swalwell in 2012 as a student at Cal State East Bay, helped raise funds for his election campaign, and placed an intern in Swalwell's office. According to American counterintelligence officials, Fang was probably a Chinese intelligence operative.[265]

Axios reported in early December 2020 that Swalwell, who sits on the House Intelligence Committee, was one of a number of politicians who were targets of a "honey trap," a very old ploy in which someone with information is lured into a physical relationship to extract intelligence, either through shared confidences or blackmail. US counterintelligence officials told *Axios* they believe Fang reported to China's Ministry of State

Security, the country's main civilian spy agency. The FBI began an investigation into her activities in 2015, about the time Fang surprised friends by suddenly returning to China. She has not returned to the US as of this writing.[266]

Given that House Speaker Nancy Pelosi has represented San Francisco in Congress since 1987, and that the Bay Area is home to one of the oldest and largest Chinese American communities, and that Silicon Valley, just south of San Francisco, is a prime target for espionage (Chinese and Russian), one might expect Mrs. Pelosi to be more sensitive to efforts by the Chinese Communist Party to use her community as a base to gather valuable intelligence against the United States. To date, however, Pelosi has refused calls from Republicans to remove Rep. Swalwell, whose district is just across San Francisco Bay from Pelosi's (and includes Hayward, home of Cal State East Bay), from the Intelligence Committee.[267]

Maybe Speaker Pelosi *is* aware of the espionage efforts by the CCP but finds it in her best interests not to care.

China's rise to the status of global superpower might seem irrelevant to the theme of this book, but it's not. First, recent revelations about the lucrative business deals between the son of our Joe Biden and his Chinese colleagues raise serious questions about the policies he will adopt toward China. Biden has talked tougher lately than he did during his campaign, when he declared that China was "not competition for us."[268] His nominee for the position of US Trade Representative, Katherine Tai, is a native Mandarin speaker and was the Trade Representative's chief counsel for China trade enforcement with the World Trade Organization between 2007 and 2014.[269] This could mean that Joe Biden now recognizes that China is, in fact, competition.

On the other hand, America's trade imbalance with China grew from $259 billion to $345 billion during that time.[270] And, in another example of this chapter practically writing itself in real time, it was reported just hours before this paragraph was committed to digital memory that Joe Biden is considering former Disney CEO Bob Iger as America's next ambassador to China. Why is that significant? Bob Iger ran Disney from

2005 to early 2020 and oversaw the company's acquisition of the Star Wars franchise, Marvel, and 21st Century Fox. He also cut the deal with China for the construction of Shanghai Disney, a resort featuring two resort hotels, Shanghai Disneyland, Disneytown, and more. To make it happen, Iger gave up a 57 percent share of the development to a state-owned company, Shanghai Shendi Group.[271]

In September 2020, Disney disclosed that it had filmed parts of its live-action remake of *Mulan* in China's western Xinjiang province, where Beijing has imprisoned about a million Muslim Uyghurs in concentration camps and forcibly sterilized Uighur women.

Worse: The credits to Mulan thank entities in the CCP including the party's Propaganda Commission in Xinjiang as well as a branch of the Xinjiang Public Security Bureau. The latter entity has a role in operating the concentration camps, while the Propaganda Commission has justified the operation of the camps.[272]

The point here is not that Disney made questionable business deals in China. There are plenty of corporate CEOs who put a higher priority on the value of their company's stock than on the impact to America's workforce. We're suggesting that Mr. Iger's lucrative relationship with the Chinese government indicates that US policy toward China may soften under a Biden administration.

The relevance to us, as Christians, is not only the threat China poses to our way of life. That's important, yes, but even more significant is the role China is poised to play as end-times prophecy unfolds before our eyes.

To preempt speculation, the author does not believe that China will field the army of two hundred million that eliminates a third of humanity at the sounding of the sixth trumpet in Revelation chapter 9. Even with a population of 1.4 billion, China's active-duty military has only about 2.2 million soldiers.[273] Besides, the mounted army is described by John in similar terms to the locust-like creatures that swarm out of the abyss when the fifth angel blows his trumpet. In other words, the two hundred million soldiers are supernatural, not human. (Humans will be involved, but they may be nothing more than "meat suits" for the dark, demonic spirits who bring hell to those left on earth.)

Despite President Xi's aspirations, China will be nothing more than a useful tool of the principalities and powers who view the middle class of America and the West as an obstacle to achieving their goal of rebuilding the kingdom of Babel.

The parallels between the modern globalists' dream of a post-Great Reset world and the failed kingdom of Nimrod, which probably collapsed around 3100 BC,[274] at the end of the Uruk Period of Mesopotamian history, are striking. As we wrote in our 2019 book *Shadowland*:[275]

Around 3800 BC, the emerging Uruk culture developed the world's first mass-produced product, a primitive type of pottery called the beveled-rim bowl.

The beveled-rim bowl is very rough compared to the pottery from the Ubaid culture, a step backward in terms of technique and quality. Beveledrim bowls are described as "the simplest and least attractive of all Near Eastern pots...among the crudest vessels in the history of Mesopotamia pottery."[276] This is odd, because other aspects of the Uruk culture, including large temples, complex administrative systems, and sophisticated art show that these were not simple, uneducated people by any means. Yet, the most common artifacts from the Uruk period by far are these crudely made mass-produced bowls. Archaeologists have found a *lot* of them. About three-quarters of all ceramics at Uruk sites are beveled-rim bowls. One of the fastest ways to confirm that an archaeological dig belongs to the Uruk period is digging up lots and lots of beveled-rim bowls.

Scholars agree that these simple, undecorated bowls were made on molds rather than wheels, probably in cone-shaped depressions in the ground. Most important for this topic, these bowls were probably used to dole out barley and oil for workers' rations.[277]

The World Economic Forum's prediction, mentioned earlier, that by 2030 "you'll own nothing, and you'll be happy" is modern marketing to sell us on the idea of the old beveled-rim bowl. In their idealized future, we'll be completely dependent on our lords and masters for our daily rations, and we'll be happy. (Or else.)

Sadly, as 2020 drew to a close, it was becoming apparent that the head of the world's largest Christian denomination—who, of all people, should know better—was on board with this program:

Pope Francis has partnered with leaders of major corporations and organizations such as BP, Johnson & Johnson, Dupont, the Rockefeller Foundation, the Ford Foundation, Visa, and Estée Lauder to form the Council for Inclusive Capitalism.

> "The Council is led by a core group of global CEOs and public leaders, known as the Guardians for Inclusive Capitalism, who convene annually with the Vatican to advance the Council's mission," the press release stated.[278]

This group is almost certain to gravitate to the top of conspiracy theorists' flow charts. Consider: It represents "more than $10.5 trillion in assets under management, companies with over $2.1 trillion of market capitalization, and 200 million workers in over 163 countries."[279] Besides the corporations named above, members include chief executives from companies like MasterCard, Salesforce, the Bank of England, Merck, Bank of America, and Saudi Aramco. There are also officials with the United Nations, CalPERS (California's state employee retirement fund) and the state of California. And to make sure we've ticked all of the conspiracy boxes, the group was founded by a Rothschild (Lady Lynn Forester de Rothschild), and its core members literally call themselves "the Guardians for Inclusive Capitalism."[280]

So, we've got international bankers, Rothschilds, Rockefellers, Big Oil, Big Pharma, and the UN meeting to invent a new form of capitalism "under the auspices of the Vatican with the moral guidance of Pope Francis,"[281] a Jesuit!

Have we left anyone out? Freemasons? Rosicrucians? Aliens from a contiguous universe?

Honestly, if we didn't have the press release, we'd be convinced that someone had made this up as a joke or as a plot device for the next film in the Marvel Cinematic Universe. But make no mistake—this isn't funny. Pope Francis has made no secret of his distaste for capitalism. Despite denials by his defenders and Vatican spokesmen, his messages tend to emphasize "global answers to local problems."[282] He has been vague enough in his statements on economic injustice that supporters and critics have been free to interpret them as they see fit. However, his most recent encyclical, *Fratelli Tutti* ("Brothers All"),[283] shows that he favors a fundamental restructuring of global political and economic systems in response to the coronavirus pandemic:

> Francis rejected the concept of an absolute right to property for individuals, stressing instead the "social purpose" and common good that must come from sharing the Earth's resources. He repeated his criticism of the "perverse" global economic system, which he said consistently keeps the poor on the margins while enriching the few—an argument he made most fully in his 2015 landmark environmental encyclical "Laudato Sii" (Praised Be).
>
> Francis also rejected "trickle-down" economic theory as he did in the first major mission statement of his papacy, the 2013 Evangelii Gaudium, (The Joy of the Gospel), saying it simply doesn't achieve what it claims.[284]

The pope's criticism of the economic inequalities of crony capitalism are not without merit, but he misidentifies the cause. The problem is *sin*, not capitalism. When Jesus said, "The poor you will always have with you,"[285] he wasn't condemning any particular economic system; he was making a statement on the fallen state of humanity. There will always be poor people because there will always be others who exploit them for their own personal gain. (Note that Jesus did not add, "Until you do away with private ownership of the means of production.")

Blaming capitalism for economic injustice is rooted in a fundamental misunderstanding of human nature. Yes, we humans tend to be selfish, pursuing our own interests at the expense of everyone else. It's the absolute opposite of loving our neighbors as we love ourselves, which both Jesus and Paul characterized as the one-line summary of the entire Law given to Moses 1,400 years earlier.[286] Indeed, "the love of money is a root of all kinds of evils,"[287] but replacing capitalism with a socialist economic system makes the masses dependent on the few, and those few are just as prone to sin as capitalists.

A hundred years of socialism's documented economic failure should be enough to convince any fair-minded person that putting control of the global economy into the hands of a few elites (who are already fabulously wealthy) is an astoundingly stupid idea. Ah, but won't these "guardians" be under the moral guidance of the Holy Father?

Yes. So what?

The Pilgrims who founded the Massachusetts Bay Colony in 1622 discovered that even a society based entirely on Christian ideals couldn't make a go of socialism. William Bradford, a signer of the Mayflower Compact and governor of the Plymouth Colony off and on for thirty-five years, wrote about the colony's near collapse in its first year:

> For the young men, that were most able and fit for labor and ser-
> vice, did repine that they should spend their time and strength to
> work for other men's wives and children without any recompense.
> The strong, or man of parts, had no more in division of victuals
> and clothes than he that was weak and not able to do a quarter
> the other could; this was thought injustice. The aged and graver
> men to be ranked and equalized in labors and victuals, clothes

etc., with the meaner and younger sort, thought it some indignity and disrespect unto them. And for men's wives to be commanded to do service for other men, as dressing their meat, washing their clothes, etc., they deemed it a kind of slavery, neither could many husbands well brook it.[288]

The colony only prospered when the governor decided:

They should set corn every man for his own particular, and in that regard trust to themselves…. This had very good success, for it made all hands very industrious, so as much more corn was planted than otherwise would have been by any means the Governor or any other could use, and saved him a great deal of trouble, and gave far better content.[289]

When the colonists were allowed to keep the fruit of their labors, *they prospered because they worked harder*. Before, when the needs of the many outweighed the needs of the few (another *Star Trek* reference), resentment and the lack of incentive for productive work very nearly led to the colony's starvation.

Bradford summarized their experiment in socialism thus:

The experience that was had in this common course and condition, tried sundry years and that amongst godly and sober men, may well evince the vanity of that conceit of Plato's and other ancients applauded by some of later times; and that the taking away of property and bringing in community into a commonwealth would make them happy and flourishing; as if they were wiser than God….

Let none object this is men's corruption, and nothing to the course itself. I answer, seeing all men have this corruption in them, God in His wisdom saw another course fitter for them.[290]

The governor concluded his observations by asserting that their experience "would have been worse if they had been men of another condition." In other words, had they not been "godly and sober," the selfishness and resentment that festered among the families of Plymouth Plantation would have been more destructive than it was. The fault was not with the colonists, Bradford wrote, since "all men have this corruption in them." The near failure of the colony was due to the socialist system that brought those destructive human failings to the surface. Capitalism can be exploited, to be sure, but at least it rewards hard work. Socialism, on the other hand, exploits those who are productive and rewards those who do as little as they can get away with.

Sadly, Pope Francis is putting the weight of the Vatican and behind making this Babelian dystopia a reality. The pope has adopted a phrase that's become all too familiar in recent months: "Build Back Better." Pope Francis (or whoever manages his social media) tweeted the phrase on December 3, 2020,[291] and his book *Let Us Dream*, published two days earlier, calls for a change that sounds a lot like the Great Reset:

> God asks us to dare to create something new. We cannot return to the false securities of the political and economic systems we had before the crisis. We need economies that give to all access to the fruits of creation, to the basic needs of life: to land, lodging, and labor.[292]

Lest we be accused of reading our prejudice into the pope's words, note that the World Economic Forum has interpreted the pope's public pronouncements on economic injustice as an endorsement. In response to his aforementioned encyclical, the WEF declared that Francis had "put his stamp on efforts to shape what's been termed a Great Reset of the global economy in response to the devastation of COVID-19."[293]

Klaus Schwab and his supporters believe their Great Reset will produce a man-made paradise. In truth, this strange partnership between a Jesuit pope and executives from some of the world's wealthiest corporations is a bold plot to cement their status at the top of the socioeconomic pyramid by making the rest of us equally impoverished. China's ruling elite, for their part, views this as a step toward the creation of a New World Order—or, more accurately, a New World *Reordered*, with the United States knocked from its perch as the world's leading power. The destruction of the middle class in the West, a consequence of the Great Reset, is essential to their goal of supplanting the United States as the world's leading geopolitical power.

It appears that President Joe Biden and his supporters don't intend to resist, preferring instead to facilitate China's rise through the WEF's Vatican-assisted technocratic takeover, a marked difference from President Trump's campaign promise to "Make America Great Again."

The tragic irony in all of this is that the groups working to use the COVID-19 pandemic to justify the Great Reset and leverage the resulting restructured world order to their advantage are themselves pawns in a much bigger game. As mentioned earlier, if they are built at all, the WEF's socialist utopia and the worldwide Chinese empire will be quickly subsumed into another global government—one led by a man who is not truly a man.

George Santayana famously wrote, "Progress, far from consisting in change, depends on retentiveness…. Those who cannot remember the past are condemned to repeat it."[294] If growing awareness of the Great Reset, and what it would mean for liberty and prosperity, delays the formation of a global government, then may this year of pandemic hysteria stand as a warning for future generations: When the Antichrist finally steps onto the world stage, his opening act will look much like 2020.

BEYOND CHINA: MORE ON THE BIDENS FROM THE LAPTOP FROM HELL

The American media played a crucial role in the apparent election of Joe Biden in 2020.[295] This is not hyperbole; without the open support of Democratic operatives with bylines at major newspapers and cable news outlets, Biden may not have won the popular vote, much less the electoral votes needed to win. (Of course, that assumes the reported results are reasonably accurate, which is not by any means an established fact.)

A survey commissioned by the Media Research Center[296] found that just over a third of Biden voters in seven key swing states (Arizona, Georgia, Michigan, Nevada, North Carolina, Pennsylvania, and Wisconsin; all except North Carolina were called for Biden) were unaware of the serious sexual assault allegation against Biden by a former staff assistant Tara Reade,[297] and over 45 percent hadn't heard about the financial scandal around the former vice president and his son, Hunter Biden, detailed in another chapter of this book.

Had the media not run interference for the former vice president by concealing this relevant information, 17 percent of Biden voters in these key states would not have voted for him. Even though most of those voters said they still would not have cast ballots for President Trump, a shift of that magnitude would have been enough to put those six key states in the president's win column,[298] giving him 311 electoral votes and a second term in the White House.

A sampling of headlines reveals that, if anything, the media's bias in the final month of the 2020 campaign was even more blatant than it had been four years earlier when Trump upset the expected winner Hillary Clinton.

- NPR: "Questionable 'N.Y. Post' Scoop Driven by Ex-Hannity Producer and Giuliani." (Why did the headline writer put the name of the *New York Post* inside scare quotes? Were they implying that the *Post*, which was founded in 1801 by Alexander Hamilton, isn't a real newspaper?)
- Vox: "Mysterious Emails and Convenient Leaks: The Trump Campaign's Hunter Biden Attacks, Explained."
- *New York Magazine*: "Trump Tries to Make 'Laptop from Hell' the New Hillary Emails. It Won't Work."
- *The Atlantic*: "You're Not Supposed to Understand the Rumors

about Biden." (The subhead: "To Raise Doubts about the Democratic Nominee, Right-Wing-Media Smears Don't Even Need to
Make Sense.")

- *Daily Beast*: "Fox News Reportedly Turned Down Hunter Biden
Story First." (The implication being that if a purportedly right-
wing, pro-Trump cable news organization passed on the "Laptop
from Hell" story, it must be fake news.)

- *The Guardian*: "Facebook and Twitter Restrict Controversial *New
York Post* Story on Joe Biden" (Social media giants suppressed news
of the laptop, a move that backfired and actually raised awareness
of it.)

- *Santa Monica Observer*: "Wikipedia Declares the Hunter Biden
Laptop a Hoax; 'Has all the Hallmarks of a Russian Intelligence
Operation.'" (Ah, it's a conspiracy theory. Bear in mind that Wikipedia receives substantial funding from Google[299] and other tech
companies[300] that were overtly anti-Trump during the campaign.)

- NBC: "Inside the Campaign to 'Pizzagate' Hunter Biden" (Anything the media wants you to ignore is linked to what they deem
a "conspiracy theory," such as Pizzagate.)

- *USA Today*: "Were Voters Manipulated by QAnon a Force behind
Trump's 'Red Wave' in 2020 Election?" (And there's the other
"conspiracy theory" routinely invoked by the media. They think
Trump voters are rubes duped by QAnon.)

It begs credulity. Republicans won the 2020 election at the local and
state levels, gaining as many as thirteen seats in the House of Representatives. President Trump won four million more votes than political rock
star Barack Obama during his historic 2008 victory,[301] setting an all-time
record for American presidential elections—yet we're supposed to believe
that Joe Biden, suffering from obvious cognitive decline and running
arguably the worst presidential campaign in history, avoiding the media
by remaining in his basement for weeks on end, drawing dozens to his
campaign rallies when he finally ventured out compared to the tens of

thousands who packed stadiums for President Trump, somehow won *six million more votes* than the president?

Patrick Basham, writing in *The Spectator*, explains the extreme improbability of these results:

> President Trump received more votes than any previous incumbent seeking reelection. He got 11 million more votes than in 2016, the third largest rise in support ever for an incumbent. By way of comparison, President Obama was comfortably reelected in 2012 with 3.5 million fewer votes than he received in 2008.
>
> Trump's vote increased so much because, according to exit polls, he performed far better with many key demographic groups. Ninety-five percent of Republicans voted for him. Catholics also supported Trump in higher numbers. He did extraordinarily well with rural male working-class whites.
>
> He earned the highest share of all minority votes for a Republican since 1960. Trump grew his support among black voters by 50 percent over 2016. Nationally, Joe Biden's black support fell well below 90 percent, the level below which Democratic presidential candidates usually lose.
>
> Trump increased his share of the national Hispanic vote by two-thirds to more than four-in-ten. With 60 percent or less of the national Hispanic vote, it is arithmetically impossible for a Democratic presidential candidate to win Florida, Arizona, Nevada, and New Mexico. Bellwether states swung further in Trump's direction than in 2016. Florida, Ohio and Iowa each defied America's media polls with huge wins for Trump. Since 1852, only Richard Nixon has lost the electoral college after winning this trio, and that 1960 defeat to John F. Kennedy is still the subject of great suspicion.
>
> Midwestern states Michigan, Pennsylvania, and Wisconsin always swing in the same direction as Ohio and Iowa, their regional peers. Ohio likewise swings with Florida. Current tallies

show that, outside of a few cities, the Rust Belt swung in Trump's direction. Yet, Biden leads in Michigan, Pennsylvania, and Wisconsin because of an apparent avalanche of black votes in Detroit, Philadelphia, and Milwaukee. Biden's "winning" margin was derived almost entirely from such voters in these cities, as coincidentally his black vote spiked only in exactly the locations necessary to secure victory. He did not receive comparable levels of support among comparable demographic groups in comparable states, which is highly unusual for the presidential victor.

We are told that Biden won more votes nationally than any presidential candidate in history. But he won a record low of 17 percent of counties; he only won 524 counties, as opposed to the 873 counties Obama won in 2008. Yet, Biden somehow outdid Obama in total votes.[302]

After reading that analysis, we're left with just one question: How stupid does the political class think we are?

Even the liberal media admits that it's unusual, to put it mildly, for a political party that loses the White House to do so well in down-ballot races. In fact, this is the first time it's happened in more than 120 years.[303]

Now, investigating the probable fraud behind the improbable election results that none dare question[304] is beyond the scope of this chapter. Instead, we're going to go back to the infamous "Laptop from Hell" to ask what the media won't: What's on it, and why were the contents almost immediately lumped together with those hot-button "conspiracy theories" QAnon and Pizzagate?

Some background first. The laptop in question is actually three. According to John Paul MacIsaac, the owner of the computer repair shop in Wilmington, Delaware, at the heart of this story, a man stumbled into his store on April 12, 2019, with three water-damaged MacBooks.[305] MacIsaac was able to repair two of the laptops, but the third was beyond saving. MacIsaac told the customer, who identified himself as Hunter Biden (and appeared to have been drinking), that it would take a few days to extract the contents of the hard drive to preserve the data. For some as-yet unknown reason, Biden never returned for the computer, despite several attempts by MacIsaac to reach him.

After ninety days, the hard drive became the legal property of the shop. Curious, MacIsaac looked at the contents—and realized he had a problem. There was information on Biden's laptop that would be very useful to foreign intelligence agencies, from private phone numbers of high-ranking members of the United States government to embarrassing photos of Hunter Biden apparently engaged in compromising intimate (and potentially illegal) activity that could provide leverage over a Biden administration.

MacIsaac contacted the FBI, which collected the laptop from his shop on December 9, 2019.[306] After months went by with no word from the Bureau, he reportedly began emailing senators about the contents of the hard drive, which MacIsaac had copied. Finally, he reached out to President Trump's personal attorney, Rudy Giuliani, who put him in touch with his attorney, Robert Costello. This is the link between the laptop's hard drive and the *New York Post*, which broke the story on October 14, 2020.[307]

As noted above, news and social media worked overtime to keep this report away from the public. Twitter locked the *Post* out of its account, preventing the newspaper from sharing the story with its 2.1 million followers. Facebook openly admitted to suppressing the story.[308] Mainstream broadcast news outlets were wholly disinterested, devoting just twenty-one minutes out of one hundred thirteen hours of news programming monitored by the Media Research Center between October 14 and October 27, 2020.[309] Given the salacious contents of the laptop, custom-made for Internet clickbait, and the potential national security risk it represented, this story should have driven the news cycle over the final three weeks of the presidential election. Instead, journalists who only *mentioned* it, even critically, were immediately condemned by their colleagues:

> Two mainstream reporters who acknowledged (and criticized) the *Post*'s scoop—*The New York Times*' Maggie Haberman and

Politico's Jake Sherman—faced thunderous denunciation on Twitter from Democratic partisans simply for discussing the story. Center for American Progress President Neera Tanden accused Haberman of promoting disinformation, and *New York Times* columnist Michelle Goldberg told Sherman that he was helping nefarious conservative activists "launder this [expletive] into the news cycle." Historian Kevin Kruse asked why they were "amplifying" the story.[310]

Criticizing the *Post*'s story was unacceptable. For the incestuous, interconnected web of political operatives and so-called journalists who believe they have the right to determine what the public should know about the workings of American government, the only correct response was to pretend that Hunter Biden's laptop didn't exist.

We deal with the political and social implications of the Biden family's shady financial dealings with businesses linked to the governments of China, Ukraine, and Kazakhstan elsewhere in this book. The question we ask here is this: Could there be reasons other an obvious preference for Joe Biden that compelled the major media outlets in the US, with few exceptions, to suppress news of the "Laptop from Hell"?

To frame a possible answer to that question, let's look at the contents of the hard drive—that is, the contents other than the emails that appear to reveal a "pay for access" scheme on the part of the Biden family.

First, we want to make it clear that we take no pleasure in sharing this information. One has to wonder why Hunter Biden, who obviously knew what was on that computer's hard drive, left it with anyone he didn't personally know and trust, much less abandon it altogether. Did he *want* that stuff to go public?

Or is it possible that the man who dropped off the computers with MacIsaac was not, in fact, Hunter Biden? Could this have been an intelligence op to derail Joe Biden's campaign? Or was it a shot across the bow by other power elites in New York or Washington DC? According to MacIsaac, the FBI has been in possession of the hard drive for nearly a year as of this writing. So, why did it fall to former Trump adviser Steve Bannon and Trump's personal attorney Rudy Giuliani to make the public aware of the shady business dealings alluded to in the emails stored on the hard drive? Was the FBI holding the information in reserve as leverage over a potential Biden administration in the tradition of the Bureau's founder, J. Edgar Hoover?

And is it possible that the leftward shift by Fox News, which has been especially noticeable since Election Night, was prompted by the *New York Post*'s receipt of the hard drive? Like Fox, the *Post* is owned by Rupert Murdoch. He hosted fundraisers for Hillary Clinton's presidential campaign, and his two sons and their wives openly support progressive causes. Maybe the *Post*'s bombshell on October 14 was a message from the Murdochs to both presidential candidates: "We don't need to be nice to Trump or his supporters anymore because we've got the goods on Joe."

Acknowledging that the preceding three paragraphs are sheer speculation, the fact remains that nobody connected to the Biden family has actually denied that the laptop and its contents are legit. And that is truly sad. The impression created by the photos, emails, and text messages is one of a desperately unhappy man. We don't pretend to be psychoanalysts, but it's hard to draw any other conclusion. Our sincere prayer is that for the sake of his family, Hunter Biden will find the peace that passes all understanding, a peace he appears to be seeking through substance abuse and empty sexual encounters, by making a sincere commitment to Jesus Christ.

The *New York Post* reported that Biden's laptop contained nearly twenty-five thousand images "loaded with sexually explicit selfies and porn."[311] Some images appear to show Hunter Biden smoking crack cocaine, which would be an outrageously irresponsible claim were it not for his acknowledged struggles with drugs and alcohol, including six stints in rehab,[312] and the public record of his discharge from the Navy Reserves after testing positive for cocaine use.[313]

His personal life seems to be one of unrestrained indulgence. Records lifted from his laptop reveal that he once dropped more than eleven thousand dollars on a single night at a New York strip club and spent more than twenty-one thousand dollars on a website that allows viewers to interact with sex workers in real time via webcam.

What's more disturbing, and perhaps more relevant, is the claim by Rudy Giuliani that the laptop contained "numerous pictures of under-age girls" and an alleged text message exchange in which Hunter Biden admitted to his father having a relationship with a fourteen-year-old girl.[314] Giuliani told NewsMax TV's Greg Kelly that he turned over the laptop to Delaware State Police; later, Republican candidate for Senate Lauren Witzke tweeted that a police source had confirmed the presence of child pornography on the laptop.[315]

And here we may have touched the raw nerve that triggered the media's reflexive dismissal of the laptop as a conspiracy theory. If an enterprising, objective journalist were to start digging, one can imagine questions about how a man whose unrestrained appetite for sex and drugs were widely known would be allowed such easy access to what passes for American royalty—our political and entertainment elites—that his computer's hard drive holds sexual images of children alongside files with the private telephone numbers of leading members of the United States Congress, nearly every member of President Obama's cabinet (including former Democratic presidential candidates Hillary Clinton and John Kerry), and entertainers like actress Gwyneth Paltrow and Coldplay singer Chris Martin.[316]

How much would Russian or Chinese intelligence pay to get their hands on that?

One of the biggest news stories of 2019, the arrest and subsequent death of billionaire financier Jeffrey Epstein, has been mostly forgotten, submerged by a flood of news around the COVID-19 pandemic, the economic crash, rioting across America, and, of course, the 2020 election. But the cone of silence that enabled Epstein and his wealthy friends to indulge their preference for underage girls may help us understand why the American media generally refused to acknowledge the relevance, if not the existence, of Hunter Biden's laptop.

Before his arrest in July of 2019, Epstein owned the largest town-house in Manhattan. He was well-known to elites in New York, Washington, DC, and Hollywood. Flight logs from his private 727, dubbed the *Lolita Express* as a reference to his fondness for young girls, reveal that his passengers were a who's who of the political and entertainment elite: Prince Andrew, former President Bill Clinton (who made at least twenty-six flights with Epstein, including at least five without his Secret Service detail),[317] actor Kevin Spacey, supermodel Naomi Campbell, comedian Chris Tucker, and attorney Alan Dershowitz, among others.[318] Epstein's "little black book," leaked by his former butler Alfredo Rodriguez, contained the phone numbers, emails, and home addresses of thousands of "celebrities, princes and princesses, high-profile scientists, artists from all over the world, all alongside some of the world's most powerful oligarchs and political leaders—people like Prince Andrew (circled), [former Israeli Prime Minister] Ehud Barak (circled), Donald Trump (circled)."[319]

Bear in mind that the presence of a name in Jeffrey Epstein's address book is not evidence of any crime, or of complicity in any crime, or of knowledge of any crime.

Incidentally, Rodriguez was sentenced to eighteen months in prison in 2011 for trying to sell the book to an undercover agent after failing to alert investigators to its existence. He claimed it was insurance against Epstein, who wanted him to "disappear." (As it happened, Rodriguez succumbed to mesothelioma, a very rare, asbestos-related cancer, shortly after completing his sentence.)[320]

Given that Epstein's activities were known to anyone who cared to know since at least 2003, when *Vanity Fair* published a piece by Vicky Ward titled "The Talented Mr. Epstein," why did world leaders like Prince Andrew (although perhaps that's stretching the definition of the term), Ehud Barak, and Bill Clinton continue to associate with him? Maybe they knew they could count on his discretion. Or maybe they were aware of his powers of persuasion; former *Vanity Fair* editor-in-chief Graydon Carter was subjected to "a flood of phone calls" from Epstein before the publication of Ward's story—as well as finding a bullet on his doorstep and the severed head of a cat in his front yard.[321]

Despite interviewing at least two of Epstein's alleged victims, the *Vanity Fair* article focused entirely on the financier's lavish lifestyle and the questionable origins of his fortune. There was no mention of his alleged sex-trafficking.[322]

This was the norm for press coverage of Jeffrey Epstein for most of his public life. Although he pleaded guilty in 2008 to charges stemming from an incident with a fourteen-year-old girl three years earlier, the agreement reached with then US Attorney Alex Acosta was stunning: Epstein was allowed to plead to soliciting a prostitute and procuring a child for prostitution,[323] and he served just thirteen months in custody—in a county jail, not state prison, and in a work-release program that allowed Epstein to spend twelve hours a day as a free man.[324] What's more, the non-prosecution agreement shut down an FBI investigation into the extent of Epstein's crimes that might have implicated other wealthy and powerful people.[325]

But aside from the conspiracy theorizing fringe of the Internet, Americans were generally unaware of that travesty of justice. Disturbingly typical was the revelation in November of 2019, through a video released by the investigative journalists at Project Veritas, that ABC News had quashed an investigation by anchor Amy Robach with Epstein accuser Virginia Roberts Giuffre. In a hot-mic moment, Robach complained to an off-camera coworker that she believed the network had caved to pressure from outside forces, including Buckingham Palace. It seems Britain's royal family intervened after Giuffre named Prince Andrew as one of the men to whom Epstein trafficked her for sex.[326]

By that time, however, it was too little coverage, too late. Jeffrey Epstein allegedly committed suicide while in custody at the Metropolitan Correctional Center in New York City three months earlier, on August 10—a death that probably surprised Epstein more than anyone else on the planet.

The autopsy found multiple broken bones in Epstein's neck, including the hyoid bone, which is near the Adam's apple. While the hyoid bone can break during a hanging, it's more common in victims of homicide by strangulation as was thoroughly documented in the bestselling book *Shadowland*.[327]

Surprising absolutely no one, the two video surveillance cameras outside Epstein's jail cell "malfunctioned" the night of his death. The FBI reportedly took in the "broken" cameras for further investigation,[328] but if results of the FBI's probe have been published in the fifteen months between then and this writing, we haven't found them. And you will no doubt be shocked to learn that surveillance video from what the media called Epstein's "first suicide attempt" on July 23, 2019 "no longer exists," according to federal prosecutors.[329]

This was too much even for some in the mainstream media:

> In a letter, federal prosecutors said the jail "inadvertently preserved video from the wrong tier" and "as a result, video from outside the defendant's cell...no longer exists."
>
> "When I read this letter I had to re-read it because I said, this just can't be happening," said CBS News legal analyst Rikki Klieman told CBS News correspondent Mola Lenghi. "This is madness."[330]

One would think it's madness, if one believed that such blatant disregard for protocol was the result of incompetence. Frankly, conspiracy theorists, who see bold, deliberate action behind the death of Jeffrey Epstein, have a more plausible explanation: Epstein had outlived his usefulness and become an unacceptable risk to people with the means to silence him.

And that's where we come back to the media blackout around the Laptop from Hell. While we can't pretend to know what was on it, we have no reason to believe that Rudy Giuliani, a former US attorney, would find it worthwhile to risk a potentially costly defamation suit by mischaracterizing the contents of the laptop's hard drive. Yet, like the media's feigned ignorance of the activities of Jeffrey Epstein and the constellation of luminaries in his orbit, the press in the United States has largely ignored the Hunter Biden story, which has since been eclipsed by the ongoing coverage of the aftermath of the presidential election (albeit without serious inquiries into the highly improbable result at the top of the ballot).

Why would this be? It's possible that the vast majority of those in the mainstream media just really, really don't like Donald Trump, and consider his defeat a higher priority than any standards of journalistic integrity they claim to uphold. It's also possible that some are savvy enough to know that the likelihood of Jeffrey Epstein killing himself was even smaller than Joe Biden winning a fair election, and they don't want to find themselves on the wrong side of an unfortunate "accident."

This was hinted at during the vetting process for President Trump's cabinet. The US attorney who cut the plea deal with Epstein in 2008, Alex Acosta, was Trump's choice for Secretary of Labor.

"Is the Epstein case going to cause a problem [for confirmation hearings]?" Acosta had been asked. Acosta had explained, breezily, apparently, that back in the day he'd had just one meeting on the Epstein case. He'd cut the non-prosecution deal with one of Epstein's attorneys because he had "been told" to back off, that Epstein was above his pay grade. **"I was told Epstein 'belonged to intelligence' and to leave it alone,"** he told his interviewers in the Trump transition, who evidently thought that was a sufficient answer and went ahead and hired Acosta[331] (emphasis added).

Public outcry compelled Acosta to resign as Labor secretary less than two weeks after Epstein's arrest July 6, 2019.

This begs some very large and disturbing questions: Which intelligence service did Epstein belong to? Was it American intelligence? What role did Epstein and his alleged sex-trafficking accomplice, Ghislaine Maxwell, play for this agency? Maxwell's late father, Robert, who built a publishing empire in the UK that included the *Daily Mirror*, had ties to the British Secret Intelligence Service (MI6), the Soviet KGB, and the Israeli intelligence service Mossad;[332] did she carry on in her father's footsteps? Was she the link between Epstein and this shadowy intelligence agency? Did these connections protect them from close scrutiny—not just from the media, but from law enforcement?

To the best of our knowledge, none of these questions have been asked publicly by any mainstream media outlet.

Now, it may seem like a stretch to connect the alleged contents of Hunter Biden's laptop to speculation about Jeffrey Epstein's activities and paymasters, but we suggest the parallels warrant closer examination. Both Epstein and Biden had multiple connections to men and women at the very top of the global power pyramid. Both men indulged overlarge appetites for physical gratification. What we don't know is how the two might fit into potential intelligence operations. We have only Ghislaine Maxwell's pedigree and an offhand remark by Alex Acosta that connect Epstein to the secretive world of intelligence, and, if anything, Hunter Biden looks like more of a blackmail target than an intelligence asset.

Still, it wouldn't be the first time American intelligence services have gotten into bed, if you'll pardon the phrase, with operatives who were depraved, to say the least.

In 2020, the Josh Peck documentary *Silent Cry: The Darker Side of Trafficking*, produced by SkyWatch Films (a division of Defender Publishing), examined the distressing frequency of child sex trafficking in the United States. The film opens with an account of a 1987 investigation by law enforcement in two states, the Customs Service, and the FBI into a cult called the Finders. It began in February of that year when a woman in Tallahassee, Florida, spotted six filthy, disheveled, underfed children accompanied by two well-dressed men, and called the police.

The *Washington Post* ran the story beneath a headline in all caps:

OFFICIALS DESCRIBE "CULT RITUALS" IN CHILD ABUSE CASE

Authorities investigating the alleged abuse of six children found with two men in a Tallahassee, Fla., park discovered materials yesterday in the Washington area that they say points to a 1960s-style commune called the Finders, described in a court document as a "cult" that allegedly conducted "brainwashing" and used children "in rituals."…

D.C. police sources said some of the items seized yesterday showed pictures of children engaged in what appeared to be "cult rituals." Officials of the U.S. Customs Service, called in to aid in the investigation, said that the material seized yesterday includes photos showing children involved in bloodletting ceremonies of animals and one photograph of a child in chains. Customs officials said they were looking into whether a child pornography operation was being conducted.[333]

Details of the case were released by the FBI in a 597-page document dump posted to the agency's website in October 2019.[334] It's too long to explain in depth here, but the relevance to this chapter is summed up in the only substantial media follow-up to the *Post*'s initial report, which was published by *U.S. News and World Report*—almost *seven years later*.

One of the unresolved questions involves allegations that the Finders are somehow linked to the Central Intelligence Agency. Customs Service documents reveal that in 1987, when Customs agents sought to examine the evidence gathered by Washington, D.C. police, they were told that the Finders investigation "had become an internal matter."

The police report on the case had been classified secret. Even now, Tallahassee police complain about the handling of the Finders investigation by D.C. police. "They dropped this case," one Tallahassee investigator says, "like a hot rock." D.C. police will not comment on the matter. As for the CIA, ranking officials describe allegations about links between the intelligence agency and the Finders as "hogwash," perhaps the result of a simple mix up with D.C. police.[335]

Contrary to the CIA's cavalier dismissal, the case mixed clear evidence of the sexual abuse of children, probably in the context of occult rituals, with travel that should have been illegal at the time. According to the final memo filed by US Customs Service Special Agent Ramon J. Martinez:

> On April 2, 1987, I arrived at MPD [Metropolitan Police Department] at approximately 9:00 a.m. Detective Bradley was not available. I spoke to a third party who was willing to discuss the case with me on a strictly "off the record" basis.
>
> I was advised that all the passport data had been turned over to the State Department for their investigation. The State Department in turn, advised the MPD that all travel and use of the passports by the holders of the passports was within the law and no action would be taken. This included travel to Moscow, North Korea, and North Vietnam from the late 1950s to mid 1970s.
>
> The individual further advised me of circumstances which indicated that the investigation into the activity of the Finders had become a CIA internal matter. The MPD report has been classified SECRET and was not available for review. I was advised that the FBI had withdrawn from the investigation several weeks prior and that the FBI Foreign Counter Intelligence Division had directed MPD not to advise the FBI Washington Field Office of anything that had transpired.
>
> No further information will be available. No further action will be taken.[336]

You can almost feel the disgust of Special Agent Martinez as he typed that last line of his final report.

Note this: Travel to Moscow, North Korea, and North Vietnam "from the late 1950s to mid 1970s"—the height of the Cold War and covering the entire Vietnam conflict—could only have been possible with approval at the highest levels of the American government or through the machinations of one of its intelligence services.

And the CIA intervened to spike what appeared to be a solid criminal case against perpetrators of truly vile activity—international sex trafficking of children—because it was "an internal matter."

There are other examples of this type of behavior at high levels around the world: The Franklin Credit Union scandal of the late 1980s, the infamous Marc Dutroux case in Belgium,[337] and the hundreds of sexual-abuse allegations against British entertainer Jimmy Savile that emerged after his death in 2012, some from victims who were as young as twelve when they were assaulted. Police sources indicated that "figures of high standing" might have shielded Savile from scrutiny.[338]

Another story of which most Americans are completely unaware is the untimely end of Craig Spence, a high-flying Washington lobbyist during the 1980s. He was known for his lavish parties, which attracted prominent politicians and journalists such as Ted Koppel, Eric Sevareid and William Safire, conservative icon Phyllis Schlafly, CIA Director William Casey, Attorney General John Mitchell, and assorted members of Congress. Friends of Spence reported that he bragged about being a CIA operative and bugging his party guests (his home reportedly had an eight-foot long, two-way mirror)[339] to collect material for blackmail.[340]

That was probably more than just big talk. Spence was under investigation at the time of his death for his connection to a well-known Washington homosexual escort service that reportedly was "patronized by government officials, military officers, congressional aides and U.S. and foreign businessmen."[341] That clientele, needless to say, would have been susceptible to blackmail.

Spence genuinely had some juice in DC. *The Washington Times* reported in June of 1989 that he'd arranged a private midnight tour of the White House for two call boys the previous July,[342] and subsequent articles in the *Times* reported at least three more late-night trips through the White House, including one with a fifteen-year-old boy Spence falsely identified as his son.[343]

Bear in mind that these tours took place during the Reagan administration. Sexual perversion and abuse of power crosses party lines.

Spence's life apparently began a downward spiral after the *Times* bombshell. He was arrested a month after the article's publication at a hotel in Manhattan and charged with possession of drugs and criminal possession of a loaded firearm. He committed suicide at the Ritz-Carlton in Boston that November—some might say conveniently—before he could testify in the escort-service case.[344]

One common thread among those cases, and many others, is the lack of interest in them until something forces the media to pay attention: The death of a child whose parents refuse to be quiet; the involvement of someone whose diminished value to those in power no longer merits protection (like Jeffrey Epstein and, presumably, Craig Spence), resulting in a high-profile death; or, as with Jimmy Savile and Michael Jackson, the perpetrators are long dead and exposing them is no longer a threat to the power elite.

During the four years of the Trump administration, hardly a month has gone by without another bust by state and federal law enforcement agencies connected to child pornography and pedophile rings. And it's not just here in the US; an operation in Germany in the summer of 2020 uncovered a ring of thirty thousand pedophiles who shared child pornography through the Dark Web along with "tips on how to sedate and abuse young children."[345]

But even with the good work of investigators and prosecutors chasing down the money trails and rescuing children from lives too horrific for most of us to imagine, the public's awareness of child sex trafficking is dangerously low. Stories are reported, but below the fold or off the front page. What grabs headlines? What attracts clicks? What drives the topics for the talking heads on cable news? Politics. The media's outraged reactions to President Trump's latest tweet or the latest "bombshell" that will prove once and for all that Vladimir Putin really pulls his strings. When a story breaks about the bust of a pedophile ring operating in our neighborhood, we're shocked—then we forget about it, like the man described by the Apostle James "who looks at his face in a mirror and, after looking at himself, goes away and immediately forgets what he looks like."[346]

So, what do we make of all of this? How do we boil down a topic that has filled books (and police files) for decades, and how does it connect back to Hunter Biden—and his father, the man who became the forty-sixth president of the United States? Without specific, verifiable information as to what's on the laptop, the best we can do is try to fit the younger Biden's alleged activities into the broader context of our debauched culture.

The media counts on us walking away from the mirror and immediately forgetting what we've seen. But they doth protest too much. Their characterizations of those who question the results of the 2020 presidential elections as believers in Pizzagate and/or QAnon have tipped their hands.

In case the term is new to you, Pizzagate is the name that's been applied to the belief that political elites in Washington, especially a group connected to Bill and Hillary Clinton, used certain code words like "pizza" and "hot dogs" in email and text messages to refer to child prostitution. The theory was connected to a pizzeria in Washington called Comet Ping-Pong, which made national news on December 4, 2016, when one Edgar Maddison Welch of Salisbury, North Carolina, fired three rounds from an AR-15 style rifle into the floor of the restaurant. He later told police that he'd come to "self-investigate" claims that Comet was a hub for child trafficking.[347]

Of course, the media immediately characterized Welch as unhinged, dangerous, and typical of the most ardent supporters of Donald Trump… and probably a believer in end-times Bible prophecy.

You could be a mother, picking leftovers off your toddler's plate. You could be the young man in headphones across the street. You could be a bookkeeper, a dentist, a grandmother icing cupcakes in her kitchen. You may well have an affiliation with an evangelical church. But you are hard to identify just from the way you look—which is good, because someday soon, dark forces may try to track you down. You understand that this sounds crazy, but you don't care. You know that a small group of manipulators, operating in the shadows, pulls the planet's strings. You know that they are powerful enough to abuse children without fear of retribution.

You know that the mainstream media are their handmaidens, in partnership with Hillary Clinton and the secretive denizens of the Deep State. You know that only Donald Trump stands between you and a damned and ravaged world. You see plague and pestilence sweeping the planet and understand that they are part of the plan. You know that a clash between good and evil cannot be avoided, and you yearn for the Great Awakening that is coming. And so you must be on guard at all times. You must shield your ears from the scorn of the ignorant. You must find those who are like you. And you must be prepared to fight.

You know all this because you believe in Q.[348]

And here we are, back to Q again. The liberal media has two clubs that they've invariably used over the last four years whenever they want to characterize something as so irrational that even entertaining the notion is evidence of disordered thinking: One is Pizzagate, and the other is QAnon.

We normally don't recommend Wikipedia as an unbiased source of information, especially when researching topics open to any sort of political interpretation. Here, however, making an exception is instructive, because it helps to illustrate how liberals view the Q phenomenon:

This article is about the baseless far-right conspiracy theory.

QAnon (/ˌkjuːəˈnɒn/) is a far-right conspiracy theory alleging that a cabal of Satan-worshipping pedophiles is running a global child sex-trafficking ring and plotting against US president Donald Trump, who is fighting the cabal. QAnon also commonly asserts that Trump is planning a day of reckoning known as the "Storm," when thousands of members of the cabal will be arrested. No part of the conspiracy claim is based in fact. QAnon supporters have accused many liberal Hollywood actors, Democratic politicians, and high-ranking government officials of being members of the cabal. They have also claimed that Trump feigned conspiracy with Russians to enlist Robert Mueller to join him in exposing the sex trafficking ring and preventing a coup d'état by Barack Obama, Hillary Clinton and George Soros.[349]

Setting aside the obvious bias, you can plainly see the intent of the author's rhetoric: By portraying the QAnon narrative as a delusional fiction completely detached from reality, any idea linked to or compared with Q, of which Pizzagate is now an integral part, is likewise to be ridiculed by anyone who wants to be accepted by the rational, cultured, sophisticated crowd that controls the levers of power.

A brief search of the Web is all you'll need to confirm that the authors of the article and Wikipedia entry cited above are not alone in pushing this despicable narrative. In their world, if you believe that a dark, barely hidden subculture of sexual perversion exists in Washington, Hollywood, and other world centers of power and high society, then you are one of the "deplorables," to borrow a term from Hillary Clinton.

The facts are these: Yes, Virginia, there *are* satanic pedophiles loose in the world today. From time to time, some of them are caught. Some of these monsters are, in fact, actors, politicians, entertainers, and high-ranking government officials. And sometimes well-intentioned officers of the law are ordered to stand down because the accused party "belongs to intelligence" or the crime is "an internal matter."

The children? Apparently, they don't matter.

We can't say what consequences, if any, will come from the Laptop from Hell. At this point, if I were pressed for a guess, I'd say nothing. It would be nice to be more encouraging, but the FBI has had the information in its possession for nearly a year and it appears that little, if anything, has been done. Admittedly, I have limited knowledge of how criminal investigations are conducted, but given what we've learned over the past year about the Bureau's approach to investigating the baseless Russian collusion allegations against President Trump, it's hard to be optimistic. Politics trumps justice in Washington, DC, as it has everywhere on earth since the first kings began to assert power over their neighbors.

And again, we have to be clear that we've only seen a few of the images, emails, and text messages from Hunter Biden's laptop. That was disturbing enough, but without specific knowledge of the rest of what the *New York Post* only described in vague terms, speculating on the depth of

Biden's involvement in anything immoral and illegal is irresponsible. We simply don't know if he's a tool of a shadowy government agency or just a broken man trying to compensate for a spiritual need that he can't meet on his own.

What we can say is this: Hunter Biden, like untold multitudes before him, has been deceived by the gods of this world into desperately trying to satisfy a deep, spiritual yearning with momentary pleasures of the flesh. The promise that money or power, and the physical gratification and altered states of consciousness that it can buy, will fill that gaping spiritual void is a lie.

Pray that Hunter Biden finds the truth before it's too late.

A TROJAN PRESIDENT, A MARXIST FUTURE, AND HOW AMERICA LEARNED TO STOP WORRYING AND EMBRACE TOTALITARIANISM

6

Editor's Note: This chapter is adapted from a 2021 Defender book by LTC Robert L. Maginnis , *Give Me Liberty, Not Marxism.*

The election of Joe Biden to the American presidency was accompanied by the banter of a number of ideological terms used in a variety of derogatory or supportive ways. We must define those terms, their origins, and consequences to establish a starting point.

These descriptive "isms" were used as both nouns and adjectives in the 2020 political discourse—capitalism, Marxism, communism, socialism, and progressivism—but too few Americans really understand the differences, much less the background and implications of each, especially from a Christian worldview perspective.

For most people, these isms became throw-away labels meant as adjectives modifying personalities (e.g., "She's a socialist" or "He's a progressive"), and ideas more often than not used in a derogatory fashion. Certainly in 2020, the political class at all levels used these isms to describe political philosophies and political figures or movements to gain support for or scandalize their opponents. However, these terms have serious meanings and implications for America's future as well as for other societies that may embrace them as the basis for governance or for influencing their way of life.

For me, an evangelical Christian, I will define and describe each of these isms from my biblical worldview perspective. These definitions and my Christian perspective suggest the consequences of their impact for the American experiment going forward into the middle of the twenty-first century, especially the immediate dangers posed by a Biden administration that may embrace or excuse the most dangerous of these isms.

CAPITALISM

> Now you know my credo: Free-market capitalism is the best path
> to prosperity. And let me add to that from our Founding Fathers:
> Our Creator endowed us with the inalienable rights to life, liberty,
> and the pursuit of happiness. In other words, freedom.[350]
> —Lawrence Kudlow, director of the National Economic Council

We begin with perhaps the most commonly understood ism associated with the American experience: capitalism. It might surprise the reader that many Americans are ignorant concerning capitalism, and many prefer alternatives like socialism.

A 2019 Pew Research poll found that 39 percent of Americans have both a positive view of capitalism and a negative view of socialism, "a quarter have positive views of both terms and 17% express negative opinions about both. Another 16% have a positive opinion of socialism and a negative opinion of capitalism."[351]

While two-thirds (65 percent) of Americans have a positive view of capitalism, they demonstrate a lack of understanding of the system. One middle-age man spoke truth to Pew by paraphrasing a famous quote attributed to the World War II-era British Prime Minister Winston Churchill: "Capitalism is the worst way to set up a society, except for all the other ways.... Free markets allow for more innovative solutions and for more people to succeed."[352] That man was the exception, however.

Criticism of capitalism among those polled included the allegation that it creates an unfair economic structure, whereby only the few benefit from the system. Others claim that capitalism "has an exploitative and corrupt nature, often hurting either people or the environment." And yet others (8 percent), according to Pew, mentioned that "corporations and wealthy people undermine the democratic process by having too much power in political matters. And 4% of those with a negative view say that capitalism can work, but to do so it needs better oversight and regulation."[353]

What is capitalism? It is the engine (economic system) that made and keeps America prosperous. I also believe it is the best economic system known to man and closest to the biblical prescription for mankind. In other words, I begin this volume with a description of the biblical "right way" to understand how wealth and means for creating wealth are controlled and owned. Capitalism is the vehicle that fuels free enterprise, allowing individuals to operate businesses with minimal government interference, but the state does have a role in enforcing laws that protect property rights and maintaining a stable currency.

David Landes, an economic historian and nonbeliever, explained that religion provided the engine behind the West's great economic success. Specifically, Landes said the Judeo-Christian religions provided the individual with the "joy in discovery" granted him by the Creator; acknowledged the value God attaches to hard and good manual work; subordinates nature to the will of man without reservation; prescribes linear time, which can result in progress for one's efforts; and grants respect for the market.[354]

Capitalism—the essence of what Landes described above—came about thanks to the Roman Catholic Church in the Middle Ages, according to historian Randall Collins. The Church found the correct mixture of rule of law and bureaucracy to resolve economic disputes, the specialization of labor and investment, and allowed for the accumulation of wealth empowered by the individual's zest for enterprise and wealth creation.[355]

Capitalism really began to fully blossom under the tutelage of the
Catholic Church at the advent of the Industrial Revolution, which
together transformed the world of enterprise. That marvelous marriage—
of Church and Industrial Revolution—sparked competition and created
markets for products like mechanical clocks, grist mills, ship rudders, and
eyeglasses, and the production of iron and much more came to fruition
thanks to human innovation and the engine of capitalism.

The coincidence of invention and the steady hand of the dominant,
bureaucratic, rule of law by the Catholic Church which owned at the
time nearly a third of all Europe, provided the environment for capitalism to flourish. The Church administered its resources via Church-based
bureaucracies of arbitrators, negotiators, and judges and a common law
that impacted every aspect of life to include economic, known in Latin as
the *jus canonicum* or canon law.[356]

The Cistercians, a Catholic religious order of monks and nuns, gave
capitalism the spark to encourage entrepreneurs by creating a system of
cost accounting, practicing the reinvestment of their profits back into
their businesses, moving capital among their various businesses to opti-
mize their return, and even cutting their losses in order to pursue better
investment opportunities. In fact, the Cistercians came to dominate iron
production in France; as historian Randall Collins wrote, they were the
first founders of "the Protestant ethic without Protestantism."[357]

The Catholic Church also brought "spontaneous order" to the emergent markets, explained Friedrich August von Hayek, one of the most
influential economists and social theorists of the twentieth century. This
was essential, because it gave way to predictable economic activity, a
necessity for markets to develop. That concept of stability thanks to economic rules meant that if France needs wool, "prosperity can accrue to the
English sheepherder who first increases his flock, systematizes his fleecers
and combers, and improves the efficiency of his shipments," according to
Michael Novak, writing for the Acton Institute.[358]

The evidence is undeniable: The Catholic Church played a critical
role in the creation and success of capitalism, especially in the Western

world. However, just because the Church helped create capitalism as an economic system does not necessarily mean that capitalism per se has a biblical endorsement. After all, economics influences many of our life choices, and those decisions should be governed for the Christian by a biblical worldview.

It is true the Bible nowhere mentions capitalism, but it does address characteristics and behaviors that are consistent with biblical principles. For example, the book of Proverbs deals extensively with economic matters and attitudes toward acquiring and handling wealth (e.g., Proverbs 10:15; 11:28; 14:20; 18:11; 19:4; 22:2; 28:11).

The Bible acknowledges the worth and dignity of every individual in the eyes of God. Capitalism as an economic model affords each person the best opportunity (dignity) to succeed subject to their talents, skills, intelligence and effort. That doesn't mean it promises equal outcomes, but it does offer equal opportunity and encourages hard work.

A number of Scripture passages address man's sin nature, which provides caution to believers when applied to their economic realm. For example, God grants to humans the right to own property, and as Genesis 1:28 states, to exercise dominion over the earth. That translates to property ownership and the opportunity to use it as one sees fit, such as exchange it for other goods and services—evidence of a free market.[359]

The Bible calls us to be good stewards of our property. After all, God committed the world's resources to humanity (Genesis 1:28–29). Obviously, capitalism grants to men, who are made in the image of God, the opportunity to be good stewards of those God-given resources that allow them to exercise their judgment to grow His property, albeit honestly. Yes, that outcome is evidence of exercising self-interest, which is supported by New Testament obligations to be accountable for ourselves and our actions (e.g., Matthew 12:36; Romans 14:12; 1 Corinthians 4:2).

We are also instructed to exercise wise stewardship within the free market, but that opportunity risks the emergence of sinful behaviors such as laziness and neglect. That is why biblically we are each held accountable for our own productivity.[360]

Capitalism also embraces the scriptural principles of equality and liberty, which influence our treatment of others (e.g., Galatians 3:28–29; Acts 2:1-47). Liberty is a key biblical principle that must not be flaunted as warned about in verses like Romans 14:22 (CSB):

> Whatever you believe about these things, keep between yourself and God.

Individually, each person enjoys the freedom to use his or her talents and gifts through entrepreneurial efforts, thanks to capitalistic economies, and without government interference. Success is more often than not a product of personal effort.

Admittedly, modern capitalism has its flaws, which are mostly attributable to the sinful nature of man. Specifically, sometimes government interferes in the marketplace by granting exclusive rights to certain entities, thus creating unfair monopolies. There are also instances of people in positions of power who use their stature for improper gain. That's a sin in God's Word, such as in Ephesians 6:9 (NASB):

> And masters, do the same things to them, and give up threatening, knowing that both their Master and yours is in heaven, and there is no partiality with Him.

The Bible calls on believers to be generous, especially to the less fortunate. This issue comes up most often when considering the human flaw of greed (Jeremiah 17:9), which is often highlighted by critics—especially when Christians appear to be greedy, thus spoiling their witness. What's not disputed in the free market capitalistic system or by the Bible is that some people use capitalism to satisfy their lust for greater wealth—but that's a moral issue, not the fault of the system. What's true, however, is that capitalism grants both the moral person and the immoral person equal opportunity.[361]

Finally, Christian charity is the opposite of greed and is encouraged for believers. The biblical concept of charity is infused in capitalism by what Dante Alighieri describes in his narrative poem *The Divine Comedy* as *caritas*, "the love that moves the sun and all the starts." *Caritas* is the glue that holds families and nations together and promotes honesty and mutual respect, which are biblical concepts and key ingredients in a functioning capitalistic economy.[362]

Also, there's nothing biblically wrong with exercising self-interest, which is starkly different from being selfish. An adult with a family to feed exercises self-interest by earning wages in a capitalistic system to support his/her family.

In conclusion, capitalism is successful because, when properly implemented, it employs the principles of liberty, equality, and numerous biblical values. Admittedly, it is abused by man's sinfulness, which is a human flaw, not a system flaw. What's clear and will become more evident as we review the other economic-related isms is that capitalism is the superior system from a biblical, productivity, and sociological perspective.

MARXISM

My object in life is to dethrone God and destroy capitalism.[363]
—Karl Marx, author of *Das Kapital*

Black Lives Matter (BLM) is a Marxist movement, according to Carol Swain, a Black conservative and former professor at Vanderbilt and Princeton universities. Ms. Swain said, "Now, the founders of Black Lives Matter, they've come out as Marxists."[364]

Patrisse Cullors, one of the three cofounders of BLM, said in a 2015 interview:

We do have an ideological frame. Myself and Alicia, in particular, are trained organizers; we are trained Marxists. We are super-versed on, sort of, ideological theories. And I think what we really try to do is build a movement that could be utilized by many, many Black folks.[365]

Black Lives Matter is known for race-based violence and alignment with the Democrat Party's radical leftist agenda. But what is Marxism that these radicals are "trained Marxists"? BLM is not the garden-variety Marxism, as I'll explain below. No, it's neo-Marxism that redefines today's fight to incorporate biological sex, race, ethnicity, and much more.

These neo-Marxists distort original Marxism to mean most everything and reduce it to a war between "oppressors" versus the "oppressed." The BLM neo-Marxists target "oppressors" for punishment. But it's important to realize as we explore Marxism to appreciate that not everyone who claims to be a Marxist is true to Marx's original intent, which is radical enough.

What is classical Marxism? It is a political philosophy developed by Karl Heidrich Marx, a nineteenth-century German philosopher, economist, historian, sociologist, political theorist, journalist and socialist revolutionary. Marx's philosophy focuses on class struggle to ensure an equal distribution of wealth for all citizens and illustrates that the inequality created by the ruling class in a capitalistic system that historically oppresses the lower (working) classes triggers a social revolution that creates a classless society, where there is no private property and every citizen gives selflessly to the good of all persons. This ideal model is variously called socialism (communism) or progressivism, examples of Marxism explored in this chapter.

Marx's theory is perhaps best known for its sharp critique of capitalism, which claims that workers in a capitalist system are little more than a commodity, "labor power." This economic clash, which is set forth in Marx's 1859 book, *Das Kapital*, creates a conflict between the proletariat (workers who transform raw commodities into goods) and the bourgeoisie (owners of the means of production), which has a "built-in" inequality. The bourgeoisie, with the help of government, according to Marx, employ social institutions against the proletariat. Marx argues in his writings that capitalism creates an unfair imbalance between the bourgeoisie and the workers whom they exploit for gain and those inherent inequalities, and exploitative relations ultimately lead to revolution that abolishes capitalism and reconstructs society into a socialist form of government.

Of course, Marxism addresses more than just the inequalities between the proletariat and the bourgeoisie. It is a comprehensive ideology, some say a religion, that expresses a broad worldview about most aspects of ordinary life and society that are contrary to a Christian, biblical worldview.

Marxist Worldview

Summit Ministries, a Christian organization, provided a thumbnail sketch of the Marxist worldview across major categories that are summarized and elaborated on below.[366]

First, Karl Marx was a devout atheist from the time he was in college. In 1844, he wrote:

> The abolition of religion as the illusory happiness of the people is required for their real happiness. Religion is the sigh of the oppressed creature, the heart of a heartless world, and the soul of soulless conditions. It is the opium of the people.

He also said religion is a "spiritual booze" and that putting his atheism into practice meant a "forcible overthrow of all existing social conditions," which included economic structures like capitalism, but Marx makes government his god—the provider, sustainer, protector, and lawgiver. Meanwhile, atheistic aspects of Marxism became a trademark of communist regimes like the old Soviet Union and the present-day Peoples Republic of China, which is known for the persecution of religious Muslims and Christians alike.

Second, Marxist philosophy is known as dialectical materialism, which is another name for naturalism. The concept says there are polar opposite states of being—one is the thesis and the other the antithesis, which inevitably clash. That struggle produces a new thesis (way things are), which eventually clashes with a new antithesis. This is an evolutionary process—a series of steps—not that different from Charles Darwin's theory of evolution (spontaneous generation): inorganic substances evolve into life; single-celled life becomes animals and then humans.

Third, Marxist ethics or proletariat morality means that whatever advances the working class is good, and by association, whatever hinders that progress is morally evil. The logical extension of class morality is evidenced by communist China's former leader Mao Zedong, who committed mass murder of perhaps forty million people who allegedly opposed the advances of the working class.

Fourth, Marxist psychology leaves no room for the spiritual dimension, because all behavior is purely based on the material. He argues that human behavior is the result of material reasons, physical makeup (genetics), and outside environmental influences. He asserts that the brain is programmed to react a certain way and our socialization (education, background, etc.) causes us, like Pavlov's dog, to respond to outside stimuli.

Fifth, a classless society is Marx's vision for sociology whereby everyone is the owner and employee—there are no class distinctions. That means there is no need for government or outside influencers, because the owner/employee will always act responsibly. Translation: The working class' (proletariat) sovereignty is the rule in Marx's world, a view traced to his concept of private property (Marxist law). The basis for this law is to protect social or state property that advances socialism and evolution. Once socialism is victorious, explains Marx, then the working class will realize its communist paradise and law is no longer needed.

Sixth, a communist world government is Marx's ultimate political vision. He believed the working class will rise up, overthrow the bourgeois oppression to seize power, and establish a worldwide "dictatorship." That is the next evolutionary step to world government, and once bourgeois ideology is vanquished and all traces of capitalism are history, then a communist society exists—a utopia on earth.

Seventh, Marx believes that economics determines the nature of all legal, social, and political institutions. He blames social problems on imperfections in the modes of production and over time, evolution makes things better—slavery became feudalism, which gave way to capitalism, which will become socialism and eventually communism. The final step in his economic determinism view is a socialist society where there is no private property whereby man is oppressed by his fellow being, which leads to a classless society, communism (the highest economic state).

Marxism the Religion

It is important to put Marx's rejection of the existence of God into proper perspective. Marxism seeks to replace all religions with itself, and a major fault with his theory is that Marx believed in the perfectibility of man while rejecting the perfect God.

Although Marxism rejects the existence of God and labels religion as an opium, Marxism is a true religion to its followers. Consider Marx's background and perhaps come to appreciate how he came about to substitute his Marxist religion for Christianity.

Karl Marx was born to a Prussian attorney who converted to Christianity in order to practice law. Marx's father introduced Karl to the greats—gods at the time—Frederick the Great and the Prussian state and Enlightenment thinkers like John Locke, who saw human nature as a blank page, and Jean-Jacques Rousseau, who wrote, "We do not know what our nature permits us to be."[367]

Marx's Christian background was thanks to religious training in the Prussian school system, which he abandoned once at the University of Bonn and then after that at the University of Berlin, where he joined the "Young Hegelians (German: *Junghegelianer*)," a group of German intellectuals who reacted to the writings of Georg Wilhelm Friedrich Hegel, the father of progressivism.

Marx wrote in his PhD dissertation at the University of Jena (Thuringia, Germany) his view of the deities: "In truth, I hate all gods."

He continued, "I shall never exchange my fetters for slavish servility." Marx spent his life arguing against the existence of the God of the Bible, and in fact he sought in his work to create an entirely new religion based circumspectly on a mirror image of Christianity.[368]

Boston college philosopher Peter Kreeft wrote:

> Marxism retains all the major structural and emotional factors of biblical religion in a secularized form. Marx, like Moses, is the prophet who leads the new Chosen People, the proletariat, out of the slavery of capitalism into the Promised Land of communism across the Red Sea of bloody worldwide revolution and through the wilderness of temporary, dedicated suffering for the party, the new priesthood.[369]

Ulster University economist Esmond Birnie shared that view:

> The deep structure of Marxism parallels that of Christianity. It has a "fall" event—the concentration of ownership of property in the hands of the capitalists—and a "chosen people," the proletarians—as well as a coming "day of judgment," when capitalism is replaced by the classless society.[370]

Marx essentially displaced Christianity with an alternative faith, Marxism, which at its core rejects God but is very much a religion. As one author states, it replaces monotheism with monostatism, whereby all authority rests with state government. In fact, Pavel Hanes, an associate theology professor at the University of Matej Bel in Slovakia, wrote:

> Marx himself insisted that an atheistic state predicted in his philosophy would be a perfect realization of the essence of Christianity.[371]

Professor Hanes' "essence of Christianity" view is shared by German philosopher Karl Löwith who believed that "Marx's historical materialism is a secularized version of Christian teleology" (the explanation of phenomena by the purpose they serve rather than by postulated causes), according to Bryan S. Turner, a British and Australian sociologist. Löwith, wrote Turner, "treats Marx's philosophy of history as a global vision that depends fundamentally on the Christian scheme of eschatology, the doctrine of the Last Days and the Restoration of man to Grace."[372]

Marxism and Christianity do not mix, however. Marxism never works. The Marxist-inspired brutality realized in communist governance is a human tragedy. Even the late Martin Luther King Jr. addressed the issue in a 1953 sermon:

> Communism and Christianity are at the bottom incompatible. One cannot be a true Christian and a true Communist simultaneously.... They represent diametrically opposed ways of looking at the world and transforming the world. We must try to understand Communism, but never can we accept it and be true Christians.[373]

Marxist-inspired communism has a documented history of failure with many anecdotal testimonies. Laura M. Nicolae, who fled communist Romania, wrote about communism in her former homeland:

> Communism cannot be separated from oppression; in fact, it depends upon it. In the communist society, the collective is supreme. Personal autonomy is nonexistent. Human beings are simply cogs in a machine tasked with producing utopia; they have no value of their own. Thankfully, we serve a God whose valuation of those he has made in his own image led him to send his Son to take the penalty for our sins as he hung on a cross. The God-man Jesus of Nazareth came gladly to save us and sent his Spirit to live within us. This is transformation. This is the beginning of a whole new humanity and a whole new world.[374]

Differences between Marxism and Christianity

The Bible doesn't use guilt as a weapon. Marxism and especially the neo-Marxists use collective guilt as a weapon, a significant contradiction with Christianity. Neo-Marxists like BLM claim all white people bear the guilt of past slave owners, and if Caucasians remain silent, they are accused of violence.

Marxism uses a broad brush to accuse large segments of society with guilt such as Marxist BLM followers who say that white people bear the guilt of sins committed by former slave owners. Yet Christianity holds that we are accountable to God alone for our sins.

No verses of Scripture tell Christians to cast guilt on entire people groups; rather, the sins of a nation are God's, not fellow humans', to address. This view is expressed in Ezekiel 18:20 (NIV):

> The one who sins is the one who will die. The child will not share the guilt of the parent, nor will the parent share the guilt of the child. The righteousness of the righteous will be credited to them, and the wickedness of the wicked will be charged against them.

God deals with humans on a personal level. We become Christians by asking Jesus to save us, forgive us of our sin, and become Lord of our lives. Issues of guilt were addressed at Calvary, and no ideology or group can replace the ultimate forgiveness Christ grants believers.

The Bible endorses the ownership of private property. Earlier, I established that Marxists embrace a materialistic worldview. Simply, the concept is that when a society shares everything in common, life becomes a utopia, according to Marx. However, the abolishing of private property runs contrary to the teachings of Bible, such as the injunction in Deuteronomy 5:19 (ESV), which commands, "And you shall not steal." Stealing presumes private property ownership. Further, 2 Thessalonians 3:10 states that people must be willing to work to eat; once again, there is no entitlement to another's property without labor in exchange. Even Jesus' parable of the bags of gold (Matthew 25:14–30) becomes nonsense as an application where there is no private property.

Marxism claims that people will reach the point at which they are solely satisfied with possessions, and God becomes irrelevant. However, common sense and decades of observing human behavior demonstrates that wealth in itself breeds sin, not satisfaction. The fact is that numerous passages of Scripture illustrate the spiritual nature of mankind (e.g., Job 32:8; Ecclesiastes 12:7; Proverbs 20:27; Romans 8:16).

Marxism is the source of much sin. After all, classical and especially neo-Marxists like the BLM movement are filled with anger and resentment. Instead of demonstrating the virtues of peace and thankfulness, they tend to be violent and coveters, sins that are specifically condemned in the Scriptures. For example, Exodus 20:17 says we must not covet our neighbor's possessions, and the New Testament encourages us to be content "in every situation" (Philippians 4:11–13).

The Bible focuses on spiritual matters. A major distinction between Marxism and Christianity are the different views of material and spiritual things. Marxism focuses on physical (material) needs while Christianity, as Jesus explained in Matthew 6:26, 33 (NIV) focuses on the spiritual: "Do not worry about your life, what you will eat or drink; or about your body, what you will wear. Is not life more than food, and the body more than clothes? ….Seek first [God's] kingdom and his righteousness."

Marxism promotes division, not equality. Marxism is divisive. For example, "group identity" is everything to neo-Marxists like BLM. By contrast, America's founders fought the British to create a level ground that promoted the first principle of equality. Further, for the Christian, Christ erased all cultural and ethnic, race barriers to God, and the Apostle Paul wrote in Galatians 3:28–29 (NLT):

There is no longer Jew or Gentile, slave or free, male and female. For you are all one in Christ Jesus. And now that you belong to Christ, you are the true children of Abraham. You are his heirs, and God's promise to Abraham belongs to you.

Karl Marx, as explained earlier, discriminated against all people of faith. He called for the abolition of religion and compared it to opium (an intoxicating drug). He also claimed, "My object in life is to dethrone God." And that view of religion is evident even today; where Marxism prevails, Christians are oppressed.

In conclusion, Marxism is an anti-Christian theory that rejects biblical freedom and personal responsibility. Besides, it sets itself up as a religion exclusively focused on the unrealistic vision of an earthly utopia and the perfectibility of mankind. It has nor ever will attain its utopian goal because of its view of man. Efforts to follow Marx's prescription in places like the old Soviet Union always will result in massive suffering at the hands of dictatorial governments.

SOCIALISM

The American people will never knowingly adopt socialism. But, under the name of "liberalism," they will adopt every fragment of the socialist program, until one day America will be a socialist nation, without knowing how it happened.[375]
—Norman Thomas, six-time presidential candidate for the Socialist Party of America

The 2020 election was a petri dish for socialism, and it came up short. A post-election analysis by Representative Abigail Spanberger (D-VA) found that Democrats shouldn't say the word "socialism...ever again." Why? It was a major political loser in the 2020 election cycle, according to Spanberger, which, evidence suggests, was one of the reasons Joe Biden lost in Florida and a major disappointment for so-called Democratic socialists like Senators Elizabeth Warren (D-MA) and Bernie Sanders (I-VT), both of whom celebrated their socialist credentials during the campaign and promised more of the same for America's future.[376]

Bernie Sanders explained his perspective for his loved socialism: "To me, democratic socialism means democracy."[377] But to conservatives like former President Ronald Reagan, "Socialism only works in two places: heaven where they don't need it and hell where they already have it."[378]

Most every astute American knows that socialism earned considerable press during the 2020 election cycle, but according to veteran pollster George Barna, that support didn't come from many Christians. He found that 98 percent of Americans who support socialism reject the biblical worldview. Barna explained, "The 2020 election is not about personalities, parties, or even politics. It is an election to determine the dominant worldview of America."[379]

What is socialism? It is the realization of the social and economic theory attributed to Karl Marx that embraces state ownership of all property and the means of production. This idea of the sharing of wealth in society theoretically results in a classless society where everyone is equal, and the distribution of the means production is the chief characteristic. Not surprisingly, it is in direct opposition to capitalism.

Socialism depends on Marx's wrongheaded assumption about life based on the Hegelian dialectic, which is explained in the earlier section on Marxism—thesis, antithesis, synthesis—which is a social evolutionary theory much like Charles Darwin's evolution of the species. The problem for Marx and socialism in particular is that, with hundreds of years of empirical evidence, it's capitalism, not socialism, that works. Economist Paul Samuelson observed, "As a prophet Marx was colossally unlucky and his system [socialism] colossally unuseful."[380]

Socialism is not just "unuseful," as Samuelson wrote, but it is dangerous because it leads to big government and, as F. A. Hayek, a twentieth-century British-Australian philosopher, observed, centralized and big government planning inevitably leads to dictatorship. A simple study of socialist leadership over the past century conclusively demonstrates that such leftist authorities promise freedom but end up delivering only misery and tyranny.

The evidence is conclusive: Socialism is an abject failure across time and continents from the Marxism-Leninism in Soviet Union, Maoism in China, so-called democratic-socialism in Sweden to national socialism in Nazi Germany. Across time, socialists who survived were forced to consistently compromise Marx's original vision by embracing aspects of capitalism such as economic zones and foreign investment, to name just a couple.

The best-known socialist experiment, the Soviet Union, couldn't be saved by Mikhail Gorbachev who tried *perestroika* (restructuring) and *glasnost* (openness). Those efforts ended with the lowering of the Soviet hammer and sickle (the Soviet's national flag) for the last time on Christmas Day 1991. Much the same outcome happened in communist China in the late 1970s when Deng Xiaoping compromised Maoist ideas of socialism to accept more capitalist ways such as enterprise and foreign investment. Unfortunately, the communist Chinese were sufficiently flexible to adjust their adherence to Marxism in order to maintain control of that nation, unlike their communist Russian peers.

Socialism also long ago failed in America when Robert Owen (1771–1858), an English philanthropist, invested much of his fortune in the experimental socialist community at New Harmony, Indiana. That nineteenth-century experiment lasted about two years before Owen returned to London.[381]

Unfortunately, empty socialist promises still inspire people today in spite of a record of total failure across the globe. Specifically, socialism manifests itself in some Western countries where there is increased reliance on big government and centralized programs such as universal healthcare and massive social welfare programs. These policies are key to modern socialism that advances the view that communal sharing helps society prosper.

Perhaps it isn't surprising that some socialist ideas regarding healthcare, climate change, free education, and government assistance for the needy all poll well today, especially among American Millennials (born 1981–1996), who tend to favor socialism thanks to a sympathetic mainstream media and the influence of the public educational establishment that more often than not advocates for leftist philosophies. By contrast, older-schooled Baby Boomers (born 1946–1964) tend to favor capitalism, a result of their histories—and not surprisingly, these Americans are often labeled by Millennials as indifferent to the needs of the common man for their opposition to socialist ideas.

Those differences in view across the generations beg the question: Just what makes someone embrace socialism? Perhaps part of the attraction is a result of personality or youthful idealism. After all, some young people who favor socialism tend to be very personable themselves and feel good about sharing and collaboration, as opposed to being competitive. They tend to believe the greatest good comes from self-sacrifice for the common good, and they aspire to redistribute resources until everyone is equal, a reflection of Marx's well-known exhortation: "From each according to his ability, to each according to his needs."[382]

Our public educational establishment tends to endorse socialism as well. After all, who hasn't heard true accounts of the socialist-leaning teacher, school administrator, and/or coach who promotes equal outcomes for all the children on sports teams? They don't keep score and don't like labels like "winner" or "loser." That's why every member of the team gets a participation trophy at the end of the season, because it's all about everyone feeling equal, no matter one's talents and contributions.

At the aggregate economic level, the socialist is passionate about the equal distribution of financial resources and he or she becomes quite upset when there are disparities in society whereby some people are obviously very wealthy while others live a meager existence. The socialist expects the strong arm of government to rectify those disparities and are upset when that doesn't happen.

The extreme version of socialism is communism, which is profiled in the next section of this chapter. However, for now, consider that these people, according to one author, are an exaggerated version of the socialist person profiled above, but with a vengeance. The communist's psychological profile is best described by terms like "defeatism," "deceptive hypocrisy," "low self-esteem," and by the tendency to be delusional about their theoretical notion of equality.[383]

These psychological characteristics are on full display most every day in the halls of the US Congress. Leading socialist activists like US House of Representatives Congresswoman Alexandra Ocasio-Cortez (D-NY), a member of the Democratic Socialists of America (DSA), earns considerable attention and support, especially among socialist-leaning younger Americans. She calls for government ownership of industries such as railroads and coal mines, and would "democratize" private businesses to give the workers total control, a Marxist idea. Not surprisingly, the DSA National Steering Committee called for the "democratization of all areas of life, including but not limited to the economy."[384]

Even though socialism may still not be an integral part of the Democrat Party's public platform, some of those closely associated with the party, like Senator Sanders, a hard-core socialist, push the party to implement socialist policies, albeit gradually—and, like what Norman Thomas said, they will press that agenda as they did with Joe Biden "until one day America will be a socialist nation, without knowing how it happened."[385]

Socialism's Worldview

Below is socialism's worldview followed immediately by a biblical perspective of this ism.

First, socialism is an expression of Marxism, a belief that the material universe is all that exists or, said otherwise, it is an atheistic belief system. It places total trust in the evolution of man to create a utopia, and asserts that once we die, there is no afterlife.

Christianity was a favorite target of Marx because of its concept of a fixed human nature. Marx's disciples, especially Vladimir Lenin (1870–1924), waged a campaign of terror against Christian churches in Russia, where he executed priests and violated nuns. For socialists like Lenin, these horrors were a necessary part of the Marxist-inspired and necessary class warfare.

Second, socialism, in spite of protests from its proponents, is a kind of faith system like most religions. Like all religions, socialism answers three key questions about ultimate reality, the nature of mankind, and what man can achieve in this life. The socialist worships his/her god, Marxist socialism.

Third, the socialist is totally focused on human existence. That doesn't mean that socialists who have a faith in God don't perhaps embrace aspects of true socialism, but it is an issue they must somehow hybridize.

Fourth, socialists believe in the evolution of man from the animal species, and their focus is on human life in this world. There is no hereafter, says the socialist. Therefore, they exclusively focus on the survival of the human race and do whatever is necessary to ensure that the species thrives.

Fifth, socialism embraces moral relativism because it doesn't believe in absolute moral laws that transcend mankind (God). However, socialists do recognize the need for moral rules imposed by their political masters to prevent chaos.

Sixth, socialism advocates central control of the economy with the goal of equality across the entire population. That means the government is expected to take resources from those who earn it and give it to others who need it. They do this by creating a centralized authority that plans the production and distribution of all products and services.

Seventh, socialists accept centralized political control in order to enforce "equality" across society, which translates into the need for a ruling class to make and enforce the rules. The result in every case of socialism is that the ruling class becomes some form of dictatorship with all power vested in a single political party or a strong-man dictator like China's President Xi Jinping and the ruling Chinese Communist Party.

The consequences of socialism are tragic. Millions of people living today can testify to the ravages of socialist tyrants like those in China. Obedience to the will of the party is expected, with no alternative.

American author Richard N. Wright (1908–1960) wrote the following about socialist tyranny:

> At that [socialist] meeting I learned that when a man was informed of the wish of the Party he submitted, even though he knew with all the strength of his brain that the wish was not a wise one, was one that would ultimately harm the Party's interests.[386]

French Nobel laureate André Gide spoke bluntly after visiting the Soviet Union:

> I doubt whether in any country in the world—not even in Hitler's Germany—have the mind and spirit ever been less free, more bent, more terrorized and indeed vassalized—than in the Soviet Union." Gide said, "The Soviet Union has deceived our fondest hopes and shown us tragically in what treacherous quicksand an honest revolution can founder."[387]

Even the American journalist Louis Fisher, who once boasted of Soviet Union's advances, provided a stark picture of that regime:

> Ubiquitous fear, amply justified by terror, had killed revolt, silenced protest, and destroyed civil courage. In place of idealism, cynical safety-first. In place of dedication, pursuit of personal aggrandizement. In place of living spirit, dead conformism, bureaucratic formalism, and the parrotism of false clichés.[388]

Eighth, socialism is not biblical but a Marxist method of execution and runs contrary to Bible teachings. Consider key areas where socialism and Christianity diverge, in spite of the fact that, according to a George Barna poll, many Americans think Jesus was a socialist (24 percent) as opposed to a capitalist (14 percent).[389]

Socialism Is Antithetical to Christian Teachings

Socialism focuses on an earthly (material) heaven and rejects a spiritual heaven. Further, it defines salvation in terms of material goals rather than the biblical teaching of a spiritual salvation. It assumes that sinful man can overcome the effects of sin through social engineering.[390]

Socialism's materialistic worldview contradicts biblical Christianity, which teaches that man's problems are mostly spiritual. The cause of human suffering is sin, and salvation is found only in Christ, who came to earth to die for mankind's sin.

Socialism also distributes resources without regard to need and effort. After all, Marx said, "From each according to his ability, to each according to his needs."[391] That means the socialist punishes those who excel in industry and rewards those who don't necessarily contribute to the common welfare by working hard. By contrast, the Bible says that anyone who refuses to work ought not eat (2 Thessalonians 3:10).

Translation: Socialism approves of stealing from the more prosperous (hard-working) and then turns over resources to the less fortunate. Famously, former president Barack Obama expressed that socialist view to a young girl: "We've got to make sure that people who have more money help the people who have less money. If you had a whole pizza, and your friend had no pizza, would you give him a slice?"[392]

Obama evidently endorses the forced redistribution of wealth, which is a socialist value, not a biblical value. After all, as illustrated above, socialists don't believe in ownership of private property. By contrast, the Bible calls on Christians to protect private ownership while encouraging believers to share their resources with the less well-to-do as God's Spirit directs.

Socialism also creates class warfare by blaming the wealthy for all problems. Socialist Senator Bernie Sanders illustrates the point. He said:

> Let us wage a moral and political war against the billionaires and corporate leaders on Wall Street and elsewhere, whose policies and greed are destroying the middle class of America.[393]

That view is contrary to the teachings of verses in Scripture such as Proverbs 14:31 (NIV), which states, "Whoever oppresses the poor shows contempt for his maker," but socialists like Sanders condemn the wealthy as a class and encourage revolution to overthrow them, what Hillary Clinton called "toppling" the top 1 percent of Americans.[394]

Socialists like Sanders and evidently Clinton misunderstand that the wealthy are not stealing from others, but create products and jobs for the broader population. Further, Scripture doesn't demand the transfer of money from the wealthy, but it teaches us not to covet (Exodus 20:17) and to be content in all circumstances (Philippians 4:11–13).

Socialists are not pro-marriage and family. Marx's coauthor of *The Communist Manifesto*, Fredrich Engels, proposed government strive for a future whereby "the single-family ceases to be the economic unit of society. Private housekeeping is transformed into a social industry. The care and education of the children becomes a public affair."[395]

Socialist Sanders said much the same. He called for a "revolution" in childcare beginning with all six-week-old children.[396] Besides he's a proponent of so-called "gay" marriage as a means, perhaps, to destroy traditional Christian marriage.[397]

In conclusion, socialism has a violent, bloody history and offers no hope for humanity either in this life or the next.

The *Black Book of Communism* (1999) chronicles that there have been at least one hundred million victims of socialism (communism). That volume documents that every Marxist socialist regime to date exclusively existed thanks to the muzzle of a gun and forced labor camps—no exceptions from Cambodia's Pol Pot to China's Mao Zedong and to the present socialist regime in Venezuela.

Let there be no doubt that socialism is a religion itself grounded in political tyranny where its god (big government) failed, a theory (Marxism) that never worked, and a social structure/political system that always fails the people it was set up to support.

COMMUNISM

There is no difference between communism and socialism, except in the means of achieving the same ultimate end: communism proposes to enslave men by force, socialism—by vote. It is merely the difference between murder and suicide.[398]
—Ayn Rand, twentieth-century Russian-American writer and philosopher

Many people use the terms "Marxism," "socialism," and "communism" interchangeably, perhaps because they mistakenly believe they are the same philosophies. It is true that these philosophies are related, and in fact Marxism provides the foundation for the economic and political philosophies of both socialism and communism.

A major distinction between socialism and communism is the necessity for the public to own all property and means of production and services. The centralization of ownership gives everyone a chance to develop their very best—or so the theory contends.

Karl Marx believed there is a natural progression from socialism to communism. The first step is for the proletariat (the workers) to push the bourgeoisie (the wealthy owners) out (translation: "kill them"), then society would evolve into a classless utopia without a government, a concept found in Marx's and Fredrich Engels' book, *The Communist Manifesto*. That text states:

> [Communists] are, on the one hand, practically, the most advanced and resolute section of the working class parties of every country, that section which pushes forward all others; on the other hand, theoretically, they have over the great mass of the proletariat the advantage of clearly understanding the line of march, the conditions, and the ultimate general results of the proletarian movement.[399]

Communism is the extreme version of socialism, which, like the original ideology, Marxism, is atheistic to its core. Invariably, socialism given license eventually morphs into communism marked by tyranny, suffering, and death.

The biblical differences noted earlier between socialism and Christianity also apply to Marxist communism, but on steroids. History exposes the bloody path of communism's march through Russia, China, Venezuela, and elsewhere. Fundamentally, that toll is the result of communism's stark failure to recognize a higher moral authority, and without a constraining god, even mass murder is permissive as the means to pursue the communist's utopian social goal.

Unfortunately, there are some rather naïve people who believe that communism is in fact somewhat acceptable. They express that view by offering a sympathetic portrayal of communist ideology and try to reconcile it with Christianity. One such person is Dean Dettloff, who wrote in *America*, a Jesuit magazine, an article that attempted to reconcile the similarities of communism and the Catholic Church's teaching.

Mr. Dettloff compares the communist view about the class struggle with that of the Catholic Church when he writes:

> For communists, global inequality and the abuse of workers at highly profitable corporations are not the result only of unkind employers or unfair labor regulations. They are symptoms of a specific way of organizing wealth, one that did not exist at the creation of the world and one that represents part of a "culture of death," to borrow a familiar phrase....
>
> Although the Catholic Church officially teaches that private property is a natural right, this teaching also comes with the proviso that private property is always subordinate to the common good.[400]

Long ago, comparisons like that above between communism and Christianity were condemned, however. Paul Kengor, the author of *The Devil and Karl Marx (2020)*, wrote:

> In 1846, Pope Pius IX released *Qui pluribus* [an encyclical subtitled 'On Faith and Religion'], affirming that communism is "absolutely contrary to the natural law itself" and if adopted would "utterly destroy the rights, property, and possessions of all men, and even society itself." In 1849, one year after the [*The Communist*] *Manifesto* was published, Pius IX issued the encyclical, *Nostis Et Nobiscum*, which referred to both socialism and

communism as "wicked theories," "perverted theories," and "pernicious fictions."

Communism and religion—especially Christianity—are incompatible, as history demonstrates. That's because communist tyrants refuse to share their authority over the people and all social institutions with any other group, especially the Christian God. This all-encompassing authoritarian focus explains why the world's best-known communist regime failed, a surprise to many.

At the beginning of 1991, the year the Soviet Union collapsed, it was the largest country in the world (one-sixth of the earth's land surface), with 290 million people. It had tens of thousands of nuclear weapons and a massive military presence that extended deep into Europe. But it failed because of many flaws directly attributable to its Marxist foundation.

First, the Soviet Union collapsed because politically it didn't have the tools to right its failing economy. Mikhail Gorbachev became the secretary of the Communist Party in 1985 and quickly tried to jump start his flagging economy. That failed, so he instituted policies of openness (*glasnost*) and restructuring (*perestroika*). Gorbachev's openness created a groundswell of criticism for the entire Soviet apparatus. That restructuring welcomed the lifting of Soviet-era price controls, but the overseeing of those controls was left to the well-embedded Soviet bureaucracy, who vigorously resisted the new approach, which resulted in its failure because the corrupt bureaucrats didn't benefit directly.[401]

Second, as late as 1990, the Soviet economy was the world's second largest, even though it suffered from major shortages of consumer goods. That explains the Soviet Union's massive black-market economy that perhaps accounted for at least 10 percent of the country's gross domestic product (GDP). Besides, the nation was crippled at the time by economic stagnation, which was exacerbated by the government's mismanaged fiscal policy (a Marxist economy) and accompanied by a sharp drop in the price of oil, the country's prime source of foreign currency.

Third, the Kremlin accelerated its defense spending in response to President Ronald Reagan's announced Strategic Defense Initiative, an ambitious project to construct a space-based anti-missile system dubbed "Star Wars." That 1983 announcement shocked the Kremlin and pushed it to invest in defense the nation could ill afford. At the time, the military budget already consumed somewhere between 10 and 20 percent of the GDP, which ignored the other critical needs of the nation, and quickly the fiscal weight of new defense spending became an unsustainable drain on the country's dwindling resources.

Fourth, Gorbachev's glasnost awakened Soviet citizens to just how bad things were at home in comparison with the West. That openness brought new ideas and experiences to a Soviet citizenry accustomed to bland food, shabby clothes, and hopeless lives. Meanwhile, Russians began to explore, thanks to glasnost, ideas about democratization, and they experimented with Western-style food and other imported goods. Quickly the population became disillusioned, mostly disgusted with the country's endemic corruption and poor quality of life.

Aleksandr Yakovlev, Gorbachev's adviser, described the problem. "The main issue today is not only economy," he said. "This is only the side of the process. The heart of the matter is in the political system...and its relation to man." That was the legacy of Marx's idea about socialism, its view about the nature of man and the state's role, and its objection to religion, a source of hope for a desperate people.[402]

Finally, the Soviet Union was humbled by its nuclear industry. Throughout the Cold War (1947–1991), the world teetered on the edge of mutual nuclear destruction, but it took the implosion of a civilian nuclear reactor, the Chernobyl power plant in Ukraine, to expose the world to Russia's serious shortfalls. That disaster released more than four hundred times the amount of radioactive fallout as the atomic bomb dropped on Hiroshima, but communist officials in Moscow at the time suppressed the truth about the disaster.

The Kremlin responded to the unprecedented catastrophe using the same approach it always employed when faced with a serious problem: It lied. After all, the entire Soviet society was based on so many lies that no one knew the truth, and thus that flaw characteristically hobbled most decision-making. Meanwhile, Western media and governments accused Moscow of "malicious lies" for what the Kremlin characterized as a "misfortune." As a direct result of Moscow's lies about the reactor incident, much of the world quickly lost all trust in the Soviet's account. According to Gorbachev, who marked the anniversary of the disaster decades later, the regime's misinformation campaign "was perhaps the real cause of the collapse of the Soviet Union five years later."[403]

In conclusion, what's clear is that communism is the most extreme version of socialism. The demise of the Soviet Union demonstrates that view in terms of its economic and political failures, especially in terms of the trust it squandered with its citizens and much of the world.

PROGRESSIVISM

Progressivism is the cancer in America and it is eating our Constitution, and it was designed to eat the Constitution, to progress past the Constitution.[404]
—Glenn Beck, an American political commentator

Contemporary progressivism is the new communism with a twist. It is a social and political movement that promotes unreason and irrationality through the guise of various social justice causes.

Progressivism didn't start out that way, however. In fact, it had many redeeming qualities in the late nineteenth and early twentieth centuries. Progressive ideology at its origin was about making use of or being interested in new ideas, findings, or opportunities. It was, as I explain in *Progressive Evil* (Defender, 2019):

...about the advancement and adoption of social reform for the amelioration of society's ills. Progressives through the ages have come from all backgrounds, claiming they promote freedom of the individual to compete in fair conditions while championing the progress and improvement of society.

That has all changed.

Modern American progressives flushed out the good from the original movement and embraced a Marxist approach to changing society not that different from past communists. Much like the old Marxists who gave the task of leading a revolution to overthrow the capitalists to revolutionaries, today's revolutionaries are progressive politicians, social justice reformers, and civil rights warriors who permeate our media, government, education establishments, and workplaces.

Their goal, like the goal of the old Marxists, is to set things right through social change in order to create a more just society by advancing equality between men and women, immigrants and citizens, people of color, heterosexuals and homosexuals, the disabled and able-bodied, and more. These postmodern progressives share a vision of a society free of all the modern social "isms"—sexism, nativism, racism, heterosexism, and other so-called perceived communal injustices.

The individual's ability is not a discriminator for the progressive, which is also an aspect of Marxist theory. For the progressive like the Marxist communist and the socialist, private property ought to become taboo in favor of state-controlled resources.

A key aspect of postmodern progressivism is the use of the central, big government to force these changes. Progressives need government to advance civil rights laws, maintain a living minimum wage, provide housing, ensure guaranteed income, and much more. After all, for the progressive, big government is the blunt instrument that advances equality for all citizens and ultimately leads to utopia.

It's not surprising that postmodern progressives are truly intolerant when it comes to conservative views. They reject our constitutional safeguards (rights)—freedom of speech, freedom of religion, and the right to bear arms—which explains their efforts to rewrite our Constitution in order to grow the government's control over every aspect of life, from healthcare to managing our economy.

They also, in the name of social justice, favor radical directives that put women in frontline ground combat and require public schools to allow K–12 transgender students to use the bathroom or locker room of their choice.

Progressives want to subordinate our national sovereignty to leftist supranational bodies like the United Nations and welcome the introduction of Islamic law (sharia) into our communities, which is contrary to our Constitution, and they also welcome oversight from international tribunals (courts) at the expense of our own sovereign judiciary. Then there is the matter of welcoming a flood of illegal immigrants, and they expect the US to embrace global strategies to address issues like climate change.

How do progressives intend to reach these lofty outcomes? As I said earlier, much like socialist and communist revolutionaries who replaced the so-called oppressive class (the bourgeoisie), progressives intend for the heavy hand of government to create overseers (bureaucrats) who inevitably become corrupt and eventually morph into little tyrants and dictators. Also, they enlist the support of nongovernment radicals like BLM and ANTIFA (so-called anti-fascists) to do their bidding.

We shouldn't expect postmodern progressives to be any better than communists at restraining the tendency to embrace tyranny, because both suffer from the same ideological deficiencies. For example, communist and progressive ideals of equality aren't realistic because they ignore the true, sinful nature of mankind. After all, fallen man is competitive by nature and he will never settle on being an equal among his peers. Rather, he will always strive to improve his lot first, whereby the stronger man always subjugates the weaker—the ingredients of dictatorships.

Just like the communists who built their utopian "proletarian state" in the former Soviet Union through a corrupted bureaucratic class that denied basic freedoms, the social justice progressives today will use the strong arm of big government to enforce affirmative action that tolerates certain types of racism and allows so-called gay liberation activists to trample the rights of Christians.

You see, progressive politics ultimately divides people through identity politics and results in intergroup conflicts across various religions, races, sexual-orientations and economic groups.

Postmodern progressivism is also as anti-biblical as its fellow isms—Marxism, socialism, and communism. It hates the true God and His followers. It will do everything the other isms endorse that advances an anti-religion future and targets Christians who are a harbinger of ill content for the dedicated progressive.

In conclusion, postmodern progressives are nothing like their forefathers who sought change to improve their lives. Rather, they are dead set on weakening our constitutional rights to fit their radical Marxist ideology. They seek to destroy our key institutions—family and faith—to fit their social justice agenda, and ultimately, they will lead this country to ruin, much like the former Soviet tyrants did to communist Russia.

CONSEQUENCES OF THE ISMS FOR FUTURE AMERICA

The consequences of this milieu of isms for future America are rather breathtaking. Literally, America's foundation could be rocked by the changes should the isms have their way with our republic.

I anticipate that Biden and his leftist advisers following their ism ideologies will certainly revise the interpretation of our Bill of Rights to address their version of faith and speech rights, our right to privacy, and our right to bear arms.

We saw in this chapter the significant social influences across ism-based societies, particularly the impact for key institutions such as family, education, the media, and the economy. No doubt, with the power of big government in their sails, leftists will pervert the definition and roles of the American family; education will be far more of a state-based mechanism for molding our children into faithful socialists or worse; the media will make no pretense about becoming the propaganda arm for Washington;

and our economy will sour as it quickly abandons capitalism in favor of socialist policies to control the means of manufacturing and distribution. They will destroy the entrepreneurial spirit and send more jobs abroad.

Leftists infatuated with these isms will cravenly embrace globalism on steroids as well. Consider that in late 2020, we learned to expect President Biden to embrace a globalist Great Reset plan to use the coronavirus pandemic as cover to transform the world's economy, according to former Secretary of State John Kerry.

Mr. Kerry told the World Economic Forum audience:

> The notion of a reset is more important than ever before. I personally believe…we're at the dawn of an extremely exciting time.

Translation: Unelected global bureaucrats will usher in a New World Order.[405]

These globalists will ride the fear and uncertainty associated with the COVID-19 lockdowns and the predicted economic downturn some economists promise will be worse than the Great Depression of the 1930s. But even if that economic tragedy doesn't happen, according to Klaus Schwab, the founder and executive chairman of the World Economic Forum, globalists elite, which include President Biden and his handlers, will act jointly and swiftly to "revamp all aspects of our societies and economies, from education to social contracts and working conditions.… In short, we need a "'Great Reset' of capitalism."[406]

The consequences for America of the imposition of the isms is radical and all-encompassing. The America we know and love may well become little more than a distant memory, and in its place will be a new reality our founders long ago sought to prevent.

THE ESSENES, 2025, AND THE FINAL AGE OF MAN

7

Much like the body of believers called Christians today, the Essenes are largely misunderstood. This is unfortunate, due to the amazing kinship Christians have had with the Essenes, spanning the last two thousand years and the end of two ages, as we will look at more throughout this chapter. Among the few who have heard of this mysterious group, many think of the Essenes as one homogeneous entity; they were either "this" or "that," or "either, or" rather than "both, and." Again, this is very similar to how the world views Christianity today. Christians are considered by many to have one specific set of beliefs or another, without much variety. This concept is clearly mistaken, but not unique. In fact, it's human nature to make such generalizations instead of adopting a more nuanced understanding. To prove this, try simply entering into Google Search "Christians are," "Republicans are," or "Liberals are," and allow the search engine to autofill for you what others have previously searched. Chances are, you won't receive autofills that say "a wide variety of unique people who all have a few common beliefs." Rather, you'll probably see words similar to "negative," "cruel," and "stupid" (three results that popped up when I did this myself). The same kind of misconception can be found in our modern understanding of the Essenes

This is only the beginning of the parallels between the Essenes and Christians today. There were Essenes who believed in the Tanakh (Old Testament) who lived throughout the various cities of Israel from around the second century BC to the first century AD.[407] However, around the same time, there were also groups of Gnostics and heretics who called themselves "Essenes," much how today's Christianity includes groups of New Agers who call themselves "Christians" but who do not in fact adhere to the tenets of authentic Christian faith. Throughout history, the Essenes have had other heretical groups take on their name as well.

Even within the Essene community in ancient Israel, at least three different factions broke off from the believing remnant. Piecing together information gathered from the works of Josephus and Hippolytus, we learn that one faction considered typically normal activities to be idol worship. Carrying coins, for example, was to be considered idol worship because he image on the coin was considered a "graven image" such as what is referenced in Exodus 20:4.[408] A modern example of this might be those who claim decorating a Christmas tree is actually a form of idol worship and no Christian should take part in the holiday celebrations and traditions.

A second faction of Essenes was violently obsessed with bringing Christian believers back under the Law of Moses, especially regarding the rite of circumcision, even to the point of slaughtering those who refused. This would be comparable to modern-day, hyper-Hebrew-roots believers who teach that Christians must submit to the Law of Moses to be saved, though admittedly in America, this group hasn't yet gone to the extreme of putting to death those who don't.

The third faction of Essenes was very careful about not calling anyone "lord," even while under torture or threat of death. At first this sounds reasonable, as we shouldn't equate any person with our Lord. However, at the time, the word "lord" was just a title, like "king" or "prince." The belief was that even calling a person who held the title of "lord" would offend God, thereby putting a heightened emphasis on the importance of names and titles. It is similar to those called "sacred-namers" today who insist that we must pronounce Jesus' Hebrew name perfectly or He won't hear our prayer. Further, they believe we must never call someone by the title "rabbi." It is interesting that the Essenes were dealing with very similar offshoots from their believing remnant that we're dealing with today.

On top of that, there were other divisions amongst the Essenes as well during those ancient days. Some groups abstained from marriage and others were married.[409]

Anyone could define all of Essenes by any one of these groups. This is why some people say "Essenes were celibate," "Essenes were mystics," or "Essenes were vegetarians." Any of these claims could be true, but not all are true of the entire group. Similarly, we could make any number of generalized claims about Christians, some of which might be true about certain groups of people calling themselves Christians, but none of which are probably true about *all* Christians. Therefore, for sake of clarity, when Essenes are discussed throughout the rest of this chapter, we're talking about the remnant of believing Essenes who did not fall into these heretical factions.

THE ESSENE CALENDAR

The first-century Essenes had a much different calendar than the one used by the Pharisees and Sadducees. In fact, according to Essene writing, the Pharisees were using a corrupt pagan lunar calendar, and the Essenes preserved the original solar calendar that God gave Adam. Even more astonishing, this was prophesied in the Dead Sea Scrolls! The Book of Jubilees, which was kept by the Essenes in Qumran, states:

> And there will be those who will make observations of the moon, for this one (the moon) corrupts the stated times and comes out earlier each year by ten days. And in this way they will corrupt the years and will observe a wrong day as the day of testimony and

a corrupted festival day, and every one will mix holy days with unclean ones and unclean with holy; for they will err as to months and sabbaths and festivals and jubilees. (Jubilees 6:34–35)

This corrupted calendar of the Pharisees would become the Hillel II calendar in the middle of the third century, which is what modern Judaism uses today.[410] The Essene calendar, however, is a bit more difficult to figure out, as much that was known about it in ancient times was lost, only to be rediscovered in the 1990s. Dr. Ken Johnson has done some amazing work with the Dead Sea Scrolls in an effort to restore the Essene calendar.[411] What he has turned up is nothing short of amazing.

The Essene calendar is based on the seven-day week. Saturday is still the Sabbath, making Sunday the first, Monday the second, and so on. Interestingly, because the sun, moon, and stars were created on the fourth day, the Essene calendar has the beginning of every year start on a Wednesday. This emphasis on the fourth day continued even in the early Church, as evidenced by some of the writings of the Church Father credited with writing the first commentary on the book of Revelation, Victorinus of Pettau, who wrote:

Victorinus, On the Creation of the World—"On the fourth day He made two lights in the heaven, the greater and the lesser, that the one might rule over the day, the other over the night," Genesis 1:16–17—the lights of the sun and moon and He placed the rest of the stars in heaven, that they might shine upon the earth, and by their positions distinguish the seasons, and years, and months, and days, and hours. Now is manifested the reason of the truth why the fourth day is called the Tetras, why we fast even to the ninth hour, or even to the evening, or why there should be a passing over even to the next day. Therefore this world of ours is composed of four elements—fire, water, heaven, earth. These four elements, therefore, form the quaternion of times or seasons. The sun, also, and the moon constitute throughout the space of the year four seasons—of spring, summer, autumn, winter; and these seasons make a quaternion. And to proceed further still from that principle, lo, there are four living creatures before God's throne, four Gospels, four rivers flowing in paradise; Genesis 2:10 four generations of people from Adam to Noah, from Noah to Abraham, from Abraham to Moses, from Moses to Christ the Lord, the Son of God; and four living creatures, viz., a man, a calf, a lion, an eagle; and four rivers, the Pison, the Gihon, the Tigris, and the Euphrates. The man Christ Jesus, the originator of these things whereof we have above spoken, was taken prisoner by wicked hands, by a quaternion of soldiers. Therefore on account of His captivity by a quaternion, on account of the majesty of His works—that the seasons also, wholesome to humanity, joyful for the harvests, tranquil for the tempests, may roll on—therefore we make the fourth day a station or a supernumerary fast.[412]

The Essene calendar is based on a 364-day year that begins on the spring equinox (when there is an equal amount of day and night). It is also set up so that everything comes out the same every year, because 364 days mean the year is exactly fifty-two weeks with no leftover days (52 x 7 = 364). For example, Passover is always on the 14th of the Hebrew month Nisan, which is always on a Tuesday. By contrast, the Pharisee and even our Gregorian calendars are imperfect, as we can't pinpoint down to the day when a holiday will occur. We can know Christmas is on December 25, of course, but every year, the day itself might change. For example, in 1998, Christmas Day was on a Friday, while in 2014 it was on a Thursday. Every year is different. There is even a reference to the 364-day year starting on the spring equinox in the Book of Enoch, which was found among the Dead Sea Scrolls:

Enoch 72:32b—…and the night is equal to the day and the year is exactly as to its days three hundred and sixty four.

Leap years on the Essene calendar are handled differently as well. Our Gregorian calendar includes 365 days per year, which generally means that every four years we add an extra "leap" day.[413] The modern Jewish calendar has only 354 days per year, meaning that once about every three years, a "leap" month is added. The Essene calendar, however, maintains the Sabbath cycle, meaning that when the calendar becomes seven days "off," a "leap" week is added. This keeps all of the Sabbaths in sync—a very important practice for the rituals of priests.

The Essene calendar is also based around the prophetic year of 360 days, such as what is used in the books of Daniel and Revelation.[414] However, to compensate for the fact that an actual earth year is longer than 360 literal days, the Essenes added four extra days called *tekufahs*. A *tekufah* was always on the two solstices and the two equinoxes of every year.[415] These were days considered outside of the calendar, so while the new year would technically begin on the spring equinox (*Tekufah Nisan,*) on a Tuesday, this day isn't considered the first calendar day of the year; *tekufahs* are more like place markers, or dividers, of the four seasons. This is why the first day of the year is actually the day after *Tekufah Nisan*, which would be Wednesday. The Essene calendar has twelve months of thirty days. Every season (spring, summer, winter, and fall) is ninety days long. A *tekufah* day splits each ninety-day season from the following one. Every year, there is a *Tekufah Nisan* (spring equinox) followed by a ninety-day period, then a *Tekufah Tammuz* (summer solstice), followed by another ninety-day period, then a *Tekufah Tishrei* (fall equinox), followed by a third ninety-day period, then lastly, a *Tekufah Tevet* (winter solstice) followed by the final ninety-day period before the start of the next year.[416]

AGES OF HUMAN HISTORY

The Essenes also had an understanding of the total number of years of human history, from Creation to the time of the establishment of the new heavens and new earth, and how this long period is to be divided. The totality of human history, according to the Essenes, is to be seven thousand years from the creation of Adam. For example, we learn from Genesis chapter 5 that Adam was 130 years old when his son Seth was born. For this way of figuring time in years, it doesn't matter how long Adam was in the Garden of Eden, how old he was when he and Eve rebelled, how old they were when they were kicked out of the Garden, etc. For our purposes here, what matters is that we know Adam was 130 years old when Seth was born. Therefore, according to Essene understanding, Seth was born in the year 130 AM (for *anno mundi,* "the year of the world").[417] Instead of having the BC/AD system we currently use, the Essenes counted their years from Creation forward. With careful calculations, and working on the assumptions that the AM calendar hasn't been tampered with over time and that certain biblical, extrabiblical, and historical data likewise hasn't changed, we can determine the date of Creation, which would be the year 1 AM (which, technically, would be a year after Creation, since we name years based on how much time has already passed and not on what year is starting; for example, a baby is considered to be one year old a full year *after* birth rather on the day of birth. "Year 1"), would correspond to our year 3926–3925 BC (depending on the month and how we are counting the years).[418]

The seven thousand years of human history were split into three periods of two thousand years and one final period of one thousand years called "ages." This final one thousand years was seen as the ultimate Sabbath. Each age was split into periods of five hundred years called *Onahs,* each of which was split into ten periods of fifty years called "jubilees." Each jubilee was split into seven periods of seven years, called *shemitahs,* and one additional "jubilee" year. Therefore, according to the Essenes, all time is understood as subsets:

- A year is 364 days.
- A *shemitah* is seven years.
- A jubilee is seven *shemitahs* plus one year, or fifty years.
- An *onah* is ten jubilees, or five hundred years.
- A millennium is two *onahs,* or twenty jubilees, or one thousand years.

- An age is two millennia, or four *onahs*, or forty jubilees, or two thousand years.
- The last age is a half-length Sabbath, or one millennium, or two *onahs*, or twenty jubilees, or one thousand years.
- All of human history is four ages (technically three and one-half ages, or three ages and one millennium), or seven millennia, or fourteen *onahs*, or 140 jubilees, or one thousand *shemitahs*, or seven thousand years.

As of the time of this writing (the end of AD 2020), we are at the end of the year 5945 AM, meaning that, in a little more than four years, we will be entering the final jubilee of our current age.

We find additional information about these ages by tying together some ancient writings by historians and Church Fathers, as well as in the Dead Sea Scrolls and the Bible. An ancient tradition recorded in a Jewish text called *Tanna Devei Eliyahu* is thought to have been written between the third and tenth centuries AD. When reading through this work, it is clear that revisions have been added throughout the centuries; however, it seems to preserve a tradition of the general understanding of ages. It reads:

> It was taught in the school of Elijah: The world will endure six thousand years: two thousand desolation, two thousand Torah, two thousand the messianic age, but because of our many sins some of [those final two thousand years] have already passed.[419]

Of course, this being a Jewish source and not a Christian one that would recognize that the Messiah has already come (teaching instead that, because of the sins of Israel, God decided not to allow the Messiah to come when He was expected), we need help from the Dead Sea Scrolls and Church Fathers to recognize what these ages are and what happened during them.

The first age was called the Age of Confusion or the Age of Chaos, and lasted from Creation to the call of Abraham (the first set of two thousand years, or 1 AM–2000 AM). The second age was the Age of Torah, lasting from the time of Abraham to the end of the sacrificial system in AD 75 (2000 AM–4000 AM). The third age is called the Age of Grace, which starts in AD 75 and ends in AD 2075 (4000 AM–6000 AM). Finally, the last age is the Messianic Kingdom, or Kingdom Age, lasting from AD 2075–AD 3075 (6000 AM–7000 AM).

The Church Fathers continued this tradition in their writings. The Epistle of Barnabas, written between AD 70 and AD 132, says:

> Give heed, children, what this meaneth; He ended in six days. He meaneth this, that in six thousand years the Lord shall bring all things to an end; for the day with Him signifyeth a thousand years; and this He himself beareth me witness, saying; Behold, the day of the Lord shall be as a thousand years. Therefore, children, in six days, that is in six thousand years, everything shall come to an end. And He rested on the seventh day. this He meaneth; when His Son shall come, and shall abolish the time of the Lawless One, and shall judge the ungodly, and shall change the sun and the moon and the stars, then shall he truly rest on the seventh day. (Barnabas 15:4–5)[420]

Irenaeus, a Greek bishop who studied under Polycarp, the last living connection to the Apostles,[421] wrote:

> For in as many days as this world was made, in so many thousand years shall it be concluded. And for this reason the Scripture says: "Thus the heaven and the earth were finished, and all their adornment. And God brought to a conclusion upon the sixth day the works that He had made; and God rested upon the seventh day from all His works." Genesis 2:2 This is an account of the things formerly created, as also it is a prophecy of what is to come. For the day of the Lord is as a thousand years; 2 Peter 3:8 and in six days created things were completed: it is evident, therefore,

that they will come to an end at the sixth thousand year. (*Against Heresies*, Book 5, 28:3)

Victorinus of Pettau, who wrote the oldest known commentary on the book of Revelation around AD 260, wrote:

He says, the thousand years should be completed, that is, what is left of the sixth day...which subsists for a thousand years. (Commentary on Revelation, 20:1–3)

Several other Church Fathers expressed a belief in the same seven thousand-year period of human history—past, present, and future. However, even earlier than the days of the Church Fathers, we find the Essene calendar referenced in the Dead Sea Scrolls, even in documents that were unique to the Essenes and were never included in the biblical canon.

The Essenes had a surprisingly large number of prophetic predictions in the Dead Sea Scrolls relating to the coming Messiah. They knew He would be God incarnate, die for our sins in AD 32, and initiate the coming Age of Grace. Modern scholarship says no one knows what happened to the Essenes; it seems they just vanished one day: "The Essenes disappear from the historical record after the first century C.E."[422]

However, when we understand what they believed and what they were looking forward to, what happened to them is obvious. The believing remnant of Essenes who did not fall into heretical factions were expecting the Messiah. When Jesus came, died, resurrected, and ascended to heaven, the Essenes became Christians and went out to preach the Gospel to the world. They became a part of those of us who are Christians!

To show what the Essenes were looking for in the Messiah within the context of their calendar and understanding of ages, we can look at some of their writings that still exists today. An interesting document called 11QMelchizedek found among the Dead Sea Scroll in the Qumran caves is believed to have been written around a century before the birth of Jesus Christ, at the latest.[423] It accurately predicts the arrival and death of the coming Messiah, right down to the exact year, and uses the Essene calendar and understanding of the ages of human history to explain it:

> And as for what he said: (Lev 25:13—In [this] year of jubilee, [you shall return, each one, to his respective property), concerning it he said: (Deut 15:2—Th]is is [the manner of the release:] every creditor shall release what he lent [to his neighbor. He shall not coerce his neighbor or his brother, for it has been proclaimed] a release for G[od) Its interpretation] for the last days refers to the captives, who...and whose teachers have been hidden and kept secret, and from the inheritance of Melchizedek, fo[r...]...and they are the inherita[nce of Melchize]dek, who will make them return. And liberty will be proclaimed for them, to free them from [the debt of] all their iniquities. And this [wil]l [happen] in the first week of the jubilee which follows the nine jubilees. And the d[ay of aton]ement is the e[nd of] the tenth [ju]bilee in which atonement shall be made for all the sons of [light and] for the men [of] the lord of Mel[chi]zedek. over [the]m... accor[ding to] a[ll] their [wor]ks, for it is the time for the (year of grace) of Melchizedek, and of [his] arm[ies, the nat]ion of the holy ones of God, of the rule of judgment, as is written about him in the songs of David, who said: (Ps 82:1—Elohim will [st]and in the assem[bly of God,] in the midst of the gods he judges). And about him he sai[d: (Ps 82:2—How long will you] judge unjustly and show part[lity] to the wicked? [Se]lah).[424] (11QMelchizedek, Col. 2, 2–11)

That might be a bit difficult to read, but it's written that way because these texts were found in fragments and had to be reconstructed over time. That aside, what we learn here is stunningly accurate and comes across as incredibly Christian, even though it was written no later than 100 BC. We first learn that, according to the writer of this text, the Law of Moses in Leviticus and Deuteronomy points to the coming Messiah. The biblical passages that are quoted are interpreted as having to do with

the last days, when the Messiah will free the captives from the debt of
their iniquities—or, in other words, will forgive sinners of their sins. It
says this will happen in the first week (seven years) of the jubilee (again, a
fifty-year period) that follows the nine jubilees. So, once we have passed
nine jubilees, in the first week of the tenth jubilee, that's when this is supposed to happen. Remember, there are ten jubilees to a five hundred *onahs*
cycle, so they are talking about the *onah* they're currently in. Additionally,
they were in the final *onah* of their age, so this tenth jubilee would have
been the final jubilee of their age. When we use their calendar (keeping in
mind that we already calculated the beginning of Creation to 3926 BC,[425]
meaning the beginning of their age would have been in 1926 BC), we
find out their age would conclude in AD 75. This means the final jubilee
of their age (the tenth jubilee, or "the jubilee which follows the nine jubilees") began in AD 25. Now we only have to add the "first week," which
is a week of years, or a *shemitah*, and we arrive at AD 32. Did something
happen in AD 32 that resulted in the sins of humanity being forgiven? Of
course—the death of Jesus Christ! Even more, it goes on to say that at the
end of the tenth jubilee, the "year" (or "Age") of Grace will begin, and it
even connects the Messiah with Elohim, who judges in the assembly of
God (or the Divine Council, for those who are familiar with the work of
Dr. Michael Heiser).[426, 427] The true, believing Essenes knew that the Messiah would be God incarnate, coming to forgive the sins of the repentant
by dying and initiating a final Age of Grace before His triumphal return
that begins the millennial reign!

Lastly, it becomes obvious the apostles and even Jesus Himself held to
this understanding of ages. This context can help us make sense of passages that are often misunderstood and become the object of disputes—
sometimes animosity—among believers:

> Now as He sat on the Mount of Olives, the disciples came to
> Him privately, saying, "Tell us, when will these things be? And
> what will be the sign of Your coming, and of the end of the age?"
> (Matthew 24:3)

But, beloved, do not forget this one thing, that with the Lord one day is as a thousand years, and a thousand years as one day. (2 Peter 3:8)

The enemy who sowed them is the devil, the harvest is the end of the age, and the reapers are the angels. Therefore as the tares are gathered and burned in the fire, so it will be at the end of this age. (Matthew 13:39–40)

So it will be at the end of the age. The angels will come forth, separate the wicked from among the just. (Matthew 13:49)

Go, therefore and make disciples of all the nations, baptizing them in the name of the Father and of the Son and of the Holy Spirit, teaching them to observe all things that I have commanded you; and lo, I am with you always, even to the end of the age. Amen. (Matthew 28:19—20)

He then would have had to suffer often since the foundation of the world; but now, once at the end of the ages, He has appeared to put away sin by the sacrifice of Himself. (Hebrews 9:26)

It is interesting to read through these with the question in mind: Are they talking about the end of their age, the end of our age, or the end of all ages? One passage that talks about the transition from the previous Age of Torah to our Age of Grace can be found in the letters of Paul:

Now these things became our examples, to the intent that we should not lust after evil things as they also lusted. And do not become idolaters as were some of them. As it is written, "The people sat down to eat and drink, and rose up to play." Nor let us commit sexual immorality, as some of them did, and in one day twenty-three thousand fell; nor let us tempt Christ, as some

of them also tempted, and were destroyed by serpents; nor complain, as some of them also complained, and were destroyed by the
destroyer. Now all these things happened to them as examples,
and they were written for our admonition, upon whom the ends
of the ages have come. (1 Corinthians 10:6–11)

In his letter, Paul states that what happened to those who didn't obey
God was an example and a warning to those for who are alive when the
end of ages has come. Paul was writing from his own perspective; he was
a convert to Christianity who was originally from the end of the Age of
Torah and who was about to enter into the Age of Grace. We, as Christians today, find ourselves in a position similar to that of Paul. If the Essene calendar is correct, we are Christians living in the end of the Age of
Grace, and we are getting ready to see the return of our Lord Jesus Christ,
who will usher in the final Kingdom Age.

THE FINAL JUBILEE OF MAN: 2025–2075

What can we expect in coming days? In just around four short years,
according to the Essenes, we will be entering the final jubilee of our age,
the final age before the return of Christ. Of course, we don't want to
become overly excited and begin setting definite dates. Speculation and
wondering "what if" is one thing, but we can fall into serious error if we
begin setting specific dates for events like the Rapture of the Church. In
fact, Jesus tell us this Himself:

But of that day and hour no one knows, not even the angels in
heaven, nor the Son, but only the Father. Take heed, watch and pray;
for you do not know when the time is. It is like a man going to a far
country, who left his house and gave authority to his servants, and
to each his work, and commanded the doorkeeper to watch. Watch
therefore, for you do not know when the master of the house is coming—in the evening, at midnight, at the crowing of the rooster, or

in the morning—lest, coming suddenly, he find you sleeping. And what I say to you, I say to all: Watch! (Mark 13:32–37)

There has been much discussion about what Jesus is referring to here. Some say this describes the Rapture, while others say it's a reference to the day Jesus returns to earth. However, the message in this passage is that this "time" is a mystery; this "day and hour" cannot be known. The angels in heaven haven't figured it out, and neither has Jesus Himself; only the Father knows the timing of these events. The books of Revelation and Daniel tell us how many days after certain events (such as the abomination of desolation) we can expect to pass before we see the end of the Great Tribulation and the return of Jesus. Also, with the ancients' understanding of ages, it would seem that they would be able to assume that Jesus would be returning in AD 2075 (though, as we will see a bit later, it could be quite a bit sooner than that). It is true, from the perspective of those living during the time of Jesus, and even from our perspective today, that we wouldn't be able to perfectly calculate the day or hour Jesus will return, because we don't know when the Antichrist will come on the scene and initiate the seven-year Tribulation with the confirmation of the "covenant with many." However, after that covenant is confirmed, as foretold by the prophet Daniel, and certainly after the abomination of desolation that Jesus mentioned, we should be able to determine exactly when to expect Jesus; at that point, it will be obvious. Therefore, if this passage is teaching of the physical return of Jesus to planet earth, some have taken the position that there will be a point in the future when this verse won't be true anymore, rendering void the teaching about being watchful.

That could be true; God, of course, can certainly do anything He wishes. However, another event, it is said, could occur at *any* moment during the period between the time of the apostles to the time of Jesus' bodily return: the Rapture of the Church. For some, a more consistent interpretation of this passage would say that Jesus is speaking of the Rapture rather than the Second Coming. For those who don't like either of those options, there is a third.

When we compare this passage with a familiar one in Thessalonians, we pick up more context that helps us more clearly understand what Jesus was talking about:

> But of the times and the seasons, brethren, ye have no need that I write unto you.
>
> For yourselves know perfectly that the day of the Lord so cometh as a thief in the night.
>
> For when they shall say, Peace and safety; then sudden destruction cometh upon them, as travail upon a woman with child; and they shall not escape.
>
> But ye, brethren, are not in darkness, that that day should overtake you as a thief.
>
> Ye are all the children of light, and the children of the day: we are not of the night, nor of darkness. (1 Thessalonians 5:1–5)

Here, Paul points out the contrast between the children of light and those of darkness (which, interestingly, is a common theme throughout the Dead Sea Scrolls). The day of the Lord comes as a thief to those in darkness, but not to those in light. Paul is telling believers in Jesus that we are children of light, so that day won't take us by surprise; we should be watchful. With that, we can understand Mark 13:32–37 in the same way. Unbelievers will know neither the day nor the hour of the day of the Lord; it will come as a surprise.

Now, that's not to suggest that we absolutely *can* know the day and the hour. One thing anyone who spends enough time in the study of Bible prophecy will say is that there are several possibilities. However, as time marches on and the end draws closer, our perception of the times and seasons can become more clear. We can pay attention to current events while we continue to study the Scripture and try to narrow down the possibilities. That way, once the Antichrist does confirm that covenant, believers who come to Christ during the Tribulation will have a better chance of understanding these things and preparing for them. Lastly, I must emphasize that this is not something we as believers in Christ should become dogmatic and divisive about.

Whether or not this verse is talking about the Rapture, most Christians who believe in any kind of Rapture (whether it's pre-, mid-, or post-Tribulation) agree that we cannot know its timing with any certainty. The best we can do is speculate and wonder. I absolutely plan on doing just that here, but it's important to keep in mind that I'm not saying it absolutely will play out this way. I'm only offering a possibility. Further, if the past speculations of many other researchers concerning the timing of the Rapture are any indication, the safest bet is to assume that the timeline I'm going to provide as a possible scenario of how it all could pan out is wrong. But, there is always that part of us that asks "what if?"

THE FINAL JUBILEE OF THE PREVIOUS AGE

The Essene calendar absolutely does put an exact year as being the end of one age and the beginning of the next; however, prophetic events that are supposed to happen around this time don't always work out so precisely. In fact, the beginning of one age tends to bleed into the end of the previous. This "bleeding through" of ages tends to occur within the final jubilee of an age. It's almost as if the old age is winding down, getting tired, and the new age is so excited to begin, it begins preparing a bit earlier than its exact starting date.

We can think of this in terms of a relay race, in which team members cover equal distances in a race where each takes a turn carrying and then handing off a baton. During that handing-off period, at the end of one runner's time and the beginning of the next, both runners are actually running together, at the same time, in a marked exchange zone. Ages work exactly like that. The marked exchange zone of ages is the final jubilee of the age that is about to end. In AD 2025, if the Essene calendar is correct, we will enter the marked exchange zone of our age and the Kingdom Age; what an exciting time to be alive!

We see many examples of this when we consider how the Age of

Torah ended and the Age of Grace began between the AD years 25 and AD 75. As Christians, of course, we agree that the Church really started with Jesus. Some would say it began at His birth, because there was finally a Messiah on earth for people to accept. Others would say the Church originated at the start of, or possibly sometime during, His three and a half years of ministry on earth. Still others still would say it started at His death, or His resurrection, or His ascension, or at Pentecost with the indwelling of the Holy Spirit. All of these events have three things in common: First, all contributed to formation of the Church; second, all were the main fulfillments of prophecies those living in that age were looking for; and third, all occurred before the technical end of the age in AD 75.

We must remember that when we say that an age begins on a certain year, we are talking about an exact number; by the time of this exact year, everything that needs to be in place for the operation of the next age should be in place. Here's an illustration of how that works. Let's say we're going to have a birthday party at three o'clock this Friday afternoon, and there's going to be cake, presents, games, and live performances. By that exact time on that exact date, every aspect of the party will already be in place. On Tuesday, I might hire the live performers. Wednesday, I could start buying all the presents. When Thursday rolls around, I can have all the games delivered, and at noon on Friday I can pick up the cake. Finally, between one o'clock and two forty-five on Friday afternoon, I might make sure all of the components of the party are together and go through my final checklist before guests start arriving. Technically, as stated on the invitation, the party starts at three o'clock on Friday afternoon, but many of the elements of the party were changing and coming to pass since the prior Tuesday. Much is the same with ages: By AD 75, everything should have been in place, without any event remaining to be completed before the Church Age could officially begin. The Messiah had to be born, teach, die, resurrect, and ascend. The Holy Spirit had to come, the Temple in Jerusalem had to be destroyed, and the sacrificial system had to be finally done away with. Then, and only then, when all of those prophecies were fulfilled, could the Age of Grace (Church Age) officially begin.

This might lead us to wonder what the final event was that occurred in AD 75. We all have at least a basic understanding of the Temple in Jerusalem being destroyed in 70 AD, but what occurred five years later? There's some really interesting history here. While the destruction of the Jerusalem Temple definitely dealt a hard blow to the sacrificial system of the Pharisees, it didn't completely demolish it. There was actually another Jewish Temple in Egypt that was destroyed by the Romans in AD 73.[428] Then, the final nail in the coffin of the Pharisaical sacrificial system was hammered in when a new type of Sanhedrin was established[429] in Yavneh that decided prayer, rather than sacrifice, was sufficient.[430] This reestablishment was the beginning of modern rabbinic Judaism. According to some sources, the last president of the old Sanhedrin (Rabban Yochanan ben Zakkai) died[431] and the first president of the new, reestablished Sanhedrin (Gamliel II of Yavneh) officially began his duties in exactly AD 75.[432, 433] This means by AD 75, everything was in place for the Age of Grace to officially begin.

We can assume that the same would be true for the end of our Age of Grace. If the Essene calendar is correct, by AD 2075, everything should be in place for the millennial reign of Christ to begin. This mean all of the prophecies should already be fulfilled—not only everything having to do with the seven-year Tribulation (Daniel 9:24), but also the return of Jesus (Revelation 19:11); the judgment of the Antichrist, the False Pphet, and everyone who took the mark of the Beast (Revelation 19:20); the binding of Satan in the abyss (Revelation 20:2); the rewards of the righteous being received (1 Corinthians 3:12–15; Revelation 20:4); and the establishment of Jesus' rule in Jerusalem (Jeremiah 3:17; Zechariah 14:9); the placement of international politics during this time (Zechariah 14:16–19); and anything else, so that in 2075, everything will be in order for the Kingdom Age to begin without any pieces left to be put into place…except enjoy the next thousand years.

Numerous prophecies still must be fulfilled prior to the Kingdom Age; however, many of them concern the seven-year Tribulation period. We also have a possible Rapture and the events after the Tribulation to deal with, and it is impossible to know exactly where to place these happenings along the prophetic timeline. However, we can look for patterns shown to us from the end of the previous Age of Torah. If Jesus came the first time relatively early in the final jubilee of the Age of Torah, is it reasonable to assume that He might return early in the final jubilee of our Age of Grace?

ENOCH'S NINTH WEEK

Another pretty amazing piece of evidence comes in the form of an ancient prophecy from the Book of Enoch, which was found among the Dead Sea Scrolls. In it, the writer organizes all of human history (seven thousand years) into ten "weeks," with each week being seven hundred years and each day being one hundred years. The whole prophecy would be worth studying because it is amazingly accurate, but for our purposes here, we focus on week nine which, if we do the math, involves our time today. About this period, the Ethiopic version of the Book of Enoch states:

> And after that, in the ninth week, The righteous judgement shall be revealed to the whole world, And all the works of the godless shall vanish from all the earth, And the world shall be written down for destruction. And all mankind shall look to the path of uprightness. (Enoch 91:14)

It is probably obvious that this is referring to the return of the Messiah, Jesus Christ. Of particular note, though, is that this "week" occurs between the years AD 1675 and AD 2375. The exact midpoint of week nine (half of 700 is 350, so 350 years after 1675) is 2025! This is, as we saw earlier, the beginning of the final jubilee of our Age of Grace before the Kingdom Age will begin. Is it coincidence that this halfway point falls at the beginning of the final jubilee of our age? Or, could it be that Enoch's ninth week is pointing exactly to the year 2025 by supreme design?

A POSSIBLE END-TIMES TIMELINE

We can piece together a few bits of information and speculate about a possible early return of Jesus to use as an example of how the rest of end-times prophecy could be fulfilled. In looking at this timeline, keep in mind that this is only hypothetical and involves many of assumptions (again, such as presuming the Essene calendar to be correct and not tampered with, and that we understand it correctly and have made accurate calculations, etc.). It is at best a guess, and most likely an incorrect one. We must keep in mind that literally 100 percent of those who have predicted specific dates for the Rapture and the beginning of the Tribulation have been wrong. Therefore, I emphasize, what is presented next to close out this chapter isn't a prediction, only a possibility.

We believe the final jubilee of our age begins in AD 2025. Interestingly enough, NASA has also predicted three dates when the asteroid Apophis will fly by the earth. These dates are in the spring of the years 2029, 2036, and 2068.[434] A possible connection between the Apophis asteroid and the Wormwood prophecy of the book of Revelation has also been well established in the past.[435] It is also believed that an Apophis/Wormwood asteroid strike could tie some of the trumpet judgments of Revelation into a chain reaction caused by a single event and could possibly occur during the middle of the seven-year Tribulation.[436] Lastly, while NASA is saying that a 2029 strike of Apophis is extremely unlikely, it has recently admitted to an unexpected acceleration of the asteroid due to what's called the "Yarkovsky effect."[437] NASA is saying that a 2068 strike is more likely sure to this acceleration, but is still maintaining that a 2029 event is unlikely. However, we don't know what could change within the next few years.

Let's say that the Apophis asteroid does strike earth on Friday, April 13, 2029 (the date NASA currently predicts Apophis to be closest to the earth), and it is, in fact, the fulfillment of the Wormwood prophecy. Amazingly, when we subtract three and a half years from the spring of 2029, we arrive at the time of Rosh Hashanah, or the Feast of Trumpets, in 2025.

Rosh Hashanah is a two-day celebration commonly associated with the Rapture of the Church. This is especially interesting when considering Jesus' words about not knowing the day or the hour of His return; if the Rapture was to take place on the Feast of Trumpets, there would be no way to know which exact day or hour, since the celebration takes place over the course of two days.

According to the Essene calendar, the Feast of Trumpets in 2025 occurs on September 16–17. We also know the Rapture is not the event that officially starts the seven-year Tribulation, as the book of Daniel states:

> Then he shall confirm a covenant with many for one week. (Daniel 9:27a)

This is referring to a week of years (or a *shemitah*)—a seven-year period. This confirmation of the covenant with many is what officially begins the seven-year Tribulation.

If we assume the middle of the Tribulation is April 13, 2029, we can subtract 1,260 days (three and a half years, or forty-two months, or "time, times, and half a time" according to biblical prophecy as given in the books of Daniel and Revelation) and arrive at November 1, 2025, as the date when the Antichrist confirms the covenant. Interestingly, on the Essene calendar, this date is Cheshvan 16, which is only one day before Cheshvan 17—the date when the Flood of Noah began. In Noah's time, Cheshvan 16 was the final date the rebellious inhabitants of the world lived in blissful ignorance, believing they were safe and at peace. Remember, 1 Thessalonians 5:3 states:

> While people are saying, "There is peace and security," then sudden destruction will come upon them as labor pains come upon a pregnant woman, and they will not escape.

After that confirmation of the covenant, the middle of the Tribulation comes.

If we were to assume Apophis is Wormwood and strikes on April 13, 2029, and this is the middle of the Tribulation, we find some interesting facts about this day. First, according to the Essene calendar, April 13, 2029, is ten days after Passover (Nisan 14) on the Hebrew date Nisan 24. According to Daniel 10:4–5, the prophet Daniel was visited by the angel on Nisan 24.[438] Also, in 1312 BC on Nisan 14, a very interesting thing happened to the children of Israel after they crossed the Red Sea:[439]

> So Moses brought Israel from the Red Sea; then they went out into the Wilderness of Shur. And they went three days in the wilderness and found no water. Now when they came to Marah, they could not drink the waters of Marah, for they were bitter. Therefore the name of it was called Marah. (Exodus 15:22–23)

We can compare this with the description of Wormwood in the book of Revelation:

> Then the third angel sounded: And a great star fell from heaven, burning like a torch, and it fell on a third of the rivers and on the springs of water. The name of the star is Wormwood. A third of the waters became wormwood, and many men died from the water, because it was made bitter. (Revelation 8:10–11)

Both passages mention the number three and, most astonishingly, both mention bitter water. Also, in the passage of Exodus, if the Israelites were traveling for three days without water, sometime after the three days but before the fourth (around the halfway point, perhaps) is when they found the bitter water. Could it be that the children of Israel found the bitter water three and a half (or so) days after their Exodus from Egypt just as the world finds their bitter water three and a half (or so) years after the Church makes its exodus from the world in the Rapture?

If we add 1,260 days (as stated in the book of Daniel) to April 13, 2029, we come right to September 24, 2032, which, on the Essene calendar, is the Day of Atonement. Jesus died in AD 32 and fulfilled all of the Spring Feasts.[440] Wouldn't it be interesting if Jesus came back, right where He left off—only exactly two thousand years later, to fulfill the Fall Feasts?

If we continue with this line of thinking, Daniel's prophecy also gives us 1,290 days and 1,335 days from the middle of the Tribulation that we have to deal with. Thus, 1,290 days after April 13, 2029, is October 24, 2032, which is Cheshvan 10, the day Noah entered the ark and the day before Methuselah died. This is clearly a great day of judgment from the Lord and, based on the wording of Daniel 12, could be the day the image of the Beast is removed and thrown into the lake of fire:

And from the time that the daily sacrifice is taken away, and the abomination of desolation is set up, there shall be one thousand two hundred and ninety days. (Daniel 12:11)

Next, 1,335 days are mentioned:

Blessed is he who waits, and comes to the one thousand three hundred and thirty-five days. (Daniel 12:12)

According to our timeline, 1,335 days after April 13, 2029, is December 8, 2032, the first day of Hanukkah. What's really interesting about that is Hanukkah is exactly seventy days after the Feast of Tabernacles. The Book of Maccabees says Hanukkah is actually modeled after Tabernacles and is considered a "delay" of Tabernacles.[441] Hanukkah originated as a reaction to the desecration of the Temple by Antiochus IV Epiphanes, a historical event that Jesus used to point to the future Antichrist and the abomination of desolation:

Therefore when you see the abomination of desolation spoken of by Daniel the prophet, standing in the holy place (whoever reads, let him understand), then let those who are in Judea flee to the mountains. (Matthew 24:15–16)

To put this into our timeline, we know that just before the thousand-year reign of Christ, the first resurrection occurs (Revelation 20:4–6) and this is probably when believers will receive their rewards (1 Corinthians 3:12). We also know there have been countless multitudes of believers throughout time, and we have no idea how long it will take for all to stand before Jesus to receive rewards. It's possible that this all happens in an instant; however, it seems more likely that Jesus will work within the physical dimension of time as it has been created to work, at least until the formation of the new heavens and new earth. If that's the case and Jesus returns in AD 2032, perhaps it takes just over forty years to get through every believer's meeting for rewards, for nations to beat their swords into plowshares (Isaiah 2:2–4), and for everyone left in the world to establish and learn the new way of doing things under the rule of Jesus Christ. Especially considering the massive, final, end-times battle of Armageddon, it seems reasonable to expect some time for "clean up" so that, in AD 2075, the Kingdom Age can officially begin with nothing left to be fulfilled.

Finally, we come to the end of the millennial reign in our hypothetical prophetic timeline. Remarkably, even here, we see a bit of the "bleeding over" between ages as, just before the end of the Kingdom Age, Satan is let loose to instigate another apostasy and war:

And when the thousand years are ended, Satan will be released from his prison and will come out to deceive the nations that are at the four corners of the earth, Gog and Magog, to gather them for battle; their number is like the sand of the sea. And they marched up over the broad plain of the earth and surrounded the camp of the saints and the beloved city, but fire came down from heaven and consumed them, and the devil who had deceived them was thrown into the lake of fire and sulfur where the beast and the false prophet were, and they will be tormented day and night forever and ever. (Revelation 20:7–10)

This is how the seven thousand years of creation history finally ends before the creation of the new heavens and new earth described in Revelation 21. We see a bit of the bleeding over after the millennial reign as well. Just before everything comes to a close, we see Satan let loose, then finally destroyed, and the great white throne judgment of Revelation 20:11–15 takes place. If we had to guess, and if the previous ages are any indication of how we could date these things, we should expect Satan to be released in the final jubilee of the Kingdom Age—that final fifty years, perhaps even exactly one thousand years from the day he was originally bound, which would mean he would see his release in AD 3032. If this is the case and following this pattern, we could even predict the time of the final day of creation as we know it. We should expect the final day to be mid-March, possibly on Adar 28, which is the Saturday before the New Year, or perhaps Tekufah Nisan, 3075, the day just before the first day of the New Year on the Essene calendar. It will be a Tuesday. Or, perhaps how God used every day in the first week of existence to create everything, He will use every day of the final week to pass everything away, ending on Friday, Nisan 3, 3075.

Then, presumably, when all of creation is exactly seven thousand years old, Revelation 21–22 will be fulfilled and the old heavens and earth with "pass away" (meaning be removed, die, or both) and a new heaven and earth will be perfectly created without sin, pain, or death, exactly as intended from the beginning. Finally, this strange, seven thousand-year detour we all had to take in order to find our way back to God will finally be completed and we'll be back at a new beginning, where we were always destined to be, forever.

Of course, as you will discover in the next and final chapter, there are those who have a different plan for your life—a *Secret Destiny* for you, America, and the world. And their plan was prophesied in the Holy Bible to unfold before the end of the age foreseen by the Essenes.

COUNTDOWN TO 2025, PROPHECY ON THE GREAT SEAL OF THE UNITED STATES, AND THE SECRET DESTINY OF AMERICA

8

Over a decade ago on a business trip to Washington, DC, my wife, Nita, and I, with help from a congressman, met with two members of the Scottish Rite Freemasonry who had unrestricted access to all but the most secret and highest-guarded documents of the Order. We joined one of them at the House of the Temple, the headquarters building of the Scottish Rite of Freemasonry, Southern Jurisdiction, where the Rite's Supreme Council, 33rd Degree, have their meetings, and the other at the George Washington Masonic Memorial in Alexandria, Virginia. While both men were very helpful and informative, they were evasive whenever I probed too deeply into certain areas. I suppose this is not surprising, given that Masons are sworn to secrecy under blood oaths of horrific repercussion, including having their throats slit, eyeballs pierced, tongues torn out, feet flayed, bodies hacked into pieces, and so on if they give up the wrong information. Perhaps this is why, at one point, one of the men I conferred with became visibly nervous as soon as I started asking specific questions about Masonic religious practices, which would include secret rituals that are performed in the Temple Room on the third floor at the House of the Temple, and the hidden meaning behind the name of their deity—the Great Architect of the Universe.

What most in the public do not understand is that, in spite of denial by some Masons, theirs is a religious institution with rituals and even prophetic beliefs concerning a human-transforming final world order, founded on and maintained by dozens of doctrines that can be defined by what "Masonry's greatest philosopher," Manly P. Hall, in *The Lost Keys of Freemasonry*,[442] called "the principles of mysticism and the occult rites." The reason lower-degree Masons would deny this is because the Masters of the Craft intentionally mislead them. Speaking of the first three degrees of Freemasonry, Albert Pike admitted in *Morals & Dogma*:

> The Blue Degrees are but the outer court or portico of the Temple. Part of the symbols are displayed there to the initiate, but he is intentionally misled by false interpretations. It is not intended that he shall understand them; but it is intended that he shall imagine he understands them. Their true explication is reserved for the Adepts, the Princes of Masonry.... It is well enough for the mass of those called Masons to imagine that all is contained in the Blue Degrees; and whoso attempts to undeceive them will labor in vain, and without any true reward violate his obligations as an Adept.[443]

At these lower degrees, most members of Freemasonry belong to what is maintained as a fraternal organization that simply requires belief in a "Supreme Being" while avoiding discussion of politics and religion in the lodge, using metaphors of stonemasons building Solomon's Temple to convey what they publicly describe as "a system of morality veiled in allegory and illustrated by symbols." I've known several of these type Masons, all of whom were sincere members of society who worked together in a brotherhood for common benefit and to pool resources for charitable goals. None of these lower-degree Masons with whom I have been acquainted would ever, insofar as I know, participate in a conspiracy toward a global world order in which people will be politically and spiritually enslaved. But as one former Freemason friend told me, "This is the veneer of the lower degrees that exists on the Order's public face. What is happening with at least some of the members at the 33rd level, or among the York Rite Knights Templar and the Shriners, is another matter altogether. When I was part of the brotherhood," he continued, "I watched as specific members with the correct disposition and ideology were identified, separated, groomed, and initiated into the higher degrees for reasons you *would* find corresponding with the goals of a New World Order."

Famous Freemason Foster Bailey once described how the Masons not included among this elite are unaware of an "Illuminati" presence among Master Masons, who in turn are the guardians of a secret "Plan":

> Little as it may be realised by the unthinking Mason who is interested only in the outer aspects of the Craft work, the whole fabric of Masonry may be regarded as an externalisation of that inner spiritual group whose members, down the ages, have been the Custodians of the Plan.... These Master Masons, to whom TGAOTU [The Great Architect of the Universe] has given the design and Who are familiar with the tracing board of the G.M. [Grand Master] on high, are...sometimes known as **the Illuminati** and can direct the searchlight of truth wherever its beams are needed to guide the pilgrim on his way. They are the Rishis of the oriental philosophy, the Builders of the occult tradition.[444]

Part of the carefully guarded Illuminati "Plan" Bailey referred to involves the need for each Mason to navigate the meaning behind the various rituals in order to discover the secret doctrine of Masonry involving the true identity of deity and what this means now and for the future (which is unveiled later in this chapter as reflected in the prophecy of the Great Seal of the United States). Manly Hall, who rightly called the Great Seal "the signature" of that exalted body of Masons who designed America for a "peculiar and particular purpose," described these two kinds of Masons as members of a "fraternity within a fraternity," the elect of which are dedicated to a mysterious *arcanum arcandrum* (a "sacred secret") unknown to the rest of the Order:

> Freemasonry is a fraternity within a fraternity—an outer organization concealing an inner brotherhood of the elect.
>
> …it is necessary to establish the existence of these two separate yet independent orders, the one visible and the other invisible.
>
> The visible society is a splendid camaraderie of "free and accepted" men enjoined to devote themselves to ethical, educational, fraternal, patriotic, and humanitarian concerns.
>
> The invisible society is a secret and most august fraternity whose members are dedicated to the service of a mysterious *arcanum arcandrum*.
>
> Those brethren who have essayed to write the history of their craft have not included in their disquisitions the story of that truly secret inner society which is to the body Freemasonic what the heart is to the body human.
>
> In each generation only a few are accepted into the inner sanctuary of the work…the great initiate-philosophers of Freemasonry are…masters of that secret doctrine which forms the invisible foundation of every great theological and rational institution.[445]

Among dedicatories to those who support this "invisible" secret doctrine, there is a memorial alcove in the heart of the House of the Temple called the "Pillars of Charity." Here, between two vaults on either side—one containing the exhumed remains of former Sovereign Grand Commander Albert Pike and the other containing Sovereign Grand Commander John Henry Cowles, marked by busts of each man on marble pedestals—a stained-glass window depicts the all-seeing eye above the words *Fiat Lux* emitting thirty-three beams of light downward onto the phrase *ordo ab chao* from ancient Craft Masonic doctrine, "order out of chaos."

Between meetings with the anonymous Masons who met with me during my research, I stepped into this shrine and read the names of those who are hallowed there on reflective golden inscriptions for contributing at least $1 million to advance the cause of Scottish Rite Freemasonry, including the George Bush family, whose work to initiate the New World Order is universally understood.

At the House of the Temple, like elsewhere, "The Brotherhood of Darkness" (as my late friend Dr. Stanley Monteith used to call it) intentionally hides in plain sight the occult aspirations of universalism, which ultimately will be conceived in a one-world order and one-world religion under the son of Lucifer—Apollo/Osiris/Nimrod—or, as Manly Hall put it:

> The outcome of the "secret destiny" is a World Order ruled by a King with supernatural powers. This King was descended of a divine race; that is, he belonged to the Order of the Illumined for those who come to a state of wisdom then belong to a family of heroes-perfected human beings.[446]

When Hall offered this astonishingly perceptive commentary about the future Masonic "King" who is "descended of a divine race" of "Illumined" (luciferic) "heroes-perfected" (half-man, half-god) human beings, he nailed exactly what the Watchers had done, and what the Cumaean Sibyl's Great Seal prophecy says will occur again with the second coming of Apollo/Osiris/Nimrod.

We cited the Cumaean's prophecy in chapter 1 of this book, which Manly Hall noted is reflected in the "mass of occult and Masonic symbols" on the Great Seal, which he believed only students of archaic or esoteric symbolism would be able to accurately decipher. But after years of research and meeting with high-level Freemasons, I believe I can help with this enigma. This requires that I back up a bit, as it starts with the signing of the Declaration of Independence and the authors of that historic document—John Adams, Thomas Jefferson, and Benjamin Franklin. Within one day of July 4, 1776, these three were assigned the task of serving what today we would call a steering committee task regarding the Great Seal's design—what it should ultimately communicate about the establishment of this nation, its objectives, and its destiny. Therefore, let us briefly examine the worldview and spirituality of these men to comprehend the visionary and prophetic occultism of the Great Seal (as partially discussed by Christian J. Pinto in the preface of my bestselling book *Zenith 2016*).

JOHN ADAMS AND THOMAS JEFFERSON

John Adams was America's second president and a close friend of Thomas Jefferson. Adams, Jefferson, and Franklin worked together on the first committee to design the Great Seal for the United States. While it doesn't appear that Adams was a member of any secret group, he was a Unitarian and shared views of Christianity not unlike those of Paine, Jefferson, and Franklin. He wrote the following to Thomas Jefferson in a letter dated September 3, 1816:

> I almost shudder at the thought of alluding to the most fatal example of the abuses of grief which the history of mankind has preserved—the Cross. Consider what calamities that engine of grief has produced![447]

Worse than his friend, John Adams, was Thomas Jefferson. Along with Thomas Paine (who also wrote that Jesus was a blasphemous fable and that the Bible was "scarcely anything but a history of the grossest vices and a collection of the most paltry and contemptible tales" whose "Almighty committed debauchery with a woman engaged to be married, and the belief of this debauchery is called faith), Jefferson typified last-days "scoffers, walking after their own lusts" warned about in the Bible (2 Peter

3:3, KJV). Jefferson said this about the book of Revelation in a letter to General Alexander Smyth dated January 17, 1825:

> It is between fifty and sixty years since I read it and I then considered it as merely the ravings of a maniac, no more worthy nor capable of explanation than the incoherences of our own nightly dreams.[448]

Through the rest of his letter, Jefferson made it clear to the general that he had not repented of his formerly held view. Some have tried to whitewash him because he thought Jesus could be considered a teacher of morality, but Jefferson believed the chronicle of Jesus as depicted in the Bible was an unmitigated fraud. Here is what he said in a letter to William Short dated October 31, 1819:

> The greatest of all the Reformers of the depraved religion of his own country, was Jesus of Nazareth. Abstracting what is really His from the rubbish in which it is buried, easily distinguished by its luster from the dross of his biographers, and as separable from that as the diamond from the dunghill.[449]

The above passage describes the approach Jefferson took in writing his so-called *Jefferson Bible* (properly titled *The Life and Morals of Jesus of Nazareth*). What he claimed he was attempting to do (and wrote about extensively) was to separate the "true" sayings of Jesus from the things he believed had been added to the Gospel accounts. But he did not really believe in the authority of the Bible, Old Testament or New. In a letter to John Adams—his Declaration of Independence coauthor and assistant in designing the Great Seal of the United States—he wrote on January 24, 1814:

> Where did we get the Ten Commandments? The book indeed gives them to us verbatim, but where did it get them? For itself tells us they were written by the finger of God on tables of stone,

which were destroyed by Moses.... But the whole history of these books is so defective and doubtful, that it seems vain to attempt minute inquiry into it.... We have a right to entertain much doubt what parts of them are genuine.[450]

As seen earlier, Jefferson's view of the New Testament was no better. In the same letter to John Adams, he wrote:

In the New Testament there is internal evidence that parts of it have proceeded from an extraordinary man; and that other parts are of the fabric of very inferior minds. It is as easy to separate those parts, as to pick out diamonds from dunghills.[451]

When one reads *The Jefferson Bible*, it becomes clear what Jefferson was referring to when he mentioned "dunghills." He specifically took a pair of scissors and a razor blade and cut out evidence of the divinity and Messianic assignment of Jesus from Scripture, including the virgin birth, the miracles of Christ, the Lord's resurrection, and His ascension into heaven. Because it details His Second Coming and the arrival of Antichrist, the entire book of Revelation was also omitted. These were among the things Jefferson believed came from "inferior minds" forming "dunghills." Concerning the Lord Jesus Himself, Jefferson wrote in another letter to Short on April 13, 1920:

Among the sayings and discourses imputed to Him by His biographers [authors of the Bible], I find many passages of fine imagination, correct morality, and of the most lovely benevolence; and others, again, of so much ignorance, so much absurdity, so much untruth, charlatanism and imposture.... I separate, therefore, the gold from the dross...and leave the latter to the stupidity of some, and roguery of others of His disciples. Of this band of dupes and impostors, Paul was the...first corruptor of the doctrines of Jesus.[452]

BENJAMIN FRANKLIN

One of the most influential Founding Fathers, and the only one of them to have signed all of the original founding documents (the Declaration of Independence, the Treaty of Paris, and the US Constitution) was Benjamin Franklin. Franklin was responsible for three important phases of America's development: 1) unifying the colonists in their rebellion against England; 2) philosophy concerning the rights of mankind; and 3) facilitating the American Revolution by publishing the writings of Thomas Paine. To Sir Walter Isaacson, Benjamin Franklin was "the most accomplished American of his age and the most influential in inventing the type of society America would become."[453]

Ben Franklin was, without question, deeply involved in Freemasonry and in other secret societies. He belonged to secret groups in the three countries involved in the War of Independence: America, France, and England. He was master of the Masonic Lodge of Philadelphia; over in France, he was master of the Nine Sisters Lodge, from which sprang the French Revolution. In England, he joined a rakish political group founded by Sir Francis Dashwood (member of Parliament, advisor to King George III) called the "Monks of Medmenham Abbey," otherwise known as the "Hellfire Club." This eighteenth-century group is described as follows:

> The Hellfire Club was an exclusive, English club that met sporadically during the mid-eighteenth century. Its purpose, at best, was to mock traditional religion and conduct orgies. At worst, it involved the indulgence of satanic rites and sacrifices. The club to which Franklin belonged was established by Francis Dashwood, a member of Parliament and friend of Franklin. The club, which consisted of "The Superior Order" of twelve members, allegedly took part in basic forms of satanic worship. In addition to taking part in the occult, orgies and parties with prostitutes were also said to be the norm.[454]

But it could have been much darker than that. On February 11, 1998, the *Sunday Times* reported that ten bodies were dug up from beneath Benjamin Franklin's home at 36 Craven Street in London. The bodies were of four adults and six children. They were discovered during a costly renovation of Franklin's former home. The *Times* reported:

> Initial estimates are that the bones are about two hundred years old and were buried at the time Franklin was living in the house, which was his home from 1757 to 1762 and from 1764 to 1775. Most of the bones show signs of having been dissected, sawn or cut. One skull has been drilled with several holes.[455]

Later reports from the Benjamin Franklin house reveal that not only human but *animal* remains as well were found, that appeared to be blackened or charred, as if by fire. Needless to say, this evidence has caused a number of researchers to suggest that Franklin's involvement with the Hellfire Club may have been connected with Satanists performing ritual killings of both humans and animals.

ONE SEAL TO RULE OVER THEM ALL

With the above brief history of the men tasked with designing the Great Seal in mind, it is important to note that besides Benjamin Franklin, as many as forty-four of the fifty-six signers of the Declaration of Independence were also Freemasons. Numerous US presidents were part of the Craft as well, including Washington, Monroe, Jackson, Polk, Buchanan, A. Johnson, Garfield, McKinley, T. Roosevelt, Taft, Harding, F. Roosevelt, Truman, L. B. Johnson, and Ford, not to mention additional elites in the Order such as Paul Revere, Edmund Burke, John Hancock, and many more.

Besides the Great Seal, the question of whether the Order of Freemasons engineered the entire US city named after America's first president according to an occult grand design is something that a growing body of historians and researchers are admitting. David Ovason, who became a Mason after writing *The Secret Architecture of our Nation's Capital: The Masons and the Building of Washington, D.C.*, argues effectively that the city's layout intentionally incorporated the esoteric belief system of Freemasonry, especially as it involved astrologically aligning the capital with the constellation Virgo (Isis). In 1793, when George Washington sanctioned the laying of the capitol building's cornerstone, he did so wearing a Masonic apron emblazoned with the brotherhood's symbols. For occult expert Manly P. Hall, this made perfect sense. "Was Francis Bacon's vision of the 'New Atlantis' a prophetic dream of the great civilization, which was so soon to rise upon the soil of the New World?" he asked in *The Secret Teachings of All Ages.* "It cannot be doubted that the secret societies...conspired to establish [such] upon the American continent."

Hall's "New Atlantis" reference was based on a utopian scheme that the European secret societies of the 1600–1700s were infatuated with wherein an "occult democracy" would be established based on men participating with ancient Greco-Roman gods to earn their favor, protection, and power, in the establishment of a government dedicated to *their* second coming at the dawn of a new Golden Age (*Novus Ordo Seclorum*).

Hall continued that historical incidents in the early development of the United States clearly bore "the influence of that secret body, which has so long guided the destinies of peoples and religions. By them nations are created as vehicles for the promulgation of ideals, and while nations are true to these ideals they survive; when they vary from them, they vanish like the Atlantis of old which had ceased to 'know the gods.'"[456]

Involvement by Freemasons for the development of early America as the New Atlantis is clearly viewed from the Great Seal to the symbolic layout of Washington DC—the capital for the New Atlantis. This has been so well documented over the last two decades that even many Masons have ceased denying the affiliation. Daily Masonic tours through services devoted to this history are now offered of the city's landmarks to illustrate the connection. For a fee, a guide will help you visit locations such as the George Washington Masonic National Memorial or the House of the

Temple, which, as stated, is the headquarters building of the Scottish Rite of Freemasonry. Designed in 1911, the House of the Temple hosts the Freemason Hall of Fame and an enormous collection of Freemason memorabilia including various artworks important to Masons and a library of two hundred fifty thousand books; it is also the location for the Rite's Supreme Council 33rd-degree meetings. Upon leaving, you can exit the House of the Temple, walk down the street, and take pictures of the enormous Masonic obelisk (phallic Egyptian symbol of fertility) in the distance known as the Washington Monument, which we will discuss later.

For obvious reasons, while modern Masons may openly admit these days to involvement by their Jacobite ancestors toward establishing the foundation for a utopian New World Order in Washington, DC, most vigorously deny that the talisman-like layout of the streets, government buildings, and Masonic monuments were meant for what researcher David Bay calls an "electric-type grid" that pulsates "with Luciferic power twenty-four hours a day, seven days a week."

Notwithstanding this denial, the government's own records explain otherwise, clearly stating that the capital city's design was "shepherded" by those who wanted it to reflect dedication to "pagan gods." For instance, the article, "The Most Approved Plan: The Competition for the Capitol's Design," on the Library of Congress's website tells how, after advertising a competition for the design of Government Center in DC, "Washington, Jefferson, and the Commissioners of the District of Colombia" were disappointed by the entries, and a design based on "The Roman Pantheon—the circular domed rotunda *dedicated to all pagan gods*—was suggested by Jefferson, who later shepherded it through several transformations [emphasis added]."[457] Freemason David Ovason adds that when the cornerstone of the US Capitol building was laid, it was done through Masonic ritual meant to procure *approval of the pagan gods*. As recorded in two bronze panels on the Senate doors of the Capitol, George Washington is seen standing in front of a Mason who holds two versions of the Masonic square, while he himself uses a Masonic trowel on the cornerstone.

It is the apron Washington so famously wore that day that bears specific Masonic symbolism, which Ovason explains as designed to please the "invisible agencies" who watched over the event. "Undoubtedly, invisible agencies were present at the cornerstone ceremony," he says, "but they were made visible in the apron's symbolism. The radiant eye represented the invisible presence of the Great Architect—the high Spiritual Being who had been invited by prayer and ritual to oversee the ceremonial. The radiant eye was…the 'sun-eye,' or Spiritual Sun [Horus/Osiris/Apollo]."

The United States thus cast on the Great Seal and within the layout of the Capitol City reflects the secret society's scheme to fulfill the Baconian dream of a New Atlantis by establishing America as the capital of the New World Order. Hall confirmed:

Here [on the Great Seal] is represented the great pyramid of Gizah, composed of thirteen rows of masonry, showing seventy-two stones. The pyramid is without a cap stone, and above its upper platform floats a triangle containing the all-seeing eye surrounded by rays of light.…

The Pyramid of Gizah was believed by the ancient Egyptians to be the shrine tomb of the god Hermes, or Thot, the personification of universal wisdom.

No trace has ever been found of the cap of the great pyramid. A flat platform about thirty feet square gives no indication that this part of the structure was ever otherwise finished; and this is appropriate, as the Pyramid represents human society itself, imperfect and incomplete. The structure's ascending converging angles and faces represent the common aspiration of humankind; above floats the symbol of the esoteric orders, the radiant triangle with its all-seeing eye.…

There is a legend that in the lost Atlantis stood a great university in which originated most of the arts and sciences of the present race. The University was in the form of an immense pyramid with many galleries and corridors, and on the top was an observatory for the study of the stars. This temple to the sciences in the old Atlantis is shadowed forth in the seal of the new Atlantis. Was it the society of the unknown philosophers who scaled the new nation with the eternal emblems, that all the nations might know the purpose for which the new country had been founded?

...The combination of the pyramid and the all-seeing eye is more than chance or coincidence. There is nothing about the early struggles of the colonists to suggest such a selection to farmers, shopkeepers, and country gentlemen. There is only one possible origin for these symbols, and that is the secret societies which came to this country 150 years before the Revolutionary War. Most of the patriots who achieved American independence belonged to these societies, and derived their inspiration, courage, and high purpose from the ancient teaching. There can be no question that the great seal was directly inspired by these orders of the human quest, and that it set forth the purpose for this nation as that purpose was seen and known to the Founding Fathers.

The monogram of the new Atlantis reveals this continent as set apart for the accomplishment of the great work—here is to arise the pyramid of human aspiration, the school of the secret sciences.[458]

Besides Manly Hall, late scholars who recognized the occult symbolism of the Great Seal as pointing to this "Secret Destiny of America" included Rhodes Scholar James H. Billington and Harvard professor Charles Eliot Norton, who described the Great Seal as hardly other than an "emblem of a Masonic Fraternity." In 1846, 33rd-Degree Freemason and noted author James D. Carter inadvertently confirmed this as well when he admitted the Masonic symbolism is clearly known whenever "an informed Mason examines the Great Seal."

Yet for all the volumes written in the early years about the arcane meaning behind the symbols and mottoes of the Great Seal, it was not until the 1930s that, perhaps by providence, the significance of the seal started finding its defining moment.

It happened when two-term President Franklin D. Roosevelt decided to run for an unprecedented third term and chose as his running mate for the vice presidency secretary of agriculture and 32nd-Degree Mason Henry Wallace. Among other things, Roosevelt needed an unyielding supporter for the fading New Deal and saw in Wallace a farm-bred intellectual whose scrubbed Midwestern looks would appeal to a cross section of Americans—from ranchers to big-city unionists. Democratic National Committee Chairman Jim Farley couldn't have disagreed more, and made his opinion known not only to Roosevelt but to his wife, Eleanor, a strong and respected civil rights activist who, after discussing the liberalism and mysticism of Wallace, phoned her husband and told him, "I've been talking with Jim Farley and I agree with him. Henry Wallace won't do." But FDR was determined to have his Masonic brother as his second in command and drafted a speech in which he would refuse the party's nomination unless Wallace was designated for VP. The first lady followed by giving a speech of her own—a first time in which a woman addressed the Democratic National Convention—asking the delegates to respect her husband's reasoning. Wallace went on to become thirty-third vice president of the United States under the thirty-second president, Franklin D. Roosevelt—himself a 32nd-Degree Mason and Knight of Pythias (Shriner) with an equal thirst for mysticism. Of course, at the time, the delegates could hardly have imagined such weird instruments as a 1938 White House interoffice memo from Wallace to Roosevelt that illustrated how deeply mysticism was already a part of the two men's relationship. It read in part:

> I feel for a short time yet that we must deal with the "strong ones,"
> the "turbulent ones," the "fervent ones," and perhaps even with
> a temporary resurgence, with the "flameless ones," who with the

last dying gasp will strive to reanimate their dying giant "Capitalism." Mr. President, you can be the "flaming one," the one with
an ever-upsurging spirit to lead into the time when the children
of men can sing again.[459]

If at first this strange language befuddles the reader, it becomes much
clearer when the history of Wallace, who openly referred to himself as a
"practical mystic," is brought to light, including his veneration of Agni
Yoga Society founder and theosophist Nicholas Roerich. Known in his
native land as Nicolai Rerikh, Roerich and his wife had migrated in the
1920s from the Soviet Union to the United States, where they made a
name for themselves on the New York scene as teachers of Madam Blavatsky's theosophical *Secret Doctrine*. Roerich's particular devotion to
mysticism was, however, increasingly focused on apocalyptic themes surrounding the coming of a new earthly order, which struck a chord with
Wallace. This came to light later when Wallace began the VP race and was
threatened with embarrassment by the Republicans, who had come into
possession of a series of letters written by Wallace in the 1930s. Some of the
communications were addressed to Roerich as "Dear Guru," and described
the anticipation Wallace felt for "the breaking of the New Day," a time
when a mythical kingdom would arrive on earth accompanied by a special
breed of people. Earlier letters by Wallace simply addressed the mystic as
"Dear Prof. R," and reflected the yearning Wallace felt to become Roerich's
disciple and to make contact with those supernatural masters who populated Blavatsky's spiritual universe. In early 1934, Wallace wrote Roerich:

> Long have I been aware of the occasional fragrance from that other
> world which is the real world. But now I must live in the outer
> world and at the same time make over my mind and body to serve
> as fit instruments for the Lord of Justice. The changes in awareness
> must come as a result of steady, earnest recollectedness. I shall strive
> to grow as rapidly as possible.... Yes, the Chalice is filling.[460]

The phrase by Wallace "I must...make over my mind and body to serve as fit instruments for the Lord of Justice" is a direct reference to Helena Blavatsky's *Secret Doctrine* to which Wallace and Roerich were dedicated. On page 332 of her related work, Blavatsky explains that "Osiris" is this Lord of Justice who rules over the "Seven Luminous Ones" or seven stars that Wallace would later speak of and under which the United States would serve following the inauguration of the New World Order and the resurrection of Osiris/Apollo.[461] The other phrase, "Yes, the Chalice is filling" corresponds to Holy Grail teachings by Roerich concerning a mystical cup, called the "Chalice of Buddha" or sometimes "the Blessed One" which was (at least metaphorically) a vessel of knowledge to those who honored the messianic figure and which would be filled by the appearance of the King of the New World Order—Osiris/Apollo to Masons. Though in the 1930s and 40s such coded letters gave Wallace an air of mystery as well as space for criticism in his political life, Roosevelt, too, was more than a casual acquaintance of Roerich. John C. Culver and John Hyde, in their biography, *American Dreamer: The Life and Times of Henry A. Wallace* note:

> Roosevelt, perhaps influenced by his mother's enthusiasm for Eastern art and mysticism, took a personal interest in the Roerichs' causes. Roosevelt met Roerich at least once, met with Roerich's associates on several occasions, and between 1934 and 1936 personally corresponded with Helena Roerich several times. "Mr. President," she wrote in a typical letter, "Your message was transmitted to me. I am happy that your great heart has so beautifully accepted the Message and Your lightbearing mind was free from prejudice."
>
> Indeed, it was Roosevelt who suggested to Wallace that he read an allegory by Arthur Hopkins called *The Glory Road*, which served as the basis for the coded language in the guru letters."[462]

BEHIND THE GURU LETTERS:
BELIEF IN THE GREAT SEAL PROPHECY

Although Roosevelt would be the one to set in motion the push to place the Great Seal of the United States on the US $1 bill, Wallace claimed it was he who first brought the seal's oracular significance to Roosevelt in the 1930s, believing the symbolism of the emblems carried inference to Roosevelt's New Deal, and, more important, a Masonic prophecy toward a New World Order. Wallace describes the meeting he had with Roosevelt:

> Roosevelt as he looked at the colored reproduction of the Seal was first struck with the representation of the All-Seeing Eye—a Masonic representation of the Great Architect of the Universe. Next, he was impressed with the idea that the foundation for the new order of the ages had been laid in 1776 but that it would be completed only under the eye of the Great Architect. Roosevelt, like myself, was a 32nd-degree Mason. He suggested that the Seal be put on the dollar bill…and took the matter up with the Secretary of the Treasury [also a Freemason].… He brought it up in a Cabinet meeting and asked James Farley [Postmaster General and a Roman Catholic] if he thought the Catholics would have any objection to the "all-seeing Eye," which he as a Mason looked on as a Masonic symbol of Deity. Farley said, "No, there would be no objection."[463]

Regardless of who between Roosevelt and Wallace first perceived the seal's Masonic prophetic significance, surviving records clearly show it was Roosevelt (and in his own handwriting no less) who instructed that the obverse side of the seal be placed on the right back of the dollar and the reverse side of the seal with the pyramid and all-seeing eye be put on the left so that it would be the first thing a person saw when reading the back of the dollar from left to right. Thus, most Americans "were left with the impression that the mysterious pyramid and its heralding of a 'new

order' were the foremost symbols of the American republic," notes Mitch Horowitz in *Occult America*.[464]

Wallace and Roosevelt viewed the all-seeing eye above the unfinished pyramid as pointing to the return (or reincarnation) of the coming savior referenced in the mottoes *Annuit Coeptis* and *Novus Ordo Seclorum*, whose arrival would cap the pyramid and launch the New World Order. The all-seeing eye on the Great Seal is fashioned after the Eye of Horus, the offspring of Osiris (or Osiris resurrected), as both men surely understood. Aliester Crowley, 33rd-Degree Freemason (the "wickedest man on earth") and a Roerich occult contemporary, often spoke of this as the "New Age of Horus" and the breaking dawn of the rebirth of Osiris. That mystics and Freemasons simultaneously used such identical language is telling, given what I pointed out in chapter 1 of this book—that the Great Seal's mottoes and symbolism relate to both Osiris and Apollo specifically, yet as one. Osiris is the dominant theme of the Egyptian symbols, his resurrection and return, while the *mottoes* of the seal point directly to Apollo, and the eagle, a pagan emblem of Jupiter, to Apollo's father. For instance, the motto *Annuit Coeptis* is from Virgil's *Aeneid*, in which Ascanius, the son of Aeneas from conquered Troy, prays to Apollo's father, Jupiter [Zeus]. Charles Thompson, designer of the Great Seal's final version, condensed line 625 of book IX of Virgil's *Aeneid*, which reads, *Juppiter omnipotes, audacibus annue coeptis* ("All-powerful Jupiter favors [the] daring undertakings"), to *Annuit Coeptis* ("He approves [our] undertakings"), while the phrase *Novus Ordo Seclorum* ("a new order of the ages") was adapted in 1782 from inspiration Thompson found in a prophetic line in Virgil's Eclogue IV: *Magnus ab integro seclorum nascitur ordo* (Virgil's *Eclogue IV,* line 5), the interpretation of the original Latin being, "And the majestic roll of circling centuries begins anew." This phrase is from the Cumaean Sibyl (you'll remember this is a pagan prophetess of Apollo, identified in the Bible as a demonic deceiver) and involves the future birth of a divine son, spawned of "a new breed of men sent down from heaven" (what Roosevelt, Wallace, and Roerich were looking for) when he receives "the life of gods, and sees Heroes with gods commingling." According to the prophecy, this is Apollo, son of Jupiter (Zeus), who returns to earth through mystical "life" given to him from the gods when the deity Saturn-Jupiter returns to reign over the earth in a new pagan Golden Age. This prophecy begins in symbolism on the front side of the Great Seal with the symbol of Jupiter, a bald eagle, which clutches a bundle of arrows in its left talon while its right claw grips an olive branch.

THE GREAT SEAL TELLS THE PROPHETIC TALE

Besides the origin of the Latin mottoes on the Great Seal being derived from Apollonian prophecies forecasting the second coming of Apollo-Osiris under the usurper-sovereignty of Jupiter-Saturn in a final occult world order, the symbols on the seal confirm the Secret Destiny of America and the desire of especially Thomas Jefferson to accommodate the magical entry of these entities at the start of what I would call the Great Tribulation period (2025?).

When gazing at the front side of the Great Seal, one is stricken with the redundancy of the number thirteen's uses—thirteen leaves in the olive branch, thirteen bars and stripes in the shield, thirteen arrows in the eagle's claw, and so on. This pattern continues on the reverse side with thirteen levels in the uncapped pyramid and the thirteen letters of *Annuit Coeptis*. Recall how Albert Pike revealed Freemasonry's two sets of meanings behind such symbols, in this case the superficial translation for Blue-Degree Masonry and the profane (you and me), which asserts the number thirteen refers to the original thirteen colonies or states. However, the deeper meaning understood by 33rd-Degree Masonry is that the mystical number thirteen reflects those parts of Osiris that Isis was able to find after he was murdered by his evil brother Set (more on this later). The same is true with the phrase in the banner *E Pluribus Unum* (Latin, "Out of Many, One") which laity are told refers to the many ethnicities that came together to form one nation, while high-degree occultists acknowledge that the true meaning of *E Pluribus Unum* echoes the god of many names (Gilgamesh, Osiris, Apollo, Nimrod) as the singular entity prophesied on the Great Seal to rule the world at the end of time. This is clearly understood whenever high-degree occultists and master freemasons observe the bald eagle, the ancient icon of the god Jupiter (whose prophesied return is captioned in the phrase *Annuit Coeptis* on the reverse side of the seal) with the thirteen stars forming a hexagram above his head. For example, 33rd-Degree Freemason and famous occultist Aliester Crowley—who claimed the incorporeal entity Aiwass elected him to be the prophet that would lead the world into the Age of Horus (second coming of Osiris-Apollo)—employed the same symbols of eagle and hexagram as a talisman to summon the second coming of Jupiter.

And then there is the accompanying layout of Washington DC itself.

David Ovason, whose works have been widely endorsed by Freemasons as well as Robert Hieronimus (considered one of the world's foremost authorities on the Great Seal) as "exceptionally well referenced," adds that the dedication of buildings such as the US Capitol building cornerstone had to be done at certain astrological times related to the zodiacal constellation Virgo (Isis), while Jupiter was rising in Scorpio, because "the cornerstone ceremonial was designed not only to gain the approval of the spiritual beings, but also to ensure that these were content that the building was being brought into the world at the right time."[465] Ovason later states more directly, "Whoever arranged for Virgo to be so consistently operative during foundation and cornerstone ceremonies, must have been alert to the fact that *they were inviting some archetype, or spiritual being, to direct the destiny of the city"* (italics in the original).[466] Finally, Ovason hints who the "spiritual being" governing the capital of the United States is: "A medieval esotericist...would have said that Washington, D.C., was governed by the intelligency Hamaliel, the spiritual entity which ruled Virgo, and which worked hand in hand with Mercury."[467] Hamaliel is an evil adversary of the cherubim of God, serving under Lilith, whose devotees gather annually with US presidents and other "dignitaries" to honor her at the Bohemian Grove.

As a result of this alignment of the Capitol buildings and streets in Washington, DC, with this constellation, every August 10, an astrological event reoccurs in the sky above the nation's capital, tying the city to the pagan Virgo—known in ancient Egypt as the goddess Isis. "At dusk, as golden light turns brick facades a dusty rose, the shimmering sun floats a few degrees just to the left of Pennsylvania Avenue, gradually inching to the right until it sets directly over the famous street," writes Julie Duin. "If the horizon remains cloudless, three stars are visible in a straight line from the Capitol to the White House to the skies in the west. Known as Regulus, Arcturus and Spica, the stars form a right-angled triangle framing the constellation of Virgo."[468] Such mysticism incorporated into the design of Washington, DC, by Freemasons for summoning the timing, presence, and approval of these "invisible agents" was a formula perfected in pagan Rome. John Fellows explains why:

> They consulted the gods, to know if the enterprise would be acceptable to them, and if they approved of the day chosen to begin the work...they invoked, besides the gods of the country, the gods to whose protection the new city was recommended, which was done secretly, because it was necessary that the tutelary gods should be unknown to the vulgar.[469]

It may come as little surprise then that when George W. Bush, in a speech the day before his second inaugural, said the United States had "a calling from beyond the stars" (a disturbing statement taken directly from the satanic *Necronomicon* fiction concerning alien creator gods) that the Capitol building had been intentionally set in the head of a Masonic owl figure, which in turn stands atop the White House, located on the chin of the pentagramic goat of Mendes. The upside-down pentagram, or Baphomet, clearly visible in the DC street layout, represents the goat's head and is considered the most powerful symbol in Satanism, while the owl figure is a well-known representative of the Masonic, Illuminati, Bohemian owl of wisdom incarnation of Athene, Minerva, Lilith, and Hecate.

THE WASHINGTON, DC, PENTAGRAM

As Christian Pinto noted in the preface of *Zenith 2016*, all serious researchers contend that the controversy over the pentagram is not about whether it is truly there. Aerial photos clearly reveal it. Even the Masons, who deny that they are responsible for it, acknowledge its presence, but argue that Rhode Island Avenue does not extend all the way to complete the figure. As such, the debate is twofold: 1) Was the pentagram intentional, or simply the coincidence of geometric lines? 2) Why is the pentagram incomplete? The answer to the second part seems to reveal the first. As explained in *Riddles in Stone*, the unfinished pentagram is a well-known symbol in Freemasonry. As Manly P. Hall records in his writings:

> The pentagram is used extensively in black magic, but when so used its form always differs in one of three ways: The star may be broken at one point by not permitting the converging lines to touch.... When used in black magic, the pentagram is called the "sign of the cloven hoof" or the "footprint of the devil."[470]

Of course, Hall was writing in the twentieth century, but was this symbolism known by Masons during the founding era? The answer is yes. One of the most famous Master Masons of all time was Johann Wolfgang von

Goethe, who made use of such a pentagram in the play, *Faust,* in which the character of Faust summons Mephistophiles (the devil) to make a pact with him. As the devil tries to leave, he is hindered. As a result, he and Faust have the following exchange:

Mephistophiles:
>   Let me go up! I cannot go away;
>   a little hindrance bids me stay.
>   The Witch's foot upon your sill I see.

Faust
>   The pentagram? That's in your way?
>   You son of Hell, explain to me,
>   If that stays you, how came you in today?
>   And how was such a spirit so betrayed?

Mephistophiles
>   Observe it closely! It is not well made;
>   One angle, on the outer side of it,
>   Is just a little open, as you see.[471]

The "open" or "broken" pentagram was used by Faust to summon the devil in a black magic ceremony. The famous author of the play, Goethe, was not only a Mason, but also a well-known member of the Bavarian Illuminati. To this day, Freemasons proudly acknowledge that his writings are filled with Masonic symbolism, while books have been written about his Illuminist involvement.

Goethe published his first edition of *Faust* in 1790 (called *Faust: ein Fragment*), and it was in the next two years that Pierre L'Enfant (with the possible help of Thomas Jefferson) came up with the street design for Washington DC (1791–1792). It is therefore provable that members of these secret orders were familiar with the idea of an unfinished pentagram *before* the street layout was complete. Admittedly, this does not, of itself, prove that the pentagram was intentional. Yet it is interesting that Goethe's play and the DC design were done during the same period. Because of the close interaction between the Freemasonry of America and that of Europe, it is entirely possible (and likely) that L'Enfant and Jefferson were familiar with the symbol and placed it intentionally.

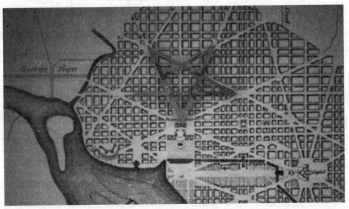

Occultists around the world understand the power of these DC symbols and rituals, and they realize they're not only for conveying psychological concepts, but actually for coercing the mysterious and potent supernaturalism invited to take residence there. This belief is deeply preserved in all of the Babylonian, Egyptian, Greek, Roman, and Kabalistic symbolism that is a part of Masonic history, and according to famous Freemason Foster Bailey, these symbols intentionally hide "a secret...which veils mysterious forces. These energies when released can have a potent effect."[472] Scottish philosopher Thomas Carlyle once famously added: "By symbols, accordingly, is man guided and commanded, made happy, made wretched." As previously pointed out, Masons, as a result, are under oath never to reveal the true meaning of their symbols, and when somehow they are compelled to offer explanation, they falsify the statement, even to lower-degree Masons.

Substantial reasons exist for why the designers of Washington's Government Center would have wanted to obscure the meaning behind the occultic layout of America's capital. If the public in general had been prematurely convinced of the end game prophesied in the DC symbolism, it would have been beyond the acceptance of prior generations who likely would have demanded change in leaders and facilities. But as time has moved forward and increasingly it has become necessary for public understanding of America's heritage and intended purpose, little by little—either by providence, promotion, or even resistance—a clearer picture has emerged of what Manly P. Hall called "the secret destiny of America" (according to the symbolism in Washington DC, this destiny includes future national and global subservience to the god of Freemasonry).

Ovason confirms how such obfuscation was deployed on the Great Seal down to the smallest detail, including how a letter was "cut" from the Latin word *saeclorum* (the usual spelling) in order to create the word *seclorum* to contribute to three sets of thirteen on the reverse side of the Great Seal.

After acknowledging that the top motto, *Annuit Coeptis*, had the obligatory thirteen letters, Ovason pointed out how *saeclorum* was letter-cut to join the bottom motto, *Nvus Ordo Seclorum*, so that the phrase would end up being seventeen letters, which, when added to the nine numerals in the Roman date, would equal a total of twenty-six, or two sets of the number thirteen. Combined with the top motto, these three sets of thirteen were very important to establish, Ovason says, in order to reflect the trinity represented in the Great Seal "Eye of Providence, and in the nominal triangle from which the pyramid is constructed."[473]

Based purely on the Great Seal's symbolism, the trinity these three sets of the number thirteen denote is authoritatively identified as Osiris, Horus, and Isis, the pagan versions of Father, Son, and Holy Spirit, respectively. The use of the number thirteen in this way also connects the Great Seal to the mythological and astrological significance of the legend of Osiris as the dying and rising god. It was evidently so important to maintain this talisman-like value, thirteen, that other phases of the design and layout of Washington, DC, were coordinated accordingly, says Ovason. This includes the laying of the White House cornerstone on October 13, 1792, by Masons, and the Fourth of July signing of the Declaration of Independence thirteen days after summer solstice, so that the sun would be on Sirius. In Egyptian mythology, the sun represented Osiris while the star Sirius symbolized Isis, and thirteen was the number of pieces of Osiris that Isis was able to find after Seth, his evil brother, murdered and threw fourteen pieces of him into the Nile. Isis searched the riverbank until she recovered every piece, except for his genitals, which had been swallowed by a fish. Isis replaced the missing organ with an obelisk and magically impregnated herself with Horus. Therefore, in Masonic as well as in ancient Egyptian mythology, the number thirteen—used a total of thirteen times on the Great Seal, counting front and back—is the number that represents the return or resurrection of Osiris.

This mythology was so meaningful to the founding of the United States and the construction of its capital—including having the missing Osiris genitalia represented by the 6,666-inches-high Egyptian obelisk known as the Washington Monument—that nearly all of David Ovason's five hundred-plus-page *Secret Architecture of Our Nation's Capital* is dedicated to establishing the singular correlation between Washington, DC, and Virgo, the constellation of Isis, or what Ovason calls "Isis, who was the chief of the feminine mystery deities and the prototype of the steller Virgo."[474]

This affiliation existed from the very day Freemasons gathered on April 15, 1791, beginning appropriately at 3:30 p.m. (reflecting the mystical value of thirty-three) because of the astrological position of Jupiter and Virgo, and what this would mean for the Secret Destiny of America:

> At exactly 3:30 PM, Jupiter…began to rise over the horizon. It was in 23 degrees of Virgo…. By this means, the zodiacal power of Virgo, which was called in later Masonic circles "the Beautiful Virgin," was able to stamp her benign influence on the building of the federal city…. A few of the many Freemasons present at this ceremony would have been only to well aware of the profound implications of what they were doing…. It is quite clear that the ceremonial placing of the stone related to more than merely the founding of the federal district: it was somehow linked to the future destiny of America itself.[475]

By dedicating the United States through its astrological alignment to the "Virgin" constellation of Isis, the founders had dedicated the "destiny" of America to fulfilling the secret doctrine of Freemasonry, as also reflected in the Osiris/Apollo symbolism of the Great Seal, concerning subservience—now and upon his return as Antichrist—to Osiris/Apollo/Nimrod.

Interestingly, the same dedication to Osiris/Isis/Apollo exists in New York where the events of September 11, 2001, initiated the push toward the *Novus Ordo Seclorum*. The Statue of Liberty in New York's Harbor, which holds the Masonic "Torch of Enlightenment," was presented in 1884 as a gift to American Masons by the French Grand Orient Temple Masons.

Designed by French Freemason and sculptor Frédéric Auguste Bartholdi and built by another French Freemason, Gustave Eiffel, the statue was originally identified as "the goddess Isis" with the statue's head formed to represent "the Greek Sun-god Apollo…as preserved on an ancient marble tablet (today in the Archaeological Museum of Corinth, Corinth, Greece)—Apollo was represented as a solar deity, dressed in a similar robe and having on its head a 'radiate crown' with the seven spiked rays of the Helios-Apollo's sun rays."[476]

The legend of Osiris and Isis, the connection with Apollo, the magical number thirteen, and the history surrounding their mythos is often openly discussed in Masonic and brotherhood-friendly literature. For instance in *Morals and Dogma*, Albert Pike enumerated the esoteric significance of the Osiris epic at length, adding that lower-level Masons (Blue Masonry) are ignorant of its true meaning, which is only known to those who are "initiated into the Mysteries."[477] Pike also spoke of the star Sirius—connected to Isis and at length to Lucifer/Satan—as "still glittering" in the Masonic lodges as "the Blazing Star." Elsewhere in *Morals and Dogma*, Pike reiterated that the "All-Seeing Eye…was the emblem of Osiris"[478] and that the "Sun was termed by the Greeks the Eye of Jupiter, and the Eye of the World; and his is the All-Seeing Eye in our Lodges."[479]

Once people understand this illuminated Masonic connection to the "trinity" on America's Great Seal, and what the prophetic symbolism, mottoes, and numerology imply, it becomes apparent why so much effort was put forward for so long by those who felt it was necessary to hide this extraordinary destiny. Ovason acknowledges this conspiracy of silence as well:

> The motto at the top of the seal, *Annuit Coeptis*, is from Virgil… from the *Aeneid*.… This is a prayer to the god Jupiter.… We should observe that while the subject matter of the reverse of the seal is undoubtedly pagan—if symbolic of hermetic Egypt—the superior motto is itself a prayer to a pagan god. Could *this* be the reason why there has been so much reluctance to bring the reverse of the seal into the light of day? Whatever the nature of the god, the prayer directed in this way is a petition that the daring undertaking [the Secret Destiny of America as symbolized in "finishing" the pyramid] may be completed, and that the new age will find fulfillment.[480]

Ovason, a Mason whose research earned praise from Fred Kleinknecht, Sovereign Grand Commander of the 33rd-Degree Supreme Council of Freemasons in Washington, DC, is to be thanked for inadvertently revealing what the Illuminatus has secretly known for ages—that the Great Seal of the United States is a pagan prophecy and petition to a pagan god (the same entity the Bible identifies by name as the end-times Antichrist) to assist in the conclusion of the great work by his return. "When we have grasped the importance of these New Age expectations," Ovason concludes, "we shall be in a better position to understand why the design for this reverse [side of the Great Seal] has remained so consistently hidden."[481]

THE DOME OF AMERICA'S TEMPLE, THE OBELISK, AND THE COMING INCARNATION

As I've written before and publicly stated in interviews, the vast majority of people, when looking at Washington, DC, and at the Vatican, never comprehend how these cities constitute one of the greatest open conspiracies of all time. There, reproduced in all their glory and right before the world's eyes, is an ancient talismanic diagram based on the history and cult of Isis, Osiris, and Horus, including the magical utilities meant to generate the deity's return.

The primeval concept—especially that of sacred domes facing obelisks—was designed in antiquity for the express purpose of regeneration, resurrection, and apotheosis, for deity incarnation from the underworld to earth's surface through union of the respective figures—the dome (ancient structural representation of the womb of Isis) and the obelisk (ancient representation of the erect male phallus of Osiris).

This layout, as modeled in antiquity, exists today on the grandest scale at the heart of the capital of the most powerful government on earth—the United States—as well as in the heart of the most politically influential Church on earth—the Vatican. Given this fact and the pattern provided by the Apostle Paul and the Apocalypse of John (the book of Revelation) that the end times would culminate in a marriage between political (Antichrist) and religious (False Prophet) authorities at the return of Osiris/Apollo, it behooves open-minded researchers to carefully consider this prophecy in stone, as it defines the spiritual energy that is knowingly or unknowingly being invoked at both locations with potential ramifications for the year 2025 and beyond.

The US capital has been called the "Mirror Vatican" due to the strikingly similar layout and design of its primary buildings and streets. This is no accident. In fact, America's forefathers first named the capital city "Rome." But the parallelism between Washington and the Vatican is most clearly illustrated by the Capitol building and dome facing the obelisk known as the Washington Monument, and at St. Peter's Basilica in the Vatican by a similar dome facing a familiar obelisk—both of which were, according to their own official records, fashioned after the Roman Pantheon, the circular domed rotunda "dedicated to all pagan gods." This layout—a domed temple facing an obelisk—is an ancient, alchemical blueprint that holds significant esoteric meaning.

For those who may not know, the US Capitol building in Washington, DC, is historically based on a pagan Masonic temple theme. Thomas Jefferson, who shepherded the antichristian "Roman Pantheon" design, wrote to the Capitol's architect, Benjamin LaTrobe, defining it as "the first temple dedicated to…embellishing with Athenian taste the course of a nation looking far beyond the range of Athenian destinies"[482] (the "Athenian" empire was first known as "Osiria," the kingdom of Osiris). In 1833, Massachusetts Representative Rufus Choate agreed, writing, "We have built no national temples but the Capitol."[483] William Henry and Mark Gray in their book, *Freedom's Gate: Lost Symbols in the U.S. Capitol*, add that, "The U.S. Capitol has numerous architectural and other features that unquestionably identify it with ancient temples."[484] After listing various features to make their case that the US Capitol building is a "religious temple"—including housing the image of a deified being, heavenly beings, gods, symbols, inscriptions, sacred geometry, columns, prayers, and orientation to the sun—they conclude:

> The designers of the city of Washington DC oriented it to the Sun—especially the rising Sun on June 21 and December 21 [the dates in 2020 that *Newsweek*[485] and other sources reported the Aztec Calendar Stone in the Capitol rotunda rolled over to a final age, followed December 21, 2020,[486] by the alignment of Jupiter and Saturn heralding the arrival of a "promised son" (Antichrist)]. The measurements for this orientation were made from the location of the center of the Dome of the U.S. Capitol, rendering it a "solar temple." Its alignment and encoded numerology point to the Sun as well as the stars. A golden circle on the Rotunda story and a white star in the Crypt marks this spot.… It is clear that the builders viewed the Capitol as America's sole temple: a solemn… Solar Temple to be exact.[487]

To understand what these statements may soon mean for the future of the world, one needs to comprehend how these apparati—the dome and the obelisk facing it—facilitate important archaic and modern protocols for invigorating *prophetic* supernatural alchemy. In ancient times, the obelisk represented the god Osiris' "missing" male organ, which Isis was not able to find after her husband/brother was slain and chopped into fourteen pieces by his evil brother Seth (or Set). The story involves a detailed account of the envious brother and seventy-two (72) conspirators tricking Osiris into climbing inside a box, which Seth quickly locked and threw into the Nile. Osiris drowned, and his body floated down the Nile River, where it snagged on the limbs of a tamarisk tree. In Byblos, Isis recovered his body from the river bank and took it into her care. In her absence, Seth stole the body again and chopped it into fourteen pieces, which he threw into the Nile. Isis searched the river bank until she recovered every piece, except for the genitals, which had been swallowed by a fish (Plutarch says a crocodile). Isis recombined the thirteen pieces of Osiris' corpse and replaced the missing organ with a magic facsimile (obelisk), which she used to impregnate herself during the very first "raising of Osiris" ceremony in which she called forth the seed of the dead god from the underworld up through the magic device, thus giving rise to Osiris again in the person of his son, Horus. This legendary ritual for reincarnating Osiris formed the core of Egyptian cosmology (as well as the Rosicrucian/Masonic dying-and-rising myths) and was fantastically venerated on the most imposing scale throughout all of Egypt by towering obelisks (representing the phallus of Osiris) and domes (representing the pregnant belly of Isis) including at Karnak, where the upright obelisks were "vitalized" or "stimulated" from the energy of the masturbatory sun-god Ra shining down upon them.

There is historical evidence that this elaborate myth and its rituals may have been based originally on real characters and events. Regarding this, it is noteworthy that, in 1998, former secretary general of Egypt's Supreme Council of Antiquities, Zahi Hawass, claimed to have found the burial tomb of the god Osiris (Apollo/Nimrod) at the Giza Plateau. In the article, "Sandpit of Royalty," from the newspaper *Extra Bladet* (Copenhagen), January 31, 1999, Hawass was quoted saying:

I have found a shaft, going twenty-nine meters vertically down into the ground, exactly halfway between the Chefren Pyramid and the Sphinx. At the bottom, which was filled with water, we have found a burial chamber with four pillars. In the middle is a large granite sarcophagus, which I expect to be the grave of Osiris, the god.... I have been digging in Egypt's sand for more than thirty years, and up to date this is the most exciting discovery I have made.... We found the shaft in November and began pumping up the water recently. So several years will pass before we have finished investigating the find.[488]

As far as we know, this discovery did not ultimately provide the physical remains of the deified person. But what it did illustrate is that at least some very powerful Egyptologists believe Osiris was a historical figure, and that his body was stored somewhere at or near the Great Pyramid. Manly P. Hall, who knew that the Masonic legend of Hiram Abiff was a thinly veiled prophecy of the resurrection of Osiris, may have understood what Zahi Hawass (not to mention Roerich, Roosevelt, and Wallace with their sacred Osiris Casket [see previous chapter]) was looking for, and why. Consider that he wrote in *The Secret Teachings of All Ages*: "The Dying God [Osiris] shall rise again! The secret room in the House of the Hidden Places shall be rediscovered. The Pyramid again shall stand as the ideal emblem of...resurrection, and regeneration."[489]

In Egypt, where rituals were performed to actually "raise" the spirit of Osiris into the reigning Pharaoh, political authority in the form of divine kingship or theocratic statesmanship was established (later reflected in the political and religious doctrine of royal and political legitimacy or "the divine right of kings," who supposedly derived their right to rule from the will of God, with the exception in some countries that the king is subject to the Church and the pope). This meant, among other things, that the Egyptian Pharaoh enjoyed extraordinary authority as the "son of the sun god" (Ra) and the incarnation of the falcon god Horus during his lifetime. At death, Pharaoh became the Osiris, the divine judge of the netherworld, and on earth, his son and predecessor took his place as the newly anointed manifestation of Horus. Thus each generation of pharaohs provided the gods with a spokesman for the present world and for the afterlife while also offering the nation divinely appointed leadership.

Yet the observant reader may wonder, "Was there something more to the Pharaoh's deification than faith in ritual magic?" The cult center of Amun-Ra at Thebes may hold the answer, as it was the site of the largest religious structure ever built—the temple of Amun-Ra at Karnak—and the location of many extraordinary mysterious rites. The great temple with its miles of walls and gardens (the primary object of fascination and worship by the nemesis of Moses—the Pharaoh of the Exodus, Ramses II) was the place where each Pharaoh reconciled his divinity in the company of Amun-Ra during the festival of Opet. The festival was held at the temple of Luxor and included a procession of gods carried on barges up the Nile River from Karnak to the temple. The royal family accompanied the gods on boats while the Egyptian laity walked along the shore, calling aloud and making requests of the gods. Once at Luxor, the Pharaoh and his entourage entered the holy of holies, where the ceremony to raise the spirit of Osiris into the king was performed and Pharaoh was transmogrified into a living deity. Outside, large groups of dancers and musicians waited anxiously. When the king emerged as the "born-again" Osiris, the crowd erupted in gaiety. From that day forward, the Pharaoh was considered to be—just as the god ciphered in the Great Seal of the United States will be—the son and spiritual incarnation of the Supreme Deity. The all-seeing eye of Horus/Apollo/Osiris above the unfinished pyramid on the Great Seal represents this event.

Fast forward to today and, at the inauguration of every American president, across town at the House of the Temple, the modern Egyptian magicians (Freemasons) simultaneously conduct the "Raising of Osiris" ceremony to call the seed of Osiris-Apollo from the underworld through the Washington monument obelisk, where it magically emits into the US Capitol Dome while America's new leader stands there accepting his role as the living representative of Osiris. This is done in anticipation of the day when events will surpass parody and "the beast that...was, and is not; shall ascend out of the bottomless pit, and go into perdition [Greek *Apollo*]: and they that dwell on the earth shall wonder, whose names were not written in the book of life from the foundation of the world, when they behold the beast that was, and is not, and yet is" (Revelation 17:8).

For a few adepts of history and secret orders, the DC ritual is deliciously staged as even the term "inaugurate" is from the Latin *inauguratio*, and refers to the archaic ceremony by which the Roman augurs (soothsayers) approved a king or ruler (or other action) through omens as being sanctioned by the god Jupiter, the same entity whose prophecies on the Great Seal herald his upcoming challenge to Yahweh-Jehovah for heavenly supremacy while his son Apollo-Osiris seizes authority over the world in a final pagan Golden Age.

As pointed out in the bestselling documentary *Belly of the Beast* and in broadcast programs on SkyWatch TV, which first aired June-August, 2021, the dome where US presidents stand during inauguration (and where they lie in state for their spirit to rise into the *Apotheosis* overhead to join George Washington in the kingdom of Osiris at death) alone is an unparalleled magical construct that openly hides the most formidable ancient supernaturalism meant for regeneration of Apollo-Osiris. In fact, it is a Satanic (Antichrist) plagiarism of the death, burial, and resurrection of Jesus Christ that I believe will play a role in the "healing" of Antichrist after he experiences a deadly head wound (see Revelation 13:3).

- Note that the 1865 *Apotheosis of Washington* painted by Greek-Italian artist Constantino Brumidi is visible through the oculus of the dome in the rotunda and bears anything but Christian symbols. It is filled with Greco-Roman gods, to whom Thomas Jefferson dedicated the United States.
- "Apotheosis" means to become a god or revived eternal being. In this depiction, Washington is becoming Osiris of the afterlife.
- The gods in the painting surrounding Washington are depicted helping the founders establish "a more perfect union" (as in the New Atlantis scheme described elsewhere in this book).

- Directly beneath the *Apotheosis* are seventy-two pentagrams forming a sorcerous gateway used by secret society members and occultists to bind and loose the seventy-two fallen angels over the heathen nations (see Psalm 82; Deuteronomy 32).
- Finally, under the floor of the rotunda is the US National Crypt, where an empty tomb resides ("He is not here, for he is risen"). This is where I argue that Antichrist will be taken after his head injury and the Freemasons will conduct the raising of Osiris ceremony, at which time he will be transmogrified into the living incarnation of Osiris-Apollo (see Revelation 17:8).

There is more to the Capitol dome, anti-Christ plagiarism of the life of Christ than these aspects of the building's design, but these points of interest clearly reveal how the architects imagined a dark parody of Jesus.

As Jesus died and rose into heaven, so Washington rises to become the Osiris.

As the seventy-two pentagrams in the Capitol dome are used to control the seventy-two kosmokrators over the nations, Jesus confronted the seventy-two fallen Watchers—from the base of Mount Hermon to His visit in the underworld and final ascension into heaven, whereby He proclaimed in Revelation 1:18: "I am he that liveth, and was dead; and, behold, I am alive for evermore [a clear denunciation of the Osiris "dying and rising god" myth so popular during His first advent], Amen; and have the keys of hell [*Hades*, the name Greeks gave to *Osiris!*] and of death." This is important because Osiris was the lord of the underworld in Greek myth and controlled who possessed the keys to the twelve gates of Egyptian afterlife.

Much has been written by historians within and without Masonry as to the relevance of the number seventy-two (72) and the alchemy related to it. In the Kabbalah, Freemasonry, and Jewish apocalyptic writings, the number equals the total of wings Enoch received when transformed into the powerful angel Metatron (3 Enoch 9:2). This plays an important role for the Brotherhood, as Metatron or "the angel in the whirl-wind" was enabled as the guiding spirit over America during George W. Bush's administration for the purpose of directing the *future* and *fate* of the United States (as also prayed by Congressman Major R. Owens of New York before the House of Representatives on Wednesday, February 28, 2001).

But in the context of the Capitol dome and the seventy-two stars that circle Washington's *Apotheosis* in the womb of Isis, the significance of this symbolism is far more important. In sacred literature, including the Bible, stars are symbolic of angels, and within Masonic Gnosticism, these seventy-two powerful entities (reflected in the seventy-two conspirators that controlled Osiris' life in Egyptian myth) currently administer the affairs of earth under Satan, the god of this world (2 Corinthians 4:4). Experts in the study of the Divine Council believe that, beginning at the tower of Babel, the world and its inhabitants were disinherited by the sovereign God of Israel and placed under the authority of seventy-two angels that became corrupt and disloyal to God in their administration of those nations (Psalm 82). These beings quickly became worshiped on earth as gods following Babel, led by Nimrod/Gilgamesh/Osiris/Apollo. Consistent with this tradition, the designers of the Capitol dome, the Great Seal of the United States, and the obelisk Washington Monument circled the *Apotheosis of Washington* with seventy-two pentagram stars, dedicated the obelisk seventy-two years after the signing of the Declaration of Independence, and placed seventy-two stones on the Great Seal's uncapped pyramid, above which the eye of Horus/Osiris/Apollo stares. These three sets of seventy-two (72), combined with the imagery and occult numerology of the Osiris/obelisk, the Isis/dome, and the oracular Great Seal, are richly symbolic of the influence of Satan and his angels over the world (see Luke 4:5–6; 2 Corinthians 4:4; and Ephesians 6:12) with a prophecy toward Satan's final earthly empire—the coming *Novus Ordo Seclorum*, or new pagan Golden Age.

In order for the "inevitable" worship of Osiris to be "reestablished" on earth, the seventy-two demons that govern the nations must be controlled, thus they are set in magical constraints on the Great Seal, the Washington obelisk, and the pentagram circles around the *Apotheosis of Washington* to bind and force the desired effect.

In *The Secret Destiny of America*, Hall noted as well that the seventy-two stones of the pyramid on the Great Seal correspond to the seventy-two arrangements of the Tetragrammaton, or the four-lettered name of God in Hebrew. "These four letters can be combined in seventy-two combinations, resulting in what is called the Shemhamforesh, which represents, in turn, the laws, powers, and energies of Nature."[490] The idea that the mystical Name of God could be invoked to bind or release those supernatural agents (powers and energies of nature, as Hall called them) is meaningful creed within many occult tenets, including Kabbalah and Freemasonry. This is why the seventy-two stars are pentagram-shaped around the deified Freemason George Washington. Medieval books of magic, or grimoires such as the Key of Solomon and the Lesser Key of Solomon, not only identify the star systems Orion (Osiris) and Pleiades (Apollo) as the "home" of these powers, but applies great importance to the pentagram shape of the stars for binding and releasing their influence. Adept Rosicrucians and Freemasons have long used these magical texts—the Key of Solomon and the Lesser Key of Solomon—to do just that.

Modern people, especially in America, may view the symbols used in this magic—the dome representing the habitually pregnant belly of Isis, and the obelisk, representing the erect phallus of Osiris—as profane or pornographic. But they were in fact ritualized fertility objects, which the ancients believed could produce tangible reactions, properties, or "manifestations" within the material world. The obelisk and dome as imitations of the deities' male and female reproductive organs could, through government representation, invoke into existence the being or beings symbolized by them. This is why, inside the temple or dome, prostitutes representing the human manifestation of the goddess were also available for ritual sex as a form of imitative magic. These prostitutes usually began their services to the goddess as children, and were deflowered at a very young age by a priest or, as Isis was, by a modeled obelisk of Osiris' phallus. Sometimes these prostitutes were chosen, on the basis of their beauty, as the sexual mates of sacred temple bulls who were considered the incarnation of Osiris. In other places, such as at Mendes, temple prostitutes were offered in coitus to divine goats. Through such imitative sex, the dome and obelisk became "energy receivers," capable of assimilating Ra's essence from the rays of the sun, which in turn drew forth the "seed" of the underworld Osiris. The seed of the dead deity would, according to the supernaturalism, transmit upward from out of the underworld through the base (testes) of the obelisk and magically emit from the tower's head into the womb (dome) of Isis, where incarnation into the sitting pharaoh/king/president would occur (during what Freemasons also call "the raising [of Osiris] ceremony"). In this way, Osiris could be habitually "born again" or reincarnated as Horus and constantly direct the spiritual destiny of the nation.

And something most people do not know and will be shocked to learn is that the Freemasons even constructed a symbolic "seed" of Osiris at the Washington Monument obelisk. If an anatomically correct phallus is placed over the Washington Monument, right in the testicular section beneath a manhole cover where it should be, is a miniature, twelve-foot-tall obelisk hidden just beneath the surface of the ground representing the seed of Osiris. The number twelve (12) is the biblical and occult numerology for perfect government—in this case that New World Order over which Osiris-Apollo will reign when:

The beast that thou sawest was, and is not; and shall ascend out of the bottomless pit, and go into (Apollo-Osiris): and they that dwell on the earth shall wonder, whose names were not written in the book of life from the foundation of the world, when they behold the beast that was, and is not, and yet is. (Revelation 17:8)

Twelve-foot-tall obelisk in testicular section of Washington Monument
representing "seed" of Osiris

This metaphysical phenomenon of deity resurrection involving mystical "seed" reminds of the Messianic protoevangelium promise, "And I will put enmity between thee and the woman, and between thy seed and her seed; it shall bruise thy head, and thou shalt bruise his heel" (Genesis 3:15), which, for occultists, was countered by Nimrod/Semiramis and was central to numerous other ancient cultures, especially developed in Egypt, where Nimrod/Semiramis were known as Osiris/Isis (and in Ezekiel chapter 8, the children of Israel set up the obelisk ["image of jealousy," verse 5] facing the entry of their temple—just as the dome faces the obelisk in Washington, DC, and in the Vatican City—and were condemned by God for worshiping the Sun [Ra] while weeping for Osiris [Tammuz]). The familiar Masonic figure of the point within a circle is the symbol of this union between Ra, Osiris, and Isis. The "point" represents Osiris' phallus in the center of the circle or womb of Isis, which in turn is enlivened by the sun rays from Ra, just as is represented today at the Vatican, where the Egyptian obelisk of Osiris sits within a circle, and in Washington, DC, where the obelisk does similarly, situated so as to be the first thing the sun (Ra) strikes as it rises over the capital city and which, when viewed from overhead, forms the magical point within a circle known as a *circumpunct*. The sorcery is further amplified, according to ancient occultic beliefs, by the presence of the Reflecting Pool in DC, which serves as a mirror to heaven and "transferring point" for those spirits and energies.

And just what is it the spirits see when they look downward on the Reflecting Pool in Washington? They find a city dedicated to and built in honor of the legendary deities Isis and Osiris complete with the thirteen gathered pieces of Osiris (America's original thirteen colonies); the required obelisk known as the Washington Monument; the Capitol dome (of Isis) for impregnation and incarnation of deity into each Pharaoh (president); and last but not least, the official government buildings erected to face their respective counterparts and whose cornerstones—including the US Capitol Dome—were dedicated during astrological alignments related to the zodiacal constellation Virgo (Isis) as required for the magic to occur.

TO SERVE THE POLITICAL—AND SPIRITUAL—LEADERS

Because the book of Revelation depicts a final global political figure (Antichrist) who gains allegiance of the world's religious community through a powerful religious leader (False Prophet), it is not surprising to find that the magical constructs in Washington, DC, necessary for Apollo-Osiris' resurrection are mirrored in the very city where the Apostle John said a global "harlot" church would lead mankind into subservience to the Man of Sin (see Revelation 17:18 regarding Rome).

To be sure, the 330-ton obelisk in St. Peter's Square in the Vatican City is not just any obelisk. It was cut from a single block of red granite during the Fifth Dynasty of Egypt to stand as Osiris' erect phallus at the Temple of the Sun in ancient Heliopolis (Ἡλιούπολις, meaning "city of the sun" or principal seat of Atum-Ra sun-worship), the city of "On" in the Bible, dedicated to Ra, Osiris, and Isis. The obelisk was moved from Heliopolis to the Julian Forum of Alexandria by Emperor Augustus and later from thence (approximately AD 37) by Caligula to Rome to stand at the spine of the Circus. There, under Nero, its excited presence maintained a counter-vigil over countless brutal Christian executions, including the martyrdom of the Apostle Peter (according to some historians). Over fifteen hundred years following that, Pope Sixtus V ordered hundreds of workmen under celebrated engineer-architects Giovanni and Domenico Fontana (who also erected three other ancient obelisks in the old Roman city, including one dedicated to Osiris by Rameses III—at the Piazza del Popolo, Piazza di S. Maria Maggiore, and Piazza di S. Giovanni in Laterano) to move the phallic pillar to the center of St. Peter's Square in Rome. This proved a daunting task, requiring more than four months, nine hundred laborers, one hundred forty horses, and seventy winches. Though worshiped at its present location ever since by countless admirers, the proximity of the obelisk to the old Basilica was formerly "resented as something of a provocation, almost as a slight to the Christian religion. It had stood there like a false idol, as it were vaingloriously, on what was believed to be the center of the accursed circus where the early Christians and St. Peter had been put to death. Its sides, then as now, were graven with dedications to [the worst of ruthless pagans] Augustus and Tiberius."[491]

The fact that many traditional Catholics as well as Protestants perceived such idols of stone to be not only objects of heathen adoration but the worship of demons (see Acts 7:41–42; Psalms 96:5; and 1 Corinthians 10:20) makes what motivated Pope Sixtus to erect the phallus of Osiris in the heart of St. Peter's Square, located in Vatican City and bordering St. Peter's Basilica, very curious. To ancient Christians, the image of a cross and symbol of Jesus sitting atop (or emitting from) the head of a demonic god's erect manhood would have been at a minimum a very serious blasphemy. Yet Sixtus was not content with simply restoring and using such ancient pagan relics (which were believed in those days to actually house the pagan spirit they represented) but even destroyed Christian artifacts in the process. Michael W. Cole, associate professor in the History of Art department at the University of Pennsylvania, and Rebecca E. Zorach, associate professor of art history at the University of Chicago, raise critical questions about this in their scholarly book, *The Idol in the Age of Art*, when they state:

> Whereas Gregory, to follow the chroniclers, had ritually dismembered the city's *imagines daemonem* [demonic images], Sixtus fixed what was in disrepair, added missing parts, and made the "idols" into prominent urban features. Two of the four obelisks had to be reconstructed from found or excavated pieces.... The pope was even content to destroy *Christian* antiquities in the process: as Jennifer Montagu has pointed out, the bronze for the statues of Peter and Paul came from the medieval doors of S. Agnese, from the Scala Santa at the Lateran, and from a ciborium at St. Peter's.
>
> [Sixtus] must have realized that, especially in their work on the two [broken obelisks], they were not merely repairing injured objects, but also restoring a *type*.... In his classic book *The Gothic Idol*, Michael Camille showed literally dozens of medieval images in which the freestanding figure atop a column betokened the pagan idol. The sheer quantity of Camille's examples makes it clear that the device, and what it stood for, would have been immediately recognizable to medieval viewers, and there is no reason to assume that, by Sixtus's time, this had ceased to be true.[492]

The important point made by Professors Cole and Zorach is that at the time Sixtus was busy reintroducing to the Roman public square restored images and statues on columns, the belief remained strong that these idols housed their patron deity, and further, that, if these were not treated properly and even placed into service during proper constellations related to their myth, it could beckon evil omens. Leonardo da Vinci had even written in his Codex Urbinas how those who would adore and pray to the image were likely to believe the god represented by it was alive in the stone and watching their behavior. There is strong indication that Sixtus believed this too, and that he "worried about the powers that might inhabit his new urban markers."[493] This was clearly evident when the cross was placed on top of the obelisk in the midst of St. Peter's Square and the pope marked the occasion by conducting the ancient rite of exorcism against the phallic symbol. First scheduled to occur on September 14 to coincide with the liturgical Feast of the Exaltation of the Cross and not coincidently under the zodiacal sign of Virgo (Isis), the event was delayed until later in the month and fell under the sign of Libra, representing a zenith event for the year. On that morning, a pontifical High Mass was held just before the cross was raised from a portable altar to the apex of Baal's Shaft (as such phallic towers were also known). While clergy prayed and a choir sang Psalms, Pope Sixtus stood facing the obelisk and, extending his hand toward it, announced: *Exorcizote, creatura lapidis, in nomine Dei* ("I exorcize you, creature of stone, in the name of God"). Sixtus then cast sanctified water upon the pillar's middle, then its right side, then left, then above, and finally below to form a cross, followed by, *In nomine Patris, et Filij, et Spiritus sancti. Amen* ("In the Name of the Father and of the Son and of the Holy Ghost. Amen"). He then crossed himself three times and watched as the symbol of Christ was placed atop Osiris' erect phallus.

Strolling from the obelisk in St. Peter's square to inside the Sistine Chapel, one finds the parallels between Washington and the prophecies of the Great Seal do not stop with the dome design and symbol of Osiris's erect manhood. But the very Cumaean Sibyl whose prophecy about the return of the god Apollo is encoded in the Great Seal of the United States is prominently depicted inside Catholicism's most celebrated chapel. On close examination of her portrait, the Cumaean of Rome unveils a secret— a magnificent clue—which her Italian Renaissance artist left concerning her and her returning Lord's origin and identity. Upon consideration, she reveals what elsewhere I have called "the sign of the sixth knuckle." The Cumaean's left thumb is inside the book and the fingers of her left hand are wrapped outside in standard book-holding fashion. But a clearly visible extra knuckle is portrayed, secreted perhaps by Michelangelo to depict a sixth digit bent under the palm, or to illustrate that a sixth finger had been lost or cut off at the knuckle. Either meaning is deeply occultic, and as students of history and the Bible clearly know, this ties both the Sibyl and her prophesied savior Apollo to the offspring of the fallen Watchers, the Nephilim (see 2 Samuel 21:20), of which Apollo/Osiris/Nimrod was chief…and will be again.

With all of this in mind, whatever happens between now and 2025, this writer firmly believes events unfolding around the world today and especially inside the United States indeed suggest a near future in which a man of superior intelligence, wit, charm, and diplomacy will emerge on the world scene as a savior. He will seemingly possess transcendent wisdom that enables him to solve problems and offer solutions for many of today's most perplexing issues. His popularity will be widespread, and his fans will include young and old, religious and nonreligious, male and female. Talk-show hosts will interview his colleagues, news anchors will cover his movements, scholars will applaud his uncanny ability at resolving what has escaped the rest of us, and the poor will bow down at his table. He will, in all human respects, appeal to the best idea of society. But his profound comprehension and irresistible presence will be the result of an invisible network of thousands of years of collective knowledge. He will, quite literally, represent the embodiment of that very old, super-intelligent spirit predicted on the Great Seal and in the layout of the Capitol of the United States. As Jesus Christ was the "seed of the woman" (Genesis 3:15), he will be the "seed of the serpent." Moreover, though his arrival in the form of a man was foretold by numerous Scripture passages, the broad masses will not immediately recognize him for what he actually is—paganism's ultimate incarnation; the "beast" Apollo-Osiris of Revelation 13:1 and 17:8.

I must ask, therefore: Are you prepared spiritually, mentally, and physically for what is just ahead? Ancient and modern occultists obviously have plans for the near future, including strategies to install the dreaded Man of Sin who will, for a short period of time, conquer and then betray the human race. Thankfully, it is the true Father of heaven and His Son, Jesus Christ, who will have the final word and ultimately determine the fate of mankind. Therefore, knowing Jesus as Savior is the first and most important "emergency planning step" you can take for your future security and survival. With Christ as your Lord, you will be able to "enter thou into thy chambers, and shut thy doors about thee: hide thyself as it were for a little moment, until the indignation be overpast" (Isaiah 26:20).

NOTES

1. Harry Lear, "Open Letter to President Trump," They Fly Blog. January 29, 2018. Accessed March 29, 2021. https://theyflyblog.com/2018/02/15/open-letter-to-president-trump/.
2. https://www.sciencedirect.com/science/article/pii/S0019103516307643.
3. https://www.youtube.com/watch?v=xaW4Ol3_M1o.
4. https://css.ethz.ch/en/services/digital-library/publications/publication.html/121625.
5. https://www.politico.com/story/2017/01/full-text-donald-trump-inauguration-speech-transcript-233907.
6. Ibid.
7. Ibid.
8. Sue Bradley, "The Fourth Turning: The Protocols and the Gray Champion," *The Sue Bradley Archives.* Last accessed May 25, 2013, http://suebradleyarchives.com/have-we-entered-the-fourth-turning/.
9. Ibid.
10. Ibid.
11. https://en.wikipedia.org/wiki/Portal:Constructed_languages/Language_of_the_month/March_2017.
12. https://www.foxnews.com/media/aoc-commission-truth-rein-in-media-slammed-unamerican.
13. https://www.americanthinker.com/blog/2021/02/trump_uncovered_a_spirit_of_racketeering_running_the_country.html.
14. https://www.foxnews.com/media/aoc-commission-truth-rein-in-media-slammed-unamerican.
15. https://www.newsmax.com/politics/randpaul-electionfraud/2021/01/24/id/1006951/.

16. https://www.faithwire.com/2021/02/11/disney-axes-mandalorian-star-for-comparing-todays-political-climate-to-nazi-germany/.

17. https://www.rt.com/usa/515452-kevin-sorbo-faceboo-removed/.

18. S. Jonathon O'Donnell (2020), "The Deliverance of the Administrative State: Deep State Conspiracism, Charismatic Demonology, and the Post-truth Politics of American Christian Nationalism, *Religion*, 50:4, 696–719, DOI: 10.1080/0048721X.2020.1810817.

19. https://news.yahoo.com/christian-nationalism-threat-not-just-110048205.html.

20. https://www.ntd.com/dennis-prager-this-is-the-reichstag-fire-relived_55387 .html.

21. https://en.wikipedia.org/wiki/Reichstag_fire

22. Andre RavenSkul Venas, *Big Black Book of Government Conspiracies*, 2018.

23. https://www.wwsg.com/news/allen-west-how-do-you-fundamentally-transform-the-united-states-of-america/.

24. https://www.foxnews.com/story/rewriting-our-history-changing-our-traditions.

25. http://signpostsofthetimes.blogspot.com/2021/01/joe-biden-sworn-in-as-americas-46th.html.

26. Thomas Horn, *Zenith 2016* (Crane, MO: Defender, August 6, 2013), 120–121.

27. https://astronomy.com/news/2020/12/the-christmas-star-appears-again-jupiter-and-saturn-align-in-the-great-conjunction-on-dec-21-2020#:~:text=Jupiter%20and%20Saturn%20will%20line,t%20occur%20again%20until%202080.

28. John Dryden, trans., as published by Georgetown University Online; also appears in: Thomas Horn, *Apollyon Rising 2012*.

29. Congressman Major R. Owens (http://www.house.gov/owens/rap010228.htm).

30. *The Possessed* (http://etext.library.adelaide.edu.au/d/Dostoyevsky/d72p/).

31. https://www.thelist.com/235714/the-surprising-meaning-of-kamala-harris-name/.

32. https://pandemic.warroom.org/2021/01/25/biden-has-lost-50-of-his-cognitive-abilities/.

33. https://www.youtube.com/watch?v=A-t3nG8uqzI&feature=emb_logo.

34. https://www.israel365news.com/161094/
    the-inner-meaning-of-bidens-name-the-hand-of-god/.

35. https://www.israel365news.com/160601/
    biden-to-bring-noah-like-flood-into-world-rabbi-warns/.

36. https://thenewamerican.com/joe-biden-on-creating-a-new-world-order/.

37. https://www.rt.com/usa/513205-biden-icon-jacobin-magazine/.

38. George Orwell, *1984* (New York: Harcourt, 1949) 21–22.

39. Ibid., 4.

40. Scott Jaschik, "More Educated, More Liberal," Insidehighered.
    com, April 27, 2016. Last accessed March 3, 2021,
    https://www.insidehighered.com/news/2016/04/27/
    study-finds-those-graduate-education-are-far-more-liberal-peers.

41. Orwell, *1984, 235.*

42. Ibid., 2.

43. Andrew Hampp, "How SpongeBob Became an $8 Billion Franchise." Adage.
    com. July 13, 2009. Last accessed March 3, 2021, https://adage.com/article/
    media/nickelodeon-s-spongebob-8b-kid-franchise/137866#:~:text=But%20
    beyond%20just%20TV%20longevity,as%20it%20were%20%2D%2D%20
    down.

44. Natalie Robehmed, "The 'Frozen' Effect: When Disney's Movie
    Merchandising Is Too Much," *Forbes,* July 28, 2015. Last accessed March 3,
    2021, https://www.forbes.com/sites/natalierobehmed/2015/07/28/the-frozen-
    effect-when-disneys-movie-merchandising-is-too-much/?sh=5d2796b222ca.

45. Nickie Louise, "These 6 Corporations Control 90% of the Media Outlets
    in America," *Tech Startups,* September 18, 2020. Last accessed February 18,
    2021. https://techstartups.com/2020/09/18/6-corporations-control-90-
    media-america-illusion-choice-objectivity-2020/.

46. Ryan Holmes, "We Now See 5,000 Ads A Day…And It's Getting Worse,"
    Linkedin.com, February 19, 2019. Last accessed March 3, 2012, https://www.
    linkedin.com/pulse/have-we-reached-peak-ad-social-media-ryan-holmes/.

47. H. D. Northrop, *Beautiful Gems of Thought and Sentiment* (Boston, MA:
    Colins-Patten Co., 1890) 248.

48. Allie Anderson, *Unscrambling the Millennials Paradox: Why the "Unreachables"
    May Be Key to the Next Great Awakening* (Crane, MO: Defender Publishing,
    2019) 82.

49. Ibid., 90.
50. Aleks Krotoski, "What Effect Has the Internet Had on Journalism?" *The Guardian*, February 19, 2011. Last accessed March 3, 2021. https://www.theguardian.com/technology/2011/feb/20/what-effect-internet-on-journalism.
51. "How the Internet Has Changed News Media Outlets," Google Sites. Last accessed March 3, 2021. https://sites.google.com/site/newsoutletsandtheinternet/.
52. Ibid.
53. "Don't Believe Everything You Read on the Internet," KnowYourMeme, TrollQuotes. Last accessed March 3, 2021. https://knowyourmeme.com/photos/1201185-troll-quotes.
54. Krotoski, "What Effect Has the Internet Had on Journalism?"
55. "How the Internet Has Changed News Media Outlets."
56. Orwell, *1984,* 207.
57. "The 5 Principles of Ethical Journalism." EthicalJournalismNetwork.org. Last accessed March 3, 2021. https://ethicaljournalismnetwork.org/who-we-are/5-principles-of-journalism.
58. Ibid.
59. "FCC Adopts Media Ownership Rules," CNN Money News, June 2, 2003, Last accessed February, 18, 2021. https://money.cnn.com/2003/06/02/news/companies/fcc_rules/.
60. Ibid.
61. Ibid.
62. Associated Press, "F.C.C. Votes to Relax Rules Limiting Media Ownership." *New York Times*, June 2, 2003. Last accessed February 18, 2021. https://www.nytimes.com/2003/06/02/business/fcc-votes-to-relax-rules-limiting-media-ownership-20030602418873791.html.
63. Ibid.
64. Ibid.
65. "FCC Adopts Media Ownership Rules."
66. Associated Press, "F.C.C. Votes to Relax Rules."
67. Ibid.
68. "FCC adopts Media Ownership Rules."
69. Ibid.
70. Ibid.

71. Way Back, "Why Is Media Consolidation Bad? Media Ownership Concentration in Markets (2003)," October 10, 2015. YouTube Video, 59:21. Last accessed March 3, 2021. https://www.youtube.com/watch?v=uj6V3YA0j7o.

72. Richard L. Worsnop, "Television and Politics," In *Editorial Research Reports 1968*, Vol. I, (Washington, DC: CQ Press, 1968) 361–84. http://library.cqpress.com/cqresearcher/cqresrre1968051500.

73. Chris Mills, "AT&T Basically Now Owns Everything Except Your Soul," *NY Post* Online, June 18, 2018. Last accessed March 3, 2021. https://nypost.com/2018/06/18/att-basically-now-owns-everything-except-your-soul/.

74. Carly Hallman, "Who Owns the News: A Closer Look at Online News Sources," TitleMax.com. Last accessed March 3, 2021. https://www.titlemax.com/discovery-center/lifestyle/who-owns-your-news-the-top-100-digital-news-outlets-and-their-ownership/#:~:text=About%2015%20billionaires%20and%20six,Amusements%20(which%20includes%20Viacom%20Inc.

75. "Brand—Licensing, Evolution and Domain Names," AT&T Online. Last accessed March 3, 2021, https://about.att.com/innovation/ip/brands/history#:~:text=The%20historical%20brands%20of%20AT%26T,synonymous%20with%20innovation%20in%20communications.&text=In%202005%2C%20SBC%20acquired%20AT%26T,in%20global%20communications%20for%20businesses.

76. Hallman, "Who Owns the News."

77. Carly Hallman, "Every Company Disney Owns: A Map of Disney's Worldwide Assets," TitleMax. Last accessed March 3, 2021. https://www.titlemax.com/discovery-center/money-finance/companies-disney-owns-worldwide/.

78. Mike Nudelman, "Here's Where Disney Really Makes Money," BusinessInsider.com. January 14, 2015. Last accessed March 3, 2021, https://www.businessinsider.com/heres-where-disney-really-makes-money-2015-1.

79. Mae Anderson, "Here's What Disney Is—and Isn't—Getting for Its $71 Billion Buy of Fox." *Chicago Tribune*, March 20, 2019. Last accessed March 3, 2021, https://www.chicagotribune.com/business/ct-biz-disney-fox-deal-details-20190320-story.html.

80. Meg James, "Disney and Fox Shareholders Approve Blockbuster $71-Billion Deal," *Chicago Tribune*, July 27, 2018. Last accessed March 3, 2021, https://www.chicagotribune.com/business/ct-biz-disney-fox-shareholders-deal-20180727-story.html.

81. "Your Complete Guide to Everything Owned by Comcast." Nasdaq.com, October 12, 2017. Last accessed March 3, 2021, https://www.nasdaq.com/articles/your-complete-guide-everything-owned-comcast-2017-10-12.

82. Hallman, "Who Owns the News."

83. "Your Complete Guide to Everything Owned by Comcast."

84. Matthew Johnston, "5 Companies Owned by Comcast," Investopedia.com. May 15, 2020. Last accessed March 3, 2021, https://www.investopedia.com/articles/markets/101215/top-4-companies-owned-comcast.asp.

85. Hallman, "Who Owns the News.".

86. "National Amusements Inc. History." FundingUniverse.com. Last accessed March 3, 2021, http://www.fundinguniverse.com/company-histories/national-amusements-inc-history/#:~:text=A%20privately%20held%20company%20owned,and%20other%20major%20entertainment%20properties.

87. "About National Amusements, 2019 Rankings." Vault.com. Last accessed March 3, 2021, https://www.vault.com/company-profiles/film/national-amusements-inc.

88. Hallman, "Who Owns the News."

89. Kate Vinton, "These 15 Billionaires Own America's News Media Companies," *Forbes*. June 1, 2016. Last accessed March 3, 2021, https://www.forbes.com/sites/katevinton/2016/06/01/these-15-billionaires-own-americas-news-media-companies/?sh=463d0cf9660a.

90. "NewsCorp: Our Leadership: Rupert Murdoch." Newscorp.com. 2021. Last accessed March 3, 2021, https://newscorp.com/leader/rupert-murdoch/.

91. Vinton, "These 15 Billionaires Own America's News Media Companies."

92. "Hearst: About." Hearst.com. Last accessed March 3, 2021. https://www.hearst.com/about.

93. "2018 Annual Hearst Properties." Hearst.com. Last accessed March 3, 2021. https://www.annual2018.hearst.com/property-list.

94. "The Hearst Corporation: At a Glance." The Vault. Last accessed March 3, 2021, https://www.vault.com/company-profiles/media-entertainment/the-hearst-corporation.

95. Nickie Louise, "These 6 Corporations Control 90% of the Media Outlets in America." *Tech Startups*, September 18, 2020. Last accessed February 18, 2021. https://techstartups.com/2020/09/18/6-corporations-control-90-media-america-illusion-choice-objectivity-2020/.

96. Orwell, *1984,* 56–57.

97. Daniel Nations, "What Is Facebook?" Lifewire.com. November 12, 2020. Last accessed March 3, 2021. https://www.lifewire.com/what-is-facebook-3486391.

98. Ryan Holmes, "We Now See 5,000 Ads A Day…And It's Getting Worse." Linkedin.com. February 19, 2019. Last accessed March 3, 2012, https://www.linkedin.com/pulse/have-we-reached-peak-ad-social-media-ryan-holmes/.

99. David Streitfeld and Jodi Kantor, "Jeff Bezos and Amazon Employees Join Debate Over Its Culture." *New York Times*, August 17, 2015. Last accessed March 3, 2021, https://www.nytimes.com/2015/08/18/technology/amazon-bezos-workplace-management-practices.html.

100. Paul Farhi, "Washington Post to Be Sold to Jeff Bezos, the Founder of Amazon," *Washington Post.* August 5, 2013. Last accessed March 3, 2021, https://www.washingtonpost.com/national/washington-post-to-be-sold-to-jeff-bezos/2013/08/05/ca537c9e-fe0c-11e2-9711-3708310f6f4d_story.html.

101. Ben Popken, "Google Sells the Future, Powered by Your Personal Data." NBCnews.com. May 10, 2018. Last accessed March 3, 2021, https://www.nbcnews.com/tech/tech-news/google-sells-future-powered-your-personal-data-n870501.

102. Naveen Joshi, "What Is Big Tech and Why We Should Care," Allerin.com. August 21, 2019. Last accessed March 3, 2021, https://www.allerin.com/blog/what-is-big-tech-and-why-we-should-care.

103. Mark McLaughlin, "Hate Crime Bill: Hate Talk in Homes 'Must Be Prosecuted.'" *The Times*, UK. October 28, 2020. Last accessed March 3, 2021, https://www.thetimes.co.uk/article/hate-crime-bill-hate-talk-in-homes-must-be-prosecuted-6bcthrjdc.

104. Ibid.

105. Orwell, *1984,* 19.

106. Bethany Blankley, "New U.S. House Rules to Eliminate Gender-Specific Terms such as 'Father, Mother, Son, Daughter.'" *Highland County Press*,

January 3. 2021. Last accessed March 3, 2021, https://highlandcountypress. com/Content/In-The-News/In-The-News/Article/New-U-S-House-rules-to-eliminate-gender-specific-terms-such-as-father-mother-son-daughter-/2/20/63644.

107. Robert Reich, "Facts Are Under Siege. Now, More Than Ever, We Need to Invest in Journalism," *The Guardian*, December 2, 2019. Last accessed March 3, 2021, https://www.theguardian.com/commentisfree/2019/dec/02/ facts-are-under-siege-now-more-than-ever-we-need-to-invest-in-journalism.

108. Ibid.

109. Ibid.

110. Ibid.

111. "Objectionable Content: Hate Speech." Facebook.com. 2021. Last accessed March 3, 2021, https://www.facebook.com/communitystandards/ objectionable_content.

112. "False News." Facebook.com. 2021. Last Accessed March 3, 2021, https:// www.facebook.com/communitystandards/false_news.

113. Chi Luu, "The Incredibly True Story of Fake Headlines." JstorDaily. November 20, 2019. Last Accessed March 3, 2021, https://daily.jstor.org/ the-incredibly-true-story-of-fake-headlines/.

114. Ibid.

115. Patrick Egan, "Elections 2020—The Role of Social Media in U.S. Elections." FPC Briefing at the Foreign Press Center, Department of State. New York City, NY. February 28, 2020. Last accessed March 3, 2021, https://2017-2021.state.gov/elections-101-the-role-of-social-media-in-us-elections/index.html.

116. Luu, "The Incredibly True Story of Fake Headlines.".

117. CNN, "Biden: Trump Skipping My Inauguration a Good Thing." January 8, 2021. YouTube Video: 15:36. Last accessed March 3, 2021, https://www. youtube.com/watch?v=JLX8N9XWojk.

118. Factbase Videos. "Speech: Donald Trump Holds a Political Rally on The Ellipse—January 6, 2021." January 6, 2021. YouTube Video, 1:11:30. https://www.youtube.com/watch?v=RTK1lm1jk60.

119. Sam Cabral, "Capitol Riots: Did Trump's Words at Rally Incite Violence?" BBC.com. February 14, 2021. Last accessed March 3, 2021, https://www. bbc.com/news/world-us-canada-55640437.

120. Ibid.
121. CNN, "Biden: Trump Skipping My Inauguration a Good Thing."
122. Ibid.
123. Andra Brichacek, "Six Ways the Media Influence Elections." University of Oregon. 2021. Last accessed March 3, 2021, https://journalism.uoregon.edu/news/six-ways-media-influences-elections.
124. Ibid..
125. Egan, "Elections 2020—The Role of Social Media in U.S. Elections."
126. Ibid.
127. Ibid.
128. Ibid.
129. Ibid.
130. Brichacek, "Six Ways the Media Influence Elections."
131. Ibid.
132. Jeffrey Winters, *Oligarchy* (New York: Cambridge University Press, 2011) Kindle Format. Location 233.
133. Ibid., 36.
134. Ibid., 239.
135. Ibid., 4.
136. Ibid., 209.
137. Ibid., 18.
138. Ibid., 206.
139. Ibid., 199.
140. Ibid., 7.
141. Ibid., 15.
142. Ibid.
143. Anne Sraders, "What Is Fintech? Uses and Examples in 2020." TheStreet.com, February 11, 2020. Last accessed March 3, 2021, https://www.thestreet.com/technology/what-is-fintech-14885154.
144. Paul La Monica, "BlackRock Now Has a Whopping $8.7 Trillion in Assets," CNN Business. January 14, 2021. Last accessed March 3, 2021, https://www.cnn.com/2021/01/14/investing/blackrock-earnings-ishares-etfs/index.html.
145. Rebecca Ungarino, "Here Are 9 Fascinating Facts to Know about BlackRock, the World's Largest Asset Manager Popping Up in

the Biden Administration," *Business Insider*. January 8, 2021.
Last accessed March 3, 2021, https://www.businessinsider.com/
what-to-know-about-blackrock-larry-fink-biden-cabinet-facts-2020-12.

146. "Global Impact: Worldwide Reach. Local Service and Relationships."
BlackRock.com. 2021. Last accessed March 3, 2021, https://www.
blackrock.com/corporate/about-us/global-impact#:~:text=With%2070%20
offices%20in%2030,the%20Middle%20East%20and%20Africa.

147. Ungarino, "Here Are 9 Fascinating Facts."

148. Meagan Day, "Joe Biden's BlackRock Cabinet Picks Show the President-
Elect Is Ready and Eager to Serve the Rich," Jacobinmag.com 2020.
Last accessed March 3, 2021, https://jacobinmag.com/2020/12/
wall-street-joe-biden-transition-cabinet-blackrock.

149. David Dayen, "How BlackRock Rules the World," American Prospect.
September 27, 2018. Last accessed March 3, 2021, https://prospect.org/
economy/blackrock-rules-world/.

150. Ungarino, "Here Are 9 Fascinating Facts.

151. Franco Ordonez, "Biden Names BlackRock's Brian Deese
as His Top Economic Aide," NPR.org. December 3,
2020. Last accessed March 3, 2021, https://www.npr.org/
sections/biden-transition-updates/2020/12/03/942205555/
biden-names-blackrocks-brian-deese-as-his-top-economic-aide.

152. Annie Massa, "BlackRock Exec Picked as Kamala Harris's Top Economic
Advisor," Bloomberg.com. January 8, 2021. Last accessed March
3, 2021, https://www.bloomberg.com/news/articles/2021-01-08/
blackrock-s-pyle-picked-as-kamala-harris-s-top-economic-adviser.

153. Ungarino, "Here Are 9 Fascinating Facts," Business Insider. January 8,
2021. Last accessed March 3, 2021, https://www.businessinsider.com/
what-to-know-about-blackrock-larry-fink-biden-cabinet-facts-2020-12.

154. La Monica, Paul. "BlackRock Now Has a Whopping $8.7 Trillion in
Assets." CNN Business. January 14, 2021. Last accessed March 3, 2021,
https://www.cnn.com/2021/01/14/investing/blackrock-earnings-ishares-
etfs/index.html.

155. La Monica, "BlackRock Now Has a Whopping $8.7 Trillion in Assets."

156. George Westlake & David Duncan, *Daniel and Revelation, 4th ed.*
(Springfield, MO: 2013) 229.

157. *The ESV Study Bible* (Wheaton, IL: 2016) 2487.

158. Westlake & Duncan, 229.

159. AreaEightyNine. "The Simpsons—Hooray for Everything 2," February 21, 2018. YouTube Video, 0:25. Last accessed March 3, 2021, https://www.youtube.com/watch?v=0RVf5oyrjaM.

160. R. L. Eisenberg, *The JPS Guide to Jewish Traditions* (Philadelphia: Jewish Publication Society, 2004) 14.

161. Ibid.

162. Ibid., 20.

163. Ibid., 20.

164. Natalia Dudareva, "Why Do Flowers Have Scents?" April 18, 2005, *Scientific American*, last accessed January 26, 2021, https://www.scientificamerican.com/article/why-do-flowers-have-scent/.

165. *Baker Encyclopedia of the Bible: Vol. 1* (Grand Rapids, MI: Baker Book House, 1988) 880.

166. V. P. Hamilton, *Evangelical Commentary on the Bible Vol. 3* (Grand Rapids, MI: Baker Book House, 1995) 22.

167. D. Brown, A. R. Fausset, & R. Jamieson, (n.d.), *A Commentary, Critical, Experimental, and Practical, on the Old and New Testaments: Genesis–Deuteronomy: Vol I* (London; Glasgow: William Collins, Sons, & Co.) 153.

168. J. D. Barry, D. Mangum, D. R. Brown, M. S. Heiser, M. Custis, E. Ritzema, … D. Bomar, *Faithlife Study Bible* (Bellingham, WA: Lexham Press, 2012, 2016), Genesis 32:28.

169. C. Brand, A. Draper, S. England, E. R. Bond, T. C. Clendenen, & Butler (Eds.), *Holman Illustrated Bible Dictionary* (Nashville, TN: Holman Bible Publishers, 2003) 1173–1174.

170. P. W. Comfort, (Ed.), *Cornerstone Biblical Commentary: Ezekiel & Daniel: Vol. 9* (Carol Stream, IL: Tyndale House Publishers; 2010) 391.

171. *The Exhaustive Dictionary of Bible Names* (North Brunswick, NJ: Bridge-Logos; 1998).

172. Brand, C., et al (Eds.), *Holman Illustrated*, 1171.

173. Manser, M. H., *Dictionary of Bible Themes: The Accessible and Comprehensive Tool for Topical Studies* (London: Martin Manser, 2009), under heading, "name of God, significance of."

174. Brand, C., et al, *Holman Illustrated*, 1172.

175. Baker Encyclopedia, 882–883.

176. Freedman, D. N. (Ed.), *The Anchor Yale Bible Dictionary: Vol. 6* (New York: Doubleday, 1992) 1,004.

177. Ibid., 1,011.

178. Ibid., 1012.

179. Ibid.

180. Ibid., 7.

181. J. A. Motyer, *Isaiah: An Introduction and Commentary: Vol. 20* (Downers Grove, IL: InterVarsity Press, 1999) 102.

182. Dr. William Menzies, *Apologetics* 4th ed. (Springfield, MO: Global University Press; 2004) 123; emphasis added.

183. *Baker Encyclopedia*, 1,983.

184. J. D. Barry, D. Bomar, D. R. Brown, R. Klippenstein, D. Mangum, C. Sinclair Wolcott, … W. Widder (Eds.), *The Lexham Bible Dictionary* (Bellingham, WA: Lexham Press, 2016), under heading "Son of Man."

185. Ibid.

186. Millard J. Erickson, *Christian Theology* (Grand Rapids: Baker Book House, 1985) 736; emphasis added.

187. Please note: This section of Scripture was taken from the KJV. Originally, "Most High" would not be capitalized, but I made that adjustment to the text because: 1) This is how it would and should appear in any modern translation since the God being referenced in this verse is undoubtedly Yahweh, and 2) so that the readers of this book could more smoothly follow along with these words in the context of this study.

188. Michael Heiser, "Naked Bible Podcast," Episode 166: Melchizedek Part 1a, July 9, 2017; transcript last accessed February 19, 2021, https://nakedbiblepodcast.com/wp-content/uploads/2017/07/NB-166-Transcript.pdf.

189. Ibid.

190. Ibid.

191. Dr. Michael Heiser, "Naked Bible Podcast," Episode 167: Melchizedek Part 1b, July 15, 2017; transcript last accessed February 19, 2021, https://nakedbiblepodcast.com/wp-content/uploads/2017/07/NB-167-Transcript-1B.pdf.

192. Ibid. Also note: Heiser uses the alternate spelling, "Tsedek," in his podcast transcript. However, because the spelling could technically go either way

and still refer to the same deity/Deity, we have changed the final letter to a "q" to match the Hebrew spelling for "righteousness" to avoid any further confusion.

193. Ibid. See previous endnote for a comment on spelling.

194. Ibid.

195. Heiser, "Naked Bible Podcast," episodes 166 (July 9, 2017), 167 (July 15, 2017), 168 (July 22, 2017), 170 (August 5, 2017), and 172 (August 19, 2017). First, route your browser to https://nakedbiblepodcast.com/episodes/, and scroll down to locate the desired episode. After you've clicked that parent link, simply pressing the "play" button on the next page will begin the podcast. However, if you're like me, and you learn better with text in front of you (instead of trying to keep up with an audio player), click the link that says "Download transcript" in red letters under the player. The entire episode will open up as a well-edited transcript, complete with citations and references, in a new window.

196. John A. Wilson, "The God and His Unknown Name of Power," in *Ancient Near Eastern Texts Relating to the Old Testament*, ed. James B. Pritchard (Princeton, NJ: Princeton University Press, 1969) 12.

197. Terence E. Fretheim, *Exodus*, ed. Jr., James Luther Mays and Patrick D. Miller, "Interpretation, a Bible Commentary for Teaching and Preaching" (Westminster: John Knox Press, 1991) 65.

198. S.K. Weber, *Holman New Testament Commentary: Matthew: Vol. 1* (Nashville, TN: Broadman & Holman Publishers; 2000) 485.

199. J. S. Exell, *The Biblical Illustrator: Matthew* (Grand Rapids, MI: Baker Book House. 1952) 682.

200. R. T. France, *Matthew: An Introduction and Commentary: Vol. 1* (Downers Grove, IL: InterVarsity Press, 1985) 420.

201. A. Roberts, J. Donaldson, & A. C. Coxe, A. C. (Eds.), *The Lord's Teaching through the Twelve Apostles to the Nations. In: Fathers of the Third and Fourth Centuries: Lactantius, Venantius, Asterius, Victorinus, Dionysius, Apostolic Teaching and Constitutions, Homily, and Liturgies: Vol. 7* (Buffalo, NY: Christian Literature Company, 1886) 379; emphasis added.

202. *Pulpit Commentary*, "Matthew 28:19," *BibleHub Online*, last accessed February 18, 2021, https://biblehub.com/commentaries/pulpit/matthew/28.htm; italics added; bold in original.

203. R. Jamieson, A. R. Fausset, & D. Brown, *Commentary Critical and Explanatory on the Whole Bible: Vol. 2* (Oak Harbor, WA: Logos Research Systems, 1997) 63.

204. E. W. Bullinger, T*he Companion Bible: Being the Authorized Version of 1611 with the Structures and Notes, Critical, Explanatory and Suggestive and with 198 Appendixes: Vol. 1* (Bellingham, WA: Faithlife; 2018) 1,380.

205. Ibid., 149.

206. *Ellicott's Commentary for English Readers,* "Matthew 28:19," *BibleHub Online,* last accessed February 18, 2021, https://biblehub.com/commentaries/ellicott/matthew/28.htm.

207. *Benson Commentary,* "Matthew 28:19," *BibleHub Online,* last accessed February 18, 2021, https://biblehub.com/commentaries/benson/matthew/28.htm.

208. *Cambridge Bible for Schools and Colleges,* "Matthew 28:19," *BibleHub Online,* last accessed February 18, 2021, https://biblehub.com/commentaries/cambridge/matthew/28.htm.

209. *Vincent's Word Studies,* "Matthew 28:19," *BibleHub Online,* last accessed February 18, 2021, https://biblehub.com/commentaries/vws/matthew/28.htm.

210. G. K. Beale, *The Book of Revelation: A Commentary on the Greek Text* (Grand Rapids, MI; Carlisle, Cumbria: W. B. Eerdmans; Paternoster Press, 1999) 254–255.

211. Virgil, Eclogue IV, lines 5–13. Found online via http://classics.mit.edu/Virgil/eclogue.4.iv.html (accessed January 14, 2021).

212. Listing for the Defender Publishing book, *Giants, Gods, and Dragons* by Sharon K. Gilbert and Derek P. Gilbert at the SkyWatchTV Store: https://www.skywatchtvstore.com/products/giants-gods-and-dragons-exposing-the-fallen-realm-and-the-plot-to-ignite-the-final-war-of-the-ages?_pos=4&_sid=bb917f061&_ss=r (accessed February 20, 2021)

213. Senator Chuck Schumer's speech of January 6, 2021, text found online at US News, https://www.usnews.com/news/elections/articles/2021-01-06/read-chuck-schumers-statement-to-the-senate-on-the-storming-of-the-capitol.

214. Full text of President Franklin D. Roosevelt's address to the Federal Council of Churches is available here: https://www.presidency.ucsb.edu/documents/

address-before-the-federal-council-churches-christ-america (accessed February 20, 2021).

215. Senator Amy Klobucher speech at inauguration, January 20, 2021. Full text found at rev.com https://www.rev.com/blog/transcripts/ amy-klobuchar-speech-transcript-at-joe-biden-inauguration.

216. Jeet Heer, *Dark Winter of Covid-19 Overshadows the Debate*, published online at *The Nation* on October 23, 2020. https://www.thenation.com/ article/politics/trump-biden-second-debate/.

217. Robert Lebacken Reynolds, *Dark Winter Is Coming*, published online at *Minot Daily News*, January 23, 2021, https://www.minotdailynews.com/ opinion/letters/2021/01/dark-winter-coming/.

218. Associated Press, published online at ABC News on January 18, 2021, https://abcnews.go.com/Health/wireStory/ bidens-test-lead-us-virus-dark-winter-75345788.

219. Associated Press, *Chattanooga Times Free Press*, posted online on January 20, 2021, https://www.timesfreepress.com/news/politics/national/story/2021/ jan/20/us-plunges-virus-dark-winter-biden/540009/.

220. Editor, *Sending Vaccines to Cities One Way out of "Dark Winter,"* published online at Express News, https://www.expressnews.com/opinion/editorials/ article/Editorial-Sending-vaccines-to-cities-one-path-15885151.php.

221. Brian Cheung, *Governments Need to Keep Providing Support through Virus "Dark Winter": IMF Economist*, published online at *Yahoo Finance*, January 6, 2021, https://finance.yahoo.com/news/governments-need-to-keep- providing-support-through-dark-winter-imf-chief-economist-173624052. html.

222. Dark Winter exercise page at Johns Hopkins website, https://www. centerforhealthsecurity.org/our-work/events-archive/2001_dark-winter/ about.html.

223. CNN staff, *China Flies Warplanes Close to Taiwan in Early Test of Biden*, published January 25, 2021 by CNN, https://www.cnn.com/2021/01/25/ asia/china-us-taiwan-military-moves-intl-hnk-mil/index.html.

224. Associated Press, *A History of Trump's Statements on the "One China" Policy*, published February 10, 2017 at apnews.com, https://apnews.com/article/ c646266824ac47dea49bd9820985af81.

225. Leonard A. Cole, *Clouds of Secrecy: The Army's Germ Warfare Tests Over*

Populated Areas (Rowman and Littlefield, January 1, 1990). Available at Amazon in print format only: https://www.amazon.com/Clouds-Secrecy-Armys-Warfare-Populated/dp/082263001X?tag=TIsafety net-20.

226. This idea comes from *Barnes's Notes on the Bible*. You'll find this information capsulized at StudyLight.org, https://www.studylight.org/commentary/revelation/6-8.html.

227. Ken Alibek served as the first deputy director of Soviet Russia's Biopreparat facility, where the scientists prepared WMD biologicals for warfare. While there, Alibek (real name Alibekov) created a "battle strain" of anthrax. He defected to the US in 1992. He is the author of *Biohazard: The Chilling True Story of the Largest Covert Biological Weapons Program in the World—Told from Inside by the Man Who Ran It*, (Random House, ISBN 0-385-33496-6) https://en.wikipedia.org/wiki/Ken_Alibek.

228. *SPARS Pandemic Scenario Booklet*, pdf available at https://www.centerforhealthsecurity.org/our-work/pubs_archive/pubs-pdfs/2017/spars-pandemic-scenario.pdf (accessed December 27, 2020 and February 20, 2021).

229. "Age of Aquarius," song by Germone Ragni, James Rado, Galt McDermot, performed by The Fifth Dimension, recorded and released in 1969 through Sony/ATV Publishing, LLC.

230. Dr. Ajal Bambi, "Jupiter-Saturn's Conjunction Will Influence Entire Century," January 19, 2021, *Teheilka Magazine*, http://tehelka.com/jupiter-saturns-conjunction-will-influence-entire-century/ (accessed February 16, 2021).

231. Catherine Neilan, "Boris Johnson Tells G7 to "Build Back Better" and Teases Joe Biden for Nicking His Slogan," *The Telegraph*, published online on February 20, 2021, via https://www.telegraph.co.uk/politics/2021/02/19/lockdown-end-roadmap-boris-johnson-schools-lord-frost-brexit/ (accessed February 20, 2021).

232 Pope Francis, *Encyclical Letter On the Care for Our Common Home*, Published May 24, 2015, Paragraph 1. Found online at http://www.vatican.va/content/francesco/en/encyclicals/documents/papa-francesco_20150524_enciclica-laudato-si.html (accessed December 27, 2020).

233. Pope Francis, *Encyclical Fratelli Tutti, on Fraternity and Social Friendship*,

October 3, 2020, Paragraph 2. Found online via http://www.vatican.va/content/francesco/en/encyclicals/documents/papa-francesco_20201003_enciclica-fratelli-tutti.html (accessed December 27, 2020).

234. Pope Francis, *Encyclical Letter On the Care for Our Common Home,* Published May 24, 2015, Paragraph 87. Found online at http://www.vatican.va/content/francesco/en/encyclicals/documents/papa-francesco_20150524_enciclica-laudato-si.html (accessed December 27, 2020).

235. Michael J. O'Loughlin, "Joe Biden Thanked Pope Francis for 'Extending Blessings and Congratulations This Morning," *America Jesuit Review,* November 12, 2020. Found online via https://www.americamagazine.org/faith/2020/11/12/pope-francis-congratulates-joe-biden-second-catholic-president (accessed December 21, 2020 and February 20, 2021)

236. David Harsanyi, "How the Media Covered up the Hunter Biden Story—Until after the Election," *New York Post,* December 10, 2020. https://nypost.com/2020/12/10/how-media-covered-up-the-hunter-biden-story-until-after-the-election/, retrieved 12/19/20.

237. A reference to presidents James K. Polk and Franklin Pierce.

238. Definitions differ, but "creative" industries include advertising and marketing, architecture, film, IT and software development, museums, publishing, music, performing arts, etc.

239. Klaus Schwab on March 3, 2020. See World Economic Forum, "The Great Reset," June 3, 2020, https://www.facebook.com/worldeconomicforum/videos/189569908956561.

240. Hilary Sutcliffe, "COVID-19: The 4 Building Blocks of the Great Reset." *World Economic Forum,* August11, 2020. https://www.weforum.org/agenda/2020/08/building-blocks-of-the-great-reset/, retrieved 12/11/20.

241. The World Economic Forum Presents: The Great Reset—"You'll Own Nothing and You'll Be Happy," https://www.youtube.com/watch?v=4zUjsEaKbkM, retrieved 12/11/20.

242. Joel Gold and Ian Gold, *Suspicious Minds: How Culture Shapes Madness* (New York: Simon and Schuster, 2015) 210.

243. Alison Adcock Kaufman, "The 'Century of Humiliation,' Then and Now: Chinese Perceptions of the International Order." *Pacific Focus* 25 (1): 1–33.

244. Lisa Dunn, "How Many People in the U.S. Own Guns?" WAMU.org,

September 18, 2020, https://wamu.org/story/20/09/18/how-many-people-in-the-u-s-own-guns/, retrieved 12/12/20.

245. Andrew Kerr and Chuck Ross, "EXCLUSIVE: Hunter Biden Called His Father and Chinese Business Partner 'Office Mates' In September 2017 Email," *Daily Caller*, December 11, 2020. https://dailycaller.com/2020/12/11/hunter-joe-biden-cefc-office-mates/, retrieved 12/12/20.

246. Ibid.

247. Alexander Bowe, "China's Overseas United Front Work: Background and Implications for the United States." U.S.-China Economic and Security Review Commission Staff Report, August 24, 2018, pp. 9–10. https://www.uscc.gov/sites/default/files/Research/China%27s%20Overseas%20United%20Front%20Work%20-%20Background%20and%20Implications%20for%20US_final_0.pdf, retrieved 12/12/20.

248. Jake Ryan, Jonathan Bucks, and Holly Bancroft, "Leaked Files Expose Mass Infiltration of UK Firms by Chinese Communist Party including AstraZeneca, Rolls Royce, HSBC and Jaguar Land Rover," *Daily Mail*, December 12, 2020. https://www.dailymail.co.uk/news/article-9046783/Leaked-files-expose-mass-infiltration-UK-firms-Chinese-Communist-Party.html, retrieved 12/14/20.

249. Ibid.

250. Keith Bradsher, "The Story of China's Economic Rise Unfolds in Switzerland," *New York Times*, January 20, 2020, https://www.nytimes.com/2020/01/18/business/davos-china.html, retrieved 12/15/20.

251. Andrew Soergel, "California, Texas among Biggest Losers of Jobs from Growing China Trade Deficit." *U.S. News & World Report*, January 30, 2020. https://www.usnews.com/news/best-states/articles/2020-01-30/us-loses-37-million-jobs-due-to-growing-china-trade-deficit-report-finds, retrieved 12/20/20.

252. "Trade in Goods with China," United States Census Bureau, https://www.census.gov/foreign-trade/balance/c5700.html, retrieved 12/15/20.

253. Yukon Huang and Jeremy Smith, "China's Record on Intellectual Property Rights Is Getting Better and Better." Foreign Policy, October 16, 2019. https://foreignpolicy.com/2019/10/16/china-intellectual-property-theft-progress/, retrieved 12/15/20.

254. James Jin Kang, "The Thousand Talents Plan Is Part of China's Long Quest to Become the Global Scientific Leader," *The Conversation*, August 31,

2020. https://theconversation.com/the-thousand-talents-plan-is-part-of-chinas-long-quest-to-become-the-global-scientific-leader-145100, retrieved 12/15/20.

255. "Threats to the U.S. Research Enterprise: China's Talent Recruitment Plans," Staff report, Permanent Subcommittee on Investigations, United States Senate. https://www.hsgac.senate.gov/imo/media/doc/2019-11-18%20PSI%20Staff%20Report%20-%20China%27s%20Talent%20Recruitment%20Plans.pdf, retrieved 12/15/20.

256. Ibid.

257. John David, "Cracking Down on Illegal Ties to China." *National Association of Scholars*, December 1, 2020. https://www.nas.org/blogs/article/cracking-down-on-illegal-ties-to-china, retrieved 12/15/20.

258. Ibid.

259. Lt. Col. Robert L. Maginnis, *Alliance of Evil* (Crane, MO: Defender, 2018), Kindle edition location 399.

260. Deb Riechmann, "Trump Administration: Confucius Institute Is Arm of Beijing," *Yahoo! Money*, August 13, 2020. https://money.yahoo.com/trump-administration-confucius-institute-arm-172441064.html, retrieved 12/19/20.

261. Yuichiro Kakutani, "Pelosi Stonewalls Bill That Would Crack Down on Chinese Influence in U.S." *Washington Free Beacon*, September 20, 2020. https://freebeacon.com/2020-election/pelosi-stonewalls-china-bill-senate-dems-unanimously-supported/, retrieved 12/19/20.

262. "H.R. 7601—CONFUCIUS Act." *Congress.gov.* https://www.congress.gov/bill/116th-congress/house-bill/7601/all-actions-without-amendments, retrieved 12/19/20.

263. S. 4049, Section 1090, "Restrictions on Confucius Institutes." https://www.govtrack.us/congress/bills/116/s4049/text, retrieved 12/20/20.

264. "Dems Water Down China Provisions in Defense Bill." *Washington Free Beacon* blog, December 18, 2020. https://free-beacon.livejournal.com/4729745.html, retrieved 12/20/20.

265. Bethany Allen-Ebrahimian and Zach Dorfman, "Exclusive: Suspected Chinese Spy Targeted California Politicians." *Axios*, December 8, 2020. https://www.axios.com/china-spy-california-politicians-9d2dfb99-f839-4e00-8bd8-59dec0daf589.html, retrieved 12/20/20.

266. Ibid.

267. Charles Creitz, "McCarthy: Anyone Who Heard What FBI Told Me 'Would Never Allow Swalwell to Be on the Intel Committee,'" *Fox News*, December 19, 2020. https://www.foxnews.com/politics/kevin-mccarthy-eric-swalwell-chinese-spy-pelosi-briefing, retrieved 12/20/20.

268. "Joe Biden's China Policy Will Be a Mix of Trump's and Obama's," *The Economist*, November 19, 2020. https://www.economist.com/china/2020/11/19/joe-bidens-china-policy-will-be-a-mix-of-trumps-and-obamas, retrieved 12/16/20.

269. Liu Zhen, "US-China Trade War: Joe Biden Hints He Will Keep up Pressure on Beijing with Pledge to Fight 'Unfair Trade Practices'." *South China Morning Post*, December 12, 2020. https://www.scmp.com/news/china/diplomacy/article/3113726/us-china-trade-war-joe-biden-hints-he-will-keep-pressure, retrieved 12/16/20.

270. United States Census Bureau, op.cit.

271. Associated Press, "For Disney, Its Shanghai Resort Is a 'Local Company'." *CBS News*. April 26, 2018. https://www.cbsnews.com/news/for-disney-its-shanghai-resort-is-a-local-company/, retrieved 12/16/20.

272. Zachary Evans, "Biden Considering Disney CEO for China Ambassador after Company Praised CCP," *National Review* (at Yahoo! News), Dec. 16, 2020. https://news.yahoo.com/biden-considering-disney-ceo-china-212646534.html, retrieved 12/16/20.

273. "The Biggest Armies in the World Ranked by Active Military Personnel in 2020." *Statista*, December 1, 2020. https://www.statista.com/statistics/264443/the-worlds-largest-armies-based-on-active-force-level/, retrieved 12/20/20.

274. Sharon K. Gilbert and Derek P. Gilbert, *Giants, Gods & Dragons* (Crane, MO: Defender, 2020) 149.

275. Thomas R. Horn, *Shadowland* (Crane, MO: Defender, 2019) 301–302.

276. A. R. Millard, "The Bevelled-Rim Bowls: Their Purpose and Significance." *Iraq*, Vol. 50 (1988), pp. 49–50.

277. Ibid., p. 50.

278. Thomas D. Williams, "Pope Francis Partners with Global CEOs to Promote 'Inclusive Capitalism'," *Breitbart*, Dec. 8, 2020. https://www.breitbart.com/economy/2020/12/08/pope-francis-partners-with-global-ceos-to-promote-inclusive-capitalism/, retrieved 12/20/20.

279. "The Council for Inclusive Capitalism with the Vatican, A New Alliance of Global Business Leaders, Launches Today," *PR Newswire*, December 8, 2020. https://www.prnewswire.com/news-releases/the-council-for-inclusive-capitalism-with-the-vatican-a-new-alliance-of-global-business-leaders-launches-today-301187931.html, retrieved 12/20/20.

280. Ibid.

281. Ibid.

282. Robert P. Barnidge, Jr., "Against the Catholic Grain: Pope Francis Trumpets Socialism over Capitalism." *Forbes*, March 11, 2016. https://www.forbes.com/sites/realspin/2016/03/11/against-the-catholic-grain-pope-francis-trumpets-socialism-over-capitalism/?sh=7e98710742d3, retrieved 12/21/20.

283. Available online: http://www.vatican.va/content/francesco/en/encyclicals/documents/papa-francesco_20201003_enciclica-fratelli-tutti.html. Retrieved 12/22/20.

284. Nicole Winfield, "Pope: Market Capitalism Has Filed in Pandemic, Needs Reform," *Associated Press*, October 4, 2020. https://apnews.com/article/virus-outbreak-pope-francis-archive-capitalism-bcde0053314e65612add0709fada5519, retrieved 12/22/20.

285. Matthew 26:11.

286. Matthew 22:36–40, Romans 13:8–10, and Galatians 5:14.

287. 1 Timothy 6:10.

288. William Bradford, *History of Plymouth Plantation*. https://sourcebooks.fordham.edu/mod/1650bradford.asp#Private%20and%20communal%20farming, retrieved 12/22/20.

289. Ibid.

290. Ibid.

291. https://twitter.com/pontifex/status/1334475219180851202?s=21, retrieved 12/22/20.

292. "'Make Space at the Table': Pope Urges Valuing All Human Life." *Catholic News Service*, December 4, 2020. https://www.thefloridacatholic.org/faith/pope-francis/make-space-at-the-table-pope-urges-valuing-all-human-life/article_0274eb32-365c-11eb-a183-f3982447671e.html, retrieved 12/22/20.

293. John Letzing, "Here's the Pope's Prescription for Resetting the Global Economy in Response to COVID-19," *World Economic Forum*, October 9, 2020. https://www.weforum.org/agenda/2020/10/here-s-the-pope-s-

prescription-for-resetting-the-global-economy-in-response-to-covid-19/, retrieved 12/22/20.

294. George Santayana, *The Life of Reason: The Phases of Human Progress, Vol. I* (1905). http://www.gutenberg.org/files/15000/15000-h/15000-h.htm#vol1, retrieved 12/22/20.

295. As of this writing, legal challenges by President Donald Trump were not resolved. Even after Biden's inauguration, it is assumed that our judicial system will be loath to challenge the veracity of the announced results of the November 3, 2020, presidential election for a variety of reasons, not least of which would be admitting to the world that for all of our moral posturing, Americans are just as susceptible to the temptation to cheat as anyone else.

296. "Biden Voter Messaging Survey Analysis." Online survey among 1,750 Biden voters in select states conducted November 9–18, 2020. States included in this survey were Arizona, Georgia, Michigan, North Carolina, Nevada, Pennsylvania, and Wisconsin. Respondents were selected randomly from opt-in panel participants. https://cdn.mrc.org/TPC-MRC+Biden+Voter+Messaging+Survey+Analysis+Nov+2020_final.pdf, access 11/27/20.

297. Lauren Gambino, " 'It happened all at once': Tara Reade Details Assault Claim against Joe Biden in Megyn Kelly Interview," *The Guardian*, May 9, 2020. https://www.theguardian.com/us-news/2020/may/08/joe-biden-tara-reade-sexual-assault-claim-megyn-kelly, retrieved 11/27/20.

298. Rich Noyes, "Special Report: The Stealing of the Presidency, 2020," *NewsBusters*, November 24, 2020. https://www.newsbusters.org/blogs/nb/rich-noyes/2020/11/24/special-report-stealing-presidency-2020, retrieved 11/27/20.

299. Megan Rose Dickey, "Google.org Donates $2 Million to Wikipedia's Parent Org." *TechCrunch*, January 22, 2019. https://techcrunch.com/2019/01/22/google-org-donates-2-million-to-wikipedias-parent-org/, retrieved 11/27/20.

300. Andrew Orlowski, "Wikipedia Doesn't Need Your Money—So Why Does It Keep Pestering You?" *The Register*, Dec. 20, 2012. https://www.theregister.com/2012/12/20/cash_rich_wikipedia_chugging/, retrieved 11/27/20.

301. "List of United States Presidential Candidates by Number of Votes Received," *Wikipedia*. Retrieved November 27, 2020.

302. Patrick Basham, "Reasons Why the 2020 Presidential Election Is Deeply Puzzling." *The Spectator*, November 27, 2020. https://spectator.us/reasons-why-the-2020-presidential-election-is-deeply-puzzling/, retrieved 11/28/20.

303. Ronald Brownstein, "Democrats' Shaky Future in the House: Joe Biden's Walloping Victory in the Popular Vote Didn't Translate Down-Ballot." *The Atlantic*, November 27, 2020. Retrieved 11/27/20.

304. A Google Trends query (https://trends.google.com/trends/explore?geo=US&q=baseless) reveals that searches for the word "baseless," as in "baseless claims of vote fraud," spiked to four times normal the week after the election. In other words, the media jumped to categorize any questions about the election results as "baseless" conspiracy theory.

305. Caroline Graham, "How Hunter Biden Became the Unkempt Man Who Left His Laptop in a Nondescript Computer Store in a Delaware Shopping Mall—and Never Returned," *Daily Mail*, November 1, 2020. https://www.dailymail.co.uk/news/article-8902229/Hunter-Biden-unkempt-man-left-laptop-computer-store-Delaware-shopping-mall.html, retrieved 11/27/20.

306. Ibid.

307. Emma-Jo Morris and Gabrielle Fonrouge, "Smoking-Gun Eail Reveals How Hunter Biden Introduced Ukrainian Businessman to VP Dad." *New York Post*, October 14, 2020. https://nypost.com/2020/10/14/email-reveals-how-hunter-biden-introduced-ukrainian-biz-man-to-dad/, retrieved 11/27/20.

308. Suhauna Hussain, Chris Megerian, and Samantha Masunaga, "Facebook, Twitter Try to Contain Hunter Biden Report amid Disinformation Crackdown." *Los Angeles Times*, October 14, 2020, https://www.latimes.com/business/story/2020-10-14/facebook-twitter-content-moderation-new-york-post, retrieved 11/27/20.

309. Geoffrey Dickens, "Still Hidin' Hunter: Nets Spend a Meager 21 Minutes Out of 113 Hours on Biden Scandals," *NewsBusters*, Oct. 27, 2020. https://www.newsbusters.org/blogs/nb/geoffrey-dickens/2020/10/27/still-hidin-hunter-nets-spend-meager-21-minutes-out-113-hours, retrieved 11/27/20.

310. Robby Soave, "The Media Do Not Want You to Read, Share, or Discuss *The New York Post*'s Hunter Biden Scoop," *Reason*, October 14, 2020. https://reason.com/2020/10/14/hunter-biden-new-york-post-story-media-facebook-burisma-ukraine/, retrieved 11/28/20.

311. Emma-Jo Morris and Gabrielle Fonrouge, "Hunter Biden Emails, Pics Reveal Wild Life, Pained Soul," *New York Post*, October 16, 2020. https://nypost.com/2020/10/16/hunter-biden-emails-pics-reveal-wild-life-pained-soul/, retrieved 11/28/20.

312. Emily Jacobs, "Inside the Life of Hunter Biden, Joe Biden's Scandal-Plagued Son." *New York Post*, October 14, 2020, https://nypost.com/article/inside-the-life-of-hunter-biden-joe-bidens-scandal-plagued-son/, retrieved 11/27/20.

313. Joe Tacopino, "Navy Kicks Out Biden's Son after Failing Coke Test," *New York Post*, October 16, 2014. https://nypost.com/2014/10/16/bidens-son-hunter-kicked-out-of-the-navy-after-failing-cocaine-test/, retrieved 11/28/20.

314. Ian Schwarz, "Giuliani: I Turned Over Hunter Biden's Laptop with Pictures of "Underage Girls" to Delaware Police," *RealClearPolitics*, October 20, 2020. https://www.realclearpolitics.com/video/2020/10/20/giuliani_i_turned_over_hunter_bidens_laptop_with_pictures_of_underage_girls_to_delaware_police.html, retrieved 11/28/20.

315. Ibid.

316. Caroline Graham, "How Hunter Biden became the Unkempt Man Who Left His Laptop in a Nondescript Computer Store in a Delaware Shopping Mall—and Never Returned," *Daily Mail*, November 1, 2020. https://www.dailymail.co.uk/news/article-8902229/Hunter-Biden-unkempt-man-left-laptop-computer-store-Delaware-shopping-mall.html, retrieved 11/28/20.

317. Malia Zimmerman, "Flight Logs Show Bill Clinton Flew on Sex Offender's Jet Much More Than Previously Known," *Fox News*, May 13, 2016. https://www.foxnews.com/us/flight-logs-show-bill-clinton-flew-on-sex-offenders-jet-much-more-than-previously-known, retrieved 11/28/20.

318. Dan Keane, "Jeffrey Epstein Flight List: Who Flew on the Paedo's Private Jet Dubbed the 'Lolita Express'?" *The Sun*, July 7, 2020. https://www.the-sun.com/news/1096305/jeffrey-epstein-flight-paedos-private-jet-lolita-express/, retrieved 11/28/20.

319. Leland Nally, "I Called Everyone in Jeffrey Epstein's Little Black Book." *Mother Jones*, October 9, 2020, https://www.motherjones.com/politics/2020/10/i-called-everyone-in-jeffrey-epsteins-little-black-book/, retrieved 11/28/20.

320. Ibid.

321. David Folkenflik, "A Dead Cat, A Lawyer's Call and a 5-Figure Donation: How Media Fell Short on Epstein," *NPR*, August 22, 2019. https://www.npr.org/2019/08/22/753390385/a-dead-cat-a-lawyers-call-and-a-5-figure-donation-how-media-fell-short-on-epstei, retrieved 11/28/20.

322. Ibid.

323. Samuel Goldsmith, "Jeffrey Epstein Pleads Guilty to Prostitution Charges." *New York Post*, June 30, 2008. https://web.archive.org/ web/20190813000524/https://nypost.com/2008/06/30/jeffrey-epstein- pleads-guilty-to-prostitution-charges/, retrieved 11/28/20.

324. Julie K. Brown, "How a Future Trump Cabinet Member Gave a Serial Sex Abuser the Deal of a Lifetime," *Miami Herald*, November 28, 2018, https://www.miamiherald.com/news/local/article220097825.html, retrieved 11/28/20.

325. Ibid.

326. David Folkenflik, "ABC News Defends Its Epstein Coverage after Leaked Video of Anchor," *NPR*, November 5, 2019. https://www.kpbs.org/ news/2019/nov/05/abc-news-defends-its-epstein-coverage-after/, retrieved 11/29/20.

327. Carol D. Leonnig and Aaron C. Davis, "Autopsy Finds Broken Bones in Jeffrey Epstein's Neck, Deepening Questions around His Death," *Washington Post*, August 15, 2019. https://www.washingtonpost.com/ politics/autopsy-finds-broken-bones-in-jeffrey-epsteins-neck-deepening- questions-around-his-death/2019/08/14/d09ac934-bdd9-11e9-b873- 63ace636af08_story.html, retrieved 11/29/20.

328. Mark Hosenball, "FBI Studies Two Broken Cameras Outside Cell Where Epstein Died: Source," *Reuters*, August 28, 2019. https://www.reuters.com/ article/us-people-jeffrey-epstein-cameras-idUSKCN1VI2LC, retrieved 11/29/20.

329. "Jail Cell Video of Jeffrey Epstein's First Suicide Attempt 'No Longer Exists'," *CBS News*, January 10, 2020. https://www.cbsnews.com/news/ jeffrey-epstein-jail-cell-video-of-sex-offenders-first-suicide-attempt-goes- missing/, retrieved 11/29/20.

330. Ibid.

331. Vicky Ward, "Jeffrey Epstein's Sick Story Played Out for Years in Plain Sight," *Daily Beast*, July 9, 2019. https://www.thedailybeast.com/jeffrey- epsteins-sick-story-played-out-for-years-in-plain-sight, retrieved 11/29/20.

332. Lydia Bell, "FO Suspected Maxwell Was a Russian Agent, Papers Reveal," *The Telegraph*, Nov. 2, 2003. https://web.archive.org/ web/20200420024613/https://www.telegraph.co.uk/news/

uknews/1445707/FO-suspected-Maxwell-was-a-Russian-agent-papers-reveal.html, retrieved 11/29/20.

333. Saundra Saperstein and Victoria Churchville, "Officials Describe 'Cult Rituals in Child Abuse Case," *Washington Post*, February 7, 1987. https://www.washingtonpost.com/archive/politics/1987/02/07/officials-describe-cult-rituals-in-child-abuse-case/11f05df1-48e0-41f7-b46d-249c0bd2bc39/, retrieved 11/29/20.

334. The PDF files are available for download here: https://vault.fbi.gov/the-finders.

335. Gordon Witkin, Peter Cary & Ancel Martinez, "Through a Glass, Very Darkly: Pedophile Networks and the CIA," *U.S. News and World Report*, December 27, 1993.

336. David McGowan, *Programmed to Kill: The Politics of Serial Murder* (Lincoln, NE: iUniverse, 2004) 66–67.

337. Dutroux and his wife were convicted in 2004 for the kidnapping, torture, sexual abuse, and murder of six girls between the ages of eight and nineteen, four of whom died, including two eight-year-olds who starved to death. The lenient treatment Dutroux received from Belgian law enforcement, which enabled him to continue his crimes even after an earlier prison term for kidnapping and rape, led to widespread allegations of corruption, if not complicity, by the government. A 2004 report in *The Guardian* revealed that more than twenty potential witnesses in the case had died under mysterious circumstances. It so enraged the public that the Belgian government was compelled to reorganize its law enforcement agencies, and nearly a third of Belgians with the surname Dutroux applied to change their names after the scope and nature of his crimes became public knowledge. Despite his life sentence, Dutroux has been eligible for early release since 2013; his next opportunity for parole will be in 2021 when he will be sixty-five.

338. "Jimmy Savile: Number of Victims Reaches 300, Police Say," *BBC News*, October 25, 2012. https://www.bbc.com/news/uk-20081021, retrieved 11/29/20.

339. Margaret Carlson, "Washington's Man from Nowhere," *TIME*, July 24, 1989. http://content.time.com/time/subscriber/article/0,33009,958213,00.html, retrieved 11/29/20.

340. Ken Franckling, "Craig Spence, Capitol Hill Scandal Figure, Found

Dead," *UPI News*, November 13, 1989. https://www.upi.com/Archives/1989/11/13/Craig-Spence-Capitol-Hill-scandal-figure-found-dead/2555626936400/?spt=su, retrieved 11/29/20.

341. Ibid.

342. Paul M. Rodriguez and George Archibald, "Homosexual Prostitution Inquiry Ensnares VIPs with Reagan, Bush," *Washington Times*, June 29, 1989, p. A1.

343. Charles Young, "Still Evil After All These Years." *Counterpunch*, Sep. 10, 2012, https://www.counterpunch.org/2012/09/10/still-evil-after-all-these-years/, retrieved 11/29/20.

344. "Figure in DC Sex Scandal Found Dead in Boston Hotel," *Deseret News*, November 12, 1989. https://www.deseret.com/1989/11/12/18832018/figure-in-d-c-sex-scandal-found-dead-in-boston-hotel, retrieved 11/29/20.

345. Jacquelin Magnay, "Germany Uncovers Pedophile Ring of 30,000," *The Australian*, June 30, 2020. https://www.theaustralian.com.au/world/germany-uncovers-pedophile-ring-of-30000/news-story/a61ce8dadc01c368a979bf658e17a531, retrieved 11/29/20.

346. James 1:23b–24 (NIV).

347. Spencer S. Hsu, "'Pizzagate' Gunman Sentenced to Four Years in Prison, as Prosecutors Urged Judge to Deter Vigilante Justice," *Washington Post*, June 22, 2017. https://web.archive.org/web/20170622171606if_/https://www.washingtonpost.com/local/public-safety/pizzagate-gunman-sentenced-to-four-years-in-prison-as-prosecutors-urged-judge-to-deter-vigilante-justice/2017/06/22/a10db598-550b-11e7-ba90-f5875b7d1876_story.html, retrieved 11/29/20.

348. Adrienne LaFrance, "The Prophecies of Q," *The Atlantic*, June 2020. https://www.theatlantic.com/magazine/archive/2020/06/qanon-nothing-can-stop-what-is-coming/610567/, retrieved 11/29/20.

349. "QAnon." Wikipedia. https://en.wikipedia.org/wiki/QAnon, retrieved 11/29/20.

350. https://www.brainyquote.com/authors/lawrence-kudlow-quotes.

351. https://www.pewresearch.org/fact-tank/2019/06/25/stark-partisan-divisions-in-americans-views-of-socialism-capitalism/.

352. Ibid.

353. Ibid.

354. https://www.acton.org/pub/religion-liberty/volume-10-number-3/how-christianity-created-capitalism.

355. Ibid..

356. Ibid.

357. Ibid.

358. Ibid.

359. https://www.gotquestions.org/capitalism-Bible.html.

360. Ibid.

361. Ibid.

362. https://www.acton.org/pub/religion-liberty/volume-10-number-3/how-christianity-created-capitalism.

363. https://www.azquotes.com/author/9564-Karl_Marx.

364. A Short History of Black Lives Matter, https://therealnews.com/pcullors0722blacklives.

365. A Short History of Black Lives Matter, https://therealnews.com/pcullors0722blacklives.

366. https://www.allaboutworldview.org/marxist-worldview.htm#:~:text=The%20Marxist%20worldview%20is%20grounded%20in%20Karl%20Marx,of%20the%20Marxist%20Worldview%20across%20ten%20major%20categories.

367. file:///C:/Users/rober/OneDrive/Desktop/C%20S%20BOOK/SECTION%20I/CHAPTER%201/MARXISM/MARXS%20NEW%20RELIGION.pdf.

368. file:///C:/Users/rober/OneDrive/Desktop/C%20S%20BOOK/SECTION%20I/CHAPTER%201/MARXISM/MARXS%20NEW%20RELIGION.pdf.

369. https://www.catholiceducation.org/en/culture/catholic-contributions/3-the-pillars-of-unbelief-karl-marx.html.

370. https://www.etsjets.org/files/JETS-PDFs/62/62-4/JETS_62.4_775-788_SchwarzwalderJr.pdf.

371. https://thoughtsofalivingchristian.wordpress.com/2010/11/21/a-christian-critique-of-marxism/.

372. file:///C:/Users/rober/OneDrive/Desktop/C%20S%20BOOK/SECTION%20I/CHAPTER%201/MARXISM/MARXS%20NEW%20RELIGION.pdf.

373. https://kinginstitute.stanford.edu/king-papers/documents/communisms-challenge-christianity.
374. https://www.intellectualtakeout.org/article/harvard-student-whose-father-escaped-communism-has-message-her-fellow-students/.
375. https://www.snopes.com/fact-check/norman-thomas-on-socialism.
376. https://reason.com/2020/11/06/socialism-2020-trump-biden-rebuke-left/.
377. https://www.brainyquote.com/quotes/bernie_sanders_830990.
378. https://quotefancy.com/quote/902961/Ronald-Reagan-Socialism-only-works-in-two-places-Heaven-where-they-don-t-need-it-and-hell.
379. https://www.westernjournal.com/survey-finds-98-americans-support-socialism-reject-bibles-key-teachings/.
380. https://www.heritage.org/progressivism/commentary/socialism-clear-and-present-danger.
381. https://en.wikipedia.org/wiki/Robert_Owen.
382. https://en.wikipedia.org/wiki/From_each_according_to_his_ability,_to_each_according_to_his_needs.
383. https://www.thehansindia.com/hans/opinion/news-analysis/the-psychology-of-communist-liberals-651426.
384. https://www.heritage.org/progressivism/commentary/socialism-clear-and-present-danger.
385. https://www.snopes.com/fact-check/norman-thomas-on-socialism.
386. https://spectator.org/what-americans-must-know-about-socialism/.
387. Ibid..
388. Ibid..
389. https://www.dailywire.com/news/poll-who-would-jesus-vote-james-barrett.
390. http://www.marketfaith.org/2020/03/a-worldview-perspective-on-socialism/.
391. https://en.wikipedia.org/wiki/From_each_according_to_his_ability,_to_each_according_to_his_needs.
392. http://usatoday30.usatoday.com/news/politics/2007-11-01-1567063266_x.htm.
393. https://www.facebook.com/senatorsanders/posts/10150781969192908.
394. https://www.businessinsider.com/report-hillary-clinton-called-for-toppling-the-1-2015-4.
395. https://thefederalist.com/2015/06/29/americans-buy-into-marxist-family-planning/.

396. https://feelthebern.org/bernie-sanders-on-children/.

397. https://www.christianpost.com/news/5-reasons-socialism-is-not-christian-opinion.html.

398. https://genzconservative.com/socialism-is-suicide-and-communism-is-murder/.

399. https://encyclopedia2.thefreedictionary.com/Communist+Manifesto.

400. https://www.cnsnews.com/index.php/commentary/rev-michael-p-orsi/communism-and-christianity-cannot-coexist.

401. https://www.britannica.com/story/why-did-the-soviet-union-collapse.

402. https://apnews.com/article/1abea48aacda1a9dd520c380a8bc6be6.

403. https://www.britannica.com/story/why-did-the-soviet-union-collapse.

404. https://www.brainyquote.com/quotes/glenn_beck_411837.

405. https://www.wnd.com/2020/11/4871642/.

406. Ibid.

407. Josephus, *The Wars of the Jews.*

408. Hippolytus of Rome, *The Refutation of all Heresies.* Book IX. Chapter XXI

409. Ibid. Chapter XXIII

410. Bernard Dickman, *The Beginning of the Jewish Calendar.*

411. Dr. Ken Johnson, *The Ancient Dead Sea Scroll Calendar: And The Prophecies It Reveals.*

412. https://www.newadvent.org/fathers/0711.htm.

413. Technically, it's not as simple as adding an extra day every four years; there's a more complicated way to figure out leap years on the Gregorian calendar. For any given year to qualify as a "leap" year, the year must be divisible by four. If the year is also divisible by one hundred, then it is not a leap year. However, if the year is also evenly divisible by four hundred, then it is a leap year. For more information, visit https://www.timeanddate.com/date/leapyear.html.

414. Daniel 7:25; 9:27; 12:7; Revelation 11:2; 11:3; 12:6; 12:14;, and 13:5 all talk about 42 months, 1,260 days, half one set of 7, or time, times, and a half. These are all based around a 360-day "prophetic year" and not on the Essene or Pharisee calendar.

415. "Tekufah" entry in Jewish Encyclopedia, http://jewishencyclopedia.com/articles/14292-tekufah.

416. To help visualize the Essene calendar, visit dsscalendar.org.

417. Johnson, *Ancient Dead Sea Scroll Calendar*..

418. Ibid.

419. Bav. Sanhedrin 97a; Bav. 'Avodah Zarah 9a; Tana de-bei Eliyyahu, ed. Shmuel Yehuda Weinfeld (Jerusalem, 1991), 2:1, p. 14.

420. Epistle of Barnabas. http://www.earlychristianwritings.com/text/barnabas-lightfoot.html.

421. Eusebius of Caesarea, *Ecclesiastical History* Book v. Chapter v.

422. *New World Encyclopedia*. Essenes. https://www.newworldencyclopedia.org/entry/Essenes.

423. Florentino García Martínez Qumran and Apocalyptic: studies on the Aramaic texts from Qumran 1992 p176 "11QMelchizedek. This is a clearly eschatological Hebrew fragment."

424. 11QMelchizedek, https://www.marquette.edu/maqom/11QMelchizedek.pdf.

425. We wouldn't say 3925 BC because, first, there's no year "0" so it goes from 1 BC to AD 1, and also the name of a year signifies the time that's already passed, so by 3925 BC, while that's technically "Year 1," the creation would have already existed for a year. The BC/AD system we use can be a bit confusing, but a good resource to find the number of years, days, and months between two time periods can be found at https://keisan.casio.com/exec/system/1247118517.

426. Dr. Michael S. Heiser, *The Unseen Re*alm.

427. Also, speaking of the work of Dr. Michael Heiser, we can confirm the date of the birth of Jesus with this as well. Based on the Essene calendar, if we assume Jesus' death at Passover of AD 32, assume His birth at September 11 of 3 BC, and calculate the time between, we arrive at 33 1/2 years (the age many have come to believe Jesus was when He died; He started His 3 ½-year ministry at age 30). According to Dr. Heiser, September 11, 3 BC, is the day the astronomical alignment mentioned in Revelation 12 occurred and is the most likely date for the birth of Jesus: https://drmsh.com/september-11-happy-birthday-to-jesus/.

428. Josephus, *Wars of the Jews*, vii.

429. Babylonian Talmud, Gittin 56b.

430. Rabbi Nathan. Avot 4.

431. Leo Baeck College Library Lecture Archives. Rabbi Akiba (25/2/55). https://lbc.ac.uk/direct-archives/lectures/L35-L53/39.pdf.

432. The Sanhedrin English. The Re-established Jewish Sanhedrin. http://www.thesanhedrin.org/en/index.php?title=Historical_Overview&mobileaction=toggle_view_desktop#Table_of_Zugos.

433. Geni: The Great Sanhedrin. Sanhedrin Presidents. https://www.geni.com/projects/The-Great-Sanhedrin/13069.

434. Earthsky. Infamous asteroid Apophis is accelerating. https://earthsky.org/space/asteroid-99942-apophis-encounters-2029-2036-2068.

435. Tom Horn, *The Wormwood Prophecy*.

436. Tom Horn, *The Messenger*.

437. Earthsky. Infamous asteroid Apophis is accelerating. https://earthsky.org/space/asteroid-99942-apophis-encounters-2029-2036-2068.

438. Daniel 10:4–5:On the twenty-fourth day of the first month, as I was standing on the bank of the great river (that is, the Tigris) I lifted up my eyes and looked, and behold, a man clothed in linen, with a belt of fine gold from Uphaz around his waist.

439. https://www.aish.com/dijh/Nisan_24.html.

440. Horn, *The Messenger*.

441. Rabbi Paul Kipnes, *Chanukah as a Second Sukkot*. https://orami.org/chanukah-as-a-second-sukkot/.

442. Hall, *Lost Keys*, 19.

443. Pike, 819.

444. Bailey, 20.

445. Manly P. Hall, *Lectures on Ancient Philosophy: An Introduction to Practical Ideals* (Philosophical Research Society, 1984), 433.

446. Hall, *Secret Destiny*, 26.

447. Richard Dawkins, *The God Delusion* (New York: Houghton Mifflin Harcourt, 2006) 43.

448. Andrew A. Lipscomb and Albert Ellery Bergh, eds., *The Writings of Thomas Jefferson*, Vol. XVI (Washington, DC: Thomas Jefferson Memorial Association, 1903) 100–101.

449. Gerard W. Gawalt, ed., Thomas Jefferson and William Short Correspondence (Library of Congress Manuscript Division).

450. Lipscomb and Bergh, Vol. XIV, 71–72.

451. Ibid.

452. Samuel E. Forman, *The Life and Writings of Thomas Jefferson* (Bowen-Merrill, 1900) 365.

ed., *Benjamin Franklin Reader* (New York: Simon and Schuster, 2003) 492.
454. "Ben Franklin and His Membership in the Hellfire Club: Founding Father or Satanic Killer?" Associated Content News, June 27, 2007 (http://www.associatedcontent.com).
455. "Benjamin Franklin, the Occult, and the Elite," *Sunday Times*, February 11, 1998 (http://www.infowars.com, January 11, 2005).
456. Manly P. Hall, *Secret Teachings of All Ages: An Encyclopedic Outline of Masonic, Hermetic, Qabbalistic and Rosicrucian Symbolical Philosophy* (Lulu.com, 2005) 589.
457. "The Most Approved Plan: The Competition for the Capitol's Design" (http://www.loc.gov/exhibits/us.capitol/s2.html).
458. Ibid.
459. Mitch Horowitz, Occult America (New York, NY: Bantam Books, 2010) 172.
460. John C. Culver and John Hyde, *American Dreamer: The Life and Times of Henry A. Wallace* (W. W. Norton & Company, 2001), 135.
461. Helena Petrovna Blavatsky, *The Secret Doctrine: The Synthesis of Science, Religion, and Philosophy*, Volume 1 (New York: NY, Newman, Cowell & Gripper, Ltd., 1893) 332.
462. John C. Culver and John Hyde, *American Dreamer*, 136.
463. "How the Great Seal Got on the One Dollar Bill," GreatSeal.com, last accessed January 23, 2012, http://www.greatseal.com/dollar/hawfdr.html.
464. Mitch Horowitz, *Occult America*, 173.
465. David Ovason, *The Secret Architecture of Our Nation's Capital: The Masons and the Building of Washington DC* (New York: HarperCollins, 2000), 71.
466. Ibid., 361.
467. Ibid., 373.
468. Julie Duin, "Ergo, We're Virgo" (October 16, 2000) (http://findarticles.com/p/articles/mi_m1571/is_38_16/ai_66241134).
469. Ovason, 71.
470. Manly P. Hall, *The Secret Teachings of All Ages, Diamond Jubilee Edition* (Los Angeles: Philosophical Research Society, 2000) CIV.
471. Johanne Wolfgang von Goethe, *Faust*, translated by George Madison Priest, The Alchemy Website (http://www.levity.com).

472. Foster Bailey, *The Spirit of Freemasonry* (New York: Lucis Press, 1957).

473. Ovason, 236.

474. Ibid., 139.

475. Ibid., 49.

476. See (http://en.wikipedia.org/wiki/Statue_of_Liberty).

477. Pike, 335.

478. Ibid., 16.

479. Ibid., 472.

480. Ovason, 237.

481. Ibid.

482. "Growth of a Young Nation," U.S. House of Representatives: Office of the Clerk, last accessed January 30, 2012, http://artandhistory.house.gov/art_artifacts/virtual_tours/splendid_hall/young_nation.aspx

483. "1964–Present: September 11, 2001, The Capitol Building as a Target," United States Senate, last accessed January 30, 2012, http://www.senate.gov/artandhistory/history/minute/Attack.htm.

484. William Henry and Mark Gray, *Freedom's Gate: Lost Symbols in the U.S.* (Hendersonville, TN: Scala Dei, 2009), 3.

485. https://sputniknews.com/viral/202006161079633514-new-interpretation-of-maya-calendar-suggests-the-world-will-end-on-21-june/.

486. https://astronomy.com/news/2020/12/the-christmas-star-appears-again-jupiter-and-saturn-align-in-the-great-conjunction-on-dec-21-2020#:~:text=Jupiter%20and%20Saturn%20will%20line,t%20occur%20again%20until%202080.

487. Ibid., 4.

488. "Sandpit of Royalty," Extra Bladet (Copenhagen, January 31, 1999).

489. Hall, *Secret Teachings*, 104.

490. Hall, *Secret Destiny of America* (Penguin Group, 2008), chapter 18.

491. James Lees-Milne, *Saint Peter's: The Story of Saint Peter's Basilica in Rome* (Little, Brown, 1967), 221.

492. Rebecca Zorach and Michael W. Cole, *The Idol in the Age of Art* (Ashgate, 2009), 61.

493. Ibid., 61.